A History of the Civil War, 1861-1865
James Ford Rhodes

Winner of the Pulitzer Prize in History in 1918

Table of Contents

Chapter I

THE GREAT factor in the destruction of slavery was the election of Abraham Lincoln as President in 1860[1] by the Republican party, who had declared against the extension of slavery into the territories. The territories were those divisions of the national domain which lacked as yet the necessary qualifications for statehood through insufficient population or certain other impediments; they were under the control of Congress and the President. The Republicans were opposed to any interference with slavery in the States where it already existed, but they demanded freedom for the vast unorganized territory west of the Missouri river. How the election of Lincoln was brought about I have already related at length in my History of the United States from the Compromise of 1850 to the Final Restoration of Home Rule at the South in 1877[2] and more briefly in the first of my Oxford Lectures.[3] It was a sectional triumph, inasmuch as Lincoln did not receive a single vote in ten out of the eleven States that afterwards seceded and made up the Confederate States. Charleston, South Carolina, an ultra pro-slavery city and eager for secession, rejoiced equally with the Northern cities over the election of Lincoln, but the Charleston crowds were cheering for a Southern confederacy.[4] Herein were they supported by the people of South Carolina generally, who saw in the election of Lincoln an attack on their cherished institution of slavery and cared no longer for political union with a people who held them to be living in the daily practice of evil. They regarded their slaves as property and believed that they had the same constitutional right to carry that property into the common territory as the Northern settlers had to take with them their property in horses and mules. Lincoln as President would deny them that privilege; in other words he would refuse them equality. In his speeches he had fastened a stigma upon slavery; believing it wrong, he must oppose it wherever he had the power, and he certainly would limit its extension. Could a free people, they asked, have a more undoubted grievance? Were they not fired by the spirit of 1776 and ought they not to strike before any distinct act of aggression? Revolution was a word on every tongue. The crisis was like one described by Thucydides when the meaning of words had no longer the same relation to things. Reckless daring was held to be loyal courage; prudent delay was the excuse of a coward; moderation was the disguise of unmanly weakness. Frantic energy was the true quality of a man.[5] The people of South

---

[1] Nov. 6. For a characterization of Lincoln, see II, 308; Lect., 46.

[2] I, II.

[3] On the Amer. Civil War, 1913.

[4] III, 115.

Carolina amid great enthusiasm demanded almost with one voice that their State secede from the Federal Union. The authorities promptly responded. A Convention duly called and chosen passed an Ordinance of secession which was termed a Declaration of Independence of the State of South Carolina.[6] This act, in view of the South Carolinians and of the people of the other cotton States, was based on the States reserved right under the compact entitled the Constitution. Martial music, bonfires, pistol firing, fireworks, illuminations, cries of joy and exultation greeted the passage of the Ordinance, which seemed to the people of Charleston to mark the commencement of a revolution as glorious as that of 1776.[7]

Meanwhile the United States Senate, through an able and representative committee of thirteen, was at work on a compromise in the spirit of earlier days. In 1820, according to Jefferson, the knell of the Union had been rung; the slavery question, said he, like a fire-bell in the night awakened and filled me with terror. But then the Missouri Compromise had saved the Union.[8] Again, in 1850 when the South and the North were in bitter opposition on the same issue of slavery and threats of dissolution of the Union were freely made by Southern men, the controversy was ended by Clays Compromise.[9] And now in 1860 the people of the Northern and of the border slave States, ardent for the preservation of the Union, believed that Congress could somehow compose the dispute as it had done twice before. The Senate committee of thirteen at once took up the only expedient that could be expected to retain the six remaining cotton States in the Union.[10] This was the Crittenden Compromise, called after its author, a senator from Kentucky; and the portion of it on which union or disunion turned was the article regarding territorial slavery. Crittenden proposed as a constitutional amendment that the old Missouri Compromise line of 36° 30′ should serve as the boundary between slavery and freedom in the Territories; north of it slavery should be prohibited, south of it protected. As phrased, the article was satisfactory to the Northern Democratic and border slave State senators, who together made up six of the committee. The two senators from the cotton States would have accepted it, had the understanding been clear that protection to slavery was to apply to all territory acquired in the future south of the Compromise line. The five Republican senators opposed the territorial article, and, as it had been agreed that any report to be binding must have the assent of a majority of these five, they defeated in committee this necessary provision of the Compromise. William H. Seward,[11] one

---

[5] Jowett, III, 82.

[6] Dec. 20, 1860.

[7] III, 114-125, 192-206; Lect., 65*et seq.*

[8] I, 39 *et ante.*

[9] I, Chap. II.

[10] I class as cotton States, South Carolina, Georgia, Florida, Alabama, Mississippi, Louisiana, Texas.

[11] See I and II.

of the thirteen, the leader of the Republicans in Congress, and the prospective head of Lincolns Cabinet, would undoubtedly have assented to this article, could he have secured Lincolns support. But Lincoln, though ready to compromise every other matter in dispute, was inflexible on the territorial question: that is to say as regarded territory which might be acquired in the future. He could not fail to see that the Territories which were a part of the United States in 1860 were, in Websters words, dedicated to freedom by an ordinance of nature and the will of God; and he was willing to give the slaveholders an opportunity to make a political slave State out of New Mexico, which was south of the Missouri Compromise line.[12] But he feared that, if a parallel of latitude should be recognized by solemn exactment as the boundary between slavery and freedom, filibustering for all south of us and making slave States of it would follow in spite of us. A year will not pass, he wrote further, till we shall have to take Cuba as a condition upon which they [the cotton States] will stay in the Union. Lincoln, therefore, using the powerful indirect influence of the President-elect, caused the Republican senators to defeat the Crittenden Compromise in the committee, who were thus forced to report that they could not agree upon a plan of adjustment. Then Crittenden proposed to submit his plan to a vote of the people. So strong was the desire to preserve the Union that, had this been done, the majority would probably have been overwhelming in favor of the Compromise; and, although only an informal vote, it would have been an instruction impossible for Congress to resist. Crittendens resolution looking to such an expression of public sentiment was prevented from coming to a vote in the Senate by the quiet opposition of Republican senators: the last chance of retaining the six cotton States in the Union was gone.[13]

Between January 9 and February 1, 1861, the conventions of Mississippi, Florida, Alabama, Georgia, Louisiana and Texas passed ordinances of secession. Early in February the Confederate States was formed. Delegates from six cotton States[14] assembled in Montgomery and, proceeding in an orderly manner, formed a government, the cornerstone of which rested upon the great truth that slavery is the negros natural and normal condition. They elected Jefferson Davis[15] President and adopted a Constitution modelled on that of the United States, but departing from that instrument in its express recognition of slavery and the right of secession.[16]

---

[12] A real slave State was impossible. Twenty-two slaves in the territory was the result of seven years' work. III, 176, 268 n., 313. In New Mexico there was a belt 30 miles wide with additional width at the eastern end which was north of 36° 30'.

[13] III, 150-179, 253-265; Lect., 68*et seq.* For a Senate vote Jan. 16, 1861, III, 266. For vote of the House Feb. 27, 1861, and of the Senate March 2 on the Crittenden Compromise, III, 313.

[14] Texas was not at first represented. III, 291, n. 4.

[15] I, 389.

When Lincoln was inaugurated President on March 4, he confronted a difficult situation. Elected by a Union of thirty-three States, he had lost, before performing an official act, the allegiance of seven. Believing that no State can in any way lawfully get out of the Union without the consent of the others and that it is the duty of the President to run the machine as it is,[17] he had to determine on a line of policy toward the States that had constituted themselves the Southern Confederacy. But any such policy was certain to be complicated by the desirability of retaining in the Union the border slave States of Maryland, Virginia, Kentucky and Missouri, as well as North Carolina, Tennessee and Arkansas, whose affiliations were close with the four border States. All seven were drawn towards the North by their affection for the Union and towards the South by the community of interest in the social system of slavery. One of Lincolns problems then was to make the love for the Union outweigh the sympathy with the slaveholding States that had seceded.

It is difficult to see how he could have bettered the policy to which he gave the keynote in his inaugural address. I hold, he said, that the union of these States is perpetual. Physically speaking we cannot separate. The power confided to me will be used to hold, occupy and possess the property and places belonging to the Government. This last declaration, though inevitable for a President in his position, outweighed all his words of conciliation and rendered of no avail his closing pathetic appeal to his dissatisfied fellow countrymen not to bring civil war on the country.[18]

During the progress of the secession, the forts, arsenals, custom-houses and other property of the Federal government within the limits of the cotton States were taken possession of by these States and, in due time, all this property was turned over to the Southern Confederacy, so that on March 4, all that Lincoln controlled was four military posts, of which Fort Sumter, commanding Charleston, was much the most important.[19] Since the very beginning of the secession movement, the eyes of the North had been upon South Carolina. For many years she had been restive under the bonds of the Union; her chief city, Charleston, had witnessed the disruption of the Democratic national convention,[20] and the consequent split in the party which made certain the Republican success of 1860, that in turn had led to the secession of the State and the formation of the Southern Confederacy. Fort Sumter had fixed the attention of the Northern mind by an occurrence in December, 1860. Major Anderson with a small garrison of United States troops had occupied Fort Moultrie; but, convinced that he could not defend

---

[16] III, 291-296, 320-325; Lect., 77*et seq.* The first session of this Provisional Congress ended March 16.

[17] Lincoln, C. W. I., 660.

[18] III, 318.

[19] III, 280, 285 n., 321.

[20] II, 450.

that fort against any attack from Charleston, he had, secretly on the night after Christmas, withdrawn his force to Fort Sumter, a much stronger post. Next morning, when the movement was discovered, Charleston fumed with rage whilst the North, on hearing the news, was jubilant and made a hero of Anderson.[21] Lincoln recognized the importance of holding Fort Sumter but he also purposed to use all means short of the compromise of his deepest convictions to retain the border slave States and North Carolina, Tennessee and Arkansas in the Union. The action of these three turned upon Virginia, whose convention was in session, ready to take any action which the posture of affairs seemed to demand. The fundamental difficulty now asserted itself. To hold Fort Sumter was to Lincoln a bounden duty but to the Virginians it savored of coercion; and coercion in this case meant forcing a State which had seceded, back into the Union. If an attempt was made to coerce a State, Virginia would join the Southern Confederacy. The Confederate States now regarded the old Union as a foreign power whose possession of a fort within their limits, flying the American flag, was a daily insult. They attempted to secure Sumter by an indirect negotiation with the Washington government and were encouraged by the assurances of Seward, Lincolns Secretary of State and most trusted counsellor. Had the President known of Sewards intimation, which was almost a promise, that Sumter would be evacuated, he would have been greatly perturbed and would have called a halt in the negotiations to the end that the Southern commissioners be undeceived. On April 1 he was further troubled by a paper, Some Thoughts for the Presidents Consideration, which Seward had privately submitted to him as an outline of the fit policy to be pursued. This was briefly: the evacuation of Fort Sumter; the re-enforcement of the other posts in the South; a demand at once for explanations from Spain and France and, if they were not satisfactory, a call of a special session of Congress to declare was against those two nations; also explanations to be sought from Great Britain and Russia. With that same rash disregard of his chief and blind reliance on his own notions of statecraft which he had shown in his negotiations with Justice Campbell, the intermediary between himself and the Southern commissioners, who had been sent to Washington by Davis, he gave the President a strong hint that the execution of this policy should be devolved upon some member of the Cabinet and that member, himself. The proposed foreign policy was reckless and wholly unwarranted. Our relations with these four powers were entirely peaceful; to use Sewards own words less than three months before, there is not a nation on earth that is not an interested, admiring friend.[22] Seward had got it into his head that, if our nation should provoke a foreign war, the cotton States would unite in amity with the North and like brothers fight the common foe under the old flag. Lincoln of course saw that the foreign policy proposed was wild and foolish but

---

[21] III, 216.
[22] Bancroft, II, 134, 136, 157.

ignored it in his considerate reply to Some Thoughts for the Presidents Consideration; he kept the existence of the paper rigidly a secret;[23] he did not demand the Secretarys resignation; he had for him no word of sarcasm or reproach.

The President submitted to another drain on his time and strength in the persistent scramble for office. The grounds, halls, stairways, closets of the White House, wrote Seward, are filled with office seekers; and Lincoln said, I seem like one sitting in a palace assigning apartments to importunate applicants, while the structure is on fire and likely soon to perish in ashes.[24] When he ought to have been able to concentrate his mind on the proper attitude to the seceding States, he was hampered by the ceaseless demands for a lucrative recognition from his supporters and by the irrational proposals of the chief of his Cabinet.

The great problem now was Sumter. What should be done about it? On the day after his inauguration, the President was informed that Anderson believed a re-enforcement of 20,000 men necessary for the defence of the post;[25] after being transported to the neighborhood by sea, they must fight their way through to the fort. For the South Carolinians had been steadily at work on the islands in Charleston harbor erecting batteries and strengthening the forts which bore on Sumter. Moreover, Andersons provisions would not last beyond the middle of April. General Scott, the head of the army, advised the evacuation of Sumter, a logical step in the course of action toward the South, which he and other men of influence had advocated and which he expressed in the pertinent words, Wayward sisters depart in peace.[26] At the Cabinet meeting of March 15 the President asked his advisers, If it be possible to provision Fort Sumter, is it wise to attempt it? Four agreed with Seward, saying, No; only two gave an affirmative answer. Lincoln undoubtedly had moments of thinking that the Fort must be evacuated.[27] With his eye upon Virginia, whose convention he hoped might adjourn without action, he may have promised one of her representatives that he would withdraw Anderson, provided the Virginia convention, always a menace of secession while it continued to sit, would adjourn sine die. The evidence is too conflicting to justify a positive assertion; but if such a proposal were made, it was never transmitted to and acted upon by the convention.[28]

In the final decision, the sentiment of the North had to be taken into account. To abandon Sumter would seem to indicate that a peaceful separation would follow;

---

[23] It was not disclosed until Nicolay and Hay printed it in their History in the *Century Magazine,* February, 1888.

[24] III, 326, 327.

[25] The full strength of the regular army was 17,000 men, N. & H., IV, 65.

[26] III, 341.

[27] *Ibid.*

[28] III, 344; the authorities cited in n. 3; J. Hay. Oct. 22, 1861, I, 47; private letters from Horace White, June 11, 1908-March 7, 1909. See Life of Trumbull, Horace White, 158.

that the principle of the sovereignty of the States and secession had triumphed. Finally, with increasing support in his Cabinet, Lincoln came to a wise decision. Re-enforcement from a military point of view was impracticable; to reach the fort the North might have to fire the first shot. But, as a political measure, he decided to send bread to Anderson,[29] so that Sumter would not have to be evacuated from lack of food. In accordance with his previous promise,[30] he sent word to the Governor of South Carolina of his intention. Beauregard, commander of the Confederate troops at Charleston, who in company with the Governor heard the formal notification, telegraphed it to the Confederate Secretary of War at Montgomery, receiving two days later [April 10] the order to demand the evacuation of Fort Sumter and, if this was refused, to proceed to reduce it.

The demand was made; and when Anderson had written his refusal to comply with it he observed to the Confederate aides, the bearers of Beauregards note, If you do not batter the fort to pieces about us, we shall be starved out in a few days.[31] Beauregard, acting with caution, transmitted this remark to Montgomery where equal caution not to precipitate hostilities was shown in the reply: Do not desire needlessly to bombard Fort Sumter. If Major Anderson will state the time at which he will evacuate Sumter you are authorized thus to avoid the effusion of blood. Evacuation was redemanded by Beauregards aides at three quarters of an hour after midnight of April 11. This was again refused, but Anderson wrote, I will evacuate Fort Sumter by noon on the 15th instant should I not receive prior to that time controlling instructions from my government or additional supplies.[32] The aides considered these terms manifestly futile[33] and, acting in accordance with the letter of their instructions, they gave the order to Fort Johnson to open fire; the first shell was fired at half past four on the morning of April 12. This shot, the signal for the bombardment to begin, caused a profound thrill throughout the United States and in point of fact it inaugurated four years of civil war.[34]

The bombardment was unnecessary. Sumter might have been had without it. Beauregard was needlessly alarmed over the relief expedition that was bringing bread to Anderson. He feared a descent upon the South Carolina coast by the United States fleet then lying at the entrance of the harbor for the supposed purpose of re-enforcing Fort Sumter. One of his aides reported that four large steamers are plainly in view standing off the bar. The people in Charleston thought that there were six men-of-war in the offing.[35] In connection with the general

---

[29] N. & H., IV, 44.

[30] Ibid., 33.

[31] III, 348.

[32] O. R., I, 14, 301. In both despatches are provisos unnecessary for this narrative.

[33] O. R., I, 60.

[34] O. R., I, 31, 306, 307.

[35] Chesnut 33, 39. "The steamer *Nashville* from New York [merchant steamer] and a number of merchant vessels reached the bar and awaited the result of the bombardment,

alarm on shore, it is interesting to note the actual mishaps of the relief expedition. This was intended to consist of four war-ships, three steam-tugs and the merchant steamer Baltic. The Baltic, with G. V. Fox, who had command of the expedition, on board, arrived off Charleston one hour and a half before the bombardment began, but found there only one warship.[36] Another[37] arrived at seven in the morning; but without the Powhatan,[38] the most important of the war-ships and the one carrying the equipment necessary for the undertaking, nothing could be accomplished, and no attempt was made to provision the fort. Administrative inefficiency, Sewards meddlesomeness and a heavy storm at sea conjoined to cause the failure of the expedition. Fox and his companions watched the bombardment, chafing at their powerlessness to render their brothers-in-arms any assistance.

Before leaving Sumter Beauregards aides notified Anderson in writing that in an hour their batteries would open on the fort. Anderson and his officers went through the casemates where the men were sleeping, waked them, told them of the impending attack and of his decision not to return the fire until after daylight. The first shell was from Fort Johnson; at half past four, it rose high in air and curving in its course burst almost directly over the fort.[39] The next shot came from Cummings Point, fired, it is said, by a venerable secessionist from Virginia who had long awaited the glory of this day. The official account does not confirm the popular impression, but the Lieutenant-Colonel in command wrote that his men were greatly incited by the enthusiasm and example of this old Virginian who was at one of the Cummings Point batteries during the greater part of the bombardment.[40] After Cummings Point all the batteries opened in quick succession; Sumter was surrounded by a circle of fire.[41] Meanwhile the men in the fort, alive to the novelty of the scene, watched the shot and shell directed at them, until, realizing the danger of exposure, they retired to the bomb-proofs to await the usual roll-call and order for breakfast. Having no more bread, they ate pork and damaged rice. At seven o'clock, Anderson gave the order and Sumter discharged its first gun at Cummings Point, following up this shot with a vigorous fire. An hour and a half later Sumter opened upon Moultrie and from that time a steady and continuous fire between the two was kept up throughout the day.[42] For the people

---

giving indications to those inside of a large naval fleet off the harbor." G. V. Fox, O. R. N., IV, 249; Chadwick, 333.

[36] *Harriet Lane,* revenue steamer.

[37] *Pawnee.*

[38] The *Powhatan* had been detached and never arrived at Charleston. The *Pocahontas* arrived at 2 P.M., April 13.

[39] Crawford, 427.

[40] O. R., I, 35, 44, 46, 54.

[41] Crawford, 427.

[42] O. R., I, 40.

of Charleston who gathered on the house-tops and thronged to the wharves and to their favorite promenade, the Battery, this artillery duel was a mighty spectacle. They had lost all love for the Union; they hated the American flag somewhat as the Venetians hated the Austrian and, though apprehensive of danger to their husbands, sons and brothers, they rejoiced that the time was drawing near when the enemy should no longer hold a fort commanding their harbor and city.

In the early afternoon the fire of Sumter slackened; cartridges were lacking, although the six needles in the fort were kept steadily employed until all the extra clothing of the companies, all coarse paper and extra hospital sheets had been used.[43] After dark Sumter stopped firing; the Confederate batteries continued to throw shells, though at longer intervals. As, during the dark and stormy night, it was almost confidently expected that the United States fleet would attempt to land troops upon the islands or to throw men into Fort Sumter by means of boats, there was ceaseless vigilance on Morris and Sullivans islands.[44] Early on Saturday morning [April 13] the bombardment was renewed. The men in the fort ate the last of the damaged rice with pork, but they sprang briskly to their work. Fort Sumter opened early and spitefully and paid especial attention to Fort Moultrie, wrote Moultries commander.[45] Soon hot shot from Moultrie and other batteries set the officers quarters on fire. The powder magazine was in danger. Anderson ordered fifty barrels removed and distributed around in the casemates, the magazine doors to be closed and packed with earth. As in the meantime the wooden barracks had taken fire, endangering the powder in the casemates, he commanded that all but five barrels should be thrown into the sea. At one o'clock the flag-staff was struck and fell; and the fallen flag, though soon hoisted again, together with the smoke and the flames gave the Confederates reason to believe that Anderson was in distress. An aide under a white flag was despatched to him from Cummings Point; three more from the city by Beauregard. Negotiations followed resulting in honorable terms. I marched out of the fort Sunday afternoon the 14th instant, reported Anderson, with colors flying and drums beating, bringing away company and private property, and saluting my flag with fifty guns.[46]

In this momentous battle, no man on either side was killed. As compared with the military writing of two years later, the crudity of the contemporary correspondence and reports is grimly significant. They told of the work of boys learning the rudiments of war boys who would soon be seasoned veterans wise in the methods of destruction. A strenuous schooling this; and the beginning of it was the artillery duel in Charleston harbor.

---

[43] O. R., I, 19, 21.
[44] O. R., I, 31.
[45] O. R., I, 41.
[46] O. R., I, 12.

Beauregards aides assumed too great a responsibility in giving the order to fire the first shot; they should have referred Andersons reply to their chief. There can be no doubt that the Confederate States would have obtained peacefully on Monday what they got by force on Sunday. If Beauregard had had Andersons last response, he would unquestionably have waited to ask Montgomery for further instructions. The presence of the United States fleet was of course disquieting; yet the danger from this source, even as exaggerated in Beauregards mind, could be averted quite as well by acting on the defensive, as by the bombardment of Fort Sumter.[47] But South Carolina was hot for possession of the fort and the aides who gave the order that precipitated hostilities were swayed by the passion of the moment.

In April, 1861, war was undoubtedly inevitable. The House divided against itself could not stand. The irrepressible conflict had come to a head; words were a salve no longer. Under the circumstances it was fortunate for Lincoln that the South became the aggressor. Davis's elaborate apology[48] and the writing inspired by it could never answer the questions put by Northern to Southern soldiers, when they met under a flag of truce or in the banter between Confederates and Federals when opportunities offered, Who began the war? Who struck the first blow? Who battered the walls of Fort Sumter?[49] At one stamp of his foot, the President called the whole nation to arms, wrote Henry Adams in 1861 while in Washington.[50] He referred to the Proclamation asking for 75,000 volunteers whose first service would probably be to repossess the forts, places and property which have been seized from the Union. Lincoln wrote this on the Sunday when Anderson marched out of Sumter (April 14) and, following closely the act of February 28, 1795, his authority, he called forth that number of militia, apportioned among twenty-seven States, to suppress, in the seven cotton States, combinations beyond the ordinary course of judicial proceedings, and he summoned Congress to meet on July 4 in special session. In the particulars communicated by the War department to the several governors, the time of service was fixed at three months, but this represented in no way the Presidents opinion as to the probable duration of the war; he was simply following the act of 1795 which provided that the militia could be held to service for only thirty days after the next meeting of Congress.

After two days full of indignant outbursts at the insult to the flag, the people of the North read the Presidents call for troops. That first gun at Sumter, wrote Lowell, brought all the free States to their feet as one man. The heather is on fire, said George Ticknor. I never before knew what a popular excitement can be. At the North there never was anything like it.[51] Governors, legislatures, wherever

---

[47] O. R. N., IV, 252, 262.

[48] III, 351 n. 3.

[49] Watson, 98; see Russell, 204.

[50] M. H. S., XLIII, 687.

these were in session, and private citizens acted in generous co-operation. Men forgot that they had been Republicans or Democrats; the partisan was sunk in the patriot. Washington was supposed to be in danger of capture by the Southern troops flushed with their victory at Sumter; armed and equipped soldiers were needed for its defence. The Sixth Massachusetts was the first regiment to respond, leaving Boston on April 17 and arriving in Baltimore two days later. The only approach by rail to Washington was through Baltimore where the strong feeling for secession was vented in threats that Northern troops, bent on the invasion of the South, would not be permitted to pass through its streets. The Colonel of the Sixth, being informed in Philadelphia of the situation, timed his arrival in Baltimore for the morning (April 19). Here a transfer was usually made by means of horses, drawing the passenger cars through the streets from the Philadelphia to the Washington station, a mile distant, where a change was made to the cars of the Baltimore and Ohio railroad, which owned the forty miles of single track to the nations capital. Seven companies were thus driven rapidly through the city. Meanwhile an angry mob had collected, torn up the railroad and erected a barricade to dispute the passage of the rest of the regiment. Informed of this the captains of the four remaining companies decided that they must march to the station; but before they had started, up came the mob, carrying a secession flag and threatening that, if an attempt were made to march through the streets, every white nigger of them would be killed. The Captain, on whom the command devolved, gave the order to march, a policeman leading the way. As the soldiers stepped forward, they received a volley of brick-bats and paving-stones from the mob; a hundred yards farther on they came to a bridge which had been partially demolished. We had to play scotch-hop to get over it, said the Captain. The order double-quick was then given, which led the mob to believe that the soldiers either had no ammunition or dared not use it. In their growing rage, they fired pistol-shots into the ranks, and one soldier fell dead. The Captain gave the order fire; a number of the mob fell. The mayor of Baltimore arrived and placed himself at the head of the column. The mob grew bolder, he wrote, and the attack became more violent. Various persons were killed and wounded on both sides. As his presence failed to allay the tumult, the mayor left the head of the column, but the four companies marched on, fighting their way through to their comrades, aided by the city marshal with fifty policemen who covered their rear. In the Baltimore and Ohio cars with the blinds closed, the regiment received a volley of stones which so infuriated one of the soldiers that he fired and killed a prominent citizen, a mere looker-on. Finally the train got away and reached Washington late in the afternoon. Of the regiment four had been killed and thirty-six wounded. The casualties in the mob were larger.

---

[51] III, 357.

In Baltimore the excitement was intense. The streets are red with Maryland blood are the marshals words. Secessionists and Southern sympathizers were rampant; stifling the Union sentiment of the city, they carried everything with a high hand and dictated the action of the constituted authorities. The excitement is fearful. Send no more troops here, is the joint despatch of the governor of Maryland and the mayor of Baltimore to the President. So great was the commotion that a part of the State and city military was called out; citizens volunteered, and, after being more or less adequately furnished with arms, were enrolled for the purpose of defence under the direction of the board of police. In Monument Square a mass-meeting assembled, whose sentiment was decidedly opposed to any attempt at coercion of the Confederate States. Apprehending a severe fight and bloodshed if more Northern troops attempted to pass through Baltimore, the mayor and city marshal ordered the burning of certain bridges on the Philadelphia, Wilmington and Baltimore railroad, the line to Philadelphia, and on the Northern Central, the line to Harrisburg; three bridges on each railroad were burned, thus completely severing the rail communication with the North.[52]

The seven days since the evacuation of Sumter had been crowded with events of a deeply ominous character. On April 17, the Virginia convention, sitting in secret, had passed an ordinance of secession, an act which became known to the authorities in Washington on the following day. As a rejoinder to Lincolns call for 75,000 troops, Jefferson Davis by proclamation invited applications for letters of marque and reprisal against the merchant marine of the United States. The President retorted (April 19) by proclaiming a blockade of Southern ports from South Carolina to Texas inclusive, and declaring that privateers acting under the pretended authority of the Confederate States would be treated as pirates. On the 18th, the United States commander at Harpers Ferry in Virginia, deeming his position untenable, abandoned it after demolishing the arsenal and burning the armory building. On the 20th the Gosport navy-yard was partially destroyed by the Union forces and left to the possession of the Virginians. On the same day Robert E. Lee, who was esteemed by Scott the ablest officer next to himself in the service, and who had been unofficially offered the active command of the Union army, resigned his commission, thus indicating that he had decided to cast his lot with the South. The gravity of the situation was heightened by the severance of communications between the national capital and the North, as a result of the trouble in Baltimore.[53] On Sunday night (April 21) the telegraph ceased to be available. The only connection the government now had with its loyal territory and people was by means of private couriers; these made their way with difficulty through Maryland, where for the moment an unfriendly element prevailed. Correct information was difficult to get, and rumors of all sorts filled the air. The

---

[52] O. R., II, LI, Pt. I, III, I; N. & H., IV; Globe, July 18, 1861; Hanson; III; Pearson.

[53] The Baltimore riot occurred on Friday, April 19.

government and citizens alike were apprehensive of an attack on the capital. They feared that Beauregards South Carolina army would be transported North as fast as the railroads could carry it and, re-enforced in Richmond by Virginia troops, would easily take Washington. Preparations were made to withstand a siege. Panic seized the crowds of office-seekers, driving them northwards. Many secessionist citizens, fearing that the whole male population of the city would be impressed for its defence, left for the South. Washington, wrote General Scott, on April 22, is now partially besieged, threatened and in danger of being attacked on all sides in a day or two or three. The arrival of the Eighth Massachusetts and Seventh New York at Annapolis, who had finished their journey to that point by water, prompted the governor to telegraph to the President advising that no more troops be ordered or allowed to pass through Maryland; and he suggested that Lord Lyons [the English minister] be requested to act as mediator between the contending parties of our country.[54]

John Hay, then one of the Presidents private secretaries, has given in his diary a graphic account of these days. Of the novel scene of the Sixth Massachusetts quartered in the Capitol, he wrote, The contrast was very painful between the grey-haired dignity that filled the Senate chamber when I saw it last, and the present throng of bright-looking Yankee boys, the most of them bearing the signs of New England rusticity in voice and manner, scattered over the desks, chairs and galleries, some loafing, many writing letters slowly and with plough-hardened hands or with rapid-glancing clerkly fingers while Grow [representative from Pennsylvania, later speaker of the House] stood patient by the desk and franked for everybody. The town is full to-night (April 20) of feverish rumors about a meditated assault upon the city. This morning (April 21) we mounted the battlements of the Executive Mansion and the Ancient (Lincoln) took a long look down the bay [troops were expected to arrive via Fort Monroe, Chesapeake bay, and the Potomac river]. It was a water-haul. A telegram intercepted on its way to Baltimore states that our Yankees (Eighth Massachusetts) and New Yorkers (Seventh New York) have landed at Annapolis (April 22). Weary and foot-sore but very welcome, they will probably greet us to-morrow. Housekeepers here are beginning to dread famine. Flour has made a sudden spring to $18 a barrel.[55]

The President was keenly alive to the importance of holding the capital and feared greatly for its safety. As Tuesday the 23d passed and no soldiers came, he paced the floor of the executive office in restless anxiety looking out of the window down the Potomac for the long expected boats; thinking himself alone he exclaimed in tones of anguish, Why don't they come! Why don't they come! That same day had brought a mail from New York three days old, containing newspapers which told that the uprising of the North continued with growing

---

[54] III, 364 *et seq.*

[55] J. Hay, I, 14 *et seq.*

strength and unbounded enthusiasm, that the Seventh New York regiment had already departed and that troops from Rhode Island were on the way. Next day (April 24), wrote Hay, was one of gloom and doubt. Everybody seems filled with a vague distrust and recklessness. The idea seemed to be reached by Lincoln when, chatting with the volunteers (Sixth Massachusetts) this morning, he said: I don't believe there is any North! The Seventh regiment is a myth! Rhode Island is not known in our geography any longer. You are the only Northern realities.[56]

Meanwhile the Seventh New York and Eighth Massachusetts were marching to Annapolis junction where they found a train which took them quickly to Washington. The Seventh regiment arrived first (April 25). Forming as soon as they left the cars, they marched up Pennsylvania avenue to the White House. To the people who noted their military bearing and to the President who reviewed them, they were a goodly sight. Their arrival indicated that a route from the loyal North to its capital was open, that other regiments were on the way soon to arrive and that Washington was safe.[57] It was not until May 9, however, that Northern troops attempted to pass through Baltimore; coming from Perryville in transports and landing under the guns of a revenue steamer, they were then carried in cars under ample police protection through South Baltimore; they were not molested. Four days later, and twenty-four after the severance of communication, the first train from Philadelphia arrived at the capital, and shortly afterwards regular railroad communication with the Northern cities, for passengers as well as for the military, was re-established.[58] The people of the Confederate States looked upon Lincolns call for 75,000 troops as a declaration of war, implying a policy of invasion of their territory, an attack upon themselves and their property. The uprising in the South was precisely similar to that in the North. The people declared that they would resist the Lincoln government as long as they could command a man or a dollar. The co-operation of governors and individuals with Davis matches the cooperation of Northerners with Lincoln. If a European, ignorant of the names of our States or of our public men in 1861, were to read the Official Records, the only way he could tell which side he was reading about would be by reference to the editors titles of Union or Confederate correspondence.

The first stakes for Lincoln and Davis to play for were Maryland, Virginia, North Carolina, Kentucky, Tennessee, Missouri and Arkansas. Despite the unfortunate demonstrations in her chief city, Baltimore, Maryland contained a

---

[56] III, 368; J. Hay, I, 23. He added, "Seward's messengers sent out by the dozen do not return." An Ass't. Adj. Gen. telegraphed from Washington, "Washington will fall from starvation alone within ten days." O. R., LI, Pt. I, 367.

[57] III, 372 *et seq.* The alarm in regard to Washington was natural but not well founded, *I bid.,* 374 *et seq.*

[58] III, 389; N. & H., IV, 172.

powerful element whose love of the Union was shared by her governor; under his guidance with the tactful help of the President she cast her lot with the North.

Two days before the bombardment of Sumter, Roger A. Pryor, a Virginia secessionist, in an impassioned speech in Charleston, said, I will tell you, gentlemen, what will put Virginia in the Southern Confederacy in less than an hour by Shrewsbury clock strike a blow. He knew his countrymen. The excitement in Virginia was equal to that in the cotton States. To the requisition for her quota of troops under the Presidents call for 75,000, her governor expressed the public opinion in a defiant refusal. Montgomery had already heard that Virginia was in a blaze of excited indignation against Lincolns proclamation.[59] On April 17, her convention, by a vote of 103 : 46, adopted an ordinance of secession, which was to be valid if ratified by a vote of the people on the fourth Thursday of May.[60] As the authorities assumed the result of the popular vote, they proceeded to join the fortunes of Virginia with the Confederate States. Having telegraphed to Montgomery the common desire, the governor received at once this despatch from Davis: Resolution for alliance received. Proposition cordially accepted. Commissioner will be sent by next train.[61] In fulfilment of this promise Alexander H. Stephens, the Vice-President of the Confederate States, went to Richmond. Although he wrote of the embarrassments and difficulties in getting the arrangement effected, the common aim and sympathy were so certain that he negotiated a military alliance between the Confederate States and Virginia, giving the control and direction of her military force to Davis.[62] On May 7, the Confederate Congress admitted her into the Confederacy and, accepting the offer of her convention (April 27), made Richmond their capital (May 21).[63]

The governor of North Carolina replied to the Secretary of War: I regard the levy of troops made by the administration for the purpose of subjugating the States of the South as in violation of the Constitution and a gross usurpation of power. I can be no party to this war upon the liberties of a free people. You can get no troops from North Carolina.[64] Before Lincoln's call for troops two-thirds of the people of North Carolina were opposed to secession;[65] now, however, as speedily as a convention could be assembled, an ordinance of secession was adopted by a unanimous vote, and North Carolina became one of the Confederate States.[66]

---

[59] O. R., LI, Pt. II, 11.

[60] On May 23 a majority of 96,750 was given for its ratification; the 32,134 votes cast against it came mostly from the western counties. III, 387.

[61] O. R., LI, Pt. II, 18.

[62] All based on ratification by the popular vote. O. R., IV, I, 242 *et seq.;* III, 379.

[63] III, 396; O. R., IV, I, 255.

[64] O. R., III, I, 72.

[65] O. R., LI, Pt. II, 831.

[66] III, 383.

On May 6, Arkansas, through her convention, passed an ordinance of secession with only one dissenting vote; soon afterwards she joined the Southern Confederacy.

In answer to Lincolns requisition for troops, Tennessees governor said, Tennessee will not furnish a single man for purpose of coercion.[67] She did not adopt an ordinance of secession, but during the month of May her legislature made a military league with the Confederate States, and she became one of them, subject to the vote of the people which was taken on June 8; by a majority of nearly 58,000, they declared in favor of separation from the Union and of joining the Southern Confederacy.[68]

Kentucky, so telegraphed her governor, will furnish no troops for the wicked purpose of subduing her sister Southern States.[69] But he could not draw her into the secession movement. A drift of conflicting opinions held her in the balance, but Lincoln knew his native State well and, by tact and forbearance, he guided the Union men so that their influence continually spread until the month of August, when, in the newly elected legislature, they had a majority of nearly three-fourths in each branch.[70]

Missouris governor was likewise favorable to secession, replying to the call for troops: Your requisition, in my judgment, is illegal, unconstitutional and revolutionary in its object, inhuman and diabolical. Not one man will the State of Missouri furnish to carry on any such unholy crusade.[71] He had, however, a resolute antagonist in Francis P. Blair, Jr., a man of extraordinary physical and moral courage, of high social position in St. Louis and personally very popular. Between him and the governor, there ensued four months of political and martial manoeuvring, but Blair won in the end and Missouri remained in the Union.[72]

The array was now complete. Twenty-three States were pitted against eleven; twenty-two million people against nine, and of the nine, three and one-half million were slaves. Each side had peculiar advantages.[73] But neither section understood the other. If the South had known that secession must result in war and that the foe would be a united North, it is doubtful if she would have proceeded to the last extremity. It is still more doubtful if the North would have fought, had she known that she must contend against a united Southern people. The remark of Chatham, Conquer a free population of three million souls? the thing is impossible, had become an axiom of the English race. But now the North confronted five and a half million earnest and brave people, supported by three and a half million

---

[67] O. R., III, I, 81.
[68] III, 384.
[69] O. R., III, I, 70.
[70] III, 391; N. & H., IV, 240.
[71] O. R., III, I, 83.
[72] III, 393.
[73] III, 397; Lect., 95.

servants, who grew the food and took care of the women and children at home while the men fought in the field. The North was contending for the Union on the theory that a strong and unscrupulous minority had overridden the majority of Southerners who had no desire for secession, loathed the idea of civil war and, if protected and encouraged, would make themselves felt in a movement looking towards allegiance to the national government. Lincoln comprehended the sentiment of the North and he never gave public expression to any opinion that he did not sincerely hold. In his fourth of July message to the special session of Congress he said: It may well be questioned whether there is to-day a majority of the legally qualified voters of any State, except perhaps South Carolina, in favor of disunion. There is much reason to believe that the Union men are the majority in many, if not in every other one, of the so-called seceded States.

I have discussed this matter so thoroughly in my History that it is unnecessary for me to recur to it at length. Nevertheless, I may observe that on returning to the subject twenty years after my first discussion of it, and on going through the original materials again, I have been more firmly convinced than before of the unanimity of the Confederate States after the Presidents call for troops. The citations from William H. Russells letters to the London Times and from his Diary, which I gave in my third volume, furnish an authoritative corroboration of the other evidence. This intelligent and fair-minded man, who sympathized with the North because he hated slavery and was convinced that the invocation of State-rights was for protection to slavery, extension of slave territory and free-trade in slave produce with the outer world, made a journey through the Southern States between April 14 and June 19, 1861, and became convinced that the people of the Confederacy were united. Summing up the results of his tour, he wrote: I met everywhere with but one feeling, with exceptions which proved its unanimity and force. To a man the people went with their States, and had but one battle-cry, States-rights and death to those who make war against them!

In spite of his supercilious criticism, Russell wished the North to win because he foresaw in her victory the destruction of slavery. But he did not believe that she could triumph. In April, while in Charleston, he wrote, I am more satisfied than ever that the Union can never be restored as it was, and that it has gone to pieces, never to be put together again in the old shape, at all events, by any power on earth. In New Orleans, on May 31, he set down in his Diary, Now that the separation has come, there is not, in the Constitution, or out of it, power to cement the broken fragments together. On the steamer on the Mississippi which brought him from a Confederate camp to Cairo, he met an Englishman who was steward of the boat and not averse to giving his opinion, which Russell quotes with apparent approval of the concluding statement. This war, the steward said, is all about niggers; I've been sixteen years in the country, and I never met one of them yet was fit to be anything but a slave; I know the two sections well and I tell you, sir, the North cant whip the South let them do their best.[74]

Mixed with the stern determination on both sides to fight out the conflict was a sincere regret that the Union should be broken. When an old gentleman, whom Russell met in Charleston, spoke of the prospect of civil war tears rolled down his cheeks, but regarding it as the natural consequence of the insults, injustice and aggression of the North against Southern rights he had no apprehension for the result. Mrs. Chesnut wrote of the separation, The wrench has been awful. When the Virginia convention was considering the ordinance of secession, one delegate, who spoke against it, became incoherent in his emotion and finally broke down sobbing. Another, who voted for it, wept like a child at the thought of rending ancient ties.[75] It is Henry Adams's opinion based on his recollections of Washington in the winter of 1861 that, Not one man in America wanted the civil war or expected or intended it. Similar was Nicolays impression at the same period in Springfield while assisting Lincoln. Nobody wanted war is the word.[76] And when it came, J. D. Cox and James A. Garfield, then members of the Ohio legislature, groaned at the shame, the folly, the outrage of civil war in our land.[77]

John T. Morse, in his biography of Lincoln, which possesses somehow the authority of a contemporary document as well as the interest of an artistic study of a great man, wrote, Historians say rhetorically that the North sprang to arms; and it really would have done so if there had been any arms to spring to; but muskets were scarce.[78] The correspondence in Volume I, Series III of the Official Records amply confirms this statement. The governors of the several States, in their communications to the United States War Department, began by asking for muskets and cannon; soon they were begging for them. Ohio was undoubtedly a fair example of the States west of the Alleghanies. McClellan, who had been appointed major-general of her volunteers, made an inspection of the State arsenal and found, a few boxes of smooth-bore muskets, rusted and damaged; two or three smooth-bore 6-pounders which had been honey-combed by firing salutes; a confused pile of mildewed harness which had been once used for artillery horses. As he went out of the door he said half humorously, half sadly, A fine stock of munitions on which to begin a great war.[79] The governor of Iowa demand of the Secretary of War, for Gods sake send us some arms, exemplified the feeling of all. All the States wanted rifled-muskets, of which the government had only a small supply; and when they received old flint-lock muskets or the same percussioned, they felt that due attention was not being paid to their necessities. Morton, the governor of Indiana, reported that the arms received by his State were of an inferior character, being old muskets rifled out; in very many instances, he added,

[74] Russell, 106, 251, 315, 329; III, 407 n., 433 n.; Lect., 157 *et seq.*
[75] Russell, 117; Chesnut, 53; III, 386.
[76] Nicolay, 153. Nicolay was Lincoln's first private secretary; see Mark Twain, I, 160.
[77] III, 359 n.
[78] Morse, I, 252.
[79] J. D. Cox, B. & L., I, 90.

the bayonets have to be driven on with a hammer and many others are so loose that they can be shaken off. Our boys, wrote the governor of Iowa, don't feel willing to carry old-fashioned muskets to the field to meet men armed with better weapons. Appreciating the impotence of the Federal government, Massachusetts sent an agent to Europe with money for the purchase of improved arms and New York bought Enfield rifles in England. The governors of the several States begged for accoutrements, uniforms and clothing. There was urgent need of forage caps, infantry trousers, flannel sack coats, flannel shirts, bootees, stockings, great coats and blankets. The government, wrote the Secretary of War to Morton, finds itself unable to furnish at once the uniforms and clothing demanded by the large force suddenly brought into service.[80]

McClellan wrote of his Ohio troops: I have never seen so fine a body of men collected together. The material is superb but has no organization or discipline.[81] A captain of the regular army who came to muster a number of these regiments into the United States service, looking down the line of stalwart men, clad in the Garibaldi red flannel shirt (for lack of uniforms) exclaimed, My God! that such men should be food for powder![82] Good-looking and energetic young fellows, too good to be food for gunpowder, wrote John Hay of the Sixth Massachusetts![83] And the same remark might have been made of nearly all the three-months men from every State.

Before the end of April, Lincoln had made up his mind that he had embarked on a long war. The quotas of three-months volunteers were rapidly filled and, as more men came forward, he determined to turn the prolonged outburst of patriotism to account by prevailing upon the late-comers to enlist for three years. On May 3, he increased the army by proclamation.[84] The response to his different calls for troops was thus described in his Fourth-of-July message: One of the greatest perplexities of the government is to avoid receiving troops faster than it can provide for them. In a word, the people will save their government if the government itself will do its part only indifferently well. Our Secretary of War (Cameron), to judge from the official correspondence during the first months of the war, appears to have been good-natured, inefficient, short-sighted, a man of narrow views. Lincoln, on the other hand, keenly alive to the situation, was repeatedly urging the War Department to accept the men who offered themselves for three years and take the chance of providing them with arms, uniforms and monthly pay; thus, in the beginning, even as in the later years of his presidency, his first thought was for the

---

[80] O. R., III, I.

[81] O. R., LI, Pt. I, 333.

[82] J. D. Cox, B. & L., I, 97.

[83] J. Hay, I, 13.

[84] 42,034 volunteers for three years; 22,714 for the regular army; 18,000 seamen for the navy. O. R., III, I, 145.

chief requirement of his side; he would have the men; the provision to be made for them could be left to the future.

The unpreparedness of the Southern people was similar to that of the Northern, but their difficulty in procuring arms and ammunition was greater. Accustomed as they had been to buy their powder from Northern factories, they were now obliged to develop this industry within their own borders. With less money and inferior credit they found it more difficult to make purchases abroad; moreover the blockade soon became a serious impediment to their commerce. On May 3, General Scott wrote, We rely greatly on the sure operation of a complete blockade of the Atlantic and Gulf ports soon to commence.[85] Mrs. Chesnut, who had dined with Jefferson Davis in Richmond on July 16, set down in her diary, We begin to cry out for more ammunition and already the blockade is beginning to shut it all out. The Confederate Secretary of War [Walker] seemed to lack geniality and showed in his correspondence with the governors more acerbity than was desirable in an officer of a new government organizing for a protracted conflict. On the other hand, Davis was at first superior in administrative capacity to Lincoln. His West Point training, army service in Mexico and efficient conduct of the War Department for four years had made him familiar with military details which Lincoln had now to master with painful effort. Lee, as commander of the Virginia forces, was an efficient aid to the governor in Richmond, which city was destined to be the most important military point in the Confederacy; but, affected by the disposition that prevailed on each side to overrate the other, he, like the governor of Iowa, thought that the enemy had much superior arms.[86]

In perusing the confidential Union and Confederate correspondence between the bombardment of Sumter and the battle of Bull Run, one is struck with the unreadiness of both South and North for war and with the contrast generally between military conditions in this country and in Europe. In 1870, the French minister of war told his colleagues and the Emperor that France was ready, more than ready, and to a commission of the Corps Legislatif, declared, So ready are we that, if the war were to last two years, not a gaiter button would be found wanting. Within ten days he had transported by railroad to the frontier nearly 200,000 men with cannon, horses and munitions. Meanwhile Bismarck was asking Moltke, What are our prospects of victory? I believe, replied Moltke, that we are more than a match for them always with the reservation that no one can foresee the issue of a great battle. And a rapid outbreak is, on the whole, more favorable to us than delay. In a little over a fortnights time, Moltke had a Prussian army more than twice as large as the French on the French frontier.[87]

---

[85] On April 27 the President had extended the blockade to Virginia and North Carolina. O. R., III, I, 122.

[86] O. R., LI, Pt. I, IV, I; Chesnut; N. & H.; IV.

[87] Ollivier, XV; de la Gorce, VI; Walpole, II; Ency. Brit. article Leboeuf; La Rousse,

Had either South or North had the comparatively imperfect preparation of France, with no similar development on the part of the other, that side would have swept everything before it. Had both South and North had the perfect organization of Prussia, the war might have been shorter. But the Prussian military system was impossible in the United States and even if possible, it would not have been considered worthwhile. The Americans, like the Athenians of the time of Pericles, then preferred to meet danger with a light heart but without laborious training.[88]

Davis, in his message of April 29 to his Congress, maintained that Lincolns call for 75,000 troops was a declaration of war against the Confederacy and he asked them to devise measures for their defence. Arguing that each State was sovereign and in the last resort the sole judge as well of its wrongs as of the mode and measure of redress, he justified secession and the formation of the Confederate States. We feel that our cause is just and holy, he declared. All we ask is to be let alone; that those who never held power over us shall not now attempt our subjugation by arms. This we will, this we must, resist to the direst extremity. Davis as President was obliged to make the best out of a situation which he regarded with considerable misgiving. He had been averse to war and had wished his Southern brethren less precipitate. Toward the end of June in Richmond, Mrs. Chesnut had with him a talk of nearly an hour, through which there ran, on his part, a sad refrain. His tone was not sanguine. He anticipated a long war. He laughed at the common brag that every Southerner was equal to three Yankees. Only fools, he continued, doubted the courage of the Yankees or their willingness to fight when they saw fit.[89]

The Confederates, said the President in his Fourth-of-July message, forced upon the country the distinct issue, immediate dissolution or blood. It was with the deepest regret that the executive found the duty of employing the war power in defense of the government forced upon him. He could but perform this duty or surrender the existence of the government. Using an expression of which he grew fond, the plain people, he addressed to them an argument in support of his position.

Lincoln of all men in 1861 was most thoroughly convinced that the Southerners would never have carried the doctrine of State-rights to the point of secession had it not been for the purpose of repelling what was considered an aggression on slavery; yet in his message there is not a word on this subject and the reason is not far to seek. Restricting the object of the war to the restoration of the Union, he had with him Democrats and Bell and Everett men as well as Republicans; a mention of slavery would at once have given rise to partisan contentions. At this early day, however, Lincoln understood the scope of the conflict and thus unbosomed

---

ibid.; von Sybel; Bismarck.

[88] Jowett, II, 39. Danger of war is meant.

[89] Chesnut; III, 299.

himself to the private secretary who was in sympathy with him: For my own part, I consider the central idea pervading this struggle is the necessity that is upon us of proving that popular government is not an absurdity. We must settle this question now, whether, in a free government, the minority have the right to break up the government whenever they choose. If we fail, it will go far to prove the incapability of the people to govern themselves. There may be one consideration used in stay of such final judgment but that is not for us to use in advance: that is, that there exists in our case an instance of a vast and far-reaching disturbing element, which the history of no other free nation will probably ever present. That, however, is not for us to say at present. Taking the government as we found it, we will see if the majority can preserve it.[90]

An official report of July 1 gives the strength of the Union army as 186,000.[91] The newspapers, especially the New York Tribune, had already been clamoring for an advance on Richmond. General Scott was urged not to lose the services of the three-months men whose time would soon expire.[92] Politicians, fearing the effect of delay on public sentiment, supported this demand; and men of experience and good judgment joined in the popular cry. As early as May Governor Andrew complained of the want of vigor, in the Northern operations and Senator Fessenden wrote, I am hoping every day to hear of some decided blow.[93] William H. Russell, basing his opinion on the European standard, with which his experience in the Crimea had made him familiar, gave an account of the wretched condition of the Union soldiers in camps near Washington, whose number, available for a campaign, he estimated at 30,000. I am opposed to national boasting, he wrote, but I do firmly believe that 10,000 British regulars (then apparently thinking he must say something for Englands ally) or 12,000 French with a proper establishment of artillery and cavalry, under competent commanders, would not only entirely repulse this army with the greatest ease but that they could attack them and march into Washington, over them or with them, whenever they pleased.[94]

The popular cry On to Richmond was dinned in the Presidents ears until he yielded to the opinion, that the Union army force a battle in eastern Virginia. A victory would maintain the unanimity of feeling that had prevailed since the firing on Sumter; it would be the earnest of a short war. With a short war in prospect patriotism would continue at its present high beat and such dissensions as might issue in an opposition party would not arise. Moreover, the good will of Europe would be preserved. Europe was now in sympathy with the Presidents assertion of

---

[90] May 7, J. Hay, I, 31.

[91] III, 360 n. 2.

[92] Russell; III.

[93] O. R., III, I, 182, 244.

[94] Russell, July 13, 403, 404.

the national authority, but it would be well to let her perceive that the United States government, to which she sent her envoys, had the stronger battalions. Furthermore, if the excellent men, who had volunteered for three months, were to be used at all in active service, they must soon take the field, as their term of enlistment was fast drawing to a close. Having taken all these considerations into account, the President called a number of generals in council with his Cabinet. McDowell, a graduate of West Point, a staff-officer during the Mexican war, and the present commander of the troops on the Virginia side of the Potomac, said that he would move against Beauregard, who had a force of 21,900 behind the stream called Bull Run, provided that Joseph E. Johnston, who was in the Shenandoah valley with 9000, could be prevented from joining Beauregard. General Scott, who felt that the army was in no condition to fight a battle in Virginia but who had deferred to the Presidents wish, said, If Johnston joins Beauregard he shall have Patterson on his heels. Patterson with 18,000 to 22,000 was depended upon to keep a sharp watch on Johnston and had been instructed to beat him or detain him in the valley.

On the afternoon of July 16 McDowells Grand Army, about 30,000 strong and composed, for the most part of three months volunteers supported by 1600 regulars, marched to the front and on the 18th occupied Centreville. No living American general had ever commanded so large a body of men, and McDowells experience as staff-officer in Mexico had been with a much smaller number. Excepting the regulars, the troops were raw as were likewise most of their officers; and this march of twenty-seven miles, which a year later would have been considered a bagatelle, was now a mighty undertaking. There was lack of discipline, wrote William T. Sherman, who commanded a brigade; with all my personal efforts, I could not prevent the men from straggling for water, blackberries or anything on the way they fancied. The troops did not know how to take care of their rations, to make them last the time they should, reported McDowell; moreover their excitement found vent in burning and pillaging. These excesses, however, were checked by McDowell.

Johnston, having received a telegram from Richmond to join Beauregard if practicable, managed to elude Patterson and started for Bull Run at noon of July 18. The discouragements of that days march to one accustomed, like myself, he wrote, to the steady gait of regular soldiers is indescribable. Because of frequent and unreasonable delays and lack of discipline he despaired of reaching Beauregard in time. He accordingly made arrangements for covering the final stage by rail. After a march of twenty-three miles, he and his infantry completed the remaining thirty-four by train; the cavalry and artillery continued on the wagon-road; on Saturday the 20th he had 6000 in union with Beauregard.

McDowell had heard rumors that Johnston had joined Beauregard but he did not credit them; so he went forward with his original plan which was to turn the Confederate left. On Sunday morning, July 21, he attacked. Owing to the inexperience of both officers and men, the delays in marching and manoeuvring made the attack three hours late, yet at ten o'clock the Union troops engaged the enemy and, being in superior force, drove him before them. The Confederates were in full retreat, but as they ran up the slope of the plateau about the Henry House, Thomas J. Jacksons brigade stood there calmly awaiting the onset. General Bee cried out in encouragement to his retreating troops, There is Jackson standing like a stone wall. As Stonewall Jackson he was known till the day of his death and ever afterwards.

Patterson had greatly overestimated Johnstons force and feared to make an attack; indeed in his alarm he marched north, directly away from the Confederates instead of following them. Unaware of his actual movement the Confederate generals thought that he would make haste to join McDowell. Beauregard therefore deemed it advisable to attack the Union forces with his right wing and centre before the expected re-enforcement came; Johnston, the ranking officer, approved the plan. A miscarriage of orders prevented the movement; at the same time McDowells attack came as a surprise and it was the sound of cannon that first told them he was trying to turn their left. It was four miles to the scene of action but Johnston and Beauregard rode thither as fast as their horses would carry them. We came not a moment too soon, said Johnston. The Confederates were demoralized; a disorderly retreat had begun; and it needed all the firmness and courage of the commanding generals to stem the tide. Beauregard remained in the thick of the fight, in command of the troops there engaged, while Johnston rode regretfully to the rear to hurry forward re-enforcements.

It was high noon when the two Confederate generals appeared on the field. The battle lasted until three. The hottest fighting was for the possession of the Henry plateau which the Union troops had seized. At two o'clock Beauregard gave the order to advance to recover the plateau. The charge was made with spirit. Jackson's brigade pierced the Union centre at the bayonets point; the other troops moved forward with equal vigor, broke the Union lines and swept them back from the open ground of the plateau. The Union troops rallied, recovered their ground and drove the Confederates from the plateau into the woods beyond. McDowell, who had this part of the field immediately under his own eye, thought this last repulse final and that the day was his.

Jefferson Davis, too anxious to remain in Richmond, went by rail to the scene of action. As he approached Manassas railroad junction he saw a cloud of dust raised by wagons that had been sent to the rear and heard distinctly the sound of firing. At the junction were a large number of men who had left the field in panic and who now gave Davis graphic accounts of the defeat of the army. He asked a gray-bearded man whose calm face and composed demeanor inspired confidence, how the battle had gone? Our line was broken, came the reply; all was confusion, the army routed and the battle lost. The conductor of the train refused to go farther but, on Davis's stern insistence, detached the locomotive and ran it to the headquarters, where Davis found horses for himself and his aide; two officers guided him thence toward the battle-field. On the way, he met a large number of stragglers and received frequent warnings that there was danger ahead; but the sound of firing was now fainter, which seemed to indicate both an advance of the Confederates and a waning of the battle. Meeting Johnston on a hill overlooking the field, he might in his question have used the words of Henry V at Agincourt, I know not if the day be ours or no? when Johnston at once assured him, that we had won the battle.

It was three o'clock when McDowell saw the Confederates retire to the woods, when he hoped that the fight was over and that his army had gained possession of the field. This hope was rudely dispelled. His men had made their last desperate effort. They had been up since two in the morning; one division had had a long fatiguing march. The day was intensely hot and the fight had lasted four and a half hours. Many of the men had thrown away their haversacks and canteens. They were choked with dust, thirsty, hungry and spent. Beauregard ordered forward all of his force within reach, including the reserve, for the purpose of making a last supreme effort to regain the plateau; he intended to lead the charge in person. Then loud cheers were heard proceeding from fresh troops. They were the remainder of the army of the Shenandoah who had followed Johnston as quickly as the railroad could bring them and who were now personally ordered by him to assail McDowells right flank. From mouth to mouth went the word, Johnstons army has come. At the same time Beauregard moved forward his whole line. The Union troops were instantly seized with one of those unaccountable panics to which great armies are liable.[95] They broke and ran down the hillside in disorder. McDowell and his officers tried to rally them but the regular infantry alone obeyed commands, covering the volunteers retreat. They crossed the fords of Bull Run and crowded the Warrenton turnpike, a confused mass of disorganized frightened men. The Confederates pursued them only a short distance;[96] and McDowell intended to make a stand at Centreville. That was found to be impossible nor could the disorderly flight be arrested at Fairfax Court-House. The larger part of the men, telegraphed McDowell from there, are a confused mob, entirely demoralized. They are pouring through this place in a state of utter disorganization. The flight of the troops was not stopped until they reached the fortifications on the southern side of the Potomac, and many of the soldiers crossed the Long bridge into Washington. All were soon to learn that they had been fleeing before an imaginary foe, as the Confederates made no effective pursuit.

Lincoln in Washington was a prey to the same anxiety as Davis in Richmond. After his return from church, he scanned eagerly the telegrams sent to him from

---

[95] Thucydides. Jowett, IV, 125.

[96] As far as Cub-run. Had the pursuit continued, McDowell's reserve stationed near Blackburn's ford and Centreville would have protected the rear of the fleeing troops.

the War Department and from the army headquarters. These despatches were from the telegraphic station nearest the battle-field and toward three o'clock became more frequent and reported the apparent course and progress of the cannonade. Impatient as he was to talk over the news, he repaired to Scotts office, where he found the aged and infirm general taking his afternoon sleep. On being waked Scott told him that such reports as had already been received possessed no value but, expressing his confidence in a successful result, he composed himself for another nap. Despatches continued to come with cheering news. It was reported that the Confederates had been forced back two or three miles. One of Scotts aides brought to the President a despatch from a lieutenant of engineers at Centreville saying that McDowell had driven the enemy before him, ordered the reserve forward and desired re-enforcements without delay. As Scott deemed the report credible, the President, thinking all doubt at an end, ordered his carriage for his usual evening drive. At six o'clock Secretary Seward appeared at the White House pale and haggard. Where is the President? he asked hoarsely of Lincolns private secretaries. Gone to drive, they answered. Have you any late news? he continued. They read him the telegrams announcing victory. Tell no one, said he. That is not true. The battle is lost. McDowell is in full retreat and calls on General Scott to save the capital.[97] Returning from his drive a half hour later, the President heard Sewards message, walked over to army headquarters and there read the despatch from a captain of engineers: General McDowells army in full retreat through Centreville. The day is lost. Save Washington and the remnants of this army. The routed troops will not reform. The President did not go to his bed that night; morning found him still on his lounge in the executive office,[98] listening to the recitals of newspaper correspondents and other civilians, who had followed McDowell to Centreville and, after the repulse, fearing for their own safety, had rushed back to Washington, beginning to arrive at midnight. Monday broke dismally in the capital, a drizzling rain adding to the gloom. But by noon it was known that the Confederates had not pursued the retreating troops in the aim of taking Washington.

The disaster caused some prominent men to lose their nerve; not so, the President. Bitterly disappointed as he was at the result, he from the first showed no discouragement or loss of control. During the week he paid visits to the camps surrounding Washington and in one of these had William T. Sherman for his guide. Sherman, standing by the roadside, was recognized by Lincoln and Seward, who rode side by side in an open hack and, on his inquiring if they were going to his camps, he received from Lincoln the reply, Yes, we heard that you had got over the big scare, and we thought we would come over and see the boys. The President asked Sherman to get into their carriage and direct their course. Sherman

[97] N. & H., IV, 353.
[98] *Ibid.,* 355.

perceived his emotion and his desire to speak to the men, so he ventured to utter a word of caution. Please discourage, he said, all cheering, noise or any sort of confusion; we had enough of it before Bull Run to ruin any set of men; what we need is cool, thoughtful, hard-fighting soldiers no more hurrahing, no more humbug. The Commander-in-chief of the army and navy of the United States took the advice of his Colonel in good part and, on reaching the first camp, stood up in his carriage and made, as Sherman characterized it, one of the neatest, best and most feeling addresses I ever listened to, referring to our late disaster at Bull Run, the high duties that still devolved on us and the brighter days yet to come. At one or two points the soldiers began to cheer, but he checked them with: Don't cheer, boys. I confess I rather like it myself but Colonel Sherman here says it is not military; and I guess we had better defer to his opinion.[99] As he went the rounds, he made the same speech to other soldiers. The effect of his visit was good and proved an earnest of the hold he was soon to acquire on the army.

Sherman thought Bull Run a well-planned battle but badly fought, and Johnston agreed with him. If the tactics of the Federals had been equal to their strategy, wrote Johnston, we should have been beaten. Ropes, on the other hand, believed McDowells tactics better than his strategy. The difference of opinion does not concern the layman, to whom the battle of Bull Run appears as the encounter of two armed mobs in an open field, fighting with the utmost courage to solve a question that had baffled the wisdom of their statesmen.

A spectator, watching Henry House hill, would have seen many of the Union companies and regiments clad in the brilliant militia uniforms which they were accustomed to wear in Fourth-of-July processions. The showy Zouave dress with fez or turban and red or yellow baggy trousers was affected by many. These uniforms as contrasted with the sober United States blue of after battles are strikingly emblematic of the difference between a holiday parade responding to the call On to Richmond and the stern purpose of subduing a united South.

At Bull Run the rank and file of both armies heard for the first time in their lives the sound of cannon and muskets in hostile combat, saw cannon balls crashing through trees and saplings above and around them striking down their friends and brothers, saw a blood-stained field strewed with dead men and horses. And fighting blood was there even though fighting craft were yet to be acquired. The numbers of the dead and wounded show hard fighting.[100]

Apart from the newspapers there seems to have been little boasting in the South. The men in authority did not for a moment believe that the North would give up the contest. On the contrary they felt that a long and hard struggle was before them.

---

[99] W. Sherman, I, 189.

[100] Ropes, I, 154. The casualties were, Union 2984, Confederate 1981, T. L. Livermore, 77.

For a while bitter discouragement prevailed at the North; and the blow was the harder to bear, inasmuch as England, from whom sympathy was ardently desired, now regarded the dissolution of the Union as an accomplished fact. Friends of the South saw in this victory a promise of her eventual triumph and to help forward her cause, endeavored to cloud the issue. It is surprising, wrote Charles Francis Adams, our minister to Great Britain, in a private letter from London, to see the efforts made here to create the belief that our struggle has nothing to do with slavery, but that it is all about a tariff. I cannot conceal from myself the fact that as a whole the English are pleased with our misfortunes.[101]

Fifty-two years after the struggle, this feeling may be accounted for by the remark of Rochefoucauld, The misfortunes of our best friends are not entirely displeasing to us; but such an attitude during the war on the part of the kin across the sea was felt bitterly by men who were risking life and fortune in what they deemed a sacred cause.[102]

---

[101] Aug. 30, Forbes, I, 234.

[102] Authorities on Bull Run, III, 437, 443-457; O. R., II; N. & H., IV; W. Sherman, I; Johnston; J. Davis, I; Ropes, I; R. M. Johnston; C. W., Pt. 2; Swinton; Chesnut; B. & L., I; Globe; Hosmer's Appeal; Seward, II; Early; characterizations of Johnston and Jackson, III, 458, 462.

Chapter II

ON the day after the battle of Bull Run, Congress met at the usual hour and transacted the usual amount of business. Outwardly at least the members were calm. The House, with only four dissenting votes, adopted a resolution of Crittenden's, introduced two days previously, which gave expression to the common sentiment of the country regarding the object of the war. This resolution declared that the war was not waged for conquest or subjugation or in order to overthrow or interfere with the rights or established institutions of the Southern States, but to maintain the supremacy of the Constitution and to preserve the Union: three days later it passed the Senate by a vote of 30:5.[103]

Congress had convened July 4, and, in response to the President's request for means to make the war short and decisive, had authorized him to accept the services of 500,000 volunteers for three years unless sooner discharged, and had empowered the Secretary of the Treasury to borrow on the credit of the United States two hundred and fifty million dollars. Although failing to use its power of taxation as effectively as the occasion required, Congress nevertheless did something in that direction, increasing some of the tariff duties, imposing a direct tax of twenty millions on the States and territories and an income tax of three per cent subject to an exemption of eight hundred dollars.

Congress showed great confidence in the President and went far toward meeting his wishes. As one of its members afterwards wrote, it was during this session only a giant committee of ways and means. But it hesitated in regard to two of his dictatorial acts: the call for three years' volunteers and the increase of the regular army and navy by proclamation; and his order to Scott, the Commanding General of the Army, authorizing him personally or by deputy, to suspend, if necessary for the public safety, the privilege of the writ of habeas corpus at any point on any military line between Philadelphia and Washington.[104] A rider to the bill, raising the pay of private soldiers passed on the last day of the session [August 6], legalized the proclamation increasing the army and navy; but senators differed so widely as to suspension of the writ of habeas corpus that they were unable to agree upon any action. Some senators thought that an act of Congress was necessary to suspend the writ and in this belief were sustained by a decision of Chief Justice Marshall, the opinions of Story and Taney and English precedents for two

---

[103] For the Confiscation act and the Confederate Sequestration act, see III, 464; Schwab, 111-120.

[104] There was also another order authorizing the suspension of the writ in Florida. Lincoln, C. W., II, 39, 45; Globe, 393.

centuries. Others agreeing that the Constitution vested this power in Congress alone were nevertheless willing to make legal and valid the President's orders for the suspension of the writ. Still other senators did not care to take any action whatever; believing that the President, as commander-in-chief of the Army and Navy, had complete power to suspend the habeas corpus, they did not wish to bring this power in question by an act of confirmation.

Encouraged by the attitude of the President and Congress, the country soon recovered from the dismay caused by the defeat at Bull Run. A second uprising took place. Men came forward in great numbers, enlisting for three years. On account of some successes in Western Virginia McClellan was placed in command of the troops at Washington [July 27], which he soon named the Army of the Potomac.[105]

Lincoln and Davis were both willing to obscure the true reason of the conflict: Lincoln, because he did not wish the border slave States, the Northern Democrats and conservative Republicans to get the idea that the war was waged for the destruction of slavery; Davis, because he knew that the Southerner's devotion to slavery, if allowed to appear in too strong a light, would stand in the way of the recognition of the Confederate States by European powers which he so ardently desired. But as the Union armies advanced southward, they came into contact with the negro who had to be dealt with. On the day after Virginia had ratified by popular vote her ordinance of secession, three negroes, who had come to Fort Monroe, were claimed by an agent of their owner. General Butler, who was in command, refused to deliver them up on the ground that, as they belonged to a citizen of a State offering resistance to the federal government and had been employed in the construction of a battery, they were contraband of war. The application of this phrase, as Butler himself admitted, had no high legal sanction; nevertheless, technical inaccuracy, as Morse wrote, does not hurt the force of an epigram which expresses a sound principle;[106] this one was promptly seized upon by the popular mind as indicating a proper attitude toward the negro. The difficulty, however, could not be solved by an epigram. Contrabands or fugitive slaves came continually within the lines of the Union armies, and the question how to dispose of them became a grave one for the President. Having carefully thought out a policy, he sent the following instructions to Butler to serve as a guide for his and other commands: the general should not interfere with the reclamation of fugitive slaves who had escaped from masters in the Union slave States but, in accordance with the Confiscation act,[107] he should respect no claim for negroes who had been employed in the military service of the Confederacy. In spite of the murmurs of the abolitionists and some radical Republicans, a large majority of the

---

[105] III; IV, 229; N. & H.; Globe; Taney; Grimes; Dewey.

[106] Morse, II, 5.

[107] Approved Aug. 6.

Northern people had already acquiesced in this policy as a wise temporary expedient, when General Frémont opened the question afresh by his proclamation in Missouri.[108]

Frémont, the pet and protégé of the Blairs,[109] as Lincoln afterwards called him, had upon the earnest solicitation of his patrons been made a major-general and been placed in command of the Western department, which included Missouri. A kind of romantic hero was he the brave pathfinder, who had planted the American flag on presumably the highest peak of the Rocky mountains. Winning the first nomination of the Republican party for president, he had polled a large electoral and popular vote; and Lincoln, undoubtedly impressed by the remembrance of this first campaign, so brilliant in many ways, thought well of him and had entertained the idea of nominating him for minister to France. He was supposed to have military talent, and his appointment to a command was very popular with earnest Republicans who had looked upon him five years earlier as the champion of a sacred cause. Lincoln and the Blairs were to suffer a grievous disappointment. The first month in his headquarters at St. Louis showed Frémont to be utterly unfit for a responsible command. Over-fond of display and wishing to maintain the state of a European monarch, he surrounded himself with dishonest men to whom he was always accessible, whilst high military and civil officers and worthy Union citizens were obliged to wait days in his anteroom for an interview. The reason was apparent. These last had the sole purpose in mind to defeat the Southern sympathizers and the Confederate army, who were disputing with them the possession of Missouri; but the others were interested in securing fat contracts, a kind of suit for which Frémont had a ready ear; and he was deaf to the entreaties of well-informed Union citizens for an order to re-enforce a capable general, who was actively engaged in the field. Distrusted by men of worth and influence in Missouri, flattered by speculators, it is little wonder that the charge was made that the department of Missouri was managed for purpose of making private fortunes rather than for the country's weal. Such was the posture of affairs on the evening of August 29, when Frémont went to bed, with an undoubted perception of the strength of anti-slavery sentiment in the North and the need of some diversion to maintain his sway. Inspiration must have come to him in the night. At all events he decided upon a proclamation freeing the slaves. Next day he issued it, declaring the slaves of all persons in the State of Missouri, taking up arms against the United States, freemen. That it was a play to retain his power was evident to hard-headed men. The truth is, wrote Montgomery Blair to Sumner, with Frémont's surroundings, the set of scoundrels who alone have control of him, this proclamation setting up the higher law was like a painted woman quoting Scripture.

[108] III, 466-468.

[109] Montgomery Blair, Postmaster-General, and F. P. Blair, Jr.

Lincoln learned through the newspapers of Frémont's proclamation and of his bureau of abolition, set up for the purpose of issuing deeds of manumission to slaves. Although this major-general of two month's standing, without careful survey of the whole field, without comprehension of the important and various interests involved had, on a sudden impulse, assumed to solve a question which the President, his Cabinet and Congress were approaching only in a careful and tentative manner, Lincoln's letter to Frémont of September 2, sent by a special messenger, was as full of kindness as of wisdom. The liberating slaves of traitorous owners, he wrote, will alarm our Southern Union friends and turn them against us; perhaps ruin our rather fair prospect for Kentucky. Allow me, therefore, to ask that you will, as of your own motion, modify that paragraph[110] so as to conform to the Confiscation act of Congress. This letter is written in a spirit of caution and not of censure. Frémont was unwilling to retract the provision objected to and asked that the President should openly direct him to make the correction: this Lincoln cheerfully did by public order.

Frémont's proclamation stirred the anti-slavery sentiment of the country to its utmost depths, receiving enthusiastic commendation from many States. Senator Sumner wrote, Our President is now dictator, imperator which you will; but how vain to have the power of a god and not use it godlike! A large number of men in Ohio were furious and found fit expression in the words of an eminent lawyer and judge: Our people are in a state of great consternation and wrath on account of the quarrel between Frémont and the administration, public opinion being entirely with General Frémont. And if the election were next fall, to displace him would be to make him president. Herndon, the old law partner and later biographer of Lincoln, living in Illinois, said, Frémont's proclamation was right. Lincoln's modification of it was wrong. Senator Grimes wrote from Iowa: The people are all with Frémont and will uphold him 'through thick and thin.' Everybody of every sect, party, sex and color approves his proclamation in the Northwest and it will not do for the administration to causelessly tamper with the man who had the sublime moral courage to issue it.[111]

These expressions in private letters represented a phase of intelligent sentiment which troubled Lincoln, as is evident from his confidential letter to Senator Browning of Illinois, who, though regarded as a conservative, had approved Frémont's proclamation. It endangers the loss of Kentucky, he wrote [September 22]. I think to lose Kentucky is nearly the same as to lose the whole game. Kentucky gone, we cannot hold Missouri, nor, as I think, Maryland. These all against us and the job on our hands is too large for us. We would as well consent

---

[110] This paragraph also confiscated the real and personal property of the Confederates in Missouri, but as the reference to slaves gave the proclamation its importance, I have confined my attention to that provision. O. R., III, 466, 469.

[111] All these letters but Herndon's were written during September.

to separation at once, including the surrender of this capital. Lincoln had such a hold upon the people that he carried with him an efficient public opinion and, after due waiting, proceeded to the next step. He never had any thought of removing Frémont on account of his proclamation; but he felt that the mismanagement and corruption in Missouri must be corrected. Proceeding with caution, he sent to St. Louis Montgomery Blair and Meigs, the Quartermaster-General of the Army, and later Secretary Cameron and Adjutant-General Thomas: the four made a thorough and candid investigation.

Meigs heard a rumor that Frémont had in mind a project resembling the conspiracy of Aaron Burr's. Somewhat more than two years later Lincoln, in an expansive mood, unbosomed himself to his private secretaries and two other friends, saying, Mrs. Frémont (who had brought a letter from the General justifying his proclamation) sought an audience with me at midnight[112] and taxed me so violently with many things that I had to exercise all the awkward tact I have to avoid quarreling with her. She more than once intimated that if General Frémont should conclude to try conclusions with me, he could set up for himself. To this, the minister of the United States to Prussia, an old Illinois friend of Lincoln's, replied: It is pretty clearly proven that Frémont had at that time concluded that the Union was definitely destroyed, and that he should set up an independent government as soon as he took Memphis and organized his army.[113] That Lincoln felt there was some basis for this report is indicated by a paper which Nicolay left in a sealed envelope endorsed: A private paper, Conversation with the President, October 2, 1861, in which one of the headings is Frémont ready to rebel.[114] Nevertheless, it is hardly probable that Lincoln was disturbed enough by the report to let it have the slightest weight in his action. It was more to the point that Montgomery Blair had recommended Frémont's removal for inefficiency and that Cameron's and Thomas's conclusions had made it imperative. These two reported that Frémont was incompetent and unfit for his extensive and important command and that he had around him in his staff persons directly and indirectly concerned in furnishing supplies. On October 24, the President issued the order for his removal. Before the removal was effected, E. B. Washburne, an intimate friend of Lincoln's, who was at the head of the House sub-committee on government contracts that spent two weeks in St. Louis, taking a large amount of testimony relative to the procedure of Frémont and his friends, wrote to Chase:[115] Such robbery, fraud, extravagance, peculation as have been developed in Frémont's department can hardly be conceived of. There has been an organized system of

---

[112] During September, 1861.

[113] J. Hay, I, 133.

[114] Nicolay, 177.

[115] Secretary of the Treasury. The date of the letter is Oct. 31. Washburne was not aware that Frémont's removal had been determined. On Nov. 2, Frémont turned over his command to Hunter.

pillage, right under his eye. He has really set up an authority over the government and bids defiance to its commands. The government in failing to strike at Frémont and his horde of pirates acknowledges itself a failure. Lincoln must have seen this letter, and if further justification for Frémont's removal were necessary, this was ample.

While the people of the country could not know of these confidential letters and reports, enough was known for Lincoln's action to receive effective support. But a large minority looked upon Frémont as a martyr in the antislavery cause. Here are two out of the many instances of worthy people who were led astray by a charlatan because he knew how to play upon the one idea dearest to their hearts. Henry Ward Beecher said in his church, I cannot but express my solemn conviction that both our government, and in a greater degree the community, have done great injustice to the cause in Missouri, in the treatment which has been bestowed upon that noble man General Frémont. Is it known to the administration that the West is threatened with a revolution? asked in a private letter Richard Smith, the editor of the Cincinnati Gazette, a very important and influential Republican journal. What meaneth this burning of the President in effigy by citizens who have hitherto sincerely and enthusiastically supported the war? Why this sudden check to enlistments? The public consider that Frémont has been made a martyr of. Consequently he is now, so far as the West is concerned, the most popular man in the country. He is to the West what Napoleon was to France; while the President has lost the confidence of the people.[116] Meanwhile, McClellan was at work with energy and talent, erecting fortifications around Washington and organizing the Army of the Potomac. He had good executive ability, and aptitude for system, and, being in robust health, an immense capacity for work. All these qualities were devoted without stint to the service. In the saddle from morning to night, he visited the several camps, mixed with the different brigades and regiments and came to know his officers and men thoroughly. Himself a gentleman of sterling moral character, having come to Washington with the respect and admiration of these soldiers, he soon gained their love by his winning personality, and inspired a devotion such as no other Northern general of a large army, with one exception, was ever able to obtain. Overrating his successes in western Virginia, he was called the young Napoleon, for he was believed by the army, the administration and the country to have military genius of the highest order. And at first he seemed to have an adequate idea of what was required of him, for he wrote to the President on August 4: The military action of the Government should be prompt and irresistible. The rebels have chosen Virginia as their battle field, and it seems proper for us to make the first great struggle there.[117]

---

[116] Oct. 20, Nov. 7, III; N. & H., IV; O. R., III; C. W., Pt. III; J. Hay, I; Nicolay; Pierce; Grimes.

[117] O. R., V, 6.

Not only was McClellan working with diligence but everyone else was co-operating with him in a way to give his talent for organization the widest scope. The President, the Treasury and the War departments, the Secretary of State, the governors of the Northern States assisted him faithfully with their full powers. The officers under him displayed zeal and devotion. He had the sway of a monarch. And at the outset this complete harmony yielded results of a most encouraging nature. Troops poured in from the enthusiastic North, swelling the army of 52,000 of July 27 to one of 168,000 three months later.

One of McClellan's limitations, however, came early into view. Although personally courageous, he feared reverses for his army. Moreover, either his intelligence of the enemy was defective or his inferences from such accurate information as he possessed were radically unsound. In August, he was haunted by the notion that the Confederates largely outnumbered him; that they would attack his position on the Virginia side of the Potomac and also cross the river north of Washington. At this time, however, Johnston did not purpose either movement; he was chafing at the smallness of his force, the lack of food and ammunition, the disorganization and sickness amongst his troops. During the month of September and well into October, he was encamped about Fairfax Court-house with strong outposts on hills six and a half miles from Washington, where the Confederate flag could be plainly seen by the President and his General. On October 19, he withdrew his army to Centreville and Manassas Junction, farther from Washington but a much stronger position.

The great object to be accomplished, wrote McClellan to the Secretary of War shortly after October 27, is the crushing defeat of the rebel army now at Manassas.[118] The Union troops were sufficient in number and fighting quality to accomplish it. All the authorities agree that McClellan's organization of the Army of the Potomac was little short of magical. The training to fit men for active service generally required six months; under McClellan it had been accomplished in three. The change from the grand army before the battle of Bull Run to McClellan's Army of the Potomac, according to William H. Russell, was marvellous. The soldiers of July, who, in his opinion, could have been overcome by one-third their number of British regulars, were in September perhaps as fine a body of men in all respects of physique as had ever been assembled by any power in the world.[119]

When McClellan and McDowell rode together from camp to camp on the south side of the Potomac, McClellan used to point toward Manassas and say, We shall strike them there. What might have been is doubtless as unprofitable a subject of speculation in war as in the other affairs of life; but it is a fact of importance that during the autumn the President and the country rightly began to lose confidence in McClellan's military ability. They had good reason for this distrust. His apology

---

[118] O. R., V, 11.
[119] *Ante;* III, 493.

in his report of August 4, 1863,[120] and in his Own Story receive little justification from the pitiless contemporary record and from other facts since brought to light. On October 27, according to his own account, his effective force was 134,000; the number disposable for an advance, 76,000:[121] Johnston had 41,000. The Union artillery was superior; the infantry had better arms. The health of the Union army was good, that of the Confederate bad. The weather was fine and dry; up to Christmas the roads were in suitable condition for military operations. On the other hand, the Confederates had an immense advantage in the moral effect of their victories at Bull Run and Ball's Bluff.[122] Nevertheless, the officers and men of the Army of the Potomac were devoted to McClellan and eager to fight. They would have been glad to follow if he would lead; it only remained for him to give the word.

The Confederate were little, if any, better disciplined than the Union soldiers; but their cautions general was willing to take the offensive. Give me 19,000 more men as good as the 41,000 that I have with the necessary transportation and munitions of war, said Johnston to President Davis on October 1, and I will cross the Potomac and carry the war into the enemy's country:[123] at that time he knew that the Union force was superior in number.

When McClellan wrote as military critic he condemned by implication his own inactivity as commander. I am induced to believe, he wrote to General Scott from Washington on August 8, that the enemy has at least 100,000 men in front of us. Were I in Beauregard's place,[124] with that force at my disposal, I would attack the positions on the other side of the Potomac and at the same time cross the river above this city in force.[125] Yet McClellan himself, with at least 76,000 to 41,000 of the enemy, would not make in November a movement similar to, but not so extended as, the one he laid down for the Confederates in August. I am not such a fool, he said to the President, as to buck against Manassas in the spot designated by the foe.[126]

---

[120] O. R., V, 5.

[121] *Ibid.*, 10.

[122] On Oct. 21, occurred on the Potomac above Washington the affair of Ball's Bluff in which, owing to mismanagement, the Union forces were defeated. Measured by subsequent battles, the casualties were not large; but the death of Colonel Baker, a dear friend of Lincoln's and a popular senator and officer, and the loss to New York, Massachusetts and Pennsylvania of some of "the very pride and flower of their young men" caused a profound feeling of discouragement all over the North; still there was little tendency to impute this disaster to McClellan, although it occurred in his department. III, 496. The victory greatly elated the Confederate soldiers.

[123] O. R., V, 884.

[124] McClellan supposed Beauregard to be in command of the Confederate army, while he commanded only its first corps.

[125] O. R., XI, Pt. III, 3.

To judge from McClellan's private letters at this time, he seemed to think that the men in authority were endeavoring to add difficulties to his task. I am thwarted and deceived by these incapables at every turn, he wrote.[127] As a matter of fact, everybody from the President to the humblest orderly who waited at his door[128] was helping him according to his means. The fault was not of the President, the Cabinet, General Scott or the senators; it was entirely his own. McClellan fed himself upon the delusion that the enemy had 150,000 men. This estimate would indeed have justified his inaction; but, after an evening's conversation with him it became painfully evident to John Hay, that he had no plan.[129]

The President's attitude towards his General was sublime. They talked sadly over the disaster at Ball's Bluff. Alluding to the death of Colonel Baker, McClellan said: There is many a good fellow who wears the shoulder-straps going under the sod before this thing is over. There is no loss too great to be repaired. If I should get knocked on the head, Mr. President, you will put another man immediately in my shoes. I want you to take care of yourself, was the reply.[130]

On the evening of October 26, the Jacobin Club represented by Senators Trumbull, Chandler and Wade came up to worry the administration into a battle. The agitation of the summer is to be renewed, wrote Hay. The President defended McClellan's deliberateness. On going over to the General's headquarters the Jacobins were discussed. The President deprecated this new manifestation of popular impatience but said it was a reality and should be taken into the account: 'At the same time, General, you must not fight till you are ready.' 'I have everything at stake,' replied McClellan; 'if I fail I will not see you again or anybody.' 'I have a notion to go out with you,' said Lincoln, 'and stand or fall with the battle.'[131]

On October 31, Scott voluntarily retired from active service and McClellan succeeded him in the command of all the armies of the United States. Next evening, at his headquarters, he read to Lincoln and Hay his General Order in regard to Scott's resignation and his own assumption of command. The President said, I should be perfectly satisfied if I thought that this vast increase of responsibility would not embarrass you. It is a great relief, Sir! replied McClellan, between whom and Scott there had been friction. I feel as if several tons were taken from my shoulders to-day. I am now in contact with you and the Secretary. I am not embarrassed by intervention. Well, rejoined Lincoln, draw on me for all the sense I have and all the information. In addition to your present command, the

---

[126] Oct. 17, J. Hay, I, 45.
[127] November. McClellan, 177.
[128] N. & H., IV, 444.
[129] Oct. 22, J. Hay, I, 46.
[130] *Ibid.*
[131] *Ibid.*, 48.

supreme command of the army will entail a vast labor upon you. I can do it all, said McClellan quietly.[132]

The country had a right to expect an offensive movement. Inasmuch as McClellan was apt to underestimate the number as well as the fighting quality of his soldiers, his 76,000 disposable for an advance could likely enough have been increased to 100,000. He ought to have fought Johnston, or manoeuvred him out of Manassas, or raised the Confederate blockade of the lower Potomac or taken Norfolk.[133] Any one of these movements attempted in the autumn of 1861 would have satisfied the country and maintained their confidence, as well as the President's, in McClellan; and this would have been an asset of great value. But he was no fighter and at this time could not have handled 100,000 men. It is doubtful if any other general in the Union army could have done so. Long after the war, Grant referred to the vast and cruel responsibility devolving upon McClellan at the outset and added, If McClellan had gone into the war as Sherman, Thomas or Meade, had fought his way along and up, I have no reason to suppose that he would not have won as high a distinction as any of us.[134] In McClellan's army was Colonel William T. Sherman, who in 1864 led an army of 100,000 with great ability; but at this time he told the President that his extreme desire was to serve in a subordinate capacity and in no event to be left in a superior command.[135] To march, manoeuvre, feed and fight to the best advantage an army of 100,000 comes near being the highest executive achievement of which man is capable.[136] Joseph E. Johnston quiet and sad[137] thought that he could now conduct 60,000 in an offensive campaign, but he had had the invaluable experience of commanding half that number at Bull Run.

If McClellan had shown modesty, so striking a characteristic of Lincoln and Grant, criticism would be tempered, but he was one of the men who cannot stand prosperity. Rapid advancement had swelled him with conceit; one manifestation of this was discourtesy to the President, of whom he once wrote in a patronizing way, he is honest and means well.[138] On the evening of November 13, the President, Secretary Seward and John Hay called at McClellan's house and were told by the servant at the door that the General was at an officer's wedding and would soon return. We went in, as Hay recorded the incident in his diary, and after we had

---

[132] J. Hay, I, 50.

[133] During October the Confederates "had blocked the navigation of the Potomac by planting batteries on the Virginia side twenty or thirty miles down the river." Webb 13, 168 *et seq.*; Ropes I, 181, 222; N. & H., IV, 450.

[134] Young, II, 217.

[135] W. Sherman, II, 193.

[136] Written before the European War of 1914.

[137] McClellan, 85. J. D. Cox wrote, "Johnston by common consent stands second and hardly second, to Lee alone of the Confederate generals." *The Nation,* XVIII, 333.

[138] McClellan, 176.

waited about an hour, McClellan came in, and without paying any particular attention to the porter who told him the President was waiting to see him, went upstairs, passing the door of the room where the President and Secretary of State were seated. They waited about half an hour, and sent once more a servant to tell the General they were there; and the answer came that he had gone to bed. I merely record this unparalleled insolence of epaulettes without comment, continued Hay. It is the first indication I have yet seen of the threatened supremacy of the military authorities. Coming home I spoke to the President about the matter, but he seemed not to have noticed it specially, saying it was better, at this time, not to be making points of etiquette and personal dignity.[139] On another occasion when the General failed to keep an appointment with the President, he said, Never mind; I will hold McClellan's horse if he will only bring us success.[140]

In December, McClellan fell ill with typhoid fever. The President, the Army of the Potomac, the country waited on his recovery.[141]

To Great Britain, it seemed that as a question merely of fact a war existed[142] between the North and South which must be officially recognized. Davis had invited applications for letters of marque and Lincoln had proclaimed a blockade; both acts being permissible only in war seemed to indicate that the conflict would extend to the ocean where it would concern all maritime nations. As a matter of course, Great Britain issued a Proclamation of Neutrality [May 13], but this natural step was by no means acceptable to the North since the Proclamation by its terms recognized the Confederate States as a belligerent power. The theory of the United States Government that the Southerners were rebels against their authority was undermined as soon as these rebels became belligerents in the eyes of Europe.[143] The censure of this declaration by Seward and by Adams was therefore in conformity with diplomatic usage. Nor was the sentiment of Boston as reported by Motley surprising. The declaration of Lord John Russell, he wrote, that the Southern privateers were to be considered belligerents, was received with great indignation by the most warm-hearted, England-loving men in this England-loving part of the country.[144] In other sections of the North where England was less liked, the feeling of resentment was still more acute; and the sum of this dissatisfaction may have served a useful purpose in helping to prevent Great Britain from

---

[139] J. Hay, I, 52.

[140] N. & H., IV, 468.

[141] O. R., V, XI, Pt. III; III, I; N. & H., IV; J. Hay, I; III; Ropes, I; Webb; Johnston; B. & L., I.

[142] Lord Russell, III, 418, n. 2.

[143] The other maritime powers waited for Great Britain to take the lead, because the extent of her dominions and commerce in North America made the question most important to her. Within a few weeks France, Spain, the Netherlands, Prussia and other nations followed her example." Bancroft, II, 176.

[144] III, 421.

acknowledging the Southern Confederacy in the following year. Nevertheless, a calm survey of the facts can hardly lead to any conclusion but that Great Britain was abundantly justified for her recognition of the belligerent rights of the Confederate States. The cogent argument for it was put in a nutshell by the foreign secretary who issued the Proclamation. Upwards of five million free men, wrote Lord Russell in a private letter to Edward Everett, have been for some time in open revolt against the President and Congress of the United States. It is not our practice to treat five millions of free men as pirates and to hang their sailors if they attempt to stop our merchantmen. But unless we meant to treat them as pirates and to hang them we could not deny them belligerent rights.[145]

The concession of belligerent rights to the Confederate States was made with no unfriendly purpose; and as repeated assurances to that effect were received from both public and private sources in England, and as a proper comprehension was gained of the wide difference between the recognition of the belligerency and acknowledgment of the independence of the Confederate States, the irritation of the North began to subside. The President showed his understanding of the attitude of England and other European powers and believed that his government had their sympathy. The feeling toward the United States, wrote Adams from London on May 31, is improving in the higher circles here. It was never otherwise than favorable among the people at large.[146]

The division of English sentiment was well expressed by Palmerston, the Prime Minister, in his words, We do not like slavery, but we want cotton and we dislike very much your Morrill tariff.[147] Punch declared sympathy with the North but confessed, That with the South we've stronger ties, Which are composed of cotton. And where would be our calico Without the toil of niggers? Then the North keeps Commerce bound; thus we perceive a divided duty. We must choose between free-trade or sable brothers free.[148] But, so Adams wrote, Our brethren in this country, after all, are much disposed to fall in with the opinion of Voltaire that, 'Dieu est toujours sur le côté des gros canons.'[149]

For our standing in England it was unfortunate that we did not win the battle of Bull Run, as our defeat caused a marked revulsion of feeling. The aristocracy and upper middle class made no secret of their belief that the bubble of democracy had burst in America. By the autumn of 1861 the commercial and manufacturing people began to realize the disaster with which they were menaced by our cutting off the supply of cotton. Ordinarily the new crop came forward during the early autumn; now practically none was being received. Stocks of cotton were rapidly

---

[145] Bancroft, II, 178 n.; C. F. A. M. H. S., XLV, 77.

[146] III, 429.

[147] This act approved March 2, 1861, was considered a measure of high protection by the English.

[148] III, 433.

[149] III, 434 n.

sinking. A manufacture, said the London Times, which supports a fifth part of our whole population, is coming gradually to a stand.[150] Mills were working short time; manufacturers were reducing wages; mill owners and laborers were dismayed at the prospect of a cotton famine. The blockade stood between them and a supply of cotton, threatening the owners with business derangement, and the workmen with starvation. The self-interest of the manufacturers and the sentimental predilections of the aristocracy were forces which, sometimes merging, sometimes reacting on one another, gave rise to a desire amongst these classes that the North should fail. It seemed more favorable to England's power and trade that the United States should be divided into two nations, especially as the Southern Confederacy would offer England practically free trade, hence a large market for her manufactured goods that would be paid for in raw cotton. The wish was father to the thought and the inference to be drawn from Bull Run settled the matter. The nobility and upper middle class came to the conclusion that the North could not conquer the South and that separation would be the result. This opinion was advocated by the Times and Saturday Review with a power of sarcastic statement that stung their Northern readers to the quick. Help us to a breath of generous strengthening sympathy from old England was Sumner's appeal to William H. Russell. Do not forget, I pray you, was Russell's reply, that in reality it is Brightism and republicanism at home which the conservative papers mean to smite. America is the shield under which the blow is dealt.[151]

The exponents of the ten-pounders, who, in their smug complacency, believed their Constitution and government to be not only now the best on earth but the best that had ever existed,[152] criticised the North freely in a tone of flippant and contemptuous serenity,[153] highly irritating to a people engaged in a life-and-death struggle. The sneers at the panic and cowardice of Northern troops at Bull Run, as the common measure of a people fighting their countrymen to suppress their desire for independence, were hard to bear. Edward Dicey when in America argued with James Russell Lowell about what seemed to him an unreasonable animosity toward England. It is possible, Lowell replied, that my feelings may be morbidly exaggerated, but, pointing to a portrait of a handsome young man, a near and dear relative, a Captain of the twentieth Massachusetts, who was shot dead at Ball's Bluff, he asked, How would you like yourself to read constantly that that lad died in a miserable cause, and, as an American officer, should be called a coward? Oliver Wendell Holmes wrote to Dicey: I have a stake in this contest, which makes me nervous and tremulous and impatient of contradiction. I have a noble

---

[150] III, 503, n. 1.
[151] III, 508.
[152] See Lecky, I, 21.
[153] III, 575, n. 3.

boy, a captain in one of our regiments, which has been fearfully decimated by battle and disease and himself twice wounded within a hair's breadth of his life.[154]

Still another drift of sentiment must not be ignored. The sympathy of the British government and public with Italy during the war of 1859, and the progress made in that war towards Italian liberty, impressed upon the English mind the doctrine that a body of people who should seek to throw off an obnoxious dominion and form an orderly government of their own, deserved the best wishes of the civilized world. Why, it was asked in England, if we were right to sympathize with Italy against Austria, should we not likewise sympathize with the Southern Confederacy whose people were resisting the subjugation of the North? This argument swayed the judgment of the liberal-minded Grote, and colored other opinion which was really determined by considerations of rank or of commerce and manufactures.[155]

But there were English statesmen and writers of ability who understood that the fight of the North was against slavery; they urged her cause without ceasing, although many times their hearts failed them as they feared she had undertaken an impossible task. They had as their followers the workingmen whom hunger stared in the face but who realized, as did the upper class, that the cause of the Union was the cause of democracy in England.

Up to the latter part of November, Great Britain preserved a strict neutrality. Louis Napoleon, the Emperor of the French, though in his American policy he did not represent the intelligent and liberal sentiment of his country, asked England officially to co-operate with him in recognizing the Confederacy and breaking the blockade. Earl Russell[156] in a letter to Palmerston took the ground that it would not do for England and France to break a blockade for the sake of getting cotton, but they might offer their mediation between the North and the South with the implied understanding that the section which refused it [the United States, of course, as the South would grasp eagerly at the offer] would be their enemy. Palmerston replied that our best and true policy seems to be to go on as we have begun and to keep quite clear of the conflict between North and South.[157] Later, Lord Palmerston, in his speech at the Lord Mayor's dinner, gave it clearly to be understood that there is to be no interference for the sake of cotton.[158]

But meanwhile the American press, apparently with no feeling of responsibility, was carrying on a duel with the English. The irritation caused by the ungenerous criticism of the London journals was vented by our own in bitter recrimination. Chief in attack was the New York Herald. Let England and Spain look well to their conduct, it said, or we may bring them to a reckoning.[159] It is unfortunate

---

[154] III, 514, n.

[155] IV, 76; Lecky, I, 488, 490.

[156] Formerly Lord John Russell.

[157] Oct. 17, 18. Earl Russell, II, 344; Palmerston, II, 218.

[158] Early in November, C. F. A. M. H. S., XLV, 53.

[159] Nov. 9.

wrote John Bright to Sumner on November 20, that nothing is done to change the reckless tone of your New York Herald; between it and the Times of London there is great mischief done in both countries.

In spite of this skirmish of journalists, the two governments were approaching diplomatically a good understanding when a rash, ambitious, self-conceited and self-willed[160] naval Captain not only undid in an hour all the advantage Adams, Seward and Lincoln had gained in six months, but brought the two countries to the brink of war.

James M. Mason and John Slidell, commissioners from the Confederate States to Great Britain and France, left Charleston on a little Confederate steamer and, evading the blockade, reached a Cuban port, whence they proceeded to Havana and took the British mail packet Trent for St. Thomas, where direct connection could be made with a British steamer for Southampton. On November 8, next day after leaving Havana, the Trent was sighted in the Bahama Channel by the American man-of-war San Jacinto, under the command of Captain Wilkes. He fired a shot across her bow without result, and then a shell; this brought her to. He ordered a lieutenant, accompanied by other officers and a number of marines, to board and search the Trent, and, if Mason and Slidell were found, to make them prisoners. The British Captain opposed anything like a search of his vessel, nor would he consent to show papers or passenger list. But Slidell and Mason announced themselves, were seized, and despite their protest as well as those of the Captain of the Trent and of a commander of the royal navy in charge of the mails, were taken by force from the Trent to the San Jacinto.

On November 15, Wilkes arrived at Fort Monroe; next day the country had the news. Rejoicing over the seizure as if a great battle had been won, the Northern people completely lost their heads. Having yearned for a victory, they now held in their hands the two Southern men[161] whom, next to Davis and Floyd, they hated the worst and they had struck a blow at Great Britain for her supposed sympathy with the South. All the members of the Cabinet, except Montgomery Blair, were elated at the seizure. The Secretary of War read aloud the telegram announcing it to the group of men in his office and led the cheers in which Governor Andrew and the rest heartily joined. Andrew, who thought that in comparison with Mason and Slidell, Benedict Arnold was a saint, said, at a dinner in Boston in honor of the Captain, that Wilkes had shown wise judgment in the act which was one of the most illustrious services that had made the war memorable; we are met tonight, he added, to congratulate a gallant officer who, to uphold the American flag, fired a shot across the bow of a ship that bore the British lion.[162] The Secretary of the Navy wrote to Wilkes a formal letter of congratulation on the great public service

---

[160] Welles's Diary, I, 87.

[161] Mason and Slidell were imprisoned in Fort Warren in Boston harbor.

[162] C. F. A. M. H. S., XLV, 49, 94; Pearson, I, 319 n. 1.

you have rendered in the capture of the rebel emissaries.[163] The House of Representatives on the first day of its session passed a resolution, thanking him for his brave, adroit and patriotic conduct.[164]

Montgomery Blair denounced the act of Wilkes as unauthorized, irregular and illegal.[165] Senator Sumner, then in Boston, said at once, We shall have to give them up.[166] The President, too, resisted the general infection. On the day that the news came to Washington, he said: I fear the traitors will prove to be white elephants. We must stick to American principles concerning the rights of neutrals. We fought Great Britain for insisting by theory and practice on the right to do precisely what Captain Wilkes has done.[167] The President ought to have acted on his first impulse and had an immediate consultation with Sumner to be sure of his law and history. It is evident from a private letter that Sumner's advice would have been to act on the case at once and to make the surrender in conformity with our best precedents.[168] And it is clear from Seward's subsequent action that, if urged by the President, he too would have consented to the surrender of Mason and Slidell before a demand for them was made. The President might then have adopted Blair's recommendation that Wilkes be ordered to take Mason and Slidell on an American warship to England and deliver them to the British government.[169] Such an act would have been graceful, astute, honorable and politic and needed no more courage in breasting popular sentiment than Lincoln had already shown in his treatment of Frémont. He would have had at his back Sumner, Seward, Blair and General McClellan;[170] and, if the surrender had been made immediately before many lawyers and statesmen had fed the public excitement by alleging that the act was justifiable according to international law the country, tersely and emphatically instructed that we were carrying out the principles for which we had always contended, would doubtless have acquiesced. Yet Lincoln clearly feared to give up Mason and Slidell, although he must have appreciated that their voices were more eloquent from their prison than they would have been in London and Paris. Indeed, as a mere matter of policy, the United States ought to have made it easy for the author of the Fugitive Slave Law to reach London and the champion of filibustering in the interest of slavery to reach Paris, since their pleading could in no way injure the Northern cause, so well was it understood, at any rate in England, that they represented slavery. Slow to act and distrustful of his impulses, Lincoln let the great opportunity slip when with a word he might have won the

---

[163] O. R., II, II, 1109.
[164] Globe, 5.
[165] Welles L. & S., 186.
[166] Pierce, IV, 52.
[167] Lossing, II, 156.
[168] Pierce, IV, 61.
[169] Welles L. & S., 186.
[170] Lothrop, 327; McClellan, 175; Russell, 575.

equivalent of a successful campaign in the field. Alike a leader and a representative of popular sentiment, he in this instance suffered his representative character to overtop the leadership. The fellow-feeling with the American public that in any dispute with Great Britain there is but one side to be considered prevented him from making a brilliant stroke. As he took no action and made no public utterance, his silence was misconstrued, and he was reported falsely as having put down his foot, with the declaration, I would sooner die than give them up.[171]

As there was then no Atlantic cable, England did not receive the news of the seizure of Mason and Slidell until November 27. The opinion was general that it was an outrage to her flag. It has made a great sensation here, wrote John Bright to Sumner from London, and the ignorant and passionate and 'Rule Britannia' class are angry and insolent as usual.[172] The excitement is so great, said Adams in a despatch to Seward, as to swallow up every other topic for the moment.[173] Charles Mackay,[174] a friend of Seward's, wrote to him for his own and for the President's information: The people are frantic with rage, and were the country polled I fear that 999 men out of a thousand would declare for immediate war. Lord Palmerston cannot resist the impulse if he would. If he submits to the insult to the flag his ministry is doomed it would not last a fortnight.[175]

The English Cabinet decided that the seizure of Mason and Slidell was an act of violence which was an affront to the British flag and a violation of international law, and that their liberation and a suitable apology for the aggression be demanded. In accordance with this decision Earl Russell on November 30 prepared a despatch to Lord Lyons,[176] the tone of which was softened and made more friendly on the suggestion of the Queen and Prince Consort: the Prince's direct words, somewhat at variance with the Queen's and his kindly spirit, were put into courteous diplomatic language, but the substance of the demand was in no way changed, and on Sunday, December 1, a Queen's messenger bearing it was on his way to Washington.

Great Britain began preparations for war. Instructions for such an eventuality were sent to Lord Lyons and to the Vice Admiral commanding the British fleet in American waters. Eight thousand troops[177] were despatched to Canada. The Queen

---

[171] Russell, 588.

[172] Nov. 29, III, 525.

[173] Nov. 29, O. R., II, II, 1106.

[174] Mackay visited the United States in 1857 and wrote a book on the country. During his visit he was entertained by Seward, who saw him again in London in 1859. Seward had a high regard and friendship for him. In February, 1862, he was appointed New York correspondent of the London*Times* to supplant Davis, whose "proclivities were entirely Northern." Life, W. H. Russell, II, 92.

[175] Nov. 29, O. R., II, II, 1107.

[176] The British minister at Washington.

by proclamation prohibited the export of arms and ammunition, and the government laid an embargo on 3000 tons of saltpetre, the whole stock in the market, which had been recently bought for immediate shipment to the United States.

Curiously enough, the English like the American government was acting in response to popular sentiment and not in accordance with its law and precedents. Four days after the seizure of Mason and Slidell, but fifteen days before the news of it reached England, Adams, on the invitation of Palmerston, had an interview with him in his library [November 12]. The Prime Minister supposed that the Confederate commissioners were then approaching England as passengers in the West Indian packet, and that a United States vessel of war, then at Southampton, was on the watch for her with the intention of taking them from her by force. I am not going into the question of your right to do such an act, Palmerston said. Perhaps you might be justified in it or perhaps you might not. Such a step would be highly inexpedient. It would be regarded here very unpleasantly if the captain should within sight of the shore commit an act which would be felt as offensive to the national flag. Nor can I see the compensating advantage to be gained by it. It surely could not be supposed that the addition of one or two more to the number of persons who had already been some time in London on the same errand would be likely to produce any change in the policy already adopted.[178]

Palmerston's friendly advice was a mystery to Adams and remained so to American writers until 1908 when the Life of Delane was published. Delane was the editor of the London Times and had a close political friendship with the Prime Minister, who thus wrote to him on the day before the interview with Adams: My dear Delane, It may be useful to you to know that the Chancellor, Dr. Lushington,[179] the three law officers, Sir G. Grey,[180] the Duke of Somerset,[181] and myself met at the Treasury today to consider what we could properly do about the American cruiser come, no doubt, to search the West Indian packet supposed to be bringing hither the two Southern envoys; and much to my regret, it appeared that, according to the principles of international law laid down in our courts by Lord Stowell, and practiced and enforced by us, a belligerent has the right to stop and search any neutral not being a ship of war and being found on the high seas and being suspected of carrying enemy's despatches; and that consequently this American cruiser might, by our own principles of international law, stop the West Indian packet, search her and if the Southern men and their despatches and credentials were found on board, either take them out, or seize the packet and carry her back

---

[177] But see Walpole, II, 44; Hansard, CLXVIII.

[178] O. R., II, II, 1078; C. F. A. M. H. S., XLV, 53. I have changed the third person to first.

[179] Judge of the High Court of the Admiralty and Dean of the Arches, a famous judge.

[180] Home Secretary.

[181] First Lord of Admiralty.

to New York for trial.[182] Consequently, as Charles F. Adams wrote, the San Jacinto might, on English principles of international law, stop the Trent, search her, and if the Southern men were on board, do exactly what Captain Wilkes had already just done, take them out and then allow the packet to proceed on its voyage.[183] Such was the opinion of the law officers in a hypothetical case on November 11, but, eighteen days later, when they considered an actual seizure, until then justified by English principles and practice, they reversed their decision and declared Wilkes's act illegal and unjustifiable by international law.[184] In other words, they abandoned the English precedent and adopted the hitherto American contention as more in accordance with the age of steam and conditions on the sea in the last half of the nineteenth century. The English public showed in its outburst of indignation that the opinion of November 11 was antiquated and demanded that the law be expounded and that the government should act in a manner to enforce their own opinion.

It is a common belief that our ministers and ambassadors to Great Britain succumb to the charm of English society, that dinners of the duchesses in London and country visits to persons of quality, distinction and influence are apt to weaken the American fibre. That was not the case with Adams. He went much into society in London and was frequently invited by persons of influence to visit them in their houses in the country. Indeed he was at Monckton Milnes's house in Yorkshire, when the news of the seizure of Mason and Slidell came. But with him the dinners, receptions and country visits were all in the line of his work, which was to do his part toward saving the republic. During the forty-two days of suspense, until he learned the settlement of the question, he maintained his equable temper, although he appreciated fully the gravity of the case. There can be not a shadow of doubt, he wrote to Seward on December 6, that the passions of the country are up and that a collision is inevitable if the Government of the United States should sustain Captain Wilkes.[185] It is evident from his private letters that if Adams had been Secretary of State he would have recommended the immediate surrender of Mason and Slidell. The uniform tendency of our own policy, he wrote to Motley, has been to set up very high the doctrine of neutral rights and to limit in every possible manner the odious doctrine of search. To have the two countries virtually changing their ground under this momentary temptation, would not, as it seems to me, tend to benefit the position of the United States. To R. H. Dana, he said, What provokes me most is that we should consent to take up and to wear Great Britain's cast off rags.[186]

---

[182] Nov. 11. Delane, II, 36; C. F. A., M. H. S., XLV, 54.

[183] M. H. S., XLV, 56.

[184] Martin, V, 419; Earl Russell II, 345.

[185] O. R., II, II, 1119.

[186] Dec. 4, 13. C. F. A. M. H. S., XLV, 93, 95

At 11:30 on the night of December 18, the Queen's messenger delivered Earl Russell's despatch to Lyons and also two private letters in which full instructions were given in words of tender consideration. Next day Lyons called upon Seward at the State Department, and in accordance with his instructions, acquainted him with the tenor of the official despatch. Seward asked Lyons informally, Was any time fixed by your instructions within which the U. S. Government must reply? I do not like to answer the question, was the response. Of all things I wish to avoid the slightest appearance of a menace. Seward still pressed for private and confidential information. On this understanding, Lyons replied: I will tell you. According to my instructions, I must have your answer in seven days. Seward then requested a copy of the despatch unofficially and informally as so much depended upon the wording of it that it was impossible to come to a decision without reading it. To this Lyons replied that if he gave him the copy officially the seven days would at once begin to run. Seward suggested that he be given the copy on the understanding that no one but the President and himself should know that it had been delivered. Lyons gladly complied with this suggestion and, on returning to the Embassy, sent a copy of the despatch to the Secretary in an envelope marked, private and confidential. This brought an almost immediate visit from Seward, who expressed himself pleased to find that the despatch was courteous and friendly and not dictatorial or menacing. Now, he asked in strict confidence, Suppose that I sent you in seven days a refusal or a proposal to discuss the question? My instructions are positive, Lyons replied, and leave me no discretion. If the answer is not satisfactory and, particularly if it does not include the immediate surrender of the prisoners, I cannot accept it.[187] On the morning of December 23, the delay having occurred to suit Seward's business engagements and his wish to master the question completely, Lyons called again, read the despatch and left with the Secretary a copy of it: from this day, the seven days of waiting began to run.

As long as the English public required that their government present an ultimatum, it could not have been couched in words more considerate to the susceptibilities of the American people, nor could the instructions in the private letters have been bettered. Lyons carried out the spirit as well as the letter of his instructions; doubtless he was glad to be supported in his sympathetic consideration for the Secretary of State's difficult position. When announcing the seizure he wrote to Earl Russell, To conceal the distress which I feel would be impossible; and during the period of suspense his attitude of reserve was irreproachable. I have avoided, he wrote, the subject of the capture on board the Trent as much as possible, and have said no more than that it is an untoward event which I very much regret.[188]

---

[187] Lyons I, 65. I have frequently changed the indirect to direct narration.
[188] Nov. 19, 22. O. R., II, II, 1095, 1097.

Apparently the President submitted the question to his Secretary of State. As long as Seward could not bring himself to Sumner's, Adams's and Blair's position and advise the immediate surrender of Mason and Slidell, he conducted himself in an exemplary manner. Reticent of speech, he was receptive of information and advice which came to him from many quarters abroad and at home; much of it was excellent.[189] In his communication to Adams, of November 27, he had explained to him that Captain Wilkes had acted without any instructions whatever and that the United States intended no action until we hear what the British Government may have to say on the subject.[190] It was undoubtedly between the two interviews with Lyons, if not before, that Seward came to the conclusion that the commissioners must be surrendered; thenceforth he conducted the affair in his most skilful manner. His own decision made, he had to convince the President, the overruling authority necessary to consult in all cases.[191] Governor Seward, Lincoln said, you will go on, of course, preparing your answer, which, as I understand it, will state the reasons why they ought to be given up. Now I have a mind to try my hand at stating the reasons why they ought not to be given up. We will compare the points on each side.[192] The President made a draft of a despatch in which he expressed his unwillingness to believe that Great Britain would now press for a categorical answer; he would like the question left open for discussion in order that the United States might present her case; she would then be willing to submit the question to a friendly arbitration; but if Great Britain would not arbitrate and, after listening to the American case, still insisted on the surrender of Mason and Slidell, the surrender would be made, provided this disposition of the matter should serve in the future as a precedent for both countries. The key to the President's attitude lay in his words, We too, as well as Great Britain, have a people justly jealous of their rights.[193] Obviously, the draft did not satisfy him as suited to the present exigency, and he did not present it to his Cabinet.

The result justified William H. Russell's entry in his Diary of December 20 to the effect that Seward would control the situation.[194] And a day earlier Charles Eliot Norton had written from New York to Lowell, There is apparently no reason to fear war as the result of any popular excitement here or of any want of temper or discretion on the part of the administration. It is a fortunate thing for us that Seward has regained so much of the public confidence. He will feel himself strong enough not to be passionate or violent.[195]

---

[189] See Bancroft, II, 234.
[190] O. R., II, II, 1102.
[191] Seward, III, 43.
[192] Bancroft, II, 234; Seward, III, 25.
[193] N. & H., V, 33.
[194] Russell, 588.
[195] C. E. Norton, I, 248.

The Cabinet met at ten o'clock on the morning of Christmas day; probably only two members of it, Seward and Blair, were at that hour in favor of the surrender. Seward submitted the draft of his answer to Lord Lyons, complying with the British demand. Sumner[196] came by invitation and read letters from Bright and Cobden, staunch friends of the North, giving an account of English public sentiment and offering advice that may be summed up in Bright's words, At all hazards you must not let this matter grow to a war with England.[197] If Sumner's opinion was asked, he doubtless expressed himself warmly in favor of Seward's decision. The discussion went on until two o'clock, when the Cabinet adjourned until next day; it was then resumed. Seward maintained that the claim of the British government was just and had not been made in a discourteous manner.[198] Bates, Attorney-General, came to his support, arguing that war with England would be ruin[199] but, as he recorded in his Diary, there was great reluctance on the part of some of the members of the Cabinet and even the President himself[200] to give up the commissioners. In the end, however, from the considerations that Wilkes had acted contrary to our precedents, violated international law and that we could not afford a war with Great Britain, all came to Seward's position and approved his answer [December 26]. He said at the end of his long despatch to Lyons, the persons in question will be cheerfully liberated.[201] The disavowal of the act was accepted as a sufficient apology.

Fearing popular excitement, Seward arranged with Lyons that Mason and Slidell should not be delivered to an English vessel in Boston harbor. An American steam tug therefore took them to Provincetown, where they were delivered to a British ship-of-war, which sailed immediately for Halifax, whence they made their way to Europe.

There was no excitement in Boston nor anywhere else in the country when Mason and Slidell left Fort Warren. Bates had explained the reluctance of the President and some members of the Cabinet in coming to Seward's position as being due to a fear of the displeasure of our own people lest they should accuse us of timidly truckling to the power of England.[202] They had misread public sentiment. During the forty days that had elapsed between the news of the seizure of Mason and Slidell and their surrender, the sober second thought had asserted itself and the decision of the government was unitedly and thoroughly sustained by the whole people.[203] This seemed to indicate that if the President and his Secretary

---

[196] Chairman of the Committee on Foreign Relations in the Senate.

[197] III, 536 n.

[198] O. R., II, II, 1076, 1154.

[199] What war with England involved was well put to the President by Sumner. Pierce, IV, 58.

[200] N. & H., V, 36.

[201] The despatch is printed O. R., II, II, 1145.

[202] N. & H., V, 36.

of State had come at once to their final decision, they might have reckoned on having the country at their back. Such a disposition of the case would have made the subsequent history of the relations between England and the North far different. As it was, the transaction left a rankling wound. Many Americans thought that their country had been humiliated by being obliged to submit to a peremptory demand. Chase, in his opinion during the Cabinet Council, expressed that view. While giving his adhesion to the conclusion at which the Secretary of State has arrived, he said, it is gall and wormwood to me. Rather than consent to the liberation of these men I would sacrifice everything I possess.[204] Pending the settlement and afterwards, there was a complete misunderstanding between the two countries. The impression prevailed abroad that the North was determined to pick a quarrel with England.[205] On the other hand, there was a general belief here that Great Britain only wanted a pretext for a quarrel with the United States. Even among those who did not hold such extreme views a spirit of grim resolution prevailed. I cannot believe, wrote Norton to Lowell, that the English ministry mean war if they do, they will get it and its consequences.[206] The misunderstanding arose from each country believing that the chauvinists represented the majority in the other. As a matter of fact, a large majority in England and at the North rejoiced at the peaceful settlement of the Trent difficulty. In the South there was bitter disappointment.[207]

---

[203] III, 539.

[204] Warden, 394.

[205] Bancroft, 231.

[206] Dec. 19.

[207] Authorities: O. R., II, II; C. F. A. M. H. S., XLV; Bancroft; N. & H.; Seward; Earl Russell; Palmerston; Delane; Martin; Lyons; Life W. H. Russell; Russell; Pierce; C. F. A. Adams; Welles, L. & S.; Lossing; Lothrop; Harris; R. H. Dana; Forbes; Pearson; Lecky; McClellan; III; Lect. I have been much indebted to Charles F. Adams's paper on "The TrentAffair." M. H. S., XLV.

Chapter III

AN unfortunate political appointment of the President's was that of Simon Cameron as Secretary of War. Unequal as he was to the task of conducting a great war, he managed his Department as if it were a political machine. He had two competent subordinates[208] whose work was efficient; yet Cameron left behind him, where his own hand could be traced, a continuous line of peculation. Contracts mounting up to enormous sums were repeatedly awarded to his political followers as a reward for past services, or in anticipation of future work. He paid exorbitant prices, gave commissions, accepted inferior goods. Early in the autumn Lincoln became aware of the defects of his Secretary and undoubtedly held the view set down in Nicolay's private paper, Conversation with the President, October 2, 1861: Cameron utterly ignorant and regardless of the course of things and probable result. Selfish and openly discourteous to the President. Obnoxious to the country. Incapable either of organizing details or conceiving and executing general plans.[209] We are going to destruction, wrote Senator Grimes to Senator Fessenden, as fast as imbecility, corruption and the wheels of time can carry us.[210] Imitating Frémont, Cameron, in order to turn the public mind from his maladministration, made an appeal to the rising tide of anti-slavery sentiment. In his report to the President of December 1, he made the suggestion, in terms which could be construed as strongly recommending the measure, that the slaves should be armed, and when employed as soldiers should be freed. Without submitting the report to Lincoln, he had it mailed to the postmasters of the chief cities with instructions to hand it to the press as soon as the President's message was read in Congress. When this act came to his knowledge, Lincoln ordered that the copies which had been sent out should be recalled by telegraph and that the report should be modified to accord with his own policy in regard to slavery.[211]

On January 11, 1862, the President sent Cameron a curt note dismissing him from the position of Secretary of War and nominating him as Minister to Russia. There was reason enough for the change. The inefficiency of his administration, the belief of the country that it was corrupt, the insubordinate act in the matter of the report, all combined undoubtedly to lead the President to his decision. He then

---

[208] Montgomery Meigs, Quartermaster-General, and Thomas A. Scott, Assistant-Secretary.

[209] Nicolay, 178.

[210] Nov. 13, III, 574.

[211] The expunged part was published by some of the newspapers that had received it and was reproduced in the Congressional Globe (Dec. 12) by Representative Eliot of Massachusetts." Horace White, 172.

appointed Edwin M. Stanton, Secretary of War. Stanton, in his private correspondence during the summer of 1861, had written freely of the painful imbecility of Lincoln and the impotence of his administration, and as he was neither politic nor reserved, he had undoubtedly been equally outspoken in conversation with his friends and acquaintances in Washington, where he was then living. If Lincoln had cared to listen to Washington gossip, he might have heard many tales of this sort, but if any actually reached his ears as he was considering the appointment of Stanton, they certainly counted as nothing against his growing conviction that, in respect of local origin, previous party association and inherent ability, this Democratic lawyer from Pennsylvania was the man for the place. The appointment was acceptable to Seward and Chase, to Congress and to the country, for Stanton had gained the confidence of all by his sturdy patriotism when a member of Buchanan's cabinet; it proved as admirable a choice as Cameron's was unfortunate. Stanton made a great war minister, bringing to his task an indomitable spirit, overpowering energy and hatred of all sorts of corruption.[212] I feel that one clear victory at home, wrote Adams to Seward on January 10, 1862, might perhaps save us a foreign war. Soon after his letter reached Washington, his wish was gratified.

Commanding two important gateways to the southwestern part of the Confederacy were Fort Henry on the Tennessee river and Fort Donelson on the Cumberland, the two rivers here being but eleven miles apart. Flag-officer Foote and General Ulysses S. Grant thought the capture of Henry feasible, and asked Halleck, the commander of the Department with headquarters in St. Louis, for permission to make the attempt. This was given by telegraph on January 30, and, two days later, detailed instructions were sent by post to Grant. Next day he and Foote started from Cairo with four iron-clad and three wooden gunboats and a number of transports carrying the advance troops of the expedition. Four days later Foote poured into Fort Henry a destructive fire which, though responded to with unabated activity, resulted in the Confederate flag being hauled down after an hour and a quarter's very severe and closely contested action. The co-operation of the Army in the attack was prevented by the excessively muddy roads and high stage of water.[213] Fort Henry is ours, telegraphed Grant to Halleck on February 6. I shall take and destroy Fort Donelson on the 8th.[214]

Albert Sidney Johnston, the departmental commander of the Confederate Army, esteemed by Jefferson Davis the ablest of Southern generals, was dismayed at the fall of Fort Henry and determined to fight for Nashville at Donelson, assigning to this enterprise the better part of his army.[215]

---

[212] III; V, 179; N. & H.; Warden; Forbes, I; M. B. Field; Gorham I; Horace White, 172; Welles's Diary, I, 127.

[213] Foote's report, O. R., VII, 123.

[214] O. R., VII, 124.

Heavy rains made the roads temporarily impassable for artillery and wagons; moreover, Grant desired the co-operation of the gunboats which were detained for needed repairs; hence he was unable to fulfil his promise to the letter; but, having sent the gunboats and some of the troops round by water, he left Fort Henry on the morning of February 12 with his main force and marched across country toward Donelson, arriving in front of the enemy about noon. Here he began the investment of the fort and, amid constant skirmishing, extended it next day on the flanks of the enemy.[216] On February 14, Foote attacked with his gunboats, hoping for a repetition of the success at Fort Henry. The same courage and determination were in evidence, but the conditions were different and fortune adverse. He proved no match for the Confederate batteries, two of the iron-clads were rendered unmanageable, drifting helplessly down the river, and the other two, badly damaged, soon followed. Foote had been wounded; the Navy was for the moment out of the contest.[217] I concluded, wrote Grant, to make the investment of Fort Donelson as perfect as possible, and partially fortify and await repairs to the gunboats.[218] That night the disappointment of the Union troops was aggravated by physical discomfort. When they had left Fort Henry, the weather was warm and springlike; many of them had left blankets and overcoats behind; next day a driving north wind brought a storm of sleet and snow, which, continuing through two nights, tried the patience and endurance of the men, who were without tents and who could not risk fires because of the proximity of the enemy.

Cast down by the fall of Fort Henry, the Confederate generals were now elated at the repulse of the gunboats which had not cost them a single man or gun, but, after observing the arrival of re-enforcements for Grant, they were satisfied that he would soon be able to beleaguer the fort completely, and that to save the garrison, they must cut their way through the besiegers and recover the road to Nashville. They determined to make the attempt early the next morning.

Re-enforcements had increased Grant's army to 27,000. McClernand's division was on the right, holding the Nashville road; Lew Wallace's was in the centre and C. F. Smith's on the left.

Extending beyond the earthwork of Fort Donelson was a winding line of intrenchments nearly two miles in length, protected at certain points with abatis. These intrenchments were occupied by the Confederates, whose total force was 21,000. At five o'clock on the morning of February 15, they fell upon McClernand, who, after a stubborn resistance to superior numbers, was obliged to fall back in some confusion. The fugitives who crowded up the hill in the rear of Lew Wallace's line brought unmistakable signs of disaster. A mounted officer

---

[215] O. R., VII, 259.

[216] Grant's report, O. R., VII, 159.

[217] Foote, O. R., VII, 166.

[218] O. R., VII, 159.

galloped down the road shouting 'We are cut to pieces.'[219] The Confederates had gained possession of the Nashville road, but were too broken and exhausted by the severe battle to retreat in order over a road covered with snow and ice. Nor were all the men provided with rations; nor had certain other precautions been taken that are generally deemed indispensable for a retreat in the face of the enemy.

Early that morning Foote had requested Grant to come to his flag-ship for a consultation, he himself being too badly injured to leave the boat. Having complied with this request, the commanding general of the Union army was not in the field when the Confederates attacked; on going ashore after his conference with Foote, he met a Captain of his staff white with fear for the safety of the national troops.[220] He rode back with the utmost speed over the four or five miles of icy roads.

Here was a critical moment in Grant's life. The war had given him an opportunity to mend a broken career; should he fail in this supreme hour, another chance might never come to him and his unfortunate absence during the morning's battle would certainly be misconstrued.

Anyone used to affairs knows that there are times when, after a bad beginning everything seems to go awry, perplexity reigns and no remedy appears; when ordinary men are bewildered and know not what to do. All at once the Master appears, takes in the situation, cheers up his associates, gives a succession of orders and the difficulty is unravelled; failure gives way to success. Such was the case on the field of Donelson. Grant arrived; out of confusion came order; determination out of despair. When he learned of the disaster to his right wing, his face flushed slightly and he crushed some papers in his hand; but, saluting McClernand and Wallace, he said in his usual quiet voice, Gentlemen, the position on the right must be retaken. Then galloping towards his left, he stopped somewhere to send a despatch to Foote, requesting his assistance.[221] While on the way he heard some of the men say that the enemy had come out with knapsacks and haversacks filled with rations. This was evidence to him that the sortie of the Confederates amounted to nothing less than an attempt to escape from the fort and he said to the staff officer who was riding with him: Some of our men are pretty badly demoralized, but the enemy must be more so, for he has attempted to force his way out but has fallen back; the one who attacks first now will be victorious.

---

[219] Wallace, O. R., VII, 237.

[220] Grant, I, 306.

[221] This is the despatch: "If all the gunboats that can will immediately make their appearance to the enemy, it may secure us a victory. Otherwise all may be defeated. A terrible conflict ensued in my absence, which has demoralized a portion of my command and I think the enemy is much more so. If the gunboats do not show themselves, it will reassure the enemy and still further demoralize our troops. I must order a charge to save appearances. I do not expect the gunboats to go into action but to make appearance and throw a few shells at long range." O. R., VII, 618.

Call out to the men as we pass, 'Fill your cartridge boxes quick and get into line; the enemy is trying to escape, and he must not be permitted to do so.'[222] Wherever Grant appeared confidence followed in his train. He rode quickly to Smith's headquarters and ordered him to charge, assuring him that he would have only a thin line to contend with. Through abatis which looked too thick for a rabbit to get through, Smith led the charge with unusual energy and courage, carried the advanced works of the enemy and effected a lodgement in his intrenchments, securing a key to his position.[223] After the order to Smith, Grant commanded McClernand and Wallace to charge; they advanced with vigor and recovered their position of the morning, regaining possession of the Nashville road. There was now no way of escape for the Confederates from Fort Donelson except by the river and by a road that had been submerged by the river's overflow. Grant made arrangements for an assault at daybreak the next morning. Hardly a doubt of its success could exist.

Inside the fort the general discouragement that prevailed led the Confederate generals to the same opinion. The two ranking officers turned over the command to Buckner.[224] One of them escaped with a number of his troops in two small steamboats that had just arrived with re-enforcements; the other crossed the river in a skiff. The cavalry rode out over the submerged road finding the water about saddle-skirt deep.[225]

At an early hour next morning [February 16] Grant received a note from Buckner proposing to capitulate and suggesting an armistice until noon. To this he made his famous reply: Yours of this date, proposing armistice and appointment of commissioners to settle terms of capitulation, is just received. No terms except unconditional and immediate surrender can be accepted. I propose to move immediately upon your works.[226] Buckner was compelled to accept what he called the ungenerous and unchivalrous terms. Grant, in his despatch to Halleck of that day, said that he had taken 12,000 to 15,000 prisoners, 20,000 stand of arms, 48 pieces of artillery, 17 heavy guns, from 2000 to 4000 horses, and large quantities of commissary stores.[227]

Judged by its moral and strategical results, wrote Ropes, the capture of Fort Donelson was one of the turning points of the war.[228] It caused the evacuation of Nashville and resulted in a Union advance of more than two hundred miles of territory before the enemy could rally or reorganize. It set at rest all doubts, if any still existed, of the permanent position of Kentucky in the civil conflict and it

---

[222] Grant, I, 307.
[223] McPherson, O. R., VII, 163.
[224] See III, 592.
[225] O. R., VII, 161.
[226] Forrest, O. R., VII, 295.
[227] O. R., VII, 625.
[228] Ropes, II, 34.

deprived the Confederates of a large part of Tennessee, a fruitful ground for recruits and supplies. The people were terrified and some of the troops were disheartened, wrote Albert Sidney Johnston to Davis. The blow was most disastrous and almost without remedy.[229] When the Governor of Tennessee proclaimed that the troops must evacuate Nashville and adjourned the legislature to Memphis, panic seized upon the people, and disorder, turbulence and rapine ensued.[230]

The magnitude of the victory was fully appreciated at the North. The underpinning of the rebellion seems to be knocked out from under it, wrote Chase. The almost universal feeling is that the rebellion is knocked on the head, said Oliver Wendell Holmes. The capture of Fort Donelson was regarded in England as a victory of high importance, and greatly helped the cause of the North.[231]

The victory was due to Grant. The more clearly one studies this campaign, the more firmly is one convinced that the great general longed for by the North had appeared. His quickness to guess the enemy's design and the predicament in which they stood; his rapidity in forming a plan and putting its several elements in operation; his ability to conceal his disappointment and alarm at the disaster to his right wing and his grim determination to snatch some advantage from it: here surely we must recognize the stamp of military genius. It is true that when he gave the order to charge the enemy he could not be certain of a complete success and that he would have liked the aid of the gunboats.[232] It may be, as Ropes has suggested, that he only did the obvious thing;[233] but how many generals in the Northern Army at that time would have acted as he did and turned a defeat into so complete a victory? After Smith had carried the trench and the position on the right had been recovered, Grant must have expected demoralization to follow in the enemy's ranks; finally Buckner's note left no room for doubt. In his reply, which by an allusion to the initials of his name made him known henceforward as Unconditional Surrender Grant, he showed that in the hour of success he would exact the whole loaf: this attitude amid the amenities of our civil war was the mark of a masterful character. Five days after the surrender he wrote to his close friend, E. B. Washburne: Our volunteers fought a battle that would figure well with many of those fought in Europe where large standing armies are maintained. I feel very grateful to you for having placed me in the position to have had the honor of commanding such an army and at such a time. I only trust that I have not nor will not disappoint you.[234]

---

[229] March 18, O. R., VII, 259.

[230] Reports and statements of Forrest, Floyd, and one other in O. R., VII, 427-432; Wyeth, Forrest, 73; John Wooldridge, Nashville, 193.

[231] III, 598.

[232] The gunboats took no part in the battle of Feb. 15.

[233] Ropes, II, 36.

[234] Grant's private letters, 4.

Halleck and McClellan[235] were too good theoretical soldiers not to understand that Donelson was a signal victory and they treated Grant in a manner that savors of professional jealousy. General Grant left his command without any authority and went to Nashville, telegraphed Halleck to McClellan. I can get no returns, no reports, no information of any kind from him. Satisfied with his victory, he sits down and enjoys it without any regard to the future. I am worn-out and tired with this neglect and inefficiency. Do not hesitate to arrest Grant at once if the good of the service requires it, was McClellan's reply, and place C. F. Smith in command. Next day Halleck telegraphed: A rumor has just reached me that since the taking of Fort Donelson General Grant has resumed his former bad habits [habits of drink]. I do not deem it advisable to arrest him at present but have placed General Smith in command of the expedition up the Tennessee.[236] These despatches were a cruel injustice to Grant. Since his victory his conduct had been proper, discreet and orderly.

Important as was the taking of Donelson, the full fruits of the victory were not garnered forthwith. Celerity was needed and Grant was the one general of the North who had shown that he could move quickly and fight an army effectively. If, instead of being unjustly criticised by Halleck, he had received the consideration that was his due and had been recommended for the active command, he could undoubtedly, if keeping himself at his best level of personal efficiency, have maintained the permanent occupation of Kentucky and Tennessee and taken Vicksburg and Chattanooga, thereby cutting off from the Confederacy a region that was considerably productive of troops and supplies.

The gloom at Richmond reflected the real dimensions of the disaster. On February 22, six days after the fall of Donelson, the provisional gave way to the permanent government of the Confederate States and Davis was inaugurated President for a term of six years. Amid the profound depression, at the darkest hour of our struggle, as he phrased it, Davis, pale and emaciated from illness and grief, delivered his inaugural address, in the course of which he admitted that we have recently met with serious disasters.[237] Adversity drove the Confederates to extreme acts. Six days after his inauguration, Davis, by authority of an Act of Congress passed in secret session, proclaimed martial law in the city of Richmond and the adjoining country for ten miles around and declared the suspension therein of the privilege of the writ of habeas corpus. Seven weeks later, in response to his recommendation, a rigorous Conscription act was passed.[238] Oh, for a Grant in command of the Army of the Potomac to take quick advantage of this demoralization in the capital of the Confederacy! And indeed it seemed for the

---

[235] McClellan was still in command of all of the armies of the United States.

[236] March 3, 4, O. R., VII, 679-682.

[237] There had been Union victories besides Henry and Donelson, III, 581.

[238] April 16.

moment as if McClellan would be spurred to action, as is evident from two of his despatches to Halleck of February 20: If the force in West can take Nashville or even hold its own for the present, I hope to have Richmond and Norfolk in from three to four weeks. The rebels hold firm at Manassas. In less than two weeks I shall move the Army of the Potomac, and hope to be in Richmond soon after you are in Nashville.[239] On February 24, Nashville was occupied by the Union troops. McClellan had a wonderful opportunity.[240] In command of 150,000 men superior so far as the average raw material of the rank and file is concerned to the armies of most European countries, with roads to traverse no worse than many of those in the south of Italy over which the Sardinian army had marched in 1860,[241] roads no more difficult of passage than were the roads in Tennessee, on which the Union troops had marched and were still marching to good purpose he should unquestionably have struck at Joseph E. Johnston at Manassas. He had three men to the enemy's one and, though the outcome of a great battle may never be predicted with certainty, especially one with a McClellan pitted against a Joseph E. Johnston, nevertheless the chances were decidedly with the Union Army. Moreover Johnston was about to retire from Manassas. He began his preparations on February 22, started the movement itself on March 7 and four days later had his army safely on the south bank of the Rappahannock river. Here had been an excellent opportunity for inflicting damage, to use McClellan's own words, on a large army that was withdrawing in the face of a powerful adversary.[242] Let us now return to Grant during the days following the capture of Fort Donelson. In a private letter to Washburne of March 22, he gave an account of his misunderstanding with Halleck. After getting into Donelson, he wrote, General Halleck did not hear from me for near two weeks. It was about the same time before I heard from him. I was writing every day and sometimes as often as three times a day. Reported every move and change, the condition of my troops, etc. Not getting these, General Halleck very justly became dissatisfied, and was, as I have since learned, sending me daily reprimands. Not receiving them, they lost their sting. When one did reach me, not seeing the justice of it, I retorted and asked to be relieved. Three telegrams passed in this way, each time ending by my requesting to be relieved. All is now understood however and I feel assured that General Halleck is fully satisfied. In fact he wrote me a letter saying that I could not be relieved, and otherwise quite complimentary.[243] But in his article in the

---

[239] O. R., VII, 640.

[240] He recovered from his illness about the middle of January, 1862.

[241] Edward Dicey, III, 604.

[242] O. R., V, 51. Authorities: O. R., V, VII, X, Pt. II; B. & L., I; Grant, I; III; Ropes, II; Grant's private letters; Life of General Rawlins, J. H. Wilson MS., kindly lent to me by General Wilson. Since the use that I made of the MS. this book has been published. Neal Pub. Co., 1916; N. & H., V; Bruce Milt. Hist. Soc., VII; Swinton; T. L. Livermore; Hosmer's Appeal; Johnston; McClellan; Webb. For a characterization of Grant, III, 594.

Century Magazine (February, 1885) and in his Personal Memoirs, both written after he had seen the whole correspondence, he criticised Halleck severely. Halleck, however, at this time had the confidence of the War Department in Washington and had been appointed to the sole command of the United States forces in the West;[244] on March 13, he restored Grant to the active command of the Army of the Tennessee from which he had been temporarily suspended.[245] In 1884 Grant wrote: My opinion was and still is that immediately after the fall of Fort Donelson the way was opened to the National forces all over the Southwest without much resistance. If one general who would have taken the responsibility had been in command of all the troops west of the Alleghanies, he could have marched to Chattanooga, Corinth, Memphis and Vicksburg with the troops we then had, and as volunteering was going on rapidly over the North there would soon have been force enough at all these centres to operate offensively against any body of the enemy that might be found near them.[246] As a matter of fact when, after the inexcusable snubbing he had received from Halleck, Grant was again placed at the head of his army, he had an opportunity for action which, if he had availed himself of it to the best of his ability would, by common consent of government and people, have pointed to him unmistakably as the one man for this work.

During the last days of March, Grant's headquarters were at Savannah. He had five divisions in camp at Pittsburg Landing, nine miles higher up and on the west side of the Tennessee river, the side toward the enemy; and also Lew Wallace's division at Crump's Landing five miles below Pittsburg Landing and on the same side of the river. General Buell, in command of the Army of the Ohio, about 36,000 strong, was marching toward Savannah to join Grant in an offensive movement against the Confederates, who were at or near Corinth.

Albert Sidney Johnston, grieved as he was over the disaster at Donelson, was always cheered by the support and friendship of Jefferson Davis, who wrote to him, My confidence in you has never wavered.[247] Beauregard, then the idol of the South, had been persuaded to leave Virginia and go to the Southwest to the aid of Johnston in the hope that, by his personal popularity, he might succeed in arousing the people to resist the invasion of their territory.[248] Through the exertions of these two, an army of 40,000 was collected at Corinth. What the people want, said Johnston, is a battle and a victory; and he hoped to crush Grant before Buell could

---

[243] Grant's private letters, 8.

[244] March 11; assumed command March 13.

[245] This was the army of Donelson with reënforcements. The title was not formally given until April 21.

[246] Grant, 317.

[247] O. R., X, Pt. II, 365.

[248] This was in January after the "crushing disaster" [Beauregard's words] of Mill Spring, Ky., when General George H. Thomas defeated the Confederates. It was before Donelson.

join him. Leaving Corinth[249] on April 3, with the idea of surprising the Union forces, he expected to make the attack two days later, but owing to a number of delays, was unable to deliver the blow until the early morning of Sunday, April 6.

On the eve of this battle, called Shiloh, Grant's remarkable faculty of divining the enemy's movements, displayed at Donelson and later during his military career, seemed to be utterly in abeyance. Grant never studied the opposing commander with the thoroughness of Lee, and this time he failed to guess that desperation would drive Johnston to the offensive. He had made up his mind that the enemy would await his attack and so obstinate was he in this belief as to ignore certain unmistakable signs of a projected movement. On the day before the attack (April 5) he telegraphed to Halleck: The main force of the enemy is at Corinth. I have scarcely the faintest idea of an attack (general one) being made upon us, but will be prepared should such a thing take place.[250] At three o'clock that afternoon, he said to a Colonel of Buell's army, there will be no fight at Pittsburg Landing; we will have to go to Corinth where the rebels are fortified.[251] At this hour Johnston's advanced corps was two miles from the Union camp and the rest of his 40,000 within supporting distance.[252]

William T. Sherman, who, in addition to his own division had general command of three others[253] at Pittsburg Landing, was even more careless than Grant, for he was in close contact with the evidence; he had, however, received no order to throw up intrenchments, although Halleck had directed Grant to fortify his position. While the utility of hasty intrenchments on the field of battle was not yet appreciated,[254] it is remarkable that with an enemy estimated at from 60,000 to 80,000[255] and, located according to their own guess, not farther than twenty-three miles away, generals as resourceful as Grant and Sherman did not put their soldiers to work with the pick and spade. At a later period of the war, wrote Sherman, we could have rendered this position impregnable in one night.[256]

Sherman, restless, ardent and enterprising[257] felt the enemy more than once; on the afternoon of Friday, April 4, he made a reconnaissance and captured ten prisoners, who said they were the advance-guard of an army commanded by Beauregard that was marching to attack the Union camp; one, who was mortally wounded, told the colonel of an Ohio regiment that the army was 50,000 strong and would certainly attack within twelve hours; of this Sherman was promptly

---

[249] Twenty-two miles from Pittsburg Landing.

[250] O. R., X. Pt. I, 89, Pt. II, 94.

[251] *Ibid.,* 331.

[252] Henry Stone, Milt. Hist. Soc. VII, 52.

[253] McClernand's was not under him.

[254] Wagner, Ropes, II, 97.

[255] Grant, O. R., X, Pt. II, 93.

[256] W. Sherman, I, 229.

[257] Henry Stone, Milt. Hist. Soc., VII, 51.

informed. Pickets of this Ohio regiment called the attention of their Captain to the rabbits and squirrels that were running into the lines; they saw a body of cavalry and a large infantry force in line: these and other facts were reported to Sherman who, clinging stubbornly to his own conception of the situation, refused to regard them as indicating anything more formidable than a reconnaissance in force. Beauregard will not attack, he said. I know him and his habit of mind well. He will never leave his own base of supplies to attack the Union army at its base.[258] On Saturday, April 5, he sent this word to Grant: The enemy has cavalry in our front and I think there are two regiments of infantry and one battery of artillery about two miles out. The enemy is saucy but got the worst of it yesterday and will not press our pickets far. I do not apprehend anything like an attack on our position.[259] At this moment one corps of the Confederate Army was deployed in line of battle, not two miles from his camp, and the other three corps were in supporting distance.[260]

If Beauregard had been in command,[261] Sherman's conjecture would not have been far wrong. He had agreed to the attack on the Union force but, when it proved impossible to make it on the Saturday, he feared that the skirmish of the day before, the drum-beat and bugle calls had given them a sufficient warning, and that they would be found intrenched to the eyes and ready for an attack; he accordingly advised that the Confederate Army be withdrawn to Corinth. Two of the corps commanders differed with him and Johnston closed the discussion with: We shall attack at daylight to-morrow. I would fight them if they were a million.[262] Even if Sherman had realized that Johnston was in command, he, like Grant, would have had no idea of the desperate energy that was pushing him forward.

An incident will show the proximity of the armies. Hearing the drum-beat at the hour of tattoo, Beauregard ordered it suppressed when, after investigation, his staff officer informed him that the drumming was in the Union camp.[263]

After the downpour of Friday and that midnight's violent storm, the sun rose on Sunday in a cloudless sky. From student to student of military campaigns went the word, the sun of Austerlitz. Johnston in the bracing air shared the exultation, declaring, To-night we will water our horses in the Tennessee river.[264] Better informed than Grant and Sherman, he knew the exact position of the Union Army and planned to turn their left, cut off their retreat to the Tennessee river and compel their surrender. While taking his coffee at 5:14, he heard the first gun, the prelude to a vigorous attack that surprised Grant, Sherman and nearly all their

---

[258] Dawes, Milt. Hist. Soc., VII, 115 *et seq.*

[259] O. R., X, Pt. II, 93.

[260] Henry Stone, Milt. Hist. Soc., VII, 52.

[261] He was second in command.

[262] W. P. Johnston, B. & L., I, 555.

[263] Dawes, Milt. Hist. Soc., VII, 136; Roman, Beauregard, I, 277.

[264] B. & L., I, 556.

officers and men. A major of an Ohio regiment was still in bed; officers' servants and company cooks were preparing breakfast; at least one sutler had opened his shop; the sentinels were pacing their beats, the details for brigade guard and fatigue duty were marching to their posts.[265] All at once the regular order of the day was changed to haste and confusion. Between seven and eight o'clock the camp of the Sixth division was carried. The surprise was complete, wrote Johnston's aide-de-camp. Colors, arms, stores and ammunition were abandoned. The breakfasts of the men were on the table, the officers' baggage and apparel left in the tents.[266]

About 8 A.M., wrote Sherman in his report of April 10, I saw the glistening bayonets of heavy masses of infantry to our left front and became satisfied for the first time that the enemy designed a determined attack on our whole camp.[267] Recovering from his surprise, wasting not a moment in vain regret, Sherman plunged into the contest, making his presence felt by command and example. In the thick of the fight he had three horses killed under him and was himself twice wounded. History may accept with only slight reservation Halleck's report sent a week later from Pittsburg Landing. It is the unanimous opinion here, he wrote, that General Sherman saved the fortune of the day.[268] He was ably supported by McClernand and the other division commanders, but, by ten o'clock, Sherman's and McClernand's camps with their supplies had been taken. As the Union soldiers were outflanked they fell back until, at the close of the day, they occupied, if McClernand's division may be taken as an example of those who had not been captured or fled, their eighth position.[269]

The Union force of 36,000 resisted in this manner the Confederate of 40,000. Johnston's troops were almost entirely raw. Twenty-five of Grant's sixty-three regiments had fought at Donelson. The stragglers and the skulkers from the Union Army were a large number. Many of the green regiments broke and ran at the sudden onset, but the soldiers who stood to their colors and supported the strenuous efforts of Sherman showed a high degree of physical and moral courage.

The Grant of Shiloh was not the Grant of Donelson; nevertheless he worked hard to retrieve, as best he might, the mistake occasioned by his careless disregard of the enemy. At six o'clock, while eating his breakfast at Savannah, he received word from a private on detached duty at headquarters that artillery firing was heard in the direction of Pittsburg Landing. Leaving the table at once, he wrote an order to General Nelson, who commanded the advance of Buell's Army, and who

---

[265] Dawes, Milt. Hist. Soc., VII, 138 *et seq.*

[266] O. R., X, Pt. I, 403.

[267] *Ibid.,* 249. The hours given by men engaged in battle are naturally not exact. A coordination of them from several honest reports is impossible. It is certain that Sherman knew that a mighty battle was on before the camp of the Sixth division was captured.

[268] O. R., X, Pt. I, 98.

[269] *I bid.,* Pt. II, 119.

had arrived the day before, to move his division to Pittsburg, and then took steamer himself for the same place, stopping on the way at Crump's Landing to tell Lew Wallace to hold his 6500 in readiness to march to the scene of action. Arriving at Pittsburg at about eight, he went to the front, and at once sent the order to Lew Wallace to come to the assistance of his army. The military critics say that Grant counted for little or nothing in the conduct of the battle.[270] The layman, unable to dissociate him from his earlier and later career, feels that during his frequent visits and verbal injunctions to his division commanders, his coolness and deportment of a courageous soldier must have helped them in their efforts to maintain confidence among their hard-pressed soldiers. At noon Grant became very anxious.[271] He sent word to Lew Wallace to hasten forward and despatched this entreaty to: Commanding officer advance forces (Buell's army), near Pittsburg: The appearance of fresh troops in the field now would have a powerful effect, both by inspiring our men and disheartening the enemy. If you will get upon the field, leaving all your baggage on the east bank of the river, it will be more to our advantage and possibly save the day to us. The rebel forces are estimated at over 100,000 men.[272] This despatch was received by Buell himself, who had arrived at Savannah the evening previous and was now proceeding up the river by steamboat.

Elated at their first success, the Confederates pressed forward with vigor encouraged by Johnston, who kept well to the front. An assault seemed necessary to occupy an important ridge for the turning of the Union left. He led the charge, escaping harm during the hottest of the fight but, as the Union soldiers retired from the crest, they kept up a desultory fire and one of their minié-balls severed an artery in his leg. The blood flowed freely; in ten or fifteen minutes he was dead. Had his surgeon, who had attended him during most of the morning, still been with him, he would have been saved, but during the advance they passed a large number of wounded, many of them Union men, and Johnston ordered his surgeon to stop, saying, These men were our enemies a moment ago; they are our prisoners now. Take care of them.[273] Johnston's death happened at half-past two in the afternoon; then Beauregard assumed command with his headquarters at Shiloh Church, a log cabin where Sherman's had been the night previous. A lull in the battle ensued, but presently the struggle was renewed with fury. The Sixth Union division had made a remarkable fight, contesting the ground as they fell back; but, surrounded, their general, to save a useless sacrifice, surrendered with 2200 men.

---

[270] Ropes, 76; Stone, Milt. Hist. Soc., VII, 74.

[271] McPherson, O. R., X, Pt. I, 181.

[272] O. R., X, Pt. II, 95.

[273] B. & L., I, 565; letter of V. Warner to H. St. George Tucker, furnished me by Mr. Tucker.

This was at half past five. A last desperate effort was made by the Confederates to turn the Union left and get possession of the Landing. It was necessary to carry a hill guarded by a battery of rifled guns and by two Union gunboats which opened fire with shot and shell on the Confederate forces. Grant sat on his horse quiet, thoughtful, almost stolid. Somebody said to him, 'Does not the prospect begin to look gloomy?' 'Not at all,' was the quiet reply. 'They can't force our lines around these batteries to-night it is too late. Delay counts everything with us. Tomorrow we shall attack them with fresh troops, and drive them, of course.'[274] Although Lew Wallace had failed to reach Pittsburg, help other than nightfall was at hand. The energetic Nelson and his division were hastening forward from Savannah. After three miles of good road they had to proceed through a black mud swamp and then through a forest where the subsiding waters left but indistinct traces of the way; they could hear the roar of cannon and, as they drew nearer, the volleys of musketry. While yet two miles away, a courier, riding at full speed, reined up at the head of the column with this word from the general, Hurry up or all will be lost; the enemy is driving our men.[275] On reaching the east bank of the river a brigade crossed in boats, climbed the bank a hundred feet in height and, in obedience to the orders of Grant and Buell, both cool and calm,[276] formed in support of the batteries. An advance was immediately made upon the point of attack, wrote Grant, April 10, and the enemy soon driven back. Darkness was close at hand. Beauregard sent orders to his troops to cease fighting and to sleep on their arms.

The contest had lasted more than twelve hours and was a Confederate victory, inasmuch as the Union troops were driven back from a mile and a half to two miles and lost Shiloh Church, the point which, as Grant wrote, was the key to our position.[277] But the victory did not meet the expectations of Johnston, who had hoped to capture the Union Army or at any rate to drive it from the field in complete rout. At the time of his death he must have felt that his hopes were in a fair way to be realized. For the demoralization of a part of Grant's army began with the sudden attack and continued to the end of the day, greatly impressing Nelson as he crossed the river in the late afternoon. I found cowering under the river bank, he wrote on April 10, from 7000 to 10,000 men, frantic with fright and utterly demoralized, who received my gallant division with cries, 'We are whipped; cut to pieces.'[278] The battle of Sunday, wrote Henry Stone, was like an old-fashioned country wrestling-match, where each combatant uses any method he chooses, or can bring to bear, to force his adversary to the ground.[279]

---

[274] Whitelaw Reid, who heard the conversation, I, 375.

[275] O. R., X, Pt. I, 332. The general was probably Buell.

[276] O. R., X, Pt. I, 333.

[277] Grant, 338.

[278] O. R., X, Pt. I, 324.

[279] Milt. Hist. Soc., VII, 95.

Next day, Monday, April 7, 20,000 of Buell's well-disciplined soldiers, Lew Wallace's 6500, and such troops of the four divisions that had borne the brunt of Sunday's battle as could be brought into line, attacked Beauregard under orders from Grant and Buell and, largely out-numbering him, drove him, after eight hours' fighting, from the field, recovering the lost positions. Beauregard's army, badly demoralized, retreated to Corinth. Bragg, who had commanded the second corps in the battle, wrote to him on April 8, during the retreat: Our condition is horrible. Troops utterly disorganized and demoralized. Road almost impassable. No provisions and no forage. The enemy up to daylight, had not pursued.[280]

Like most victories of our Civil War, whether Confederate or Union, no effective pursuit was made. Grant himself and his army, except Lew Wallace's division, were too fatigued for immediate active service and he did not exercise the authority over Buell's army for which he had the warrant from Halleck. Any later pursuit was rendered impossible by Halleck's instructions and by his project of joining the army in person and taking over the command.

The Union casualties during the two days were 13,047; the Confederate, 10,694[281]. Never before had a battle of such magnitude been fought on this continent. The Confederates failed to repair the disaster of Donelson; on the other hand, Grant might have crushed Johnston had he anticipated the attack. His lack of correct information is evident from his despatch to Halleck two days after the battle, saying that he had been attacked by one hundred and sixty-two regiments, which was a much larger number than he had actually to contend with.

It was a battle between men from the Southwest and Northwest and these sections went into deep mourning over their dead and wounded. The hilarity in Chicago at Donelson gave place to grief over Shiloh. Private letters from soldiers to their homes in the Western States told of the useless slaughter and aroused a feeling of indignation toward Grant. The press and members of Congress faithfully reflected this sentiment. Washburne in the House and John Sherman in the Senate alone defended him. There is much feeling against Grant, wrote the Senator to his brother the General, and I try to defend him but with little success.[282] All sorts of charges were made against him. Stanton telegraphed to Halleck at Pittsburg Landing, The President desires to know whether any neglect or misconduct of General Grant or any other officer contributed to the casualties that befell our forces on Sunday.[283] Halleck, in his immediate answer, was evasive; and in his despatch of May 2, as printed, there is a tantalizing ellipsis,[284] but, so far as I have been able to discover, there is no evidence in the printed record of misconduct on

---

[280] O. R., X, Pt. II, 398.

[281] T. L. Livermore, 79.

[282] Sherman Letters, 147.

[283] Apr. 23, O. R., X, Pt. I, 98.

[284] *I bid.*

the part of Grant[285]. It was the tragedy of his career that whenever he was at fault, the popular judgment harked back to his early record in the regular army and charged his shortcoming to intemperance in drink[286]. A large number in the North believed this to be the cause of his recklessness at Shiloh and exerted a strong pressure on the President for his removal. A. K. McClure related that, carried along as he was by the overwhelming tide of popular sentiment and backed by the almost universal conviction of the President's friends, he urged this course upon Lincoln. Late one night, in a private interview of two hours at the White House, during which he did most of the talking, McClure advocated with earnestness the removal of Grant as necessary for the President to retain the confidence of the country. When I had said everything that could be said from my standpoint, McClure proceeded with his story, we lapsed into silence. Lincoln remained silent for what seemed a very long time. He then said in a tone of earnestness that I shall never forget, 'I can't spare this man; he fights.'[287] In his private letter to Washburne, Grant is pathetic and at the same time obstinate in his determination to defend his conduct if the battle and his procedure anterior to the Confederate assault. To say, he wrote, that I have not been distressed at these attacks upon me would be false, for I have a father, mother, wife and children, who read them and are distressed by them and I necessarily share with them in it. Then, too, all subject to my orders read these charges and it is calculated to weaken their confidence in me and weaken my ability to render efficient service in our present cause. Those people who expect a field of battle to be maintained for a whole day with about thirty thousand troops, most of them entirely raw, against fifty thousand, as was the case at Pittsburg Landing while waiting for re-enforcements to come up, without loss of life, know little of war. Looking back at the past I cannot see for the life of me any important point that could be corrected.[288]

General Halleck arrived at Pittsburg Landing on April 11; he did not displace Grant until the 30th, when, on reorganizing the army, he deprived him of any actual command of troops, but made him second to himself. Grant chafed at this, asked more than once to relieved from duty under Halleck and then decided to quit this semblance of active service, saying to General Sherman: You know that I am in the way here. I have stood it as long as I can endure it no longer. Sherman, with whom had begun that fast friendship which endured throughout Grant's whole life, urged him to stay. If you go away, he said, events will go right along and you will be left out, while, if you remain, some happy accident will restore you to favor and

---

[285] The Official Records are so voluminous that any general remark must be made with the reservation in the text. J. H. Wilson in his Life of General Rawlins, M.S., wrote "Grant was entirely guiltless of anything to his discredit."

[286] See III, 595.

[287] III, 627.

[288] May 14, Grant's private letters, 10.

your true place[289]. Grant acted upon this reasonable counsel and staid with the army.

This conversation followed the occupation of Corinth by the Union troops. Halleck had concentrated a force of 100,000, with which he moved slowly and cautiously upon Corinth, intrenching at every halt so that Sherman described the advance as one with pick and shovel.[290] He forced the evacuation of Corinth, a place of strategic importance, and worth having, but the crushing of Beauregard's army, which was possible, would have been a far more profitable achievement.[291] The navy at the outbreak of the war was small and many of the ships were on distant cruises where orders to return were long in reaching them. Through the indefatigable exertions of the Secretary, Gideon Welles, and his chosen assistant, Gustavus V. Fox, and the purchase and charter of merchant steamers, a navy was improvised which was powerful enough to maintain a reasonably effective blockade. Bases for the blockading fleet and for other naval and military operations were needed and Hatteras Inlet, Port Royal and Roanoke Island were successively captured by joint naval and army expeditions[292]. The English, wrote Adams from London, must abide by the blockade if it really be one. They will set it aside if they can pick a good flaw in it.[293] Ever present to the English and American mind was the cotton crop of 1861, which England and France wanted and which the South was eager to exchange for cannon, rifles, munitions of war, iron in many forms and general merchandise. The bar to this trade was the blockade, which to be binding must be effective. One day in March, 1862, the blockade at Norfolk was broken, which gave rise to the apprehension lest it should be raised at all the Atlantic ports.

Until 1858, the navies of the world were wooden vessels, but, in that year, the French applied armor-plating to the steam frigate La Gloire, whereupon the British admiralty speedily constructed the 9200-ton iron steamship, Warrior. Probable though it was that an immense change was imminent in naval construction, the United States Navy department was slow to make a venture in the direction indicated. Richmond was in advance of Washington. As early as May 8, 1861, the Confederate Secretary of the Navy wrote, I regard the possession of an iron-armored ship as a matter of the first necessity;[294] and in July, he gave an order to raise the steam frigate Merrimac (one of the ships partially burned and sunk when the Gosport navy-yard was destroyed[295]) and convert her into an ironclad: this was

---

[289] W. Sherman, I, 255.

[290] O. R., XVII, Pt. II, 83.

[291] Authorities: O. R., X, Pts. I, II; Milt. Hist. Soc., VII; B. & L., I; Ropes; Grant; W. Sherman; III; N. & H.; Swinton; Hosmer's Appeal.

[292] III, 489, 581.

[293] Forbes, I, 235.

[294] B. & L., I, 631.

[295] April 20, 1861, III, 364.

accomplished as rapidly as could be expected under the imperfect manufacturing and mechanical conditions in the South.

By an act of August 3, 1861, the United States Congress constituted a naval board; four days later the Navy Department advertised for plans and offers of iron-clad steamboats of light draught suitable to navigate the shallow rivers and harbors of the Confederate States.[296] John Ericsson submitted a plan which was rejected but, on the persuasion of a friend, he went to Washington and demonstrated to the entire satisfaction of the board that his design was thoroughly practical and based on sound theory.[297] His proposal was accepted and Secretary Welles told him to begin the construction forthwith without awaiting the execution of the formal contract, inasmuch as the knowledge of the progress on the Merrimac had impressed the naval people with the necessity for speed. Ericsson's ironclad was the Monitor; her keel was laid on October 25, 1861; she was launched on January 30, 1862, and on March 6 left New York for Fort Monroe.

On Saturday, March 8, a fine day with a calm sea, the blockading fleet in Hampton Roads were on their usual watch; off Newport News the frigate Congress of fifty guns and the sloop of-war Cumberland of twenty-four, both sailing vessels, swung lazily at anchor. Soon after noon a monster, resembling a huge half-submerged crocodile, belching out smoke was descried coming from the direction of Norfolk. No such ship had ever before been seen in American waters; few, if any, of the Union men had ever looked upon her like elsewhere, but all knew at once that she was the Merrimac. The Congress and the Cumberland cleared their decks for action. The Merrimac opened with her bow gun on the Congress, received a broadside and gave one in return. The Cumberland and the shore batteries fired at the monster and their balls rebounded from her iron sides as if they had been of india rubber. Passing the Congress, the Merrimac steered directly for the Cumberland, brought her guns to bear upon the Union sloop-of-war, killing and wounding men at every shot, and, steaming on under full headway, rammed the Cumberland, opening her side wide enough to drive in a horse and cart. Water poured into the hold; the ship canted to port, the masts swaying wildly. She delivered a parting shot and sank with the American flag at the peak.[298] This action had lasted thirty minutes. Seeing the fate of her sister ship, the Congress slipped her anchor, set her jib and top-sails and, assisted by a tug, ran ashore, hoping in the shoal water to escape the Merrimac, which drew twenty-two feet. But she did not get beyond the Confederate range of fire. The Merrimac raked her fore and aft with shells.[299] Being now on fire she hauled down her colors and hoisted a white flag. A misunderstanding that ensued with regard to her surrender

---

[296] B. & L., I, 730.

[297] *Ibid.*, 731

[298] B. & L., 698, 712; O. R., N., VII, 21.

[299] O. R. N., VII, 23.

led to the Merrimac firing hot shot into the Congress; this completed her destruction.

As soon as the Merrimac was sighted, the frigate Minnesota left her anchorage at Fort Monroe and steamed toward Newport News to the support of the Congress and the Cumberland. She ran aground and, as there still remained two hours of daylight she was apparently at the mercy of the ironclad, but the pilots were afraid to attempt the channel at ebbtide. The Merrimac therefore returned to Sewell's Point and anchored, to await the light of next day when the commander expected to return to destroy the Minnesota and the rest of the fleet at Fort Monroe.

That night there was consternation in the Union fleet and among the Union troops in Fort Monroe and at Newport News. The stately wooden frigates, in the morning deemed powerful men-of-war, had been proved absolutely useless to cope with this new engine of destruction. The following day in Washington, a Sunday, was one of profound disquietude. Seward, Chase, Stanton and Welles hastened to the White House to confer with the President, who was much perturbed. Stanton, wrote Hay in his Diary, was fearfully stampeded. He said they would capture our fleet, take Fort Monroe, be in Washington before night.[300] The President and Stanton went repeatedly to the window and looked down the Potomac the view being uninterrupted for miles to see if the Merrimac was not coming to Washington.[301] The despatches from the War Department that day reflect the general excitement and apprehension. The capability of the Merrimac for future performance was much exaggerated, but one consideration could not rationally be ignored. She had broken the blockade at Norfolk and might do as much at other ports. During the excited meeting at the White House, Welles said to the President and his advisers: The Monitor is now in Hampton Roads. I have confidence in her power to resist and, I hope, to overcome the Merrimac.[302]

The Monitor had been towed from New York and, despite a gale and stormy passage, had reached Hampton Roads on the Saturday evening at nine. Thence, in obedience to further orders, she proceeded two and a half hours later to a point alongside the Minnesota. At daylight on March 9, the Confederates saw a craft such as the eyes of a seaman never looked upon before an immense shingle floating on the water, with a gigantic cheese box rising from its centre: no sails, no wheels, no smoke-stack, no guns:[303] they knew it was the Monitor. At eight o'clock the Merrimac bore down upon the Minnesota and opened fire on her. The Monitor, which was commanded by Lieut. John L. Worden, steered directly for the Merrimac, laid herself right alongside and opened fire. The Monitor was of 776 tons burden, drew only ten and a half feet and had two 11-inch Dahlgren guns

---

[300] J. Hay, I, 54.
[301] Welles's Diary, I, 65.
[302] Welles's Diary, I, 63.
[303] O. R. N., VII, 53.

fired from a revolving turret; the Merrimac was a ship of 3500 tons carrying ten cannon. It was said that a pigmy strove against a giant; David had come out to encounter Goliath.

Then, for nearly four hours ensued a fierce artillery duel at close range; the distance between the two vessels varied from half a mile to a few yards. Gun after gun was fired by the Monitor without result except to draw broadsides from the Merrimac, which apparently had no more effect than so many pebble stones thrown by a child.[304] At one time Lieutenant Jones, who was in command of the Merrimac, inquired, Why are you not firing, Mr. Eggleston? Why, our powder is very precious, was the reply, and after two hours' incessant firing, I find that I can do her about as much damage by snapping my thumb at her every two minutes and a half.[305] Jones determined then to ram the Monitor as the Cumberland had been rammed the previous day. But the engines and boilers of the Merrimac were defective; her speed was only five knots; she was unwieldy and her iron prow had been twisted off and lost in her encounter with the Cumberland. Opportunity offering, however, she made for her antagonist at full speed, but the Monitor being easily handled, got out of her way, receiving only a glancing blow. She gave us a tremendous thump, wrote the Chief Engineer, but did not injure us in the least.[306] The Merrimac got the worse of the collision, springing a leak; she had, also wrote Jones, received a shot which came near disabling the machinery.[307] But Worden was hurt. In the pilot house, which was constructed of iron logs in the manner of a log cabin, he used a look-out chink to direct the movements of his vessel. A shell struck and exploded just outside, severely injuring his eyes and leading him to believe that the pilot house was seriously damaged. He gave orders to put the helm to starboard and sheer off.[308] Jones, either because he thought the Monitor had given up the contest or because his own boat was leaking badly, steered towards Norfolk and the struggle was over. The Monitor was uninjured and in condition to engage the Merrimac if she appeared on the morrow. But the Merrimac was too badly damaged for further operations; she had to dock for repairs and did not re-enter Hampton Roads until a month later.

Captain Ericsson, wrote the Chief Engineer of the Monitor from Hampton Roads on the day of the fight, I congratulate you upon your great success. Thousands have this day blessed you. I have heard whole crews cheer you. Every man feels that you have saved this place to the nation by furnishing us with the means to whip an iron-clad frigate that was, until our arrival, having it all her own way with our most powerful vessels.[309]

---

[304] O. R. N., VII, 11.
[305] B. & L., I, 702.
[306] O. R. N., VII, 26.
[307] *Ibid.*, 59.
[308] B. & L., I, 727.
[309] O. R. N., VII, 27.

This momentous encounter demonstrated that the naval ships of the future must be iron-clad. The wooden walls of England were no longer her security.[310]

The performance of the Monitor on Sunday did not entirely dispel the apprehensions in Washington and throughout the country, occasioned by the destructive work of the Merrimac on Saturday. McClellan had decided to transport his army to Fort Monroe and, using that as his base, advance on Richmond by the Peninsula between the York and James rivers. But this movement required the control of the sea in Hampton Roads and at Fort Monroe by the Union Navy and this was rendered dubious by the possibility of the Merrimac appearing again. He therefore asked Assistant Secretary of the Navy, Fox [March 12], who was still at Fort Monroe, Can I rely on the Monitor to keep the Merrimac in check so that I can make Fort Monroe a base of operations? Fox replied: The Monitor is more than a match for the Merrimac, but she might be disabled in the next encounter. I cannot advise so great dependence upon her. Meigs, still alarmed, wrote from Washington [March 13]: I would not trust this city to the strength of a single screw bolt in the Monitor's new machinery. If one breaks, the Merrimac beats her. As late as March 15, Welles confessed, There is a degree of apprehension in regard to the armored steamer Merrimac which it is difficult to allay.

The Merrimac made two more appearances in Hampton Roads, the first one on April 11, when she directed the capture of three merchant vessels by a Confederate armed steamer and a gunboat. The Monitor was on the watch, but neither ventured to attack the other. Her second appearance was on May 8, when, in the words of her commander, she stood directly for the enemy for the purpose of engaging him, but the Monitor and her consorts would not give battle. Secretary Chase, who with the President and Secretary of War was at Fort Monroe on a brief visit, wrote this account of the incident: The Merrimac came on slowly and in a little while there was a clear sheet of water between her and the Monitor. Then the great rebel terror paused then turned back and having finally attained what she considered a safe position, became stationery again. On May 11, as a consequence of the evacuation of Norfolk by the Confederates due to McClellan's advance, she was fired and, after burning fiercely for upward of an hour, blew up.[311] The opportune appearance of the Monitor was a piece of good fortune for the Navy Department, but her construction was due to its foresight. Nevertheless, her restraint of the Merrimac was in the nature of defensive warfare, whilst the conditions of the war required offensive work on the part of the Union forces. In this the Navy now bore

---

[310] Authorities: The Correspondence and several reports in O. R. N. VII; B. & L., I; III; Welles's Diary; J. Hay; Swinton; Chesnut. Other Confederate vessels and gunboats, Union frigates and tugs, Confederate and Union shore batteries had a part in this contest but, as their action did not seem to me material, I have omitted the mention of them in the narrative to avoid burdening it with too much detail.

[311] O. R. N., VII, 99, 100, 101, 127, 220, 335, 336, 337, 342, 387; Warden, 428; N. & H., V. In December, the *Monitor* foundered off Cape Hatteras.

its share under the leadership of a man of sixty who had been in the naval service from boyhood up, had thirsted for fame but had not achieved it. This was Farragut, whose opportunity had now come. From Washington he wrote to his home, I am to have a flag in the Gulf and the rest depends upon myself.[312]

The importance of the Mississippi river had been appreciated from the first. If the North could get possession of it, the Confederate States would be cut in twain and the rich supplies from the West could not reach the East. New Orleans, one hundred miles from its mouths, commanded the lower part of the river and was moreover the chief commercial city of the South: its capture would be a damaging blow to the Confederacy. Gustavus V. Fox, the assistant Secretary of the Navy, though drawn from civil life by Welles, had been in the Navy eighteen years, and afterwards commanded mail steamers, acquiring the practical knowledge wherewith to support his fertile thought. Fox now conceived a plan for accomplishing the desired object. The main defences of New Orleans were two strong fortifications, St. Philip and Jackson, situated on opposite sides of the river about seventy-five miles below the city. Fox proposed that an armed fleet should run by these forts, after which, as the navigation of the river was not difficult, the great city would be at their mercy. He won the approval of his chief and the two broached the plan in conference with the President, McClellan and Commander David D. Porter, who had been engaged in the blockade of the southwest pass of the Mississippi. Porter suggested that the naval fleet be accompanied by a mortar flotilla which should reduce the forts before the passage was made. The Chief Engineer of the Army of the Potomac, whom McClellan designated to represent him in the adjustment of the details, agreed emphatically with Porter's suggestion, writing, To pass these works merely with a fleet and appear before New Orleans is a raid, no capture.[313] In spite of his high opinion of Porter, Fox stuck to his original plan and thus the matter stood when the commander of the expedition was decided upon. Welles and Fox selected Farragut for the command, basing their choice on Porter's knowledge of the man due to an intimate personal acquaintance from his youth up. Farragut was summoned to Washington, where he learned from Fox the object of the expedition, the number of vessels he should command and the plan of attack. He entered into the affair with enthusiasm, had no doubt that the fleet could run by the forts, but had little faith in the bombardment by the mortar flotilla, which would occasion delay, but, as it seemed to have been decided upon, he was willing to give it a trial. I expect, he said, to restore New Orleans to the Government or never come back.[314] Welles's letter of instructions was far from possessing the definiteness of Fox's verbal explanation to Farragut; it stated in a

---

[312] Dec. 21, 1861. N. & H., V, 257.

[313] O. R. N., XVIII, 23.

[314] N. & H., V, 257.

general way that he should reduce the defenses which guard the approaches to New Orleans before he should appear off that city.[315]

While at Ship Island, the base of operations, about a hundred miles from the mouth of the Mississippi, Farragut wrote to Welles that the capture of Donelson and the surrender of Nashville had caused fear and demoralization in New Orleans. There could not be a better time, he added for the blow to be struck by us and you may depend upon its being done the moment the mortar boats arrive.[316]

By the middle of April, Farragut with six ships and twelve gunboats and Porter with a mortar flotilla of nineteen schooners and six armed steamships for guard and towing service, were before Forts Jackson and St. Philip. On April 18, the bombardment of Fort Jackson by the mortar boats began[317] and continued for two days, inflicting considerable damage, but not sufficient to compel the Confederates to entertain the idea of surrender. At ten o'clock in the morning of April 20, while the bombardment was at its height, Farragut signalled from his flag-ship, the Hartford, that he wished a conference with the commanding officers of his fleet. All who were not engaged in active work came.[318] Porter, who commanded the mortar flotilla subject to Farragut, was unable to be present, but sent a communication in which he advised against running by the forts; We should first capture the forts, he said, and then we may easily take New Orleans; but if we run the forts we should leave an enemy in our rear.[319] Some of the commanders agreed with Porter. As Farragut had promised Fox, he had given the bombardment by the mortar boats a trial; but, as forty-eight hours' firing had failed to reduce the forts, he reverted to his original plan which, at the end of the conference, he put into a general order. The flag-officer, he wrote, having heard all the opinions expressed by the different commanders, is of the opinion that whatever is to be done will have to be done quickly and that the forts should be run.[320] With all possible celerity, he proceeded to execute his plan. On the night after the conference, he sent a force to remove an obstruction in his way opposite Fort Jackson, a chain which crossed the river, supported by eight hulks, which were strongly moored.[321] Not all that he intended was accomplished, but enough was done to enable his ships to pass up the river.

Farragut needed all his nerve and resolution. His trusted friend Porter, a man of conspicuous naval capacity, did not believe in his plan. His instructions from the

---

[315] O. R. N., XVIII, 8.

[316] March 5, O. R. N., XVIII, 47.

[317] Fort Jackson was one half mile below Fort St. Philip and nearer the mortar boats.

[318] That is, of the fleet under Farragut's immediate command. Only one of the commanders of the mortar flotilla came and he "was laughingly told that the signal was not intended for me." O. R. N., XVIII, 143.

[319] O. R. N., XVIII, 146.

[320] Ibid., 160.

[321] O. R. N., XVIII, 156.

Secretary of the Navy were ambiguous. If he failed, he would be regarded as a foolhardy Captain who had run counter to the orthodox principles of naval strategy in breasting a current of three and a half miles an hour, in front of strong fortifications and in the face of the enemy's fire-rafts and gunboats. During the next days and nights of anxiety, however, though he neglected no precaution and availed himself of every condition in his favor, he moved straight towards his goal. By April 23, his arrangements were completed. In the afternoon, he wrote, I visited each ship in order to know positively that each commander understood my orders for the attack and to see that all was in readiness. I had looked to their efficiency before. Everyone appeared to understand their orders well and looked forward to the conflict with firmness but with anxiety. At about five minutes of 2 o'clock A.M. April 24 signal was made to get under way.[322] At once was heard in every direction the clank-clank of the chains as the seamen hove the anchors to the bows.[323] An hour and a half was consumed in getting all the vessels under way. During the days of preparation, Porter had kept up the bombardment from his mortar boats, and now aided the movement by pouring a terrific fire of shells into Fort Jackson, the first to be passed. As the fleet advanced, they fired at the forts which briskly returned the fire. The passing of the forts, Jackson and St. Philip, wrote Farragut next day was one of the most awful sights and events I ever saw or expect to experience. The smoke was so dense that it was only now and then you could see anything but the flash of the cannon and the fire-ships on rafts. The fire-rafts were immense flatboats piled loosely with wood twenty feet high and saturated with tar and resin, from which the flames rose a hundred feet into the air.[324] In the effort to avoid one of these, Farragut's flag-ship, the Hartford, was run ashore, but a tug pushed the fire-raft alongside and in a moment the Hartford was one blaze all along the port side half way up to the main and mizzen tops.[325] Thinking it was all over with them, Farragut exclaimed, My God is it to end in this way![326] But the fire department poured streams of water on the flames and put them out; at the same time the Hartford backed off and got clear of the raft. She was then opposite Fort St. Philip. The fierce fight continued and, at this time, if not before, the Confederate gunboats and two iron-clad rams took part in the contest; but most of these were destroyed. At length the fire slackened, wrote Farragut, the smoke cleared off and we saw, to our surprise, that we were above the forts. We had a rough time of it, was his word to Porter, but thank God the number of killed and wounded was very small considering.[327]

---

[322] *Ibid.*
[323] Mahan's Farragut, 151.
[324] B. & L., II, 60.
[325] O. R. N., XVIII, 154.
[326] B. & L., II, 64; O. R. N., XVIII, 142.
[327] O. R. N., XVIII, 142, 154; 37 were killed, 147 wounded. B. &. L., II, 73.

Thirteen of his little fleet were now assembled above the forts; four were missing, but only one had been sunk. Leaving two gunboats to protect the landing of the troops who were part of the expedition, he proceeded up the river to New Orleans, seeing on the way ships laden with burning cotton floating down-stream and other signs of the destruction of property, all evidence of the panic which had seized upon the city. During the morning of April 25, he reached the Chalmette batteries, three miles below the city and, by a vigorous attack, silenced them in thirty minutes. His despatch is headed, At anchor off New Orleans; the town was at his mercy. The levee, he wrote, was one scene of desolation; ships, steamers, cotton, coal, etc., were all in one common blaze.[328] As he had divined, the passage of the forts compelled the evacuation of New Orleans by the Confederate military force and its surrender, and furthermore, since the enemy's communications were now severed, the surrender of the forts. On April 29, he sent this despatch to the Secretary of the Navy, Our flag waves over both Forts Jackson and St. Philip and at New Orleans over the custom-house.[329] The passage of the forts and the possession of the Mississippi river made the way clear for General Butler and his troops to reach New Orleans by boat. On May 1, Farragut formally turned over to him the city.

After any successful achievement, nothing is so grateful as the appreciation of experts; this Farragut received. From Fox came, Having studied up the localities and defenses in conceiving this attack, I can fully appreciate the magnificent execution which has rendered your name immortal.[330] And from Captain Mahan: The conquest of New Orleans and of its defenses was wholly the work of the United States Navy. It was a triumph won over formidable difficulties by a mobile force, skillfully directed and gallantly fought.[331]

It was the crowning stroke of adverse fortune wrote later the Confederate Secretary of War.[332] A less just estimate was formed generally at the North, where the victory was not considered so great a one as the capture of Fort Donelson. At all events the two victories had this important point in common, that each had brought forward a great commander possessed of original thought and the nerve and energy to carry it into execution.[333] A naval victory is none the less striking than one by the army, once the reason of the lesser casualties is comprehended; and the cool Northern attitude may have been due to the apparent ease with which a very difficult task was accomplished.

---

[328] O. R. N., XVIII, 158.

[329] Ibid., 148.

[330] Ibid., 245.

[331] Mahan's Farragut, 172.

[332] O. R., IV, II, 281.

[333] See Captain Mahan's striking comparison between New Orleans and Vicksburg. Mahan's Farragut, 137.

The capture of New Orleans, a city of 168,000, the chief commercial port and the largest city of the South, a place well known in Europe as an important trading point, made Emperor Napoleon III waver from his intention to recognize the Confederate States; and it caused Palmerston to abandon for the moment a project which he may have had constantly in mind of joining with the Emperor in taking steps toward the breaking of the blockade.[334]

On April 7, General John Pope and Flag-officer Foote captured Island No. 10, an important fort on the Mississippi river. The occupation of Corinth compelled the evacuation of Fort Pillow, which opened the river below. In a battle off Memphis [June 6], the Union gunboats defeated the Confederate, securing the occupation of that city. Only the strongholds of Vicksburg and Port Hudson remained to the Confederacy wherewith to dispute the control of the Mississippi river. McClellan, who had failed to take advantage of the demoralization in Richmond after the fall of Donelson, was further delayed by the performance of the Merrimac, but, on the assurance that the Navy Department would hold the iron-clad in check by the Monitor and other war vessels, he proceeded to the execution of his plan a plan over which he and the President had differed from the first. The President desired the advance to be made directly overland, while McClellan proposed to go by water to Fort Monroe and advance on Richmond up the Peninsula. It was evident from the discussion that good service could not be had from the General unless the strategy as well as the active command were left to him; Lincoln therefore yielded. But lacking sufficient confidence in McClellan to give him supreme authority, the President relieved him of the command of all military departments except the Potomac [March 11] and directed the organization of the army into four corps, naming the corps commanders himself. Through a misunderstanding with McClellan as to the force necessary to cover Washington, he withheld from him McDowell's corps of 35,000 men in order to insure the safety of the capital. He had previously detached from the Army of the Potomac a division of 10,000 and sent it to Frémont who had, owing to the pressure of the radicals upon Lincoln, been unfortunately intrusted with a command in the Shenandoah mountains. It is difficult now to see any way out of the unlucky situation in so far as the command of the Army of the Potomac was concerned. No general in sight was fitted to replace McClellan, who possessed in an eminent degree the love and confidence of his soldiers; moreover Lincoln still held to the belief that when once in the field he would accomplish important results.

During April, 1862, McClellan with 100,000 men was besieging Yorktown; the Confederates were reorganizing their army and strengthening their fortifications about Richmond. On April 6, the President telegraphed to McClellan, I think you better break the enemy's line at once,[335] a suggestion which the General received

---

[334] O. R. N., XVIII; B. & L., II; Mahan's Farragut; Mahan's Gulf; N. & H., V; III; Chesnut.

with contempt, writing to his wife, I was much tempted to reply that he had better come and do it himself.[336] Three days later the President wrote to him in great kindness: Once more let me tell you it is indispensable to you that you strike a blow. I am powerless to help this.[337] Suggestion and entreaty were of no avail. Glorious news comes borne on every wind but the South Wind, wrote Hay to Nicolay [April 9]. The little Napoleon [McClellan] sits trembling before the handful of men at Yorktown, afraid either to fight or run. Stanton feels devilish about it. He would like to remove him if he thought it would do.[338] No one but McClellan, wrote Joseph E. Johnston to Lee, would have hesitated to attack.[339] It is the mature judgment of almost all military authorities that, outnumbering the Confederates as he did three to one, he could at this time have broken their line from the York river to the James and have reached his position on the Chickahominy a month earlier than he did. He missed his opportunity. By April 17, the Confederates at Yorktown numbered 53,000, and Johnston himself was in command. From this time on, nothing but scientific siege operations was feasible and, as McClellan was a capable engineer, these were undoubtedly as good as could have been devised. On May 3, Johnston evacuated Yorktown; he was followed on the retreat by the Union forces who brought on a battle at Williamsburg resulting in their defeat. On May 21, McClellan was in camp on the Chickahominy, seven to twelve miles from Richmond; he had in the meantime received a re-enforcement by water of Franklin's division of McDowell's corps and the promise of the rest of this body, 35,000 to 40,000 strong, who were now opposite Fredericksburg preparatory to joining him by an overland march.

Shortly previous to this, directly after the destruction of the Merrimac, an advance of the Monitor and a number of gunboats up the James alarmed Richmond. Fearing the fate of New Orleans, people packed their trunks and crowded the railroad trains in their flight from the city. The government archives were packed for removal to Lynchburg and Columbia. The families of the Confederate cabinet officers fled to their homes and Davis sent his wife and children to Raleigh. He himself received baptism at his house and the rite of confirmation in St. Paul's Church; he appointed by proclamation a day for solemn prayer. The Richmond Examiner, a bitter critic of Davis's acts, spoke of him as standing in a corner telling his beads and relying on a miracle to save the country. Had McClellan realized the importance of celerity as did Grant and Farragut, he would have made an attack upon Richmond in co-operation with the Navy. He had

---

[335] O. R., XI, Pt. I, 14, the line between the York and James rivers.

[336] McClellan, 308.

[337] O. R., XI, Pt. I, 15.

[338] J. Hay, I, 57.

[339] Apr. 22, O. R., XI, Pt. III, 456.

a good chance to take it but in case of failure he had behind him the authority of the President who had written to him that he must strike a blow.[340]

While McClellan dallied before Richmond, Robert E. Lee[341] planned, and Stonewall Jackson conducted, a series of manoeuvres in the course of which, playing on Lincoln's anxiety for Washington, they succeeded in bringing to naught the plan for the re-enforcement by McDowell of the Army of the Potomac. On May 8, Jackson defeated a detachment of Frémont's, sending this word to Richmond, God blessed our arms with victory. Having bigger game in sight than Frémont's army, he retraced his steps for the purpose of co-operating with Ewell in an attack upon Banks in the Shenandoah Valley; when he made this junction he had 17,000 men.

An index of Jackson's character is to be found in two of the books he had constantly with him, the Bible and Napoleon's Maxims of War.[342] He interpreted the Bible literally and was guided by its precepts. Piety pervaded his being; religion was the affair of every moment; he prayed frequently for divine guidance in the most trivial affairs of life. But for his strategy he had recourse not to Joshua but to Napoleon. He read and re-read these Maxims so that he had for the theory of his profession, the best of masters.[343] The result of his study was seen in the Shenandoah campaign, which was truly Napoleonic. Celerity and secrecy were his watch-words. He sometimes marched with his whole army thirty miles in twenty-four hours and his infantry became known as Jackson's foot cavalry. Himself apparently incapable of fatigue, he seemed to think that everybody should equal his endurance. After a sleepless night, a long march, hard fighting, he would say to his officers, 'We must push on we must push on!' Moreover, he converted his cavalry into mounted riflemen. To mystify, mislead and surprise was his precept; to hurl overwhelming numbers at the point where the enemy least expects attack was his practice.[344]

On May 23, he swooped upon a detachment of Banks's force at Front Royal and put it to rout, capturing a large part of it. Banks himself was then at Strasburg with 6800; but next day, fearing that his retreat would be cut off, he ran a race with Jackson to Winchester. The pursuit was hot, but the fighting of his rear-guard prevented his capture, and he reached Winchester first. During these two days,

---

[340] The *Monitor* and gunboats were repulsed in their attack on the batteries at Drewry's Bluff, eight miles below Richmond [May 15].

[341] Lee at this time was military adviser to President Davis.

[342] He carried these two, and one other, *Webster's Dictionary,* in his haversack.

[343] Read and re-read," said Napoleon, "the eighty-eight campaigns of Alexander, Hannibal, Cæsar, Gustavus, Turenne, Eugéne and Frederick. Take them as your models, for it is the only means of becoming a great leader and of mastering the secrets of the art of war. Your intelligence, enlightened by such study, will then reject methods contrary to those adopted by these great men." ;Lieut. Col. Henderson, I, 504.

[344] Lieut.-Col. Henderson, I, 308, 518, 519, 539.

however, Jackson had produced big results. The War Department in Washington received despatch after despatch from the theatre of operations, each more alarming than the last. Re-enforcements were ordered to Banks from Baltimore; Harper's Ferry sent him a portion of its garrison.

Until May 24, the faulty disposition of the Union forces was largely due to orders from the War Department, coming in Stanton's name. Now the President tried his hand at strategy. He directed Fremont to move into the Shenandoah Valley to a point in Jackson's rear. He suspended the order which had been given to McDowell to unite with McClellan and instructed him to send 20,000 men to the Shenandoah Valley to assist Frémont in the capture of Jackson; or, if Frémont should be late, he suggested that McDowell's force alone would be sufficient to accomplish the object.

At daybreak, on Sunday, May 25, Jackson routed Banks at Winchester, gave hot pursuit to the mass of disordered fugitives, was at one time on the point of destroying the entire force and finally drove them across the Potomac river. There were never more grateful hearts in the same number of men, wrote Banks, than when at midday of the 26th we stood on the opposite shore.[345]

The despatches sent to Washington on the Sunday came chiefly from panic-stricken men and greatly alarmed the President and Secretary of War. The main objective, which on Saturday had been the capture of Jackson's army, was now mixed with fear for the safety of the capital. Intelligence from various quarters leaves no doubt that the enemy in great force are marching on Washington, telegraphed Stanton to the several governors of the Northern States. You will please organize and forward all the militia and volunteer force in your State. This despatch and the response to it reflecting the alarm at the capital, caused wild excitement at the North which was afterwards spoken of in Massachusetts as the great scare, elsewhere as the great stampede. The militia and home guards of many of the States were called out; a number of regiments, among them the Seventh New York, were hurried to Baltimore and to Harper's Ferry; it was called the Third uprising of the North. The President took military possession of all the railroads in the country. I think the time is near, said Lincoln in a despatch to McClellan, when you must either attack Richmond or give up the job and come to the defense of Washington. Part of McDowell's force was recalled to the capital city. Our condition is one of considerable danger, wrote Stanton, as we are stripped to supply the Army of the Potomac and now have the enemy here.[346]

By May 26, the President and Secretary of War deemed Washington secure. In fact, the capital had at no time been in danger. Lee and Jackson had no further design than to threaten it and so cause the President to withhold the re-enforcements intended for McClellan. The result fully realized their expectation.

---

[345] O. R., XII, Pt. I, 551.
[346] IV, 19; General Meade, I, 269.

But now Jackson himself was in danger. Hearing of the movements for his capture, he began on May 30 a rapid retreat. Through the blessing of an ever kind Providence, he wrote, I passed Strasburg before the Federal armies effected the contemplated junction in my rear. By June 1, his safety was practically assured. Followed by the Union troops, he was successful in two engagements with them, after which they desisted from pursuit.

Jackson, so Lieutenant-Colonel Henderson wrote, fell as it were from the skies into the midst of his astonished foes, struck right and left before they could combine and defeated in detail every detachment which crossed his path.[347] With an effective force of but 17,000 men he had within the space of a month won five battles, taken rich spoil and many prisoners, given Washington a scare and prevented 40,000 men from joining the Union Army before Richmond.[348]

McClellan seemed to be aware that, while Jackson was making havoc in the Shenandoah Valley, he should embrace the opportunity to strike at Johnston. On May 25, he telegraphed to the President, The time is very near when I shall attack Richmond. McClellan had an army of 100,000; Johnston had 63,000. Yet it is doubtful if McClellan would really have taken the initiative. He never reached his ideal completeness of preparation; while he overestimated the enemy's force, he, at the same time, depreciated the energy of the Confederate commander. Richmond papers, he telegraphed on May 27, urge Johnston to attack now he has us away from gunboats. I think he is too able for that.[349]

Johnston had exact intelligence of the positions, movements and numbers of the Union armies; he knew that McClellan had three corps on the north side of the Chickahominy river and two on the side toward Richmond, and that the purposed re-enforcement of the Army of the Potomac by McDowell had been abandoned. He therefore resolved to strike on May 31 at the two corps nearest to Richmond. On the night of the 30th, there was a heavy rain turning the treacherous and already high Chickahominy into a torrent and increasing the danger of the divided Union Army and the eagerness of Johnston to give battle, despite the roads deep with mud and the consequent difficulty of moving his artillery. At some time after midday, he attacked the two corps with vigor, drove them back and came near inflicting on them a crushing defeat [Battle of Fair Oaks or Seven Pines]. But General Sumner saved the day. Receiving the order from McClellan to be ready to move at a moment's notice but, comprehending the danger better than his chief and construing the order freely, he at once marched his two divisions to his two

---

[347] Lieut.-Col. Henderson, I, 516.

[348] McDowell's corps, after Franklin's division had been sent to McClellan, is variously given at 35,000 or 40,000. Authorities: O. R., XI, Pt. I, III, XII, Pt. I, III; IV; Ropes, II; Lieut.-Col. Henderson, I; B. & L., II; McClellan; N. & H., V; Johnston; C. E. Norton, I, 253; See Correspondence between Lincoln and Carl Schurz, O. R., XII, Pt. III, 379, 398; General Meade, I, 270.

[349] IV, 23, 24.

bridges, halted and anxiously awaited further commands. Word at last came to cross the river. Sumner's corps went over the swaying and tossing bridges and preserved the Union left wing from rout. The Southern Army suffered a grievous loss in the severe wounding of General Johnston, who was knocked from his horse by the fragment of a shell near the end of the fight, and borne unconscious from the field.

On the next day the battle was renewed. The Confederates were driven back and some of the Union troops pushed forward to within four miles of Richmond. These were from the left wing; receiving no orders to advance farther, they fell back to the lines they had occupied before the battle. The action of the two days may be summed up as a partial success of Johnston and in the end a repulse of the Confederates.[350]

For nearly a month, the Union Army lay quietly in camp on the Chickahominy. Their line of pickets ran to within six miles of the city, and the sentinels guarding the Mechanicsville bridge could read on the guide post, To Richmond 4.5 miles. McClellan's soldiers could see the spires of Richmond, hear the church bells and even the clocks striking the hour. The Confederate outposts were within musket range; the people of Richmond could see the reflection of the Union camp fires and at times could hear the enemy's bugle calls.[351] The heavy rains continued and the Chickahominy became a flood. Movements of artillery were difficult. The Union camps were in a swamp and much illness was caused by the damp and malarious atmosphere and by the soldiers drinking the water of the marshes. For this reason, there was from June 1 to 20 a perceptible lowering of the morale of the army. McClellan begged for re-enforcements and in response obtained 21,000 men who came to him by the water route. By the middle of June the weather was fine and the roads dry. It looked as if the offensive movement, so often promised by McClellan, would at last be made. Having brought all of his corps but one over to the south side of the river, he probably intended to move by gradual approaches within shelling distance of Richmond, shell the city and possibly attempt to carry it by assault. McClellan's plan to take Richmond by a siege, wrote Longstreet, was wise enough and it would have been a success if the Confederates had consented to such a programme.[352]

On account of Johnston's disability, Robert E. Lee was placed in command of the Army of Northern Virginia (as it became known shortly afterwards). Johnston had been a capable commander, but Lee at once began to show that genius for leadership which distinguished him throughout the war. Furthermore, he had none of the arrogance that sometimes accompanies great military parts. He got on well with everybody and it was especially important that complete harmony should

---

[350] IV, and authorities cited, 23 *et seq.*

[351] Lieut.-Col. Henderson, II, 2; O. R., XI, Pt. III, 233. General Meade I, 276.

[352] B. & L., II, 404; see General Meade, I, 275.

exist between himself and Jefferson Davis and Jackson. Johnston had quarreled with his President and their correspondence bristled with controversy; but no one could quarrel with Lee who, in his magnanimity and deference to his fellow workers, resembled Lincoln. When Stonewall Jackson, who had been eager for re-enforcement, heard of Lee's appointment, he said to a friend, Well, Madam, I am reinforced at last.[353]

Lee had a talent for organization equal to that of McClellan. In reading the orders, the despatches, the history of the army at this time, one seems to feel that he infused a new energy into the management of affairs. Making a careful survey of the position of his army, he directed that it be at once strongly fortified. He had some difficulty in overcoming the aversion to manual labor which obtained among the Southern soldiers, but his constant personal superintendence and his pleasing authoritative manner accomplished wonders; soon his defensive works were well under way. At the same time he was becoming better acquainted with his officers and winning their respect, for he was unremitting in industry and rode over his lines nearly every day. He decided that an assault upon McClellan's left wing, the corps on the south side of the river, was injudicious if not impracticable; it would be, to use Davis's words, putting the breasts of our men in antagonism to the enemy's heaps of earth. On the other hand information gained by his cavalry and a personal reconnaissance of the Union position north of the Chickahominy led him to form the plan of striking at the Union force on that side of the river. He re-enforced Jackson, who was still in the Shenandoah Valley, and asked him to move toward Richmond in order to join in the attack. Jackson, leaving his army fifty miles away, with orders to continue their swift and stealthy march, rode rapidly to Richmond, where at midday on June 23 he met Lee, Longstreet, D. H. Hill and A. P. Hill in council. Lee set forth his plan of battle and assigned to each of his generals the part he should play. Jackson said that he would be ready to begin his attack on the morning of the 26th.

Fitz-John Porter, commanding the Fifth corps,[354] held the Union position on the north side of the Chickahominy [the right wing] where he protected the line of communication with the base of supplies at White House. At him and his communications Lee struck.

Through unavoidable delays, Jackson was half a day late. A. P. Hill waited until three o'clock in the afternoon of June 26 for Jackson to perform his part; then fearing longer delay, he crossed the river and came directly in front of Porter, bringing on a battle in which the Confederates met with a bloody repulse.

McClellan went to Porter's headquarters in the afternoon or early evening, while the battle was still on. They knew that the attack had come from Lee's immediate

---

[353] This was previously when Lee was appointed military adviser to Davis.

[354] A corps commander named by McClellan on the authorization of the President May 9. O. R., XI, Pt. III, 154.

command and also that Jackson was near, would unite with the other Confederate forces and probably give battle on the morrow. On returning to his own headquarters on the south side of the river, McClellan made up his mind that Porter's position was untenable and ordered him to withdraw to ground that had been selected east of Gaines's Mill, where he could protect the bridges across the Chickahominy, which connected the Union right and left wings and were indispensable should a further retreat become necessary. Porter received this word at about two o'clock in the morning and at daylight began the movement, which was executed without serious molestation and in perfect order. He sent word by Barnard, the chief engineer of the army, who had conducted him to the new position, that he needed additional troops. This request, although of the utmost importance, as matters turned out, never reached McClellan. Barnard came to headquarters about nine or ten in the morning and being informed that the commanding general was reposing made no attempt to see him.[355] Different from the habit of most generals when a morning battle is imminent, McClellan was not stirring at an early hour; nevertheless it is remarkable that Barnard, having apparently no special duty elsewhere, did not await his general's convenience to impart Porter's reasonable request. Conditions were different on the Confederate side. Jackson had neither rest nor sleep but, reviewing his preparations, paced his chamber in anxious thought, wrestling with God in prayer.[356]

On this Friday, June 27, was fought the battle of Gaines's Mill.[357] Porter, who had under him at the commencement of the battle but 25,000 men contended against Jackson, Longstreet and the two Hills whose combined forces amounted to 57,000.[358] Lee was in immediate command. In their first onset the Confederates met with a stubborn resistance and were driven back. At two o'clock in the afternoon, Porter called for re-enforcements and McClellan, who did not visit the field of battle that day but remained at the headquarters on the south side of the Chickahominy, sent a division of 9000 men to his support. Cool and collected as on parade,[359] his tactics seemingly without defect even in the heat of the contest, Fitz-John Porter was everywhere inciting his officers and men to supreme efforts; he succeeded in repelling the assaults of nearly double his numbers, directed by the genius of Lee and Stonewall Jackson and led by the courage and determination of the Hills and Longstreet. Higher praise no general can receive than that which Lee and Jackson unconsciously gave Porter in their reports. The principal part of the Federal army was now on the north side of the Chickahominy, wrote Lee; both

---

[355] O. R., XI, Pt. I, 118. "To sleep all night through beseemeth not one; to whom peoples are entrusted and so many cares belong." *Iliad* II. On this same day, however, McClellan telegraphed to his wife that he had had "no sleep for two nights." ;McClellan, 442.

[356] Dabney, 439, 440. Jackson was 38, McClellan 36.

[357] Or the Chickahominy.

[358] T. L. Livermore, 82. I reckon Slocum's division as 9000.

[359] Francis A. Walker, 62.

speak of the superior force of the enemy.[360] All accounts agree as to the discipline and bravery of the soldiers of both armies. The impetuous attack of the Confederates may be described in the words that Jackson used of one of his regiments as an almost matchless display of daring and valor; he well characterized the defence as stubborn resistance and sullen obstinacy. George G. Meade and John F. Reynolds, commanders of brigades, made their mark that day.

From Lee's statement, the principal part of the Federal army was now on the north side of the Chickahominy, the inference is clear that, had he been in McClellan's place, he would have had it there. McClellan's error was due to his overestimate of the Confederate force. Relying upon the report of the Chief of the Secret Service corps, he believed it to be 180,000, of whom 70,000 were attacking Porter, while 110,000 lay behind intrenchments between him and Richmond. As matter of fact, 57,000 were assailing Porter, while about 30,000 held the earthworks protecting Richmond: these last led McClellan and his corps commanders into a gross exaggeration of their number by attacking their pickets from time to time and by frequently opening fire on their works with artillery. McClellan's timid tactics are revealed in his hesitation in re-enforcing Porter. He loved Porter and would have rejoiced without a spark of envy to see him win a glorious victory. His despatches show how anxious he was to give him efficient support; and purely military considerations should have induced him to send large re-enforcements to Porter's aid. His telegram to the Secretary of War at the close of the day that he was attacked by greatly superior numbers in all directions on this side[361] (the Richmond side of the Chickahominy) remains an ineffaceable record of his misapprehension.

Skilful though the leader, brave though the men, 34,000 without intrenchments, with barriers only erected along a small portion of their front, could not finally prevail against 57,000 equally brave and as skilfully led. The end came at about seven o'clock. Lee and Jackson ordered a general assault; the Confederates broke the Union line, captured many cannon and forced Porter's troops back to the woods on the bank of the Chickahominy. Two brigades of Sumner's corps, who had been tardily sent to the support of their comrades, efficiently covered the retreat of the exhausted and shattered regiments who withdrew dejectedly to the south side of the river.

In his despatches during the battle, McClellan does not betray panic. At five o'clock he thought Porter might hold his own until dark and three hours later his confidence was only a little shaken; but by midnight he had reached a state of demoralization, which revealed itself in his famous Savage Station despatch to the Secretary of War. I now know the full history of the day, he wrote. On this side of the river (the right bank) we repulsed several strong attacks. On the left bank our

---

[360] O. R., XI, Pt. II, 492, 556. Jackson said "superior numbers." See also Chesnut, 197.
[361] 8 P.M. O. R., XI, Pt. III, 266.

men did all that men could do, all that soldiers could accomplish but they were overwhelmed by vastly superior numbers, even after I brought my last reserves into action. The loss on both sides is terrible. The sad remnants of my men behave as men. I have lost this battle because my force was too small. I feel too earnestly to-night. I have seen too many dead and wounded comrades to feel otherwise than that the government has not sustained this army. If you do not do so now the game is lost. If I save this army now, I tell you plainly that I owe no thanks to you or to any other persons in Washington. You have done your best to sacrifice this army.

The news was a terrible blow to the President. His finely equipped army costing such a tale of treasure and labor, had gone forth with high hope of conquest and bearing, so it seemed, the fate of the Union, on its shoulders; now it was defeated and in serious danger of destruction or capture. This calamity the head of the nation must face, and he failed not. Overlooking the spirit of insubordination in his general's despatch, he sent him a reply as wise as it was gentle. With equal forbearance and circumspection he offered the most charitable explanation possible of the disaster. Save your army at all events, he wrote. Will send reinforcements as fast as we can. I feel any misfortune to you and your army quite as keenly as you feel it yourself. If you have had a drawn battle or a repulse, it is the price we pay for the enemy not being in Washington. We protected Washington and the enemy concentrated on you. Had we stripped Washington he would have been upon us before the troops could have gotten to you. It is the nature of the case and neither you nor the government are to blame.[362]

As the battle of Gaines's Mill ended the offensive attitude of the Army of the Potomac, some general considerations will here be in place. Nearly all writers agree that McClellan should have strongly re-enforced Porter, who in that event could have held his own until night when he could have made an orderly retreat; he might even have won the battle. If McClellan had known of Lee's division of the Confederate force, he would of course have followed the plan of the military critics. Nevertheless there is no doubt that his judgment was bad on the basis of such information as he possessed; this may be affirmed after conceding that by no possible means could he have gained the correct knowledge of the enemy which Lee had of the Union forces. If I were mindful only of my own glory, wrote Frederick the Great, I would choose always to make war in my own country, for there every man is a spy and the enemy can make no movement of which I am not informed.[363] This advantage was Lee's; but in addition he understood McClellan. Only in dealing with a timed commander would he have so divided his force. When Lee was planning the campaign Davis said, If McClellan is the man I take him for as soon as he finds that the bulk of our army is on the north side of the Chickahominy, he will not stop to try conclusions with it there but will

362 IV, 43, 44 with authorities cited.
363 Lieut.-Col. Henderson, I, 497.

immediately move upon his objective point, the city of Richmond. Lee replied, If you will hold him as long as you can at the intrenchment and then fall back on the detached works around the city I will be upon the enemy's heels before he gets there.[364] No doubt Lee would have been as good as his word, but McClellan neither re-enforced Porter properly, nor did he take advantage of his general's gallant fight to advance on Richmond. The despatches between McClellan and his officers on the south side of the river during the day of the battle show that they were paralyzed, so far as an offensive movement was concerned, by vigorous demonstrations of the troops guarding the Confederate capital. Some writers have thought that while Porter was engaged with the larger Confederate force, McClellan could easily have gone into Richmond; but as Lee's entire army was now fully equal in number to McClellan's, it is difficult to regard such a movement as other than extremely hazardous. The re-enforcement of Porter was more prudent; moreover, to take toll from the Army of Northern Virginia, was, as Lincoln perceived, quite as effective offensive work as the capture of Richmond.

No speculation is necessary to explain why the Confederates were successful. Their victory was due to the greater ability of Lee and Jackson. Lieutenant-Colonel Henderson, in his enthusiasm over Jackson's Valley campaign, wrote, The brains of Lee and Jackson did more for the Confederacy than 200,000 soldiers for the Union.[365] Although this remark need not be taken literally, the germ of the truth is in it. They greatly excelled their adversary both in strategy and tactics. McClellan was never on the battle-field, not through a lack of physical courage, since, in making reconnaissances, he was cool under fire, but because he could not endure the sight of blood. Jackson, wrote Lieutenant-Colonel Henderson, rode along the line of battle with as much composure as if the hail of bullets was no more than summer rain.[366] Lee loved the fight and yearned to be in it. His own son, as well as President Davis and other friends, remonstrated with him for exposing himself to danger, and once, when he was for leading a charge himself, his men cried out, General Lee to the rear! It is well war is so terrible, he once said; we should grow too fond of it.[367]

The match between Lee and Jackson on one side and McClellan on the other was unequal, and McClellan of course went down. Into the dispute between him and Lincoln's friends touching the withdrawal of troops from his command and the alleged failure properly to re-enforce him we need not go further than to refer to one point which the General made. But for an unwise order of the Secretary of War, there would have been troops enough for all. Emboldened by the Union successes, he stopped recruiting on April 3, at a time when it was not difficult to

---

[364] IV, 36.

[365] Lieut.-Col. Henderson, I, 502.

[366] *Ibid.,* 539.

[367] Fitzhugh Lee, 260; 294; Long, 338; O. R., XI, Pt. III, 632.

get men and when the impulse to volunteer should not have been checked.[368] But no matter how many troops had been given to McClellan, he could not have handled them in such a manner as to get the better of Lee and Jackson. It is certain that Lincoln and Stanton desired his success as ardently as he did himself.

Although McClellan could not manage 100,000 men on the offensive, he made a masterly retreat.[369] He was able to carry out Lincoln's injunction, Save your army, when a lesser man might have lost it. Lee expected to capture or destroy the Union force, but failed to divine McClellan's plan until too late to frustrate it. Convinced as he was that the retreat would be down the Peninsula, he neglected to interfere immediately with the movement for a change of base to the James river, which McClellan had determined on making should his communications with White House be severed. On the night of Gaines's Mill, he gave the necessary orders to his corps commanders, who began their preparations next morning and wrought the whole day without molestation. Six hundred tons of ammunition, food, forage, medical and other supplies were the daily requirements of this army[370] and the change of base in presence of a victorious foe of equal number was attended with great difficulty and could not have been made had not the United States had the command of the sea. By sunrise of June 29, the Confederates discovered that the Union Army had fled toward the James river, and they started in immediate pursuit, bringing on a fight at Savage's Station in which they were repulsed. Next day was fought the stubborn battle of Glendale or Frayser's Farm, in which neither side prevailed, although the Union troops continued their retreat in good order. It was thought that, if Jackson had come up at the time he was expected, a portion of McClellan's army would have been destroyed or captured.[371]

The morning of July 1 found the whole Union Army posted on Malvern Hill, a strong position near the James river. By noon the Confederates appeared and attacked with bravery but were mowed down by the fire of the splendid artillery and the efficiently directed infantry of the Union Army. Porter was in the fight and his generalship was of a high order. The Confederates were repulsed at all points with a loss double that of the Federals.[372] McClellan was not with his fighting troops in any one of the battles during the retreat, but was doing engineer's work in preparing the position for the next day. In the Seven Days' Battles, as the fighting is called from June 25 to July 1 inclusive, McClellan's loss was 15,849, Lee's 20,614.[373] Lee's was naturally the greater as he fought constantly on the

---

[368] III, 636; see General Meade, I, 268.

[369] "A retreat is the most exhausting of military movements. It is costly in men, more so,' says Napoleon, than two battles.'" Lieut-.Col. Henderson, I, 534.

[370] Lieut.-Col. Henderson, II, 37.

[371] Dabney, 466; Allan, 121 Sometimes used for the Union troops.; Ropes, II, 195; Lieut.-Col. Henderson, 59 *et seq.*

[372] Sometimes used for the Union troops.

[373] T. L. Livermore, 86. There was a skirmish in front of Seven Pines on June 25.

offensive, but the victory was his, as he had driven the enemy away from Richmond. In these seven days Lee's soldiers began to love him and to acquire a belief that he was invincible, a belief which lasted almost to the very end of the war.

Next day after Malvern Hill, McClellan with his army retired to Harrison's Landing, a safe position on the James river, where he might have the help of gunboats and where the navy ensured him constant communication with the North. But from being in sight of the steeples of Richmond, he was now twenty to twenty-five miles away. His Peninsular campaign had been a failure. McClellan, wrote Meade privately of his friend six months later, was always waiting to have everything just as he wanted before he would attack, and before he could get things arranged as he wanted them, the enemy pounced on him and thwarted all his plans. Such a general will never command success, though he may avoid disaster.[374]

On July 8, Lee fell back to his old quarters in the vicinity of Richmond. Our success, he wrote to his wife, has not been so great or complete as we could have desired, but God knows what is best for us.[375] Nevertheless all conditions united to brighten the hopes of the South. To the work of conscription which was urged with vigor, a response seemed assured that would show the enthusiasm of the people to have been quickened by their army's success.[376]

---

[374] General Meade, I, 345.

[375] Lee's *Recollections,* 75.

[376] Authorities: O. R., XI, Pts. I, II, III, IV; Lieut.-Col. Henderson, II; Ropes, II; B. & L., II; McClellan; Allan; N. & H., V; Long; Fitzhugh Lee; Johnston; Chesnut; Hosmer's Appeal; Lee's*Recollections.*

Chapter IV

THAT war is an economic waste is a commonplace; that the man is much more valuable than the dollar a truism, for the great evil of war is the killing of men. Homer's thought when speaking of a lusty stripling who was smitten to the death cannot fail to occur, He repaid not his dear parents the recompense of his nurture.[377] It is the tragedy of war that the high-spirited men are at the front and the skulkers in the rear; that the hearts of a large number of men are not in the fight. And these flee from danger, saying with Falstaff, The better part of valor is discretion; in the which better part I have saved my life.[378]

In the course of this story we have seen how civilians were made into soldiers to fight bloody battles which presaged still greater sacrifices and a carnage of nearly three more years. We have now to consider another factor in the situation: to wit, money, which has come to mean the sinews of war. It was indispensable that the United States should keep up its credit among nations, and this, in view of its daily expenditure having increased from $178,000 to a million and a half dollars,[379] was work requiring the highest kind of financial ability. Until December 31, 1861, the war had been carried on by the placing of loans through the co-operation of the United States Treasury and the banks and by the issue of about 25 millions of United States notes payable on demand without interest; all transactions had been on a specie basis. But the loans had exhausted the resources of the banks and at the end of the year 1861, they were obliged to suspend specie payments, leaving the government in the same plight. At home and in England it was thought that national bankruptcy was threatened. By the end of January, 1862, there were 100 million of accrued indebtedness and further requirements to June 30 of 250 to 300 millions. Both popular sentiment and congressional resolution approved heavy direct and indirect taxation, but it was certain that no tax bill could be framed and got to work in time to meet the pressing exigency. The expedient finally adopted was a striking innovation in finance. Congress authorized the Secretary of the Treasury to issue 150 million United States treasury notes, payable to bearer, not bearing interest, and made these notes a legal-tender for all debts public and private.[380]

---

[377] *Iliad,* IV.

[378] I Henry IV, V, 4.

[379] Dewey, 267, 329.

[380] Except duties on imports which should be paid in coin; this coin was pledged for the payment of the interest on the bonds. Included in the 150 millions were 50 million United States notes, authorized in July, of which about 25 millions had been issued.

Action so unprecedented was not taken without serious consideration and debate. Chase, the Secretary of the Treasury, came with reluctance to the conclusion that the legal-tender clause is a necessity.[381] The two best financial authorities in the Senate, John Sherman and William Pitt Fessenden, the chairman of the Committee on Finance, differed, Sherman favoring the clause, Fessenden opposing it. Fessenden wrote in a private letter: This legal-tender clause is opposed to all my views of right and expediency. It shocks all my notions of political, moral and national honor.[382] The argument which prevailed was urged by Thaddeus Stevens, chairman of the House Committee of Ways and Means, This bill is a measure of necessity, not of choice. Sumner came to its support, but warned the Senate that the medicine of the Constitution must not become its daily bread. Sumner, Sherman and many others, perhaps most of the senators and representatives favoring it, regarded the measure as only a temporary expedient. But the apparent ease of solving a financial difficulty by making irredeemable paper a legal-tender acted like a stimulant which called for repeated doses; additional legal-tender, which became known as greenbacks, were authorized and issued until January 3, 1864, when the amount reached but a little short of 450 millions.[383] The act of February 25, 1862, under which the first legal-tenders were issued, authorized also the issue of 500 million 20 six per cent bonds, into which these legal-tender notes might be funded; interest on these bonds was payable in coin, for which the duties on foreign imports, payable in the same medium, were pledged.

It is impossible to read the debates covering the legal-tender act without recognizing the patriotic note. The advocates felt that it was necessary to avoid bankruptcy and to carry on the military and naval operations. True enough, we see its ill effects in increasing the cost of the war and in debauching the public mind with the idea that the government could create money by its fiat; and we know not what would have been the result of the alternative scheme. But as the legal-tender clause was opposed to sound principles of finance and to valuable precedent, it might have been worthwhile to try the other plan first. It was generally conceded that Treasury notes must be issued; the difference arose on the proposition to make them a full legal-tender. With the issue of the amount deemed necessary, and made legal-tender only as between the government and the public, even as Pitt had restricted that quality of the Bank of England notes during the Napoleonic wars, it is reasonable to suppose that the war might have been carried on for six months or a year longer and possibly to the end; provided also that the Secretary of the Treasury had made a proper construction of section 2 of the Act of February 25, which authorized him to dispose of the 500 million 20 six per cents at their market

---

[381] Spaulding, 59.
[382] Fessenden, I, 194.
[383] $449,338,902. Knox United States notes, 139.

value for coin or for Treasury notes. Chase construed market value to mean par, the result of this construction being very different from what would have been obtained if the bonds had been sold in the market for what they would fetch. The difference of the plans was the difference between a forced loan without interest and a voluntary loan secured by selling the bonds at their real market value. Our financiers who carried through their scheme were victims of the illusion that to make money by legislation was cheaper and better than to obtain it by bargaining.[384]

Congress at this session[385] authorized the President to take possession of the railroads and telegraph lines when necessary for the public safety,[386] and it created a comprehensive and searching scheme of internal taxation, which became a law by the President's approval on July 1 and may be briefly described as an act taxing everything, framed on the principle, Whenever you find an article, a product, a trade, a profession or a source of revenue tax it.[387] This Congress was further notable in imposing for the first time in our history a graduated federal income tax. A tax of three per cent on incomes less than $10,000 and of five per cent on incomes over $10,000, with an exemption of $600 was laid,[388] although certain deductions were permitted in making the return. The tax upon the incomes of citizens residing abroad was five per cent, without the usual exemptions. The duties on imports were increased by an act approved by the President on July 14.[389] Lincoln was not an adept in finance and left this department to his Secretary of the Treasury who, in spite of mistakes and some personal failings, made a good finance minister. In diplomatic matters Lincoln's hand may be traced and generally for the good. He was a hard student of the art of war and, through untoward circumstances and miserable failures, groped his way to the correct method of conducting large military operations. But from the first, he handled the slavery question with scarcely a flaw.

The action of Congress during the spring and early summer of 1862 indicated the progress of public sentiment since the first shot at Sumter. The Republicans, in neither of their national platforms, had deemed it prudent to demand the abolition of slavery in the District of Columbia but, in April, Congress enacted this, providing at the same time for compensation to the loyal owners of slaves, which was duly made. In June, it crystallized in a formal statute the cardinal principle of the Republican party, the very reason of its existence, by prohibiting slavery in all the Territories of the United States.[390] Lincoln went further than Congress. As

---

[384] Spaulding; III; Dewey; Fessenden, I; J. Sherman Rec., I; Hart's Chase.

[385] 2d Sess. 37 Cong. lasting from Dec. 2, 1861 to July 17, 1862.

[386] Approved Jan. 31.

[387] Wells, Dewey, 301.

[388] Income derived from interest on notes or bonds of the United States was taxed only one and one-half per cent.

[389] IV, 58 *et seq.* For the Confiscation Ace, *see* 60; Horace White, 173 *et seq.* J. G. Randall, *Am. Hist. Rev., Oct., 1912.*

early as March, 1862, he proposed the gradual abolishment of all slavery with compensation for the slave-owners and Congress adopted his recommendation. This offer was made during the military successes of the North and though, as a practical measure, there was no expectation that any but the Union border slave States would avail themselves of it, the offer was open to all; and, if the people of any or all of the Confederate States had at this time laid down their arms and respected the authority of the national government they would have received, in a plan of gradual emancipation, about four hundred dollars for each slave set free.

Lincoln measured the steps forward with discretion and kept the determination of the slavery question entirely in his own hands. On May 9, General Hunter, who commanded the Department of the South, issued an order declaring free all the slaves in South Carolina, Florida and Georgia. Lincoln heard of this a week later through the newspapers and at the same time received a letter from Chase, saying that in his judgment the order should be suffered to stand. The President replied to his Secretary, No commanding general shall do such a thing upon my responsibility without consulting me, and, on May 19, he issued a proclamation declaring Hunter's order void. In this proclamation, he made an earnest appeal to the people of the Union border slave States to give freedom gradually to their slaves and accept the compensation proffered them by himself and Congress. I do not argue, he said; I beseech you to make arguments for yourselves. You cannot, if you would, be blind to the signs of the times. The abolition of slavery contemplated would come gently as the dews of heaven, not rending or wrecking anything.

Then came the utter failure of McClellan's campaign, which convinced the President that slavery must be struck at. He grew eager to develop his policy of gradual emancipation of the slaves, compensation of their owners by the Federal government and colonization of the freed negroes in Hayti, South America and Liberia; for he believed that the abolition of slavery by the slave States in the Union would make it difficult for the Southern Confederacy to maintain the contest much longer. Before Congress adjourned, he invited the senators and representatives of the Union border slave States to the White House [July 12] and asked them earnestly to influence their States to adopt his policy. If the war continues long, he said, slavery in your States will be extinguished by the mere incidents of the war. It will be gone and you will have nothing valuable in lieu of it. How much better for you and for your people to take the step which at once shortens the war and secures substantial compensation for that which is sure to be wholly lost in any other event! He told them of the pressure upon him to interfere with slavery and of the dissatisfaction with him by the Radical supporters of the government, threatening division among those who united are none too strong. Our common country is in great peril, he continued; and as lofty views and bold

---

[390] MacDonald, 35, 42.

action on their part would bring speedy relief, he begged them to emancipate their slaves. But Lincoln was unable to secure the assent of the border States to his plan. Bound up as was slavery with their social and political life, they could not understand that its doom was certain.

The lack of military success hampered the President in this as in all other action. It was a part of the plan that payment for the slaves should be made in United States six per cent bonds, and, though property in negroes had become admittedly precarious, the question must have suggested itself, in view of the enormous expenditure of the government, the recent military reverses and the present strength of the Confederacy, whether the nation's promises to pay were any more valuable. Gold, now become a measure of the Union fortune, sold on June 3 at three and one-half per cent premium; on July 12, owing to McClellan's defeat and the further authorized issue of paper money,[391] it fetched fourteen per cent. But it is certain that, if the border slave States had acted promptly, they would have received for their slaves a fair compensation in United States bonds instead of having subsequently to sustain a flat monetary loss through the gift of freedom to the negroes.

During a drive to the funeral of Secretary Stanton's infant son on the day after his interview with the border State representatives, Lincoln broached to Seward and Welles the subject which was uppermost in his mind. The reverses before Richmond, the formidable power of the Confederacy, convinced him of the necessity of a new policy. Since the slaves were growing the food for the Confederate soldiers and served as teamsters and laborers on intrenchments in the army service, he had about come to the conclusion that it was a military necessity, absolutely essential for the salvation of the nation, that we must free the slaves or be ourselves subdued.[392] As he afterwards described the situation, Things had gone on from bad to worse, until I felt that we had reached the end of our rope on the plan of operations we had been pursuing; that we had about played our last card and must change our tactics or lose the game![393]

On July 22, Lincoln read to his Cabinet, to the surprise of all probably, except Seward and Welles, a proclamation of emancipation which he purposed to issue. Reiterating that the object of the war was the restoration of the Union, he proposed emancipation as a fit and necessary military measure for effecting this object. Seward pleaded for delay, fearing that on account of the depression of the public mind the proclamation might be viewed as the last measure of an exhausted government, a cry for help, the government stretching forth its hands to Ethiopia in a last shriek on the retreat. Now while I approve the measure, he added, I suggest

---

[391] The act approved July 11 authorized the additional issue of 150 million United States legal-tender notes.

[392] Welles's Diary, I, 70; IV, 69 n. 2.

[393] Carpenter, 20.

sir that you postpone its issue until you can give it to the country supported by military success instead of issuing it, as would be the case now, upon the greatest disasters of the war. The President had not seen the matter in this light; struck with the wisdom of Seward's objection, he put the draft of the proclamation aside waiting for a victory.[394]

The secret of this conference was well kept and the Radicals, not knowing that Lincoln was disposed to go as far as they wished, continued their criticism. What a pity, wrote Charles Eliot Norton, that the President should not have issued a distinct and telling Proclamation![395] Thaddeus Stevens characterized Lincoln's proposal of compensated emancipation as the most diluted milk-and-water gruel proposition that was ever given to the American nation, and declared that the blood of thousands moldering in untimely graves is upon the souls of this Congress and Cabinet. The administration, he said, should free the slaves, enlist and arm them and set them to shooting their masters if they will not submit to this government.[396] Sumner, restlessly pacing up and down his room, exclaimed with uplifted hand: I pray that the President may be right in delaying. But I am afraid, I am almost sure, he is not. I trust his fidelity but I cannot understand him.[397] Carl Schurz sympathized with Sumner and criticized the President for not adopting the policy of immediate emancipation, but afterwards frankly confessed that Lincoln was wiser than he.[398] Greeley, in his Prayer of Twenty Millions, printed in the New York Tribune, said to the President, We complain that the Union cause has suffered and is now suffering immensely from your mistaken deference to rebel slavery. This gave the President an opportunity for a public reply [August 22]. My paramount object in this struggle, he wrote, is to save the Union and is not either to save or destroy slavery. What I do about slavery and the colored race, I do because I believe it helps to save the Union; and what I forbear, I forbear because I do not believe it would help to save the Union.

Lincoln and Greeley may be looked upon as representative exponents of the two policies. There was in their personal relations a fundamental lack of sympathy; they could not see things alike. Lincoln knew men, Greeley did not; Lincoln had a keen sense of humor, Greeley had none; indeed, in all their intercourse of many years, Lincoln never told the serious-minded editor an anecdote or joke, for he knew it would be thrown away. Greeley and the Tribune, though not so powerful at this time in forming public opinion as they had been from 1854 to 1860, exerted still a far-reaching influence and gave expression to thoughts rising in the minds of many earnest men. No one knew this better than the President, who, in stating his

---

[394] Carpenter, 22.

[395] July 31, C. E. Norton, I, 255.

[396] March 11, July 5, 1862. Globe, 1154, 3127; Woodburn, 183 *et seq.*

[397] Schurz. Reminiscences, II, 314.

[398] *Ibid.* Schurz. Speeches, etc., I, 206; Schurz's Lincoln, 93.

policy in a public despatch to Greeley, complimented the editor and those for whom the Tribune spoke. Lincoln's words received the widest publication and were undoubtedly read by nearly every man and women at the North. They were sound indeed. His position could not have been more cogently put. His policy was right and expedient, appealed to the reason of his people and inspired their hopes.[399] The months of July and August, 1862, were one of the periods of gloom when the Northern people would probably have abandoned the contest had they not had at their head an unfaltering leader like Abraham Lincoln. The retreat to the James was a rude shock to their confidence in McClellan and the Army of the Potomac. When Norton asked George William Curtis, Do you think the Army on the James river is safe?[400] he was expressing the anxious solicitude of many, as Lowell put into words the apprehensions of countless others when he wrote, I don't see how we are to be saved but by a miracle.[401]

History has answered Norton's question, Will Lincoln be master of the opportunities or will they escape him? Is he great enough for the time?[402] Schurz wrote to Lincoln that his personal influence upon public opinion, his moral power was immense:[403] this he now used to raise the men necessary to continue the war. From McClellan's despatch of June 28[404] he was convinced that the plan for taking Richmond had failed and that the Union armies must be increased. With a view to starting fresh enlistments he furnished Seward with a letter, making clear the need of additional troops. This letter was used by the Secretary, during his journey to New York City, Boston and Cleveland, in his conferences with men of influence and with the governors of several States. In it Lincoln declared, I expect to maintain this contest until successful, or till I die, or am conquered, or my term expires, or Congress or the country forsakes me; and I would publicly appeal to the country for this new force were it not that I fear a general panic and stampede would follow, so hard is it to have a thing understood as it really is. The result of Seward's conferences and of his counsel by wire with the President and Secretary of War was a telegram to the governors of the States of the Union, asking them to unite in a letter to the President, in which they should request him to call upon the several States for men enough to speedily crush the rebellion. The governors fell in with the plan; the President accepted the patriotic offer and, after a free interchange of thought between him and Seward and between Seward and the governors, made the call for 300,000 men.[405]

---

[399] IV; Lect. with their references.

[400] July 31. C. E. Norton, I, 255.

[401] Lowell, I, 322.

[402] July 31. C. E. Norton, I, 255.

[403] May 16. Schurz, Speeches, etc., I, 206.

[404] *Ante.*

[405] July 1. The call was for three years' men.

From June 28 to July 1, Lincoln had no news of McClellan, and was in doubt as to the safety of his army for yet two more days; during this period, he grew thin and haggard. Sumner in despair wrote to Schurz: I wish you were here to tell the President the true way. In vain will he appeal for troops at the North, so it seems to many of us. I have insisted that the appeal shall be made to the slaves and the rear-guard of the rebellion be changed into the advance-guard to the Union.[406] A month later, Sumner appreciated the hold Lincoln had on the people, writing to John Bright: The last call for three hundred thousand men is received by the people with enthusiasm, because it seems to them a purpose to push the war vigorously. There is no thought in the Cabinet or the President of abandoning the contest. We shall easily obtain the new levy, wrote Lincoln in a private letter (August 4). In spite of the misfortunes of the Army of the Potomac, he had the support of the plain people, who shared the enthusiasm of a mass meeting in Chicago that listened to the reading of a poem whose theme was, We are coming Father Abraham three hundred thousand more.[407]

Gloomy as was the outlook, worse was yet to come owing to further blunders in generalship. What General Meade wrote in May, We must expect disaster so long as the armies are not under one master mind,[408] Lincoln knew perfectly well, and gladly would he have devolved the military conduct of affairs on one man could he have found that master mind for whom he made a painful quest during almost two years. The armies of the West, as contrasted with the Army of the Potomac, had accomplished positive results and to the ability there developed he looked for aid. He brought John Pope from the West where he had achieved an inconsiderable victory and made him commander of the Army of Virginia, composed of the corps of McDowell, Banks and Frémont. At the same time he appointed Halleck General-in-chief of the whole land forces of the United States with headquarters in Washington. It is difficult to comprehend the assignment of Pope, whose reported wonderful military operations on the Mississippi and at Corinth had not somehow been fully substantiated. Admiral Foote used to laugh at his gasconade and bluster.[409] Halleck's promotion is easily understood. He had received much more than his share of the glory for the capture of Forts Henry and Donelson: this and his advance upon Corinth gave him the confidence of the country and of most of the army.[410] It is remarkable that there was apparently no thought of three really able generals in the West, Grant, William T. Sherman and George H. Thomas, whose achievements at the time were greater than Pope's and Halleck's.

---

[406] July 5, Schurz, Speeches, etc., I, 209.

[407] On Aug. 4 the President ordered a draft of 300,000 nine-months' militia additional to call mentioned page 156. This brought 87,588.

[408] General Meade, I, 269.

[409] Welles's Diary, I, 120.

[410] See W. Sherman, I, 254; Sherman Letters, 153.

Pope began his brief career as commander with a tactless address to his army. I have come to you from the West, he said, where we have always seen the backs of our enemies. I presume that I have been called here to pursue the same system and to lead you against the enemy. It is my purpose to do so and that speedily. He followed his address with four published orders, one of which was unjustifiable and impossible of execution and the other three unnecessary. Lee at once began the study of Pope.

Frederick the Great, wrote Carlyle, always got to know his man, after fighting him a month or two; and took liberties with him or did not take accordingly. Learning to comprehend one's adversary was commanders easy in our civil war as most of the opposing commanders had been acquainted at West Point or during service in Mexico. Longstreet was graduated in the same class with Pope and undoubtedly conveyed to Lee his judgment of West Point days that Pope was a handsome, dashing fellow and a splendid cavalryman, who did not apply himself to his books very closely. At all events Lee accepted the general academic estimate of the new commander as a boastful, ambitious man and not a hard student or a close thinker. When he heard of Pope's address to the army, his estimate was lowered: the Federal general had shown contempt for the military maxim of centuries, Do not despise your enemy.

McClellan's army was at Harrison's Landing on the James river. He desired that it should be re-enforced, after which he would again take the offensive against Richmond; at first the President inclined to the General's view, but he returned from his visit to the Army (July 8) perplexed in mind. In May he had told General Meade, I am trying to do my duty but no one can imagine what influences are brought to bear on me.[411] Conditions in this respect were worse in July. The Radicals not only pressed him to make a declaration against slavery but urged him to remove McClellan, whom they denounced as incompetent or disloyal and utterly out of sympathy with any attack upon slavery. They had induced the President to give Frémont another command after he had shown his incapacity in Missouri; they had another favorite in Benjamin F. Butler; but Pope had a military education which the others lacked and seemed to be equally zealous against slavery. Stanton and Chase desired the President to remove McClellan and send Pope to take command of the army on the James river; this he declined to do but he offered the command of the Army of the Potomac to Burnside, who peremptorily declined it.

On July 23, Halleck reached Washington, went next day to the headquarters of the Army of the Potomac and had a frank talk with McClellan, who, eager to remain on the James river, said that with a re-enforcement of 20,000 to 30,000, he would cross the James river, attack Petersburg, an important railway centre, and cut the communication between Richmond and the States farther South. Halleck

---

[411] General Meade, I, 267.

did not approve this plan and, on his return to Washington, the President, guided by his and other advice, determined to withdraw McClellan's army to Aquia Creek in spite of the General's warm protest. Then Lee decided to attack Pope who, well-informed and wary, retreated before the superior Confederate force. Lee, watching the movement from a hill, said to Longstreet, with a sigh of disappointment, General, we little thought that the enemy would turn his back upon us thus early in the campaign.

The rest of Pope's campaign consisted of a series of blunders on his part aggravated by the indecision of Halleck, who evinced an utter incapacity for directing the movements of the two armies. There was also a lack of hearty co-operation with Pope by the Army of the Potomac. Halleck, Pope, the President, Stanton, Chase and McClellan, all had a hand in the management of the troops. Against these contended one able head, Lee, who had two powerful arms in Jackson and Longstreet. By a swift march Jackson got in Pope's rear, tore up the railroad and cut the telegraph wires, severing his line of supplies and direct telegraph communication with Washington, but before Pope could catch him, he had fled and taken up a position to await calmly Longstreet's arrival. Pope, re-enforced by two corps from the Army of the Potomac, attacked the Confederates on August 29 and was repulsed, although he thought that he had gained a victory. In pursuance of this illusion, he brought on next day the Second Battle of Bull Run, wherein acting as if in obedience to Lee's own wishes, he delivered himself into the enemy's hands, met with a crushing defeat, which became a rout, the men fleeing in panic from the field.

The common belief in Washington was that Pope had on August 29 won a great victory. Everything seemed to be going well and hilarious on Saturday (August 30), wrote John Hay in his Diary, and we went to bed expecting glad tidings at sunrise. But about eight o'clock the President came to my room as I was dressing and calling me out said: 'Well, John, we are whipped again, I am afraid. The enemy reinforced on Pope and drove back his left wing, and he has retired to Centreville where he says he will be able to hold his men. I don't like that expression. I don't like to hear him admit that his men need holding.'[412] The despatches from Pope were indeed alarming. In one of them he asked whether Washington were secure if his army should be destroyed; in another he disclosed his lack of confidence in the Army of the Potomac and its officers' lack of confidence in him. McClellan, who was now at Alexandria, did not regard Washington as safe against the rebels. If I can quietly slip over there, he said in a letter to his wife, I will send your silver off.

September 2 was an anxious day in Washington. Early in the morning came a despatch from Pope telling a sad tale of demoralization of his own army and of excessive straggling from many regiments of the Army of the Potomac. Unless

---

[412] J. Hay, I, 62.

something can be done, he continued, to restore tone to this army, it will melt away before you know it. The President knew the one remedy and, in spite of the bitter opposition and remonstrance he was certain to encounter, placed McClellan, who in the shifting of troops had been deprived of all actual authority, in command of all the soldiers for the defence of the capital. Halleck had already ordered Pope to bring his forces within or near the lines of the fortifications; there his authority passed to McClellan. In view of the great danger to Washington, Halleck asked that all the available troops be sent as rapidly as possible to the capital. A number of gunboats were ordered up the river, and anchored at different points in proximity to the city, and a war steamer was brought to the Navy Yard. All the clerks and employees of the civil departments and all employees in the public buildings were called to arms for the defence of Washington. The sale of spirituous liquors at retail within the District of Columbia was prohibited. It was a moment of acute anxiety.

McClellan, elated at being called to the rescue, went forward to meet his soldiers. Encountering J. D. Cox, he said, Well, General, I am in command again. Warm congratulations ensued. The two rode on until they met the advancing column of the army, Pope and McDowell at its head. When it became known that McClellan had been placed in command, cheers upon cheers from the head to the rear of the column were given with wild delight. Inspired by the confidence of his men, he wrought with zeal. His talent for organization had full play and in a few days he had his army ready for an active campaign. Lincoln's comment was, McClellan is working like a beaver. He seems to be aroused to doing something by the sort of snubbing he got last week.

At the Cabinet meeting of September 2, the opposition to McClellan broke forth. Stanton, trembling with excitement, spoke in a suppressed voice.[413] Chase maintained that as a military commander McClellan had been a failure, that his neglect to urge forward re-enforcements to Pope proved him unworthy of trust and that giving command to him was equivalent to giving Washington to the rebels. This and more I said, set down Chase in his diary. All the members of the Cabinet except Seward (who was out of the city) and Blair expressed a general concurrence. Lincoln was distressed and perplexed; he would gladly resign his place; (the presidency) but he could not see who could do the work wanted as well as McClellan. Chase replied that either Hooker, Sumner or Burnside could do it better.[414]

The President again offered the command of the army in the field to Burnside, who again declined it, saying, I do not think that there is anyone who can do as much with that army as McClellan, if matters can be so arranged as to remove your and the Secretary of War's objection to him.

---

[413] Welles's Diary, I, 104.
[414] Warden, 459.

At the Cabinet meeting two days later (September 4) all the members present except Blair were unanimous against McClellan and almost ready to denounce the President for reinstating him in command. On the morrow, Lincoln said to John Hay: McClellan has acted badly in this matter, but we must use what tools we have. There is no man in the army who can man these fortifications and lick these troops of ours into shape half as well as he. Unquestionably he has acted badly toward Pope. He wanted him to fail. That is unpardonable. But he is too useful now to sacrifice. And at another time Lincoln said, If he can't fight himself he excels in making others ready to fight.[415]

The intelligence came that Lee with his army was crossing the Potomac into Maryland. The Union troops must be sent in pursuit and a commander for them must be designated. The President said to McClellan, General, you will take command of the forces in the field. To Pope was sent an order which ended his service as a general in the Civil War.

Nothing is easier than to point out the mistakes in a military campaign after the event, but some contemporary expressions disclose the belief that, in trusting so much to Halleck and to Pope, the President was leaning on broken reeds. Welles thought that Halleck's mind was heavy and irresolute, that he did not possess originality and had little real military talent. Admiral Foote, who was under Halleck in the West, insisted that he was a military imbecile though he might make a good clerk. Montgomery Blair, who knew Pope intimately, said of him in the Cabinet meeting of September 2, He is a braggart and a liar, with some courage, perhaps, but not much capacity; and, in the meeting of September 12, he declared that Pope ought never to have been intrusted with such a command as that in front. McClellan, Blair also said, is not the man, but he is the best among the major-generals. We have officers of capacity, depend upon it, and they should be hunted out and brought forward. The Secretary of War should dig up these jewels; and one of the men Blair had in mind was William T. Sherman.[416] Let us take a look at Lee, as Longstreet saw him in these days. Instead of the well-formed, dignified soldier, mounted at the head of his troops, and exhibiting in every movement the alertness and vigor of rich manhood, we have now before us the closet-student, poring over his maps and papers, with an application so intense as sometimes to cause his thoughts to run no longer straight. Often on these occasions he would send for Longstreet and say that his ideas were working in a circle and that he needed help to find a tangent. He was now at Chantilly in the midst of one of these perplexities. He had no intention of attacking the enemy in his fortifications about Washington, for he could not invest them and could not properly supply his army. He must either fall back to a more convenient base or invade Maryland. In that State, so allied in sympathy with his own, he even hoped for a rising in his favor,

---

[415] J. Hay, I, 64.
[416] Welles's Diary, I, 104, 119, 120, 125, 126; IV.

but at all events deemed it likely that he could annoy and harass the enemy. Should success attend this movement, he proposed to enter Pennsylvania. Perhaps in the chances of war he might destroy McClellan's weakened and demoralized troops and thus conquer a peace. His soldiers were ragged and many of them were destitute of shoes. The army lacked much of the material of war, is feeble in transportation. Still, Lee wrote, we cannot afford to be idle; and he decided to cross the Potomac. Nothing occasioned him uneasiness but supplies of ammunition and subsistence. Desiring the friendly collision with another mind, he talked with Longstreet who, relating how during the Mexican War Worth's division had marched around the city of Monterey on two days' rations of roasting-ears and green oranges, thought they now could as safely trust themselves to the fields of Maryland laden with ripening corn and fruit.

On September 3, Lee began his march northward and next day wrote to his President that he should proceed with his expedition into Maryland unless you should signify your disapprobation; but before this word could have reached Richmond the Army of Northern Virginia had crossed the Potomac singing Maryland, my Maryland and had continued their rollicking march to Frederick City, which was reached on the 6th by the van led by Jackson.

We have seen that one of Lee's designs in crossing the Potomac was to give the people of Maryland an opportunity of liberating themselves; he accordingly issued an address to them declaring that the South had watched with deepest sympathy their wrongs and had seen with profound indignation their sister State deprived of every right and reduced to the condition of a conquered province. To aid you in throwing off this foreign yoke is the object of our invasion. But he soon perceived that, if the people of Maryland were oppressed, they kissed the rod of the oppressor, as they gave no signs of rising. The most serious effect of the cold welcome he received was the difficulty in procuring subsistence. Lee proposed to pay for his supplies, but all that he had to pay with was Confederate currency or certificates of indebtedness of the Confederate States, and these the farmers, millers and drovers would not take for their wheat, their flour and their cattle. The army which had defeated McClellan and Pope could not make the farmers thresh their wheat and the millers grind it, nor prevent the owners of cattle from driving them into Pennsylvania. The citizens of Frederick caring not for the custom offered them by the officers and soldiers, closed their shops.

Lee was hoping to place the Confederacy in a position to propose peace to the Northern government and people on the condition that the independence of the Southern States should be recognized: the rejection of the offer might help the Democratic party at the coming fall elections when a new House of Representatives was to be chosen and might even induce the people to declare for a termination of the conflict. He purposed to attack neither Washington nor Baltimore, but he probably aimed at Harrisburg and the destruction of the long bridge of the Pennsylvania railroad across the Susquehanna river, which, as communication by the Baltimore, and Ohio had been severed, would leave no land connection between the eastern and western States except the railroad line along the lakes. At the same time, by drawing the Union forces away from the capital, he might, if he defeated them, prevent them from falling back upon the intrenchments of Washington.

At no time during the war were Confederate prospects so bright. Kirby Smith had defeated a Union force in Kentucky, had occupied Lexington and was threatening Louisville and Cincinnati, having pushed a detachment of his army to within a few miles of Covington, one of the Kentucky suburbs of Cincinnati. Bragg with a large army had eluded Buell, and was marching northward toward Louisville in the hope that Kentucky would give her adhesion to the Confederacy. Cincinnati and Louisville were excited and alarmed.

Lee found out that he could not live upon the country and decided that he must open a line of communication through the Shenandoah valley if he would secure adequate supplies of flour. But Harpers Ferry, commanding the valley, was held by a Federal garrison although, according to the principles laid down in military books, it should have been abandoned when the Confederate army crossed the Potomac. Lee had expected and McClellan had advised its evacuation, but Halleck would not give it up. It was a lucky blunder, for Lee was forced on September 10 to divide his army, sending Jackson back into Virginia to capture Harpers Ferry, while he proceeded with Longstreet toward Hagerstown.

The state of feeling at the North now approached consternation. That Lee should threaten Washington and Baltimore, then Harrisburg and Philadelphia, while Bragg threatened Louisville and Cincinnati, was a piling up of menace that shook the nerves of the coolest men, and those who were in a position to receive the fullest information were more anxious than the general public, for it was the inner councils of the nation that were the most sorely perturbed. Although the number of the Confederates was exaggerated, their power as an invading army, by virtue of their mobility and the genius of their leaders, was rated none too high. Considering that 55,000 veteran soldiers led by Lee, Jackson and Longstreet marched out of Frederick with high spirits and confidence of victory, the alarm which spread over the North was no greater than a community so gravely imperilled might be expected to feel. In Washington the anxiety was no longer so much for the safety of the capital, which was well fortified and garrisoned, as for the danger to the cause. Stanton's uneasiness showed itself in the fear that communication with the North might be cut off. The President said he had felt badly all day (September 8).[417] He was sadly perplexed and distressed. Men in New York City were terrified and panic-stricken.[418] When Lee left Frederick and made directly for Pennsylvania, the farmers on the border sent away their women and children, then their cattle, then

---

[417] Warden, 466.
[418] Welles's Diary, I, 123, 131.

armed themselves for the protection of their homes against ̇
despatches from Governor Curtin at Harrisburg manifest conce
he called out 50,000 militia for the defence of the State. The ̇
from Philadelphia were such as one expects from a wealthy cit
The country is very desponding and much disheartened, wrote Welles. It is
evident, however, that the reinstatement of McClellan has inspired strength, vigor
and hope in the army. Officers and soldiers appear to be united in his favor and
willing to follow his lead.[419] The peril in which the country lay could be averted
only by McClellan and his army.

McClellan started his troops from Washington on September 5, he himself
following two days later. The necessity of reorganizing his depleted army and of
covering Baltimore and Washington, together with his own habitual caution and
his uncertainty as to the enemy's movements, caused him to proceed slowly. The
morale of the army is very much impaired by recent events; the spirits of the
enemy proportionately raised, wrote General Meade.[420] But fortune turned
McClellan's way. Lee's written order, disclosing the division of the Confederate
army and the exact scheme of their march, was sent to three generals, of whom
one pinned it securely in an inside pocket, another, Longstreet, memorized it and
then chewed it up; whilst the third copy was lost, found by a private soldier of the
Union Army and at once taken to McClellan, who showed his elation in his
despatch to the President, I have all the plans of the rebels and will catch them in
their own trap if my men are equal to the emergency.

McClellan acted with energy but not with the energy that Lee or Jackson would
have shown under similar circumstances. He marched his army forward, and on
September 14 won the battle of South Mountain, securing a passage over the
South Mountain range to the field of Antietam; by this victory he restored the
morale of the Union Army and gave heart to the President and people of the North.
He did not, however, relieve the Harpers Ferry garrison which fell without a
struggle.

A citizen friendly to the Confederate cause had been present when Lee's lost
order was brought to McClellan; he got an inkling of its importance to the Union
Army, made his way through the lines and after nightfall gave the information to a
cavalry officer who at once transmitted it to the Confederate commander. Having
this knowledge before daylight of September 14, Lee, who was disappointed and
concerned at the rapid advance of McClellan, left Hagerstown, disputed the passes
of South Mountain and took up a strong position behind Antietam Creek, around
the village of Sharpsburg. In the order for the division of the Confederate army,
Jackson and the different detachments acting with him for the capture of Harpers
Ferry were directed to join the main body of the army after accomplishing their

---

[419] Ibid., I, 129.
[420] General Meade, I, 309.

ject. Lee awaited them with his small force. His Maryland campaign so far was a failure. Circumstances had beaten him and only a decisive victory could bring back that prestige which was his when he marched out of Frederick. Philadelphia and Harrisburg were no longer in danger, but his own army stood in jeopardy.

The general opinion is that McClellan should have fought Lee before the Harpers Ferry detachments rejoined him, instead of waiting until September 17 when he had to contend with the whole army. On this day was fought the battle of Antietam, a day of isolated attacks and wasted efforts. Seventy-five thousand Union soldiers endeavored to overcome fifty-one thousand Confederates, Lee handling the inferior force in a manner absolutely above criticism. The Union loss in killed and wounded was 11,600, the Confederate about the same.[421]

The Victory was McClellan's as, on September 19, Lee withdrew from the field and re-crossed the Potomac into Virginia. At the time it was exasperating to think how much more McClellan might have accomplished but, as we see it now, no other result was probable as long as McClellan was McClellan was McClellan and Lee and Lee; still, to overcome Lee in any way and on any terms was matter for congratulation. His army had marched through the streets of Frederick full of pride and hope, singing The Girl I Left Behind Me; now it was a horde of disordered fugitives. And the state of feeling at the North had changed from despondency before South Mountain to positive buoyancy after Antietam.[422] The chief historical significance of the battle of Antietam is that it furnished Lincoln the victory which in his opinion must precede the issuance of his proclamation of emancipation. This, as we have seen, he had laid aside on July 22 until some military success should give support to the policy. The working of his mind in the interval of two months is an open page to us of to-day. Although he had already come to a decision, he showed the true executive acumen in not regarding the policy of striking directly at slavery as absolutely and finally determined until it had been officially promulgated. From the Cabinet meeting of July 22, when he announced his purpose, to that of September 22, when he informed his advisers that he should issue the irrevocable decree, he endeavored, in his correspondence, formal interviews and private conversation, to get all possible light to aid him in deciding when the proper moment had come to proclaim freedom for the slaves. To Conservatives he argued the Radical side of the question; I shall not surrender this game leaving any available card unplayed, he wrote to Reverdy Johnson. To Radicals he put forth the conservative view or laid stress on the necessity of proceeding with caution. He said to a committee of clergymen, who presented a memorial in favor of national emancipation, I do not want to issue a document that the whole world will see must necessarily be inoperative like the Pope's bull against the comet.

---

[421] T. L. Livermore, 92.

[422] IV, with various authorities cited and verified.

There was pressure on the President to issue a proclamation of emancipation and there was pressure against it. He talked with Conservatives and Radicals, listened to their arguments, reasoned with them and left different impressions on different minds. Much of his talk was after his characteristic manner of thinking aloud when the stimulus of contact with sympathetic or captious men afforded him an opportunity to revolve his thoughts and see the question on all sides. There was indeed much to be considered. His warrant was the war powers of the Constitution. There must be a reasonable probability that the proclamation would help the operations of his army in spite of the strong opposition among many officers of high rank to a war for the negro; that it would weaken the Confederates by fostering in the slaves their inborn desire for freedom and so making of them all the secret friends of the North; that it might further lead to the employment of blacks as soldiers. But these considerations being granted, Lincoln must then satisfy himself that public opinion at the North would sustain him in the action. He could not doubt that the cavilling support of the Radicals would turn to enthusiasm and that their influence in the work of raising men and money would be very powerful. But was the sentiment of the plain people, the mass of steady Republicans and war Democrats, ripe for an edict of freedom? Again, the possibility that the policy might alienate the border slave States which had clung to the Union was in Lincoln's mind a serious objection; but the difficulty was as great not to act as to act. On the other hand, emancipation would help him in Europe. England and France could not recognize the Southern Confederacy when the real issue between the two sections was thus unmasked. Yet there was reason to fear that an avowed war against slavery would revive the opposition of the Democrats and give them a club to use against the administration; but the President did not regard this an objection of great moment, since party opposition in the North must be expected in any event. In sum, it was only by turning the question over and over in his mind that he finally settled his doubts. He believed that a proclamation of freedom was a military necessity and that the plain people of the North would see this necessity even as he did. As the days went on, he was confirmed in the conclusion to which he had come in July and felt that public sentiment was growing in that direction.

Calling his Cabinet together on September 22, the President read from a book which Artemus Ward had sent to him the story entitled, High-Handed Outrage at Utica: In the Faul of 1856, I showed my show in Utiky, a trooly grate sitty in the State of New York.

The people gave me a cordyal recepshun. The press was loud in her prases.

1 day as I was givin a descripshun of my Beests and Snaiks in my usual flowry stile what was my skorn & disgust to see a big burly feller walk up to the cage containin my wax figgers of the Lord's Last Supper, and cease Judas Iscarrot by the feet and drag him out on the ground. He then commenced fur to pound him as hard as he cood.

'What under the son are you about?' cried I.

Sez he, 'What did you bring this pussylanermus cuss here fur?' & he hit the wax figger another tremenjis blow on the hed.

Sez I, 'You egrejus ass, that air's a wax figger a representashun of the false 'Postle.'

Sez he, 'That's all very well fur you to say, but I tell you, old man, that Judas Iscarrot can't show hisself in Utiky with impunerty by a darn site!' with which observashun he kaved in Judassis hed. The young man belonged to 1 of the first famerlies in Utiky. I sood him, and the Joory brawt in a verdick of Arson in the 3d degree.

Lincoln thought the story very funny and greatly enjoyed the reading of it, while the members of the Cabinet except Stanton laughed with him. Then he fell into a grave tone and told of the working of his thoughts since the meeting of July 22. The rebel army is now driven out of Maryland, he said, and I am going to fulfil the promise I made to myself and my God. I have got you together to hear what I have written down. I do not wish your advice about the main matter; for that I have determined for myself. He then read his proclamation of freedom: On the first day of January, 1863, all persons held as slaves within any State or designated part of a State, the people whereof shall then be in rebellion against the United States, shall be then, thenceforward and forever free. In the case of the loyal slave States he declared again for his policy of compensated emancipation and colonization of the freed negroes, and said that he should in due time recommend compensation also for the loss of their slaves to loyal citizens of the States in rebellion. All the members of the Cabinet except Blair approved the proclamation on the whole and Blair's objection was on the ground of expediency, not of principle. On the morrow, September 23, this edict was given to the country.

Chapter V

THE JUDGMENT of the people at the ballot-box was unfavorable to the President. At the October and November elections, New York, New Jersey, Pennsylvania, Ohio, Indiana, Illinois and Wisconsin, all of which except New Jersey had cast their electoral votes for Lincoln, now declared against him. The Democrats made conspicuous gains of congressmen and, if they had had a majority in the other States, would have controlled the next House of Representatives. From such a disaster, Lincoln was saved by New England, Michigan, Iowa, California, Minnesota, Kansas, Oregon and the border slave States. The Emancipation Proclamation was a contributing cause to this defeat: that the war begun for the Union was now a war for the negro was held up as a reproach; and, in contravention, the Constitution as it is and the Union as it was, became a maxim to conjure with. And there were other contributing causes.[423] But the chief source of dissatisfaction was the lack of success in the field. Elation over the victory of Antietam had been followed by disappointment at Lee's army being suffered to recross the Potomac without further loss. But if McClellan had destroyed it and if Buell had won a signal victory in Kentucky, Lincoln would certainly have received a warm approval at the polls.

The view of a Radical, who had a remarkable way of putting things, will give us an idea of the criticism Lincoln had to undergo. The result of the elections was a most serious and severe reproof to the administration, wrote Carl Schurz from the army to the President, and the administration is to blame. It placed the Army, now a great power in this Republic, into the hands of its enemies. What Republican general has ever had a fair chance in this war? Did not McClellan, Buell, Halleck and their creatures and favorites claim, obtain and absorb everything? The system should be changed. Let us be commanded by generals whose heart is in the war. Let every general who does not show himself strong enough to command success be deposed at once. If West Point cannot do the business let West Point go down.[424] Another Radical was more hopeful. The Administration, wrote Charles Eliot Norton, will not be hurt by the reaction (the defeat in the fall elections) if the war goes on prosperously.[425]

While Lee was advancing the cause of the Confederacy in Virginia, Bragg and Kirby Smith, by their operations in Kentucky, were endeavoring to retrieve the Confederate losses in the West. Smith, defeating the Union force which opposed

---

[423] See IV, 164.

[424] Schurz, Speeches, etc., I, 209, 210, 211, 217, 218.

[425] C. E. Norton, I, 258.

him, occupied Lexington, the home of Henry Clay and the centre of the Blue-grass region, the garden of the State. The loss of Lexington, telegraphed Governor Morton of Indiana to the Secretary of War, is the loss of the heart of Kentucky and leaves the road open to the Ohio river. Smith's army did indeed threaten Cincinnati and Louisville, causing great alarm. In Cincinnati martial law was declared, liquor shops were closed, all business was ordered to be suspended, every man who could fight or work was commanded to assemble at his voting place for the purpose of drill or labor. The street cars ceased to run and long lines of men were drilled in the streets, among them prominent citizens, ministers and judges, many beyond the age of forty-five. A newspaper alleged to be disloyal was suppressed. Tod, the governor of Ohio, hastened to Cincinnati and called out for military service all the loyal men of the river counties. Meanwhile Kirby Smith pushed a detachment to within a few miles of the city. Consternation reigned. Bells were rung in the early morning to summon men to arms and hundreds of laborers were put to work in the trenches. Women were asked to prepare lint and bandages for the approaching battle. The war has come home to us, was the thought of all. The alarm spread through the State. The call of the governor for all the armed minute-men met with a prompt response and thousands with double barrelled shot guns and squirrel rifles, known henceforward as Squirrel-hunters, poured into the city. But Smith did not deem himself strong enough to attack Cincinnati; awaiting a junction with Bragg, he withdrew the threatening detachment much to the city's relief.

Bragg and Buell had a race for Louisville, but the Confederate, who had the shorter line of march, got ahead and placed himself between the city and the Union Army. It is thought that if he had pressed on vigorously he might have captured Louisville. But Bragg procrastinated. Overawed perhaps by the magnitude of his enterprise, he lost heart and would not press forward. Then Buell came up in his rear. The two armies confronted each other, and, while each commander was willing to fight if he had the advantage of position, neither would risk attacking the other on his chosen ground. There ensued a contest in manoeuvring. Buell feared that defeat would result in the fall of Louisville; Bragg feared the serious crippling of his army. Both were short of supplies. Finally when reduced to three days' rations, Bragg turned aside from the direct road north leaving the way open for Buell, who moved rapidly to Louisville. Thus the Kentucky campaign of the Confederates was a failure even as was their Maryland campaign and mainly for the same reason: that in each case the denizens of the invaded territory were for the most part favorable to the Union. We must abandon the garden spot of Kentucky to its cupidity, wrote Bragg. The love of ease and fear of pecuniary loss are the fruitful sources of this evil.

Buell, having insured the safety of Louisville, started in pursuit of the enemy; they met in a severe battle at Perryville, both generals claiming the victory. Next day Bragg fell back and soon afterwards took up his march southward. Buell did not make a vigorous pursuit. He failed to overtake the Confederates and bring them to battle but he drove them out of Kentucky.

Western Radicals opposed Buell as their Eastern fellow-laborers opposed McClellan and they had at their head Oliver P. Morton of Indiana, who was the ablest and most energetic of the war governors of the Western States. The governors of the Northern States were important factors in the early conduct of the war because the national Administration was at first dependent on the State machinery for furnishing troops, and, to some extent, their equipment. Owing to the geographical position of his State and the bitterness of the Democratic opposition within its borders, Morton had more obstacles to surmount than any other governor; he threw himself into the contest with a vigor and pertinacity that could not be excelled. Wishing to see operative in military affairs the same force which he put into the administration of his State, he made no secret of his contempt for the generalship of Buell, whom he even accused in his communications with Washington of being a rebel sympathizer. Morton, though personally incorrupt, took his coadjutors from amongst the vulgar and the shifty, making his test of fitness for civil and military office a personal devotion and unscrupulous obedience to himself rather than intrinsic honesty and high character. He and Buell became enemies and he held it a duty to his country as well as an offering to his self-interest to crush the man whom he could not use.

Lincoln had been dissatisfied with Buell's slowness and, influenced by the pressure of Morton and Stanton and the manifestations of public sentiment in Ohio, Indiana and Illinois, took the general at his word when, aware of the Government's discontent, he suggested on October 16 that, if it were deemed best to change the command of the army, now would be a convenient time to do it. Buell was relieved and Rosecrans put in his place. In this decision the President erred, as the opinion expressed by Grant fourteen years after the war is doubtless sound, Buell had genius enough for the highest commands.[426] If, now, the scene be changed to the banks of the Potomac, the leading actor is McClellan, the action, much the same: the General did not take the aggressive promptly enough to satisfy the President and the people of the North. On October 1, Lincoln went to see McClellan, remained with the army three days and, as a result of the conferences and observations of his visit, directed the general, after his return to Washington, to cross the Potomac and give battle to the enemy or drive him south. Still McClellan procrastinated, aiming always at his ideal completeness of preparation. On October 13, Welles recorded, the mortifying intelligence that the Rebel cavalry rode entirely around our great and victorious Army of the Potomac, crossing the river above it and recrossing the Potomac below McClellan and our troops.[427] This will be a mortifying affair to McClellan, wrote Meade, and will do him, I fear,

---

[426] IV; Foulke, I.
[427] Welles's Diary, I, 169.

serious injury.[428] On October 22, Welles set down in his diary: It is just five weeks since the Battle of Antietam and the Army is quiet, reposing in camp. The country groans but nothing is done. McClellan's inertness makes the assertions of his opponents prophetic. He is sadly afflicted with what the President calls the 'slows.'[429] Meade had a high respect for McClellan, but held the opinion that he errs on the side of prudence and caution and that a little more rashness on his part would improve his generalship.[430]

On October 26, the army, 116,000 strong, began to cross the Potomac and six days later the last division was over. The Confederates fell back. On November 7, the Union Army was massed near Warrenton and received word from the President that he had relieved McClellan and placed Burnside in command. The Army is filled with gloom, wrote Meade next day. Burnside, it is said, wept like a child and is the most distressed man in the Army, openly says he is not fit for the position and that McClellan is the only man we have who can handle the large army collected together.[431] The pressure of the Radicals led by Stanton and Chase undoubtedly influenced the President to remove McClellan, but he ought not to have issued the order unless he and his Secretary of War knew of a general of equal ability for the command. This obligation he seemed indeed to feel. In a letter to Carl Schurz, he intimated that the war should be conducted on military knowledge, not on political affinity;[432] and he said to Wade, a leading Radical senator, who pressed him to remove McClellan: Put yourself in my place for a moment. If I relieve McClellan, whom shall I put in command? Why, said Wade, anybody; to which came the reply: Wade, anybody will do for you but not for me. I must have somebody.[433]

Meade, Reynolds and the other generals of their corps called upon McClellan, expressed their deep regret at his departure and sincerely hoped he would soon return. McClellan was very much affected, almost to tears, Meade wrote, and said that separation from this Army was the severest blow that could be inflicted upon him. The Army, Meade added, is greatly depressed. The officers and soldiers undoubtedly felt, as General Francis A. Walker afterwards wrote, that he who could move the hearts of a great army was no ordinary man; nor was he who took such heavy toll of Joseph E. Johnston and Robert E. Lee an ordinary soldier. This judgment may be supported by a comparison of the losses in battles between McClellan and the Confederates; in nearly every one of them their loss was greater than his. Inasmuch as the number of men fit for military service was greater at the North than at the South, the Confederacy must, if continuing to suffer equal losses

---

[428] General Meade, I, 320. On 318 is a partial apology for McClellan.

[429] Welles's Diary, I, 176, 177.

[430] General Meade, I, 319.

[431] *Ibid.,* I, 325.

[432] Schurz, Speeches, etc., I, 213.

[433] Nicolay, 255.

in battle, be thrust to the wall provided the Union could and would maintain the contest. While the Confederacy was young and fresh and rich and its armies were numerous, wrote Francis W. Palfrey, McClellan fought a good, wary, damaging, respectable fight against it. Grant's candid expression fourteen years after the war is of great value: In any judgment on McClellan, he asserted, there must be considered the vast and cruel responsibility which at the outset of the war devolved upon him, a young man watched by a restless people and Congress. If he did not succeed, it was because the conditions of success were so trying. If McClellan had gone into the war as Sherman, Thomas or Meade, had fought his way along and up, I have no reason to suppose that he would not have won as high distinction as any of us. Nineteen days after the removal, Lincoln confessed his mistake, writing to Carl Schurz, I certainly have been dissatisfied with the slowness of Buell and McClellan; but before I relieved them I had great fears I should not find successors to them who would do better; and I am sorry to add, that I have seen little since to relieve those fears.[434]

Even though Lincoln felt that he must yield his better judgment to political considerations he might have exercised greater discretion in the choice of McClellan's successor. A certain Radical, reflecting deeply in his quiet retreat at Cambridge, suggested the test that William T. Sherman afterwards applied [in January 1865][435] a test that should have been seriously considered by the President, his Secretary of War and Halleck. Burnside may be able to command one hundred thousand men in the field but is he?[436] Burnside had given no proof of his fitness, had refused the place twice and had told the President and Secretary of War over and over again that he was not competent to command so large an army and that McClellan was the best general for the position. Had he simply been asked to take it, he would have refused; but as the promotion came to him in the form of an order, he deemed it his duty to obey.

Ropes thought that Franklin should have been given the command.[437] It is among the possibilities that Meade or Reynolds or Humphreys may have been considered. Meade had served with distinction as a brigade commander during the seven days' fighting in Virginia; at Antietam he and his division were in the thickest of the battle and, when Hooker was wounded, he was placed by McClellan in command of the corps. During the President's visit to Antietam after the battle Meade accompanied him and McClellan on their survey of the battle-field, on which occasion McClellan highly commended the work of his subordinate.[438] If Meade created a favorable impression in the President's mind, it

---

[434] Schurz, Speeches, etc. I,220.

[435] I have commanded one hundred thousand men in battle," wrote General Sherman to the Senator on Jan. 22, 1865, "and on the march, successfully and without confusion, and that is enough for reputation." Sherman Letters 246.

[436] C. E. Norton, I,258.

[437] Ropes, II, 442.

is surprising that McClellan's comments did not lead to his being considered for the post of commander of the Army of the Potomac. He would probably have proved as capable at this juncture as he did eight months later.[439]

Burnside was a man of high character and gentle nature; he deserved a better fate but he had not a happy hour during the eighty days of his command. He soon gave evidence of the incompetence to which he had so often confessed. The removal of McClellan implied the ascendancy of the Radicals and the assumption of a vigorous offensive in the conduct of the war. Burnside lent himself to that policy, but neither he nor the President took sufficiently into account the great ability of the commander whom they opposed. By the last week of November, Burnside, with his army 113,000 strong, was on the north bank of the Rappahannock river opposite Fredericksburg where Lee had 72,000. Burnside proposed to cross the river and strike at the enemy in his chosen, strong position. No movement could have given Lee greater satisfaction. The night before the battle, Burnside was bewildered as he found himself committed to a greater undertaking than he had the ability and the nerve to carry through. Contrary to his habit of mind, he became headstrong, irritable, and rash; in a muddled sort of way, he thought out the semblance of a plan and gave a confused order for an attack by his left which, in the manner of its execution was certain to fail. His right with even greater madness he sent forward to a useless butchery. These regiments retiring slowly and in good order, many of the soldiers singing and hurrahing, ended the battle. The Confederate loss was 5309, the Union 12,653.

Next day Burnside was wild with grief. Oh, those men! those men over there! he wailed, pointing across the river where lay the dead and wounded. I am thinking of them all the time. In his frenzy he conceived a desperate plan. He thought of putting himself at the head of his old corps, the Ninth, and leading them in person in an assault on the Confederates behind the stone wall, from which they had done such deadly execution on the soldiers of his right. Generals Sumner, Franklin and a number of corps and division commanders dissuaded him from this undertaking, and, on the night of December 15, during a violent storm of rain and wind, he successfully withdrew his army to the north side of the river.

Burnside's loss in killed, wounded and missing was heavy but, with regard to the army's fighting power, this was a small matter in comparison with the loss in morale. Officers and soldiers, feeling that they had been put to a useless sacrifice, lost confidence in their commander. At a review of the Second Corps, Couch[440] and the division commanders called upon the men to give a cheer for their general; they rode along the lines waving their caps or swords but failed to elicit a single encouraging response. Some soldiers even gave vent to derisive cries. Indeed the

---

[438] General Meade, 1,317.

[439] See Meade's idea of an offensive campaign. General Meade, 1,330.

[440] Now commander of the Second Corps.

demoralization of the army was complete. Officers resigned and great numbers of men deserted.[441]

The President was exceedingly perturbed[442] and depressed at the repulse before Fredericksburg, the responsibility for which he must share with his general since he had placed him in command. Nearly three months earlier, he had confessed to his Cabinet that he was losing his hold on the Northern people, which he knew, as we all now know, was the prime requisite of success. Since then he had suffered defeat at the ballot-box and in the field; and the defeat of his army was aggravated in the popular estimation by his mistaken change of generals. Had McClellan appeared to take command once more, those soldiers who had received Burnside so coldly would have rent the air with joyful shouts.

When the full story of Fredericksburg became known, grief wrung the hearts of the Northern people at the useless sacrifice of so many noble lives. Gloom and despondency ensued, taking the religious tinge so common during our Civil War. An Ohio congressman spoke for many people in his diary, It would almost seem that God works for the rebels and keeps alive their cause. Some time earlier, Lincoln had given utterance to a similar thought, Being a humble instrument in the hands of our Heavenly Father if I find my efforts fail, I must believe that for some purpose unknown to me He wills it otherwise.[443] And thus Meade, It does seem as if Providence was against us.[444]

The remainder of Burnside's service is marked by desperate energy on his part, making plans to retrieve the disaster by recrossing the river and attacking the Confederates again, by his officers' and soldiers' distrust of him and opposition to his projected offensive movement, by the inefficiency of Stanton and Halleck and the painful perplexity of the President, who restrained his general with this order, You must not make a general movement of the Army without letting me know. Lincoln had a conference with Burnside in Washington at which Stanton and Halleck were present; but, being sadly in need of expert guidance which his Secretary and General-in-Chief were unable to supply, failed to reach a positive decision. Afterwards he gave a qualified consent to Burnside, who was still bent on crossing the river and delivering another attack. Very different now was his counsel from that which he had been accustomed to give McClellan. Be cautious, he wrote to Burnside, and do not understand that the country or government is driving you. Burnside moved his army four miles up the river. The pontoons, artillery and all other accessories were up in time, wrote Meade, and we all thought the next morning the bridges would be thrown over and we should be at it. But man proposes and God disposes. About 9 P.M. a terrific storm of wind and

---

[441] Contrariwise. General Meade, I,348.

[442] Forbes, I,343.

[443] Lincoln, C. W., II, 243.

[444] Nov. 13, General Meade, I,327.

rain set in and continued all night.[445] For the next two days it rained incessantly, rendering the roads deep with mud and any movement impossible. But the interference of the elements was most undoubtedly to the advantage of the Union side; for an attack of Burnside's demoralized soldiers on Lee's compact and devoted army would have been merely a further wanton sacrifice of men. Carl Schurz wrote from the army to the President: I am convinced the spirit of the men is systematically demoralized and the confidence in their chief systematically broken by several of the commanding-generals. I have heard generals, subordinate officers and men say they expect to be whipped anyhow, 'that all these fatigues and hardships are for nothing and that they might as well go home.' Add to this, that the immense army is closely packed together in the mud, that sickness is spreading at a frightful rate, that, in consequence of all these causes of discouragement, desertion increases every day and you will not be surprised if you see the army melt away with distressing rapidity.[446]

The disaster of Fredericksburg brought about a Cabinet crisis as it is called by the contemporary authorities in conformity with English political phraseology. But the procedure when a national calamity calls for prompt administrative action reveals a difference between the English and American constitutions. Lincoln was the head of the Administration, the Commander-in-Chief of the army, and, if anyone other than Burnside was responsible for the defeat on the Rappahannock, it was he. So declared the Democrats without reserve. The Republicans, too, in private conversation and confidential letters, expressed the same conviction, although in public they were cautious and reticent. If the American Government had been like the English, with Lincoln Prime Minister, Congress would probably have voted a want of confidence in him and he would then have resigned or appealed to the country. But as Lincoln had said on September 22, and might now have reiterated with equal force: If I was satisfied that the public confidence was more fully possessed by anyone else than by me, and knew of any constitutional way in which he might be put in my place, he should have it. I would gladly yield it to him. But though I believe that I have not so much of the confidence of the people as I had some time since, I do not know that all things considered, any other person has more; and, however that may be, there is no way in which I can have any other man put where I am. I am here. I must do the best I can and bear the responsibility of taking the course which I feel I ought to take.[447] In view of this constitutional limitation, the Republican senators in two successive caucuses, assuming to speak for a majority of their party and the nation, reverted unconsciously to earlier English precedents, and by word and deed plainly indicated their belief that the failure to prosecute the war with vigor and success

---

[445] General Meade, I,348.
[446] Schurz, Speeches, etc., 1,221.
[447] Warden, 482.

arose from the President being badly advised and dominated by his Secretary of State. A committee of nine was appointed to present their view to the President, who arranged the meeting for the evening of December 18, and who was prepared for the attack, having received Seward's resignation on the previous day: this the Secretary had sent him immediately on learning of the proceedings of the Senate caucus.

The conversation between the President and the senators was animated and free. Wade said that the conduct of the war was left mainly in the hands of men who had no sympathy with the cause, and that the Republicans of the West owed their defeat in the recent elections to the President having placed the direction of our military affairs in the hands of bitter and malignant Democrats (meaning McClellan, Buell and Halleck). Fessenden said that the Senate had entire confidence in the patriotism and integrity of the President, but that Republican senators were inclined to believe that the Secretary of State was not in accord with the majority of the Cabinet and exerted an injurious influence upon the conduct of the war. The officers of the regular army, largely pro-slavery men and strongly imbued with the Southern feeling, he continued, had little sympathy with the Republican party. It was singularly unfortunate that almost every officer known as an anti-slavery man had been disgraced; he instanced Frémont, Hunter, Mitchell and others. Sumner, Grimes and other senators expressed their lack of confidence in Seward.[448]

Next day the President told his Cabinet, who were all present except the Secretary of State, that the point and pith of the senators' complaint was of Seward; they charged him if not with infidelity, with indifference, with want of earnestness in the war, with want of sympathy with the country and especially with a too great ascendancy and control of the President and measures of administration.[449] In more homely phrase he described the senators' attitude: While they seemed to believe in my honesty, they also appeared to think that when I had in me any good purpose or intention Seward contrived to suck it out of me unperceived.[450] Finally the President requested the members of his Cabinet to meet the senatorial committee that evening (December 19) at the White House. The senators came in response to his summons to continue the conference of the previous evening, although somewhat surprised at having to treat with the members of the Cabinet (except Seward) as well as with the President. He opened the meeting with a defence of the Cabinet and the Administration. Secretary Chase endorsed the President's statement fully and entirely.[451] This was a surprise to the Radical senators who regarded Chase as their leader and had been influenced by

---

[448] Fessenden, 1,240.
[449] Welles's Diary, 1,195.
[450] N. & H., VI, 265.
[451] Welles's Diary, I, 196.

his strictures of the President and the Secretary of State. But Chase when thus brought to bay found himself swayed by esprit de corps and by the thought that he and Seward had for many years wrought together in the anti-slavery cause; he therefore stood up manfully for the Secretary of State and for the rest of his associates. Grimes, Sumner and Trumbull were pointed, emphatic and unequivocal in their opposition to Seward, whose zeal and sincerity in this conflict they doubted; each was unrelenting and unforgiving. The President managed his own case, speaking freely and showed great tact, shrewdness and ability. He considered it most desirous to conciliate the senators with respectful deference whatever may have been his opinion of their interference.[452] Fessenden objected to discussing the merits or demerits of a member of the Cabinet in the presence of his associates, whereupon the members of the Cabinet withdrew; though it was nearly midnight, Fessenden and some of the senators remained. Fessenden said to the President: You have asked my opinion upon Mr. Seward's removal. There is a current rumor that he has already resigned. If so, our opinions are of no consequence on that point. The President admitted that Seward had tendered his resignation, but added that he had not yet accepted it. Then, sir, said Fessenden, the question seems to be whether Mr. Seward shall be requested to withdraw his resignation. Yes, from Lincoln. I feel bound to say, then replied the Senator, that as Mr. Seward has seen fit to resign, I should advise that his resignation be accepted. It was 1 A.M. when the senators left the White House.[453]

On this Saturday morning, December 20, the President sent for Chase, telling him on his arrival, This matter is giving me great trouble. Chase replied that painfully affected by the meeting last evening he had prepared his resignation of the office of Secretary of the Treasury. 'Where is it?' said the President quickly, his eye lighting up in a moment. 'I brought it with me,' said Chase, taking the paper from his pocket. 'I wrote it this morning.' 'Let me have it,' said the President, reaching his long arm and fingers toward Chase, who held on seemingly reluctant to part with the letter which was sealed and which he apparently hesitated to surrender. The President was eager took and hastily opened the letter. 'This,' said he with a triumphal laugh, 'cuts the Gordian knot. I can dispose of the subject now without difficulty; I see my way clear.'[454] Then Stanton, who was in the President's office with Chase, offered his resignation. You may go to your Department, Lincoln replied, I don't want yours. This, holding out Chase's letter, is all I want; this relieves me; my way is clear; the trouble is ended; I will detain neither of you longer.[455] Soon after Chase, Stanton and Welles (who was also present at the interview) had left, Lincoln, still holding Chase's letter in his hand

---

[452] *Ibid.,* I, 197.

[453] Fessenden, I, 247.

[454] Welles's Diary, I, 201.

[455] *Ibid.,*

said to Senator Harris who had called, Now, I can ride; I have got a pumpkin in each end of my bag.[456]

Lincoln's elation at having in his hands the resignation of the chief of the Radicals at the same time as that of the chief Conservative is easy to understand. The Radical Senators who had attacked Seward would have viewed with great displeasure the retirement of Chase, but they it was who had brought it to pass that both must go or both remain. If I had yielded to that storm, said Lincoln nearly a year later, and dismissed Seward, the thing would all have slumped over one way and we should have been left with a scanty handful of supporters. When Chase sent in his resignation, I saw that the game was in my own hands and I put it through.[457] He declined both resignations and asked both men to resume the duties of their Departments, which Seward did cheerfully and Chase reluctantly. The Cabinet crisis was over.[458]

Lincoln had displayed rare political sagacity in retaining in the service of the State the men who could best serve it, notwithstanding the lack of harmony in the Cabinet and the knowledge Congress had of it. His decision that the public interest does not admit of the retirement of the State and Treasury secretaries is justified by a study of the existing crisis in the light of subsequent events. In the misfortune and dejection which had fallen upon the country, no voice could be slighted that would be raised for the continued prosecution of the war and, since Seward and Chase represented the diverse opinions of two large classes of men who were at least in concord on the one all-important policy, it was desirable that they should remain in the Cabinet. The loss of either or both of them would have meant a subtraction from the popular support of the Administration that could in no other way be made good.

There were also other reasons why the President did not wish to part with them. Since April, 1861, Seward had rendered him a loyal support; sinking his ambition for the Presidency, he had come to appreciate Lincoln's ability and to acknowledge in him the head of the Government in reality as in name. He had been an efficient minister. Although slavery in the Confederacy was a stumbling-block in the way of its recognition by England and France, and whilst the influence of Lincoln, Adams and Sumner in foreign relations was of great weight, much credit is still due the Secretary of State for managing the affairs of his Department in such a way as to avert the interference of Europe in our struggle.

Chase was supreme in his own Department and wrote the financial part of the President's message of December 1, 1862. Lincoln had had no business training and, like many lawyers had little or no conception of the country's resources and

---

[456] N. & H., VI, 271.

[457] J. Hay, I, 114.

[458] Welles's Diary, I; Fessenden, I; N. & H., VI; IV; J. Hay, I; Bancroft, II; Hart's Chase; Forbes, I.

sustainable outlay. Having no taste for the subject, he did not try to grasp the principles of finance, and being obliged to master, as a layman may, the arts of war and diplomacy, he was wise to attempt no more. But Lincoln though unversed in finance had a first-rate knowledge of men, and this it was that led him to retain as his Secretary of the Treasury one whose inflexible honesty and receptive mind justify the popular estimate of him as a strong finance minister. That the war had gone on for nearly two years with an immense expenditure of money, and that the Government could still buy all it needed of food and munitions of war and could pay its soldiers, was due primarily to the patriotism and devotion of the Northern people, but honor should also be given to the manager of the country's finances.

The Secretary of the Treasury was probably not a pleasant man at the council board. Moreover, his temperament differed so essentially from the President's that sympathetic relations between the two men were impossible. Chase was handsome, of commanding presence, careful in dress, courtly in manner. A graduate of Dartmouth, he had a fair knowledge of Latin and Greek and the reverence for them of an educated lawyer. He was widely read, and even in his busy life as member of the Cabinet, found his recreation in improving his acquaintance with good English and French literature. He cared neither for cards nor for the theatre. A serious, thoughtful man in every walk of life, he brought to the business of his Department a well thought-out method.

Lincoln, plain and ungainly, gave no thought to the graces of life and lacked the accomplishments of a gentleman, as no one knew better than himself. He had no system in the disposition of his time or in the preparation of his work. During his term of office he confined his reading of books mainly to military treatises and to works which guided him in the solution of questions of constitutional and international law, although he occasionally snatched an hour to devote to his beloved Shakespeare and revealed in his state papers an undiminished knowledge of the Bible. He found recreation in the theatre and has left on record his pleasure at Hackett's impersonation of Falstaff. As Hamlet had a peculiar charm for him, Edwin Booth's presentation of the rôle must have afforded him a rare delight. Possessed of a keen sense of humor he was a capital storyteller and in this capacity must often have grated on the serious temper of his finance minister who had no humor in him and but little knowledge of men.

Chase's private correspondence reveals him to our surprise in friendly communication with many cheap persons, mainly, it is true, political followers, on whose help he counted for obtaining the much-desired Presidency. This ambition, or rather the unseemly manifestations of it, became the greatest hindrance to his usefulness. His opinion of Lincoln's parts was not high, and could hardly have remained unperceived by the President, who in return made no attempt to conceal his judgment that Chase was a very able man.

At this time the Secretary was by no means alone in his estimate of the President. In the minds of many senators and representatives existed a distrust of his ability and force of character, which had been created in those who met him frequently by his lack of dignity, his grotesque expression and manner and his jocular utterances when others were depressed. These eccentricities, when viewed in the damning light of military failure, could not but produce in certain quarters a painful impression. Of the interview between Lincoln, the Cabinet and the senators during the Cabinet crisis, Fessenden wrote sarcastically, The President related several anecdotes, most of which I had heard before.[459] While his popularity was waning, he was stronger with the country than with the men at Washington. The people did not come in personal contact with him, and judged him by his formal state papers and his acts. Posterity, having seen his ultimate success, judges him on the same ground and looks with admiration on the patience and determination with which he bore his burden during this gloomy winter. The hand that draws the grotesque traits of Lincoln may disappoint the hero-worshipper, but veracity in the narrative demands the inclusion of this touch which helps to explain the words of disparagement so freely applied to him, and serves as a justification for those who could not in the winter of 1862/63 see with the eyes of to-day. Had his other qualities been enhanced by Washington's dignity of manner, not so many had been deceived; but as it was we cannot wonder that his contemporaries failed to appreciate his greatness. Since his early environment in fostering his essential capabilities had not bestowed on him the external characteristics usually attributed to transcendent leaders of men, it was not suspected that, despite his lowly beginning, he had developed into a man of extraordinary mental power.

Seward, with his amiable and genial manners, was an agreeable man in council. Fertile in suggestion, he must, in spite of his personal failings, have been exceedingly helpful to Lincoln, whose slow-working mind was undoubtedly often assisted to a decision by the various expedients which his Secretary of State put before him; for it is frequently easier for an executive to choose one out of several courses than to invent a policy. The members of the Cabinet who filled the public eye were Seward, Chase and Stanton and they demand a proportionate attention from the historian. It was either on Seward or Stanton that the President leaned the most; and the weight of evidence, confirmed by the fact of his urbanity, points to the Secretary of State as his favorite counsellor.

Though Lincoln made up his mind slowly, once he had come to a decision, he was thenceforth inflexible. By gradual steps he had evolved the policy of emancipation and he was determined to stick to it in spite of the defeat of his party at the ballot-box and of his principal army in the field during the hundred days that intervened between the preliminary proclamation of September 22 and the necessary complement of January 1, 1863. Although the form of the preliminary proclamation implied that some of the Confederates or all might lay down their arms to avoid the loss of their slaves, no such outcome was seriously regarded as

---

[459] Fessenden, I, 245.

possible. Doubt no longer existed that a united people in the South were earnest in their desire to secure their independence and that, if the Proclamation had affected them at all, it had only stiffened them in their resistance by adding force to the argument that the war of the North was a crusade against their social institutions. Regarding the Proclamation as a fit and necessary war measure, the President wrote on January 1, 1863, I do order and declare that all persons held as slaves in the States or parts of States resisting the United States Government are, and henceforward shall be, free. Upon this act, sincerely believed to be an act of justice, warranted by the Constitution upon military necessity, I invoke the considerate judgment of mankind and the gracious favor of Almighty God.

Lincoln had the American reverence for the Constitution and the laws and he could find no authority for the Proclamation in the letter of the Constitution or in any statute; but he thought out what were satisfying reasons to his own mind. My oath to preserve the Constitution to the best of my ability, he wrote afterwards, imposed upon me the duty of preserving, by every indispensable means, that government that nation, of which that Constitution was the organic law. I felt that measures otherwise unconstitutional might become lawful by becoming indispensable to the preservation of the Constitution through the preservation of the nation. I could not feel that to the best of my ability, I had even tried to preserve the Constitution, if, to save slavery or any minor matter, I should permit the wreck of government, country and Constitution all together. I think the Constitution invests its Commander-in-Chief with the law of war in time of war. The most that can be said if so much is that slaves are property. Is there has there ever been any question that by law of war, property, both of enemies and friends, may be taken when needed? The Proclamation, making clear as it did, the real issue of the war, was of incontestable value in turning English sentiment into a favorable channel. It already had the approval of the House of Representatives and, when enforced by victories in the field, received the support of the majority of the Northern people.

In addition to military emancipation, the President purposed giving the slaves their freedom in a strictly legal manner and insuring the compensation of their owners by the Federal Government. In his annual message to Congress of December 1, 1862, he took as his text the sound and now familiar proposition that Without slavery the rebellion [as he and the North called the Civil War] could never have existed; without slavery it could not continue and showed in his argument a grasp of the subject which, in the light of our subsequent experience, has proved him a consummate statesman. He pleaded for gradual emancipation, appointing January 1, 1900 as the time when it should be completed to spare both races from the evils of sudden derangement. It is to be regretted that this prophetic appeal was not re-enforced by victories in the field such as were wont to point the utterances of Cæsar and Napoleon. As matters stood, distrust of Lincoln pervaded both the Senate and the House, and for the moment his personal prestige amongst the people had paled because his armies had made no headway; so it was hardly surprising that his policy of gradual and compensated emancipation failed to receive the approval of either Congress or the country. Nevertheless he had been happy in seizing the right moment for issuing his Proclamation of Emancipation, as from Antietam in September, 1862 to Gettysburg in July, 1863 the North gained no real victory and her Army of the Potomac suffered two crushing defeats.[460]

A glimmer of hope from the West lightened the intense gloom following the disaster at Fredericksburg. Influenced undoubtedly by the President's desire for a victory, and deeming the conditions auspicious, Rosecrans moved out of Nashville the day after Christmas with the intention of attacking the Confederates. For a number of days he advanced, skirmishing as he went, and finally took up a position within three miles of Murfreesborough, Tennessee, where Bragg's army had gone into winter quarters. On the last day of the year he determined to make the attack; but Bragg had resolved to take the offensive at the same time, and obtained the advantage of the initial onset. The bloody battle of Stone's River [or Murfreesborough] ensued, wherein 41,000 Union troops were pitted against 34,000 Confederates.[461] The Confederates won the day, but Rosecrans stubbornly maintained his ground. On January 2, 1863, Bragg again attacked the Union Army and met with repulse. On the night of the following day, his troops being somewhat demoralized, he retreated from Murfreesborough. This gave Rosecrans a chance, of which he at once availed himself, to claim the victory in the campaign. The President telegraphed to him God bless you. Halleck called it one of the most brilliant successes of the war. Throughout the North it was proclaimed a victory. At last, ran the sentiment of the people, our great general has appeared. The loss on both sides was heavy[462] and both armies were so crippled that a long time was required to repair the damage. Although the casualties of Rosecrans were the larger, the superior resources of the North inclined the balance against the Confederates, who sustained moreover the loss in morale. In 1865, however, Grant declared that Murfreesborough was no victory for the North;[463] and William T. Sherman wrote at the time that Rosecrans's victory at Murfreesborough is dearly bought.[464]

If the student confines himself to the literature of this campaign alone, he will feel that the extensive claims of a victory made by the President and the people of the North were a clutching at straws; but if he looks ahead he will see that they were wiser than they knew, for he will then comprehend that to hold Tennessee Bragg needed a decisive success, and that his failure and the serious crippling of

---

[460] IV; Lect.

[461] T. L. Livermore, 97.

[462] Union 12,906, Confederate 11,739. T. L. Livermore, 97.

[463] N. & H., X, 281.

[464] Sherman Letters, 182.

his army opened the way for the Union advance to Chattanooga the following summer. The campaigns of Perryville and Stone's River were moreover a favorable augury to the cause of the North, inasmuch as they showed that in the Army of the West an education of generals was going on, that native military talent was in the process of development. George H. Thomas, a Virginian of the same good stuff as Washington and Robert E. Lee, was serving as second in command to Buell and to Rosecrans; he joined to ability in his profession and a scrupulous loyalty to his superiors, a conviction of the justice of the cause which, contrary to the example of his State, he had espoused. Although at first he had not unreasonably believed that injustice had been done him in that he was not made commander of the Army of the Cumberland at the time of Buell's displacement, he gave a magnanimous and efficient support to Rosecrans, who could say of him that he was as wise in council as he was brave in battle. Philip H. Sheridan had distinguished himself at Perryville and now did gallant work at Stone's River.

The immediate results of the campaign were not sufficiently important to lift Congress and the country for more than a brief period out of the dejection into which they had fallen. Sumner, although he realized the peril, had not lost heart. These are dark hours, he wrote to Lieber. There are senators full of despair, not I. But I fear that our army is everywhere in a bad way. Greeley in his journal advocated the mediation of a European power between the North and the South, and to further this end he held private interviews and opened a correspondence with Mercier, the French Minister, intimating that the people would welcome any foreign mediation which should look to a termination of the war. I mean to carry out this policy, he said to Raymond, and bring the war to a close. You'll see that I'll drive Lincoln into it. An offer of mediation between the two sections from Napoleon, the Emperor of the French, was communicated on February 3, 1863 to the Secretary of State. It was declined at once by the President, the offer and response being published at the same time. Despite the rumors which had somehow prepared the public mind for this step, the actual fact that a powerful nation impelled by motives of material interest was eager to interfere in the struggle startled the people and deepened the gloom.

The President tells me, wrote Sumner to Lieber, that he now fears 'the fire in the rear,' meaning the Democracy especially at the Northwest more than our military chances. Governor Morton of Indiana telegraphed to the Secretary of War, I am advised that it is contemplated when the Legislature meets in this State to pass a joint resolution acknowledging the Southern Confederacy, and urging the States of the Northwest to dissolve all constitutional relations with the New England States. The same thing is on foot in Illinois. The legislatures of these States were Democratic, having been chosen the previous autumn during the conservative reaction. Morton's grave apprehensions were far from being realized, but his legislature quarreled with him and refused its support to his energetic measures for carrying on the war. The Republican members took his part, and the wrangle became so bitter that finally the legislature adjourned without making the necessary appropriations for the maintenance of the State government during the next two years. In Illinois, resolutions praying for an armistice and recommending a convention of all the States to agree upon some adjustment of the trouble between them, passed the House, but failed to obtain consideration in the Senate. This legislature likewise fell out with its Republican governor.

The Congress which sat from December 1, 1862 to March 4, 1863 gave the President the control of the sword and the purse of the nation. Discouragement over the defeats in the field and a general feeling of weariness over the prolongation of the war combined, with the improved condition of business which opened many avenues of lucrative employment, to bring volunteering practically to an end. To fill the armies some general measure of compulsion was necessary, for the efforts at drafting by the States had not proved satisfactory. The Conscription Act, approved March 3, operated directly on the people of the nation instead of through the medium of the States, which had previously employed their own machinery for raising troops. The country was divided into enrolment districts, corresponding in general to the congressional districts of the different States, each of which was in charge of a provost-marshal. At the head of these officers was a provost-marshal-general, whose office in Washington formed a separate bureau of the War Department. All men fit for military duty were to be enrolled and, as necessity arose, were to be drafted for the service. Anyone drafted could furnish a substitute or pay three hundred dollars to the Government as an exemption.

Financial legislation was equally drastic. One year before the country had been started on the road of irredeemable legal-tender paper: there was now no turning back. The maw of our voracious treasury was again clamoring to be filled. Spaulding, who spoke for the Committee of Ways and Means, said in the House: Legal-tender notes are not plenty among the people; they are continually asking for more. Why then should we be alarmed at a further issue of legal-tender notes. It is much better to stimulate, make money plenty, make it easy for people to pay their taxes and easy for Government to make loans. Spaulding made it clear to the House that in the next eighteen months $1,000,000,000 must be borrowed. The expenses of the Government were $2,500,000 a day, Sundays included. The receipts from customs taxes and other sources would not probably exceed $600,000, leaving the balance, a daily deficit of $1,900,000, to be met by borrowing of some kind. Congress, in what is known as the nine hundred million dollar loan act, authorized more bonds, more Treasury notes, bearing interest, which might be made a legal tender for their face value, more non-interest bearing United States legal-tender notes and a large amount of fractional currency to replace the existing imperfect substitutes issued for silver change, silver having long since disappeared from circulation. This act gave large discretionary powers to the Secretary of the Treasury. Before the constitutional meeting of the next

Congress, he might issue of the different forms of paper obligations authorized a total of $900,000,000.

Congress, in pursuance of the recommendation of the President and Secretary of the Treasury, also passed at this session an act creating National Banks, which was the nucleus of our present system.

It is easier to criticise the legislative body of a democracy than to praise it. Especially is this true in as large a country as our own, with interests apparently so diverse; for even in 1863 when the West and the East were knit together in devotion to the common purpose of the war, the two sections were nevertheless at times involved in disagreement. Under the circumstances, the broadest conception of, and most loyal adherence to, the policy of give and take which is the essence of all legislative theory would have failed to satisfy the ideal of any individual or party, yet as a whole the work of the Republican majority of Congress at this session deserves high commendation. They realized that only by victories in the field could the prevailing gloom be dispelled and confidence revived and that they must show the country an agreement among themselves upon such measures as might contribute to military success. Their distrust of the President's ministers did not cease with the termination of the so-called Cabinet crisis of December. Thaddeus Stevens thought at one time of moving in a Republican caucus of the House a resolution of want of confidence in the Cabinet. The Radicals were far from being reconciled to the retention of Seward, and continued their efforts to have him removed, but, in spite of the President's firm resolve to keep him, they voted the Administration ample powers. Most of the Republicans in Congress were of the mind of John Sherman, whose views inclined for the most part to moderation. I cannot respect some of the constituted authorities, he wrote to his brother the general, yet I will cordially support and aid them while they are authorized to administer the Government. Military success could be obtained only by giving the President extraordinary powers, and both senators and representatives perceived the inevitable and submitted to it. With all its faults and errors, wrote Fessenden, this has been a great self-sacrificing Congress. We have assumed terrible responsibilities, placed powers in the hands of the government possessed by none other on earth save a despotism. Future times will comprehend our motives and all we have done and suffered.[465]

The country's response to the work of Congress was heard in enthusiastic war or Union meetings held in many cities and towns of different States. Those in New York were characteristic. Distinguished and popular Democrats addressed a magnificent uprising of the people at Cooper Institute. Loyal National Leagues or Union Leagues were formed, of which the test for membership was a brief emphatic pledge that was subscribed to by many thousands. These Leagues held one large meeting at the Academy of Music, another at Cooper Institute, and still

---

[465] Fessenden, I, 254.

another to celebrate the anniversary of the firing on Fort Sumter. To this period belongs the organization of the Union League Clubs of Philadelphia and New York and the Union Club of Boston, the object of their formation being distinctly patriotic. But nothing will do for the country, wrote Norton to Curtis neither Clubs nor Conscription Bills nor Banking Bills nothing will do us much good but victories. If we take Charleston and Vicksburg we conquer but if not?[466] Nevertheless, a feeling of comparative cheerfulness began to manifest itself, owing to the energy with which Congress had buckled to the task of rescuing the country from the depression which followed Fredericksburg, to the excellent reorganization of the Army of the Potomac and to the known confidence of the President and his Cabinet in ultimate success.

When Congress had assembled in December, the nation's finances were at a low ebb. Many of the soldiers had not been paid for five months, and to them all the paymaster was at least three months in arrears, so that by January 7, 1863, the amount due the army and navy had probably reached the sum of sixty millions. The bonds of the government were not selling. Now all was changed. The Secretary of the Treasury had devised a plan for offering the five-twenty bonds to popular subscription through the employment of a competent and energetic general agent, who, by a system of sub-agencies, wide advertising, and other business methods, appealed to the mingled motives of patriotism and self-interest and induced the people to lend large sums of money to the Government. An impetus was given to this process by the general character of the financial legislation of Congress, and in particular by the clause in the nine hundred million dollar loan act which limited to July 1 the privilege of exchanging legal-tender notes for five-twenty bonds. Immediately after the adjournment of Congress the confidence of the people began to show itself through the purchase of these securities. By the end of March, Chase told Sumner that he was satisfied with the condition of the finances, and ere three more months had passed, he could see that his popular loan was an assured success. The subscriptions averaged over three million dollars a day. The Germans were likewise buying our bonds. On April 26, Sumner wrote to the Duchess of Argyll: The Secretary of War told me yesterday that our rolls showed eight hundred thousand men under arms all of them paid to February 28, better clothed and better fed than any soldiers ever before. Besides our army, we have a credit which is adequate to all our needs. On January 1, 1863, Burnside told the President that neither Stanton nor Halleck had the confidence of the officers and soldiers and in effect urged their removal, saying at the same time that he himself ought to retire to private life. Four days afterward by letter from his headquarters, he offered his resignation as Major-General, to which the President replied, I do not yet see how I could profit by changing the command of the Army of the Potomac.

---

[466] C. E. Norton, I, 261.

Shortly after midnight of January 23, Burnside had an interview with the President, in which he asked him to approve an order dismissing Hooker from the military service of the United States on account of having been guilty of unjust and unnecessary criticisms of the action of his superior officers and of having made reports and statements which were calculated to create incorrect impressions and in short being a man unfit to hold an important commission during a crisis like the present. The order further punished by dismissal three brigadier-generals and relieved from duty Generals Franklin, W. F. Smith and a number of others. Approve this order, said Burnside, or accept my resignation as major-general. On the morning of January 25, the President summoned Stanton and Halleck to the White House and told them that he had decided to relieve Burnside and place Hooker in command of the Army of the Potomac. He asked no advice from either and none was offered.[467]

Previously Lincoln had talked more than once with members of his Cabinet concerning Hooker. Who can take command of this Army? he asked Welles after the second Battle of Bull Run. Who is there among all these generals? Without much consideration Welles replied, Hooker. The President looked approving, but said, I think as much as you or any other man of Hooker but I fear he gets excited. Blair remarked, He is too great a friend of John Barleycorn; whereupon Welles: If his habits are bad, if he ever permits himself to get intoxicated, he ought not to be trusted with such a command. After the appointment, Welles wrote in his Diary, I am surprised at his selection.

In his discouragement and growing irritability, Lincoln permitted himself to be guided by public sentiment which had been so serviceable in political affairs; he felt that a vote of the rank and file of the army and of the Northern people would have plainly indicated, Fighting Joe Hooker. It is true, as Lincoln wrote in a private letter, that in considering military merit the world has abundant evidence that I disregard politics;[468] and up to this time and afterwards, he showed his respect for the West Point education, although he did not rate it as high as we do at the present day. But in forming our opinion we have behind us the total experience of the Civil War and the records of both sides which attest by severe and thorough practice the in-estimable value of the training of our Military Academy.

Although Hooker was a graduate of West Point and had proved an excellent division and corps commander, his appointment to the chief command should never have been considered. Halleck was opposed to it and Stanton, it is said, backed him in his opposition.[469] Most of the old regular officers were decided in

---

[467] O. R., XXI, 941, 944, 954, 998, 1004, 1009; C. W., Pt. 1, 718. Burnside was persuaded to withdraw his resignation and the order therefore ran that he was relieved at his own request from the command of the Army of the Potomac.

[468] Lincoln, C. W., II, 252.

[469] C. W., 1865, I, 175; B. & L., III, 239.

their hostility to him. Meade, whose opinion was more favorable than that of his associates, thought Hooker a very good soldier and a capital officer to command an army corps, but doubted his qualifications to command a large army.[470]

All the objections to Hooker were known in Washington, and it is surprising that they were not formulated to the President, inasmuch as there were two generals in the Army of the Potomac, John F. Reynolds and George G. Meade, either of whom in respect of character, training and ability was properly qualified for the command. After Fredericksburg it was evident that a change should be made and these generals were both talked of for the place. Reynolds did not want the command and probably would not have accepted it, but if he, Couch and Sedgwick[471] had been called in council by the President or by Stanton and Halleck (an easy matter, as they were only a few hours' journey from Washington), they would unanimously have recommended Meade and, though his seniors,[472] would have offered cheerfully to serve under his command. Meade's correspondence with his wife and son[473] is crowning evidence that he would have been an admirable selection. Devotion to his wife and children and religious faith were the distinguishing marks of his private character; and his earnest thought on the conditions of the conflict remind one of the commonsense view of Lincoln and of Grant. This war will never be terminated, he wrote, until one side or the other has been well whipped and this result cannot be brought about except by fighting. He was popularly known as a fighting general and stood well with the officers of the army. On the other hand, Wade, Chandler and Covode, Radical members of the Committee on the Conduct of the War, treated him with great distinction, for he was sound according to the Radical touchstone by virtue of his willingness to command negro troops.[474] Meade could have been better known in Washington in January, 1863, than we can now know him up to that time through his private correspondence; hence it must be concluded that Hooker's appointment was an instance of the popular voice overbearing expert opinion. A superior intellect and long and hard study are required to make an efficient commander, wrote William R. Livermore. Doubt could not exist on January 1, 1863, that, as tried by this standard, Meade's worth was much greater than Hooker's.

When Hooker took command, the Army of the Potomac was depressed to a degree that seemed almost hopeless. Desertions were of alarming frequency.[475]

---

[470] General Meade, I, 318, 351.

[471] Sedgwick commanded the 9th corps at the time of Burnside's resignation. Hooker took command on Jan. 26, 1863, and Sedgwick was transferred to the 6th Corps (with which his name is usually associated) on Feb. 5.

[472] Sedgwick and Couch having been made major-generals on July 4, 1862 outranked Meade. Reynolds and Meade became major-generals on Nov. 29, 1862; but Reynolds is placed just ahead of Meade in the rank list.

[473] Published in 1913.

[474] General Meade, I, 340, 347, 349, 356, 365.

The new general went energetically to work to alter this condition and made his eminent talent for organization felt throughout the army. The sullen gloom of the camps soon disappeared, wrote Schurz, and a new spirit of pride and hope began to pervade the ranks.[476] The morale of our Army is better than it ever was, wrote Meade to his wife on March 30, so you may look out for tough fighting next time.[477] Early in April the President looking careworn and exhausted paid Hooker a visit, reviewed the whole army and said that he was highly delighted with all that he had seen.[478] The people of the North, too, gained some comprehension of the general's work and its results and showed the resiliency of their temper by taking fresh hope and talking of success to come.

Soon after the President's visit, Hooker considered his army in condition to take the offensive. He had been somewhat hurried in his preparations because the term of service of 23,000 nine months' and two years' men was soon to expire. Encamped on the north bank of the Rappahannock River, he had 130,000 troops to oppose Lee's 60,000, who were at Fredericksburg: the Army of Northern Virginia had been weakened by the detachment of Longstreet and part of his corps. Hooker ordered his cavalry to advance towards Richmond for the purpose of severing the Confederate communications, but owing to heavy rains and high water in the river these troops were delayed and proved of no assistance to him in his operations. On April 27, unable to wait longer for them to perform their part, he set in motion three corps who crossed the Rappahannock about twenty-seven miles above Fredericksburg, then forded the Rapidan and marched to Chancellorsville on the south side of these rivers. The Army was in superb condition and animated by the highest spirits, wrote Carl Schurz. Officers and men seemed to feel instinctively that they were engaged in an offensive movement promising great results. There was no end to the singing and merry laughter relieving the fatigue of the march.[479] In order to mask the main movement, General John Sedgwick with the Sixth Corps forced the passage of the Rappahannock a short distance below Fredericksburg. On April 30, Couch with the Second Corps crossed the river at the United States ford, marching to Chancellorsville, and next day Sickles with the Third Corps followed. By the morning of May 1, Hooker, had assembled five corps under his immediate command.[480] We are across the river and have out-manoeuvred the enemy, wrote Meade to his wife, but we are not yet out of the woods.[481] Hooker, however, was full of confidence[482] and issued a boastful order.

---

[475] Letterman, 101.

[476] Schurz, Reminiscences, II, 403.

[477] General Meade, I, 362.

[478] General Meade, I, 364.

[479] Schurz, Reminiscences, II, 408.

[480] Sedgwick with the Sixth Corps was about 11 1/2 miles away. Reynolds with the First Corps about 13, but the enemy was between. Their marching distance was probably 23 miles.

The operations of the last three days, he said, have determined that our enemy must either ingloriously fly or come out from behind his defences and give us battle on our own ground, where certain destruction awaits him. Hooker had said to the President, I have under my command the finest army on the planet[483]; and on May 1 he began to use it by attacking the Confederates, of whose strength he had a pretty correct idea.[484]

Lee was nowise perturbed at the successful crossing of the Rappahannock by the Union troops, although he wished that he had Longstreet and his two divisions back; he had Jackson, however, and the two wrought together in perfect accord. They feared Hooker no more than they had feared McClellan and, if they knew of his boastful order, must have felt that they had a braggart to deal with like Pope. The story of May 1 is a simple one. Hooker attacked. Lee made a counter-attack. Hooker lost his nerve and ordered his men to fall back. Meade wrote of his own corps, Just as we reached the enemy we were recalled. Had Hooker rested on his first order for an advance and left it to be carried out by his corps and division commanders, a sharp battle would have ensued, of which the result would of course have been dubious; but the army would not have been demoralized by having to retreat so soon after they had taken the offensive, and Hooker would not have lost the confidence of his officers by the vacillation exhibited in his actual orders of that day. Couch saw him soon after the retreat and got the impression that he was a whipped man.

The story of May 2 is that of a contest between Lee's and Hooker's brains; between Jackson's and Howard's execution. In the course of this History, we have gained some acquaintance with the two Confederates; but if more is needed, William R. Livermore's technical analysis of their qualities and Hooker's[485] should enable us to realize that the result could have been no other than the one we have actually to record. History seemed to be repeating itself, for here was another general who knew not how to handle a hundred thousand and more men, who made furthermore an unfortunate choice for the commander of a corps (the Eleventh) that was to be terribly exposed in the ensuing action.[486] Howard did not impress Schurz who commanded a division under him as an intellectually strong man. A certain looseness of mental operations, a marked uncertainty in forming definite conclusions became evident in his conversation.[487]

After his retreat Hooker decided to remain on the defensive. He expected that Lee would make a frontal attack on his centre, to repel which he had made

---

[481] April 30. General Meade, I, 370.

[482] J. Bigelow Jr., 130, 236, 237. General Meade, I, 369.

[483] J. Bigelow, Jr., 130.

[484] *Ibid.,* 112.

[485] W. R. Livermore, I, 114, 178.

[486] J. Bigelow, Jr., 41.

[487] Schurz, Reminiscences, II, 405.

adequate preparation. But Lee was not the man to do what his enemy desired. He saw that such an attack would be attended with great difficulty and loss in view of the strength of Hooker's position and superiority of numbers.[488] Indeed, if a study of efficiency is desired, it may be found in the Confederate camp. Lee and Jackson considered an attack on Sedgwick in the plain of Fredericksburg but abandoned this as impracticable.[489] But they were bent on an attack at some point, for they had no idea of an inglorious flight. On the night of May 1, sitting on two old cracker boxes, they had their last conference. Lee had resolved to endeavor to turn Hooker's right flank and gain his rear, leaving a force in front to hold him in check and conceal the movement; the execution of this plan he intrusted to Jackson.[490] He could not more strikingly have evinced his contempt for the generalship of his adversary, as, in the presence of superior numbers, he was willing to divide his own force.

Early on the morning of May 2, Jackson, the great flanker, started on a march which took him part way around the Union Army to carry out the design of attacking its right, which was held by Howard and his Eleventh Corps. Jackson had 31,700 men; Lee was left with 13,000. Lee had given to his lieutenant two-thirds of his infantry and four-fifths of his artillery, retaining the rest in order to demonstrate against Hooker's centre.[491] Never can I forget, wrote Dr. McGuire, the eagerness and intensity of Jackson on that march to Hooker's rear. His face was pale, his eyes flashing. Out from his thin compressed lips came the terse command, Press forward, press forward![492] The commander in dingy clothes and wearing an old cap, the men ragged and unkempt, bearing tattered flags, had the appearance of an undisciplined rabble; yet steadily they marched through the heat of the day suffering from thirst and hunger.[493] Three times the column halted for a rest of twenty minutes. During one of the halts, Fitzhugh Lee, commanding a cavalry brigade, took Jackson to the top of a hill, whence could be seen a line of entrenchments of the Eleventh Corps, and behind them the soldiers, some of whom, having stacked their arms, were chatting, smoking and playing cards, whilst others were butchering cattle for the supper near at hand. Jackson's eyes flashed and his cheeks colored, as he perceived the unreadiness of his foe for the imminent fray, but his lips moving in silent prayer showed that he was supplicating the God of Battles.[494] From this hilltop he reckoned that, by a farther march of two miles or more, he would be able to take Howard's corps in the rear. Forward then was the word and when he had completed his fifteen miles of march,

---

[488] Lee's report, O. R., XXV, Pt. 1,798.

[489] Lieut.-Col. Henderson, II, 512.

[490] Lee's report, O. R., XXV, Pt. 1,798.

[491] J. Bigelow Jr., 273.

[492] Russell; III.

[493] Hamlin, 13; J. Bigelow Jr., 276.

[494] Fitzhugh Lee, 247.

he wrote the last note that he ever sent to General Lee: I hope, so soon as practicable, to attack. I trust that an ever kind Providence will bless us with success. He was now west of the Union Army, on the side of it directly opposite to the position occupied by General Lee.

Meanwhile Hooker was up at daybreak making an examination of his right wing and when he returned to headquarters he found couriers waiting to tell him of Jackson's movement; he could himself see a portion of Jackson's column on the march turning southward which was suggestive of a retreat toward Richmond. Nevertheless, he thought for the moment that the aim of the Confederates might be to attack his right, a natural conclusion, as Lee was playing with him as he had played with Pope during the previous year. At 9:30 A.M., Hooker sent a word of warning to Howard,[495] and a little later a joint despatch to Howard and Slocum (the commander of the Twelfth Corps), suggesting that they be prepared for a flank attack, as We have good reason to suppose that the enemy is moving to our right.[496] Additional reports of the Confederate movement continued to be received. This continuous column infantry, artillery, trains and ambulances was observed for three hours moving apparently in a southerly direction, wrote Sickles in his report. Acting on information to this effect, Hooker ordered Sickles to harass the movement. Sometime after noon the impression gained ground in the army that the Confederates were in full retreat and Hooker, vacillating as ever and ignoring the importance, if he were to act on the defensive, of being defended at all points, finally adopted this hopeful view, sending at 4:10 P.M. this despatch to Sedgwick: We know that the enemy is fleeing, trying to save his trains. Two of Sickles' divisions are among them.

An able and vigilant corps commander could have done much to repair this error of his chief, but Howard was no less infatuated than Hooker. Schurz, the general of a division in his corps, plainly observed large columns of the enemy moving from east to west two miles or more away and urged Howard to make arrangements to repel a flank attack. Our right wing stood completely in the air with nothing to lean upon, he wrote in his report of May 12. Our rear was at the mercy of the enemy. He suggested a certain disposition of the force, if it was really the intention that we should act on the defensive and cover the right and rear of the whole army. As we were actually situated, an attack from the West and Northwest could not be resisted for any length of time without a complete change of front on our part.[497] Schurz urged such a disposition upon Howard who, believing that Lee was in full retreat, was averse from the trouble of preparing for an attack that he had no idea would ever be made. Feeling very tired, he composed himself for a noonday nap, asking Schurz to wake him, if any important despatch should arrive.

---

[495] J. Bigelow Jr., 276.

[496] O. R., XXV, Pt. 2,360.

[497] O. R., XXV, Pt. 1,651.

135

When Hooker's first warning came of a possible attack on the flank, Schurz roused Howard, read the despatch aloud and put it in his hands. While they were discussing it a young officer delivered the second.[498] Here was warrant enough for the action that Schurz desired, but Howard was unmoved; later on, in response to an order from Hooker, he sent his strongest brigade to the assistance of Sickles, who had now been despatched on the fruitless mission of harassing the supposed Confederate retreat. That the retreat was actually in progress seemed clear to Howard after the perusal of Hooker's third order, and he accompanied the supporting brigade to assist in the capture of Lee's rear. Nevertheless, warning after warning of Jackson's real movement came from different points and the danger gathering about the Federal right flank should have been well known to Howard and to Hooker.[499]

Meanwhile Jackson had formed his troops in battle array. The men took their positions in silence, orders were transmitted in a low voice, the bugles were still; the soldiers abstained from saluting their general with their usual cheers.[500] The Eleventh Corps lay quietly in position, with no sense of the impending disaster. The opinion at headquarters which was shared by their own commander governed the men, and with a few exceptions, their officers. Some of the men were getting supper ready, others were eating or resting, some were playing cards. Shortly before six o'clock the Confederate bugles sounded. Jackson hurled most of his 31,000 upon the hapless 9000 of the Eleventh Corps, whose first warning was the wild rush of deer and rabbits driven by the quick march of the Confederates through the wilderness. Then came the rebel yell and a withering fire from cannon and rifles. After a brief resistance they ran. No troops could have acted differently, wrote General Alexander, who was with Jackson. All of their fighting was of one brigade at a time against six.[501]

For the Confederates the victory was dearly bought. Jackson, busy in the endeavor to re-form his troops who had fallen into confusion from the charge through the thick and tangled wood, then eager to discover Hooker's intentions, rode forward with his escort beyond his line of battle. When fired upon by Federal troops the little party turned back, and as they rode through the obscurity of the night, were mistaken for Union horsemen and shot at by their own soldiers, Jackson receiving a mortal wound.[502] The disability of the general undoubtedly prevented his victory from being more complete. Sickles was in jeopardy, but the night being clear and the moon nearly full, he managed to fight his way back and re-occupy his breastworks.

---

[498] Schurz, Reminiscences, II, 416.
[499] J. Bigelow Jr., 287.
[500] *Ibid.*, 292.
[501] Alexander, 337.
[502] He died eight days later.

Hooker, anxious and careworn, despondent at the rout of the Eleventh Corps, was in mind and nerve unfit to bear his great responsibility. On Sunday, the 3d of May, we find our general, incompetent at his best and now reduced to a state of nervous collapse, blundering through a hopeless contest with his able and confident adversary. Early in the morning Jackson's corps, yelling fiercely and crying Remember Jackson, delivered an attack, supported by the troops under Lee's immediate command. The Union soldiers resisted bravely. Officers and men made praiseworthy efforts, but there was no guiding head; nothing was effective that emanated from headquarters. Thirty to thirty-five thousand fresh troops, near at hand and eager to fight, were not called into action. Lincoln's parting injunctions to Hooker on his visit to the Army of the Potomac in April, In your next battle put in all your men had gone unheeded.

Shortly after 9 o'clock in the morning, Hooker was knocked senseless by cannon-ball striking a pillar of the Chancellor House veranda against which he was leaning;[503] but at that time the battle was practically lost. By 10 A.M., said Lee in his report, we were in full possession of the field.

The rest of the Battle of Chancellorsville need not detain us. At midnight of May 4, Hooker assembled his accessible corps commanders to consider the question whether he should withdraw the army to the north side of the river. Couch and Sickles voted for its withdrawal. Meade, Reynolds and Howard favored an advance which would bring on another battle. Then Hooker said he should take upon himself the responsibility of recrossing the river.[504] This movement was accomplished safely and without molestation. The loss of the Union Army in the Chancellorsville campaign was 16,792; that of the Confederate 12,764.[505]

Hooker throughout was free from the influence of alcohol. Accustomed as he was to the use of whiskey, he had entirely stopped drinking probably at the outset of this campaign or, at all events, not later than the day when he reached Chancellorsville.[506] His defeat was due to lack of ability and nerve. Meade's account of him at this time explains the whole episode. General Hooker has disappointed all his friends by failing to show his fighting qualities at the pinch, Meade wrote to his wife on May 8. He was more cautious and took to digging quicker than even McClellan, thus proving that a man may talk very big when he has no responsibility, but that it is quite a different thing, acting when you are responsible and talking when others are. Who would have believed a few days ago that Hooker would withdraw his army, in opposition to the opinion of a majority of his corps commanders? Poor Hooker himself, after he had determined to withdraw, said to me, in the most desponding manner, that he was ready to turn

---

[503] Hooker recovered and directed the retreat of his army.

[504] Couch, B. & L., III, 171.

[505] T. L. Livermore, 98.

[506] IV, 264 n.; General Meade, I, 365.

over to me the Army of the Potomac; that he had enough of it and almost wished he had never been born.[507]

But when all is said Chancellorsville remains a brilliant victory for Lee. To have overcome with his hungry ill-clad troops an army double their number and abundantly supplied could only be the work of one who mastered men by his intellectual and moral greatness. Sound reasoning, ceaseless vigilance and unusual self-sacrifice were conspicuous on the Confederate side; not on the Union. Jackson, on the night before his flanking march, lay down to sleep at the foot of a pine tree and was covered by his adjutant with the cape of his overcoat; but when the adjutant fell asleep the general arose, spread the cape over him and slept without covering, awakening chilled and with a cold. Then declining a family breakfast that was being prepared for him, he gave his whole attention to pushing forward his troops.[508] Howard, on the eve of a ridiculous and stupid surprise,[509] although only in his thirty-third year, could not forego his noonday nap.

While calmly awaiting the result of Jackson's flank movement and on the alert for any chance, Lee wrote a remarkable letter to Davis, from which may be seen his appreciation of the risk that he was taking and his resource in the event of failure. If I had with me all my command, he wrote, and could keep it supplied with provisions and forage, I should feel easy, but, as far as I can judge, the advantage of numbers and position is greatly in favor of the enemy.[510] While Jackson was crushing the right of the Union Army, Hooker with his two aides, sat on the veranda of the Chancellor House, enjoying the summer evening[511]; his first warning of the actual disaster was the flight of disordered fugitives from his Eleventh Corps.[512]

The news from the battle-field received by the War Department and the President was meagre and unsatisfactory. Welles wrote in his Diary on May 4, I this afternoon met the President at the War Department. He said he had a feverish anxiety to get facts; was constantly up and down, for nothing reliable came from the front. There is an impression which is very general that our Army has been successful, but that there has been great slaughter, and that still fiercer and more terrible fights are impending.[513] When the President received the telegram announcing the withdrawal of the army to the north side of the Rappahannock, he

---

[507] General Meade, I, 372, 373.

[508] Dabney, 675, 677.

[509] Hamlin, 50.

[510] O. R., XXV, Pt. II, 765.

[511] J. Bigelow Jr., 301.

[512] Authorities: O. R., XXV, Pts. I, II; W. R. Livermore, I; J. Bigelow Jr.; General Meade, I; Hamlin; B. & L., III; C. W., 1865, I; Welles's Diary, I; Schurz, Reminiscences, II; Alexander; IV; Dabney; Lieut.-Col. Henderson; Fitzhugh Lee; Pennypacker; Bache; Smith, Milt. Hist. Soc., V.

[513] Welles's Diary, I, 291.

cried out, My God! My God! What will the country say! What will the country say![514] On the same day [May 6] Sumner came from the extremely dejected President to Welles's office and raising both hands, exclaimed 'Lost, lost, all is lost!'[515]

Owing to the censorship of the telegraph by the War Department, the news of the disaster at Chancellorsville reached the North slowly. When its full extent became known, discouragement ruled. Many men who were earnest in support of the war now gave up all hope that the South could be conquered. Nothing demonstrates more painfully the sense of failure of the North to find a successful general than the serious and apparently well-considered suggestion of the Chicago Tribune that Abraham Lincoln take the field as the actual commander of the Army of the Potomac. We sincerely believe, the writer of this article concluded, that Old Abe can lead our armies to victory. If he does not, who will?[516]

Nevertheless, the gloom and sickness at heart so apparent after the first and second Bull Run, the defeat of McClellan before Richmond and the battle of Fredericksburg, are not discernible after Chancellorsville in nearly the same degree. It is true that the newspapers were now become a less accurate reflection of public sentiment than in the earlier stages of the war. A great deal of editorial writing was being done unmistakably for the purpose of keeping up the readers' hope; but even after the evidence of the newspapers is corrected by the recollections of contemporaries as printed or as existing only in tradition, it is impossible to escape the inference that the depression was different in kind and in measure from that which had prevailed on other occasions. Business, which had begun to improve in the autumn of 1862, was now decidedly brisk. An era of money-making had opened, manifesting itself in wild speculation on the stock exchanges, in the multiplication of legitimate transactions and in the savings of the people finding an investment in government bonds. A belief is also noticeable that the war had helped trade and manufactures. The Government was a large purchaser of material; one activity was breeding another; men honestly, and in some cases dishonestly, were gaining profits, although the State was in distress. When the news of the defeat at Chancellorsville reached New York, gold rose in price temporarily, but railroad stocks, at first unsettled, soon resumed their active advance, while government bonds remained steady and the subscription of the public to the five-twenties still went on. That men had ceased to enlist was an indication not alone of the people's weariness of the war, but also of the many opportunities of lucrative employment offered by the improvement in business. The war, so far as getting privates into the army was concerned, had become a

---

[514] Noah Brooks, 58.
[515] Welles's Diary, I, 293.
[516] May 23.

trade. Men were induced to shoulder the musket by bounties from the national government, States, towns and city wards.

Chapter VI

CHANCELLORSVILLE demonstrated Hooker's incompetence to command a large army and would have justified his removal. That he was kept in his place by an intrigue of Chase and his Radical followers has (I think) little evidence to support it. It is true that Chase was devoted to the general but, if Lincoln was to be swayed by advice, Halleck's on a military matter would have carried the greater weight, and it is notorious that the General-in-Chief lacked confidence in Hooker a feeling that was probably shared by the Secretary of War. Hooker's steadfast friend was the President himself. He visited the army soon after the battle and, taking the view that no one was to blame and it was a disaster that could not be helped, so cheered up Hooker that the general came to feel secure in his position and to show apparent unconcern at the prevalent distrust in which he was held by the army. Hooker is safe, I think, wrote Meade, from the difficulty of finding a successor and from the ridiculous appearance we present of changing our generals after each battle.[517] The President, wrote Welles in his Diary, has a personal liking for Hooker and clings to him when others give way.[518] Reynolds, when in Washington, was informed by a friend that he was being talked of for the head of the Army of the Potomac; he immediately went to the President and told him he did not want the command and would not take it. But during the interview he spoke freely of Hooker's defects, whereupon Lincoln replied, I am not disposed to throw away a gun because it missed fire once.[519]

After the Battle of Chancellorsville, Lee gave his troops a rest of some weeks. He employed this time in reorganization, dividing the army into three corps of three divisions each, commanded respectively by Longstreet,[520] Ewell and A. P. Hill. Believing that nothing was to be gained by his army remaining quietly on the defensive, he decided on the invasion of Pennsylvania. In any case this movement, by threatening Washington and drawing Hooker in pursuit of the invading force, would relieve Virginia of the presence of a hostile army. But after such victories as Fredericksburg and Chancellorsville, he would have been modest past belief had not his expectations gone far beyond so simple an achievement. He hoped to fight the Army of the Potomac on favorable conditions. With his own well-disciplined troops in high spirits and full of confidence in their leader, he could hardly have doubted that the result of such a battle would be other than a Confederate victory;

---

[517] General Meade, May 20, I, 379. Also 373. 374, 375, 382.

[518] June 14, Welles's Diary, I, 329.

[519] June 13, General Meade, I, 385.

[520] After the battle of Chancellorsville, Longstreet with his detachment joined Lee.

he might even destroy the Union Army, in which case Washington would be at his mercy and he could conquer a peace on Northern soil. Nothing at this time so perturbed the Southern high councils as the operations of Grant against Vicksburg. More than one project was proposed to save it from capture, but no diversion in its favor could be so effectual as the taking of the Federal capital. If ever an aggressive movement with so high an object were to be made, now was the time. Not only was there the flush of Confederate success to be taken advantage of, but on the other hand the South by delay would lose in efficiency for the offensive. Our resources in men are constantly diminishing, wrote Lee to Davis, and the disproportion in this respect between us and our enemies, if they continue united in their efforts to subjugate us, is steadily augmenting. Lee's extraordinary industry and attention to detail included a constant and careful reading of Northern newspapers; from the mass of news, comment and speculation he drew many correct inferences and seldom lost sight of any of the conditions which were material to the Confederates' conduct of the war. He meditated on the weariness of the contest so largely felt at the North and on the growing Democratic strength since Fredericksburg and Chancellorsville. We should neglect no honorable means of dividing and weakening our enemies, he wrote to Davis. We should give all the encouragement we can, consistently with the truth, to the rising peace party of the North.[521]

On June 3, Lee began to move his army from the vicinity of Fredericksburg, and one week later put Ewell's corps in motion for the Shenandoah Valley. Ewell drove the Union troops from Winchester and Martinsburg, and on the 15th a portion of his corps crossed the Potomac, the remainder soon following. Hill and Longstreet moved forward and by June 26 their corps had passed over the river and were in Maryland.

When Lee's northward movement became well defined, Hooker broke up his camps on the Rappahannock and marched to the Potomac, keeping to the east of the Blue Ridge and covering Washington constantly; in this manoeuvre he managed his army well. Ewell, waiting at Hagerstown, Maryland, received orders on June 22, permitting him to move forward. If Harrisburg comes within your means, wrote Lee, capture it. Advancing into Pennsylvania and halting one day at Chambersburg to secure supplies, Ewell reached Carlisle on June 27 and sent Early with one division to seize York. On the formal surrender of the town by the chief burgess and a deputation of citizens, Early laid it under contribution, receiving 1000 hats, 1200 pairs of shoes, 1000 socks, three days' rations of all kinds and $28,600 United States money. Having already burned the railroad bridges on the way to York, he now sent an expedition to take possession of the

---

[521] June 10, O. R., XXVII, Pt. III, 881. What follows shows that Lee favored no peace except on the condition of the acknowledgment of the independence of the Southern Confederacy.

Columbia bridge over the Susquehanna, a wooden structure on stone pillars, one mile and a quarter long and bearing the railroad, a wagon-road and a tow-path for the canal. He intended to march his division across this bridge, cut the line of the Pennsylvania railroad, take Lancaster, lay it under contribution and attack Harrisburg in the rear while the remainder of Ewell's corps assailed it from the front. But a regiment of Pennsylvania militia, in fleeing before the Confederates, set fire to the bridge and Early's men found it impossible to arrest the flames.

Ewell, meanwhile, through requisitions and search of shops, had secured ordnance, medical and other valuable stores; had collected near 3000 head of cattle and located 5000 barrels of flour. In the course of a reconnaissance his cavalry, supported by a section of artillery, approached to within three miles of Harrisburg and engaged the pickets of the militia forces assembled under General Couch for its defence. By June 29, he had everything ready and purposed moving on Harrisburg. Two days earlier Longstreet and Hill had reached Chambersburg and Lee was there in command. His whole army numbering 75,000 was on Pennsylvania soil.

While there was some anxiety for Washington and Baltimore it was in the Cumberland Valley of Pennsylvania that the presence of the enemy was actually and painfully felt. Yet the Confederates under Lee's immediate command committed little or no depredation or mischief. In his order of June 21, he enjoined a scrupulous respect for private property and in that of the 27th, after he had reached Chambersburg, he made known his satisfaction with the troops for their general good behavior, but mentioned that there had been instances of forgetfulness and gave warning that such offenders should be brought to summary punishment. This attitude of Lee's was prescribed alike by considerations of military discipline, mercy and by the desire to do everything possible to promote the pacific feeling at the North. It is true that payment for supplies was made in Confederate money, which proved worthless in the end, but in estimating his motives it must be remembered that he paid with the only currency he had, a currency which bade fair to have a considerable value, should his confident expectation of defeating the Union Army on Pennsylvania soil be realized.[522]

No matter how mercifully war may be carried on it is at the best a rude game. As Lee's army advanced in the Cumberland Valley alarm and distress ruled. The whole region was alive with wild rumors. Men, women and children fled before the enemy and their horses were driven out of the path of the invader. The Yanks, wrote Pickett, have taken into the mountains and across the Susquehanna all the supplies they could, and we pay liberally for those which we are compelled to take, paying for them in money which is paid to us, our own Confederate script.[523]

---

[522] At Gettysburg and on the retreat the Confederates did not behave so well. See Frank Haskell, 176; Alexander, B. & L., III, 367.

[523] Pickett's Letters, 89.

The refugees deemed themselves and their property safe once they had crossed the broad Susquehanna. The bridge over the river, the communication between the Cumberland Valley and Harrisburg, was thronged with wagons laden with furniture and household goods. Negroes fled before the advancing host, fearing that they might be dragged back to slavery. On June 26, Curtin, the Governor of Pennsylvania, issued a proclamation calling for 60,000 men to come forward promptly to defend their soil, their families and their firesides. Harrisburg, the capital of the State, was indeed in danger, as was realized by the authorities and the citizens. Thirty regiments of Pennsylvania militia, besides artillery and cavalry and nineteen regiments from New York were assembled under the command of General Couch, who disposed his forces to the best advantage, assigning a large portion of them to the defence of Harrisburg. In that city all places of business were closed, and citizens labored on the fortifications with the pick and the spade. Men were enrolled by wards and drilled in the park and on the streets. The railroad station presented a scene of great excitement, owing to the continuous arrival of volunteers and the departure of women and frightened men. The progress of the enemy was pretty accurately known. Reports ran that he was twenty-three miles from the city, then eighteen; on June 28, cannonading was heard for two hours, and everyone knew that the Confederates were within four miles of the Capitol. On that evening a rumor circulated in Philadelphia that the Confederates were shelling Harrisburg. Chestnut and Market streets were filled with thousands of men eager for news. The next day two prominent citizens telegraphed to the President that they had reliable information to the effect that the enemy in large force was marching upon Philadelphia. Other men of influence desired him to give the general in command authority to declare martial law. Business stopped. Merchants, iron manufacturers, proprietors of machine shops and coal operators held meetings, and offered inducements to their workmen to enlist for the defence of the State. The members of the Corn Exchange furnished five companies. A meeting of the soldiers of the War of 1812 and another of clergymen were held to offer their services for home defence. It was said that bankers and merchants were making preparations to remove specie and other valuables from the city. Receipts and shipments on the Pennsylvania Railroad were suspended. Notwithstanding the acute apprehension and general derangement of affairs, there was nothing resembling panic. The excitement was at its height from June 27 to July 1. On July 1 the sale of government five-twenties for the day amounted to $1,700,000. Few trains were running on the eastern division of the Pennsylvania Railroad and it was expected that the track would in many places be destroyed, yet the shares of this company sold in Philadelphia at 61.75 on June 27 and at 60 on July 1 on a par basis of 50 a record as noteworthy as Livy's story that the ground on which Hannibal was encamped three miles from Rome, happening at that very time to be sold, brought a price none the lower on account of its occupation by the invader. Although gold advanced in New York there was no panic in the stock market.

While the alarm at the invasion of Pennsylvania was at its height, when the Northerner took up his morning newspaper with dread in his heart or watched with grave misgivings the periodical bulletins of the day, the intelligence came that there had been a change in commanders of the Army of the Potomac. Those in authority depended for the salvation of Harrisburg, Baltimore and Washington on this army which the public with its half-knowledge of the situation also felt to be their mainstay.

On account of a difference with Halleck, Hooker asked to be relieved from his position [June 27]. His request came at a fortunate moment, since only the day before, as Welles records in his Diary, The President in a single remark betrayed doubts of Hooker to whom he is quite partial. 'We cannot help beating them,' he said, 'if we have the man. How much depends in military matters on one master mind! Hooker may commit the same fault as McClellan and lose his chance. We shall soon see but it appears to me he can't help but win.'[524]

Hooker's request for relief was received at three o'clock in the afternoon of June 27 and referred to the President, who quickly made up his mind and sent an officer to the Army of the Potomac with an order relieving Hooker and appointing in his place George G. Meade.

Although at this time the merit and experience of two men, Reynolds and Meade, clearly pointed them out for the command, it is nevertheless to Lincoln's credit that he resisted the strong pressure on the one side for McClellan and on the other for Frémont and chose wisely. Reynolds being eliminated by his own refusal, the choice fell upon Meade. Three days previously in a letter to his wife Meade discussed the possibility of his own appointment to the command with attractive modesty but with insufficient comprehension of Lincoln's wisdom in a great emergency. Replying to hypothetical criticism, Meade wrote, It is notorious no general officer, not even Fighting Joe himself, has been in more battles, or more exposed than my record evidences. The only thing that can be said, and I am willing to admit the justice of the argument, is that it remains to be seen whether I have the capacity to handle successfully a large army. I do not stand however any chance, because I have no friends, political or others, who press or advance my claims or pretensions, and there are so many others who are pressed by influential politicians that it is folly to think I stand any chance upon mere merit alone.[525]

Meade can best tell the story of his promotion. It has pleased Almighty God, he wrote to his wife on June 29, to place me in the trying position that for sometime past we have been talking about. Yesterday morning at 3 A.M. I was aroused from my sleep by an officer from Washington entering my tent, and after waking me up, saying he had come to give me trouble. At first I thought it was either to relieve or arrest me. He handed me a communication to read, which I found was an order

---

[524] Welles's Diary, I, 344.
[525] General Meade, I, 388.

relieving Hooker from the command and assigning me to it. As it appears to be God's will for some good purpose at any rate as a soldier, I had nothing to do but accept and exert my utmost abilities to command success. I am moving at once against Lee. A battle will decide the fate of our country and our cause. Pray earnestly, pray for the success of my country (for it is my success besides).

Frank Haskell, a staff officer in the Second Corps, who wrote during July, 1863 a graphic account of the Battle of Gettysburg, recorded his belief that the Army in general, both officers and men, had no confidence in Hooker, in either his honesty or ability. When the change of command became known, he wrote: We breathed a full breath of joy and of hope. The Providence of God had been with us General Meade commanded the Army of the Potomac. The Army brightened and moved on with a more elastic step.[526] Reynolds at once went to see Meade and assured him of his hearty support.[527]

The President conferred upon his general full power. Meade advanced northward in his aim to find and fight the enemy. He had been prompt to command, his subordinates zealous to obey. The officers, sinking for the moment all their rivalries and jealousies, were careful and untiring in their efforts, while the soldiers showed extraordinary endurance in their long and rapid marches in the hot sun and sultry air of the last days of June.

Meade's advance northward caused Lee to concentrate his army east of the mountains; he called Ewell back from his projected attack on Harrisburg to join the army at Cashtown or Gettysburg as circumstances might require.[528] In the meantime Hill and Longstreet had been ordered to Cashtown, which was eight miles west of Gettysburg. Both Lee and Meade hoped and expected to fight a defensive battle and their manoeuvres were directed to this end.

The circumstances that led to a collision at Gettysburg on July 1 between a number of the Confederates and Reynolds commanding the left wing need not be detailed. Reynolds was killed and afterwards his troops met with a serious reverse. When Meade heard of his death, which was for him as great a disaster as the loss of Stonewall Jackson had been to Lee, he sent forward to take command, Hancock, who restored order out of the existing confusion. Nevertheless, the first day of the Battle of Gettysburg was a decided Confederate success.

By six o'clock on the afternoon of July 1, Meade had arrived at the opinion that a battle at Gettysburg is now forced on us;[529] and he issued orders to all of his corps to concentrate at that point. He himself arrived on the battle-field about midnight, pale, tired-looking, hollow-eyed and worn out from loss of sleep, anxiety and the weight of responsibility.

---

[526] Frank Haskell, 3, 6, 8.
[527] General Meade, II, 33.
[528] O. R., XXVII, Pt. II, 317.
[529] O. R., XXVII, Pt. III, 466.

At about eight o'clock on the morning of July 2, accompanied by a staff-officer and orderly, he rode forth on a visit to his right wing. Schurz, who spoke with him on this occasion, was struck with his long-bearded, haggard face, his care-worn and tired look, as if he had not slept that night. His mind was evidently absorbed by a hard problem, Schurz went on. But this simple, cold, serious soldier with his business-like air did inspire confidence. The officers and men as much as was permitted crowded around and looked up to him with curious eyes and then turned away not enthusiastic but clearly satisfied. With a rapid glance he examined the position of our army and nodded seemingly with approval. After the usual salutations I asked him how many men he had on the ground. I remember his answer well, 'In the course of the day I expect to have about 95,000 enough I guess for this business.' After another sweeping glance over the field, he added, as if reflecting something to himself, 'Well we may fight it out here just as well as anywhere else.'[530]

By the afternoon of July 2, Lee and Meade had their whole forces on the field,. Lee mustering 70,000, Meade 93,000,[531] less the losses of the first day, which had been much greater on the Union than on the Confederate side. The armies were about a mile apart, the Confederates occupying the eminence concave in form called Seminary Ridge, whilst the Federals were posted in a convex line on Cemetery Ridge a position admirably adapted for defence. Meade decided to await attack, and if he had studied closely the character and record of his energetic adversary, he must have been almost certain that it would come. Longstreet, however, differed with his commander. In a conversation at the close of the first day's fight, he expressed his opinion that their troops should be thrown round Meade's left; they would then be interposed between the Union Army and Washington and Meade would be forced to take the offensive. Lee, in the anxiety and excitement of the moment, was somewhat irritated at this suggestion of a plan contrary to the one he had already determined and said, No the enemy is there and I am going to attack him. From the beginning of his invasion he had made no secret of the poor esteem in which he held his foe. While recognizing in Meade a better general than Hooker, he believed that the change of commanders at this critical moment would counterbalance the advantage in generalship; and impressed as he was by the rapid and efficient movements of the Army of the Potomac since Meade had taken command, he must on the other hand have felt that he and his army were almost invincible, a confidence shared by nearly all his officers and men, for his success on his own soil had been both brilliant and practically unbroken. There were never such men in an army before, Lee said. They will go anywhere and do anything if properly led.[532]

---

[530] Schurz, Reminiscences, III, 20.

[531] T. L. Livermore, 102; The Nation, July 11, 1901, 36.

[532] C. F. Adams, Milt. & Dip. Studies, 310; Oxford Lect., 149.

Lee was up betimes on the morning of July 2, but, owing to the slow movements of his soldiers, he lost much of the advantage of his more speedy concentration than Meade's. He did not begin his attack until the afternoon was well advanced when the last of the Union Army, the Sixth Corps, was arriving after a march of thirty-two miles in seventeen hours. He told accurately the result of the tremendous fighting and heavy loss that afternoon on both wings of each army. We attempted to dislodge the enemy, and, though we gained some ground, we were unable to get possession of his position.[533] The Confederate assaults had been disjointed: to that mistake is ascribed their small success.

Meade claimed the victory. The enemy attacked me about 4 P.M. this day, he telegraphed to Halleck on July 2, and after one of the severest contests of the war was repulsed at all points.[534] That Meade in this despatch was not consciously resorting to the time-honored device in war by stretching the claim beyond the fact is to be inferred from the note to his wife written at 8:45 on the following morning, We had a great fight yesterday, the enemy attacking and we completely repulsing them: both armies shattered.[535]

From the reports of the several corps commanders at the council of war which Meade called on the night of July 2, it was evident that the Union Army, having incurred a loss of 20,000 men, was indeed seriously weakened, but the generals had not lost spirit and all voted to stay and fight it out. As the council broke up, Meade said to Gibbon, who was in temporary command of the Second Corps, If Lee attacks to-morrow it will be in your front. Why, asked Gibbon. Because he has made attacks on both our flanks and failed, and, if he concludes to try it again it will be on our centre. I hope he will, replied Gibbon. If he does we shall defeat him.[536]

In the early morning of July 3, there was fighting on the Union right. At it again, wrote Meade to his wife, with what result remains to be seen. Army in fine spirits and everyone determined to do or die.[537] On the other side, after Lee and Longstreet had made a reconnaissance of the Union position, Lee said that he was going to attack the enemy's centre. Great God, said Longstreet, Look, General Lee, at the insurmountable difficulties between our line and that of the Yankees the steep hills, the tiers of artillery, the fences, the heavy skirmish line and then we'll have to fight our infantry against their batteries. Look at the ground we'll have to charge over, nearly a mile of that open ground there under the rain of their canister and shrapnel. The enemy is there, General Longstreet, and I am going to strike him, said Lee in his quiet, determined voice.[538]

---

[533] O. R., XXVII, Pt. II, 298. On the Union side Warren and Humphreys distinguished themselves.

[534] O. R., XXVII, Pt. I, 72.

[535] General Meade, II, 103.

[536] B. & L., III, 314.

[537] General Meade, II, 103.

All the events of the past month invasion and answering manoeuvre, marching and countermarching, the fighting of two days were the prelude to a critical episode; three or four terrible hours were now imminent which should go far toward deciding the issue of the war. From 11 A.M. until 1 P.M. there was an ominous stillness.[539] Suddenly from the Confederate side came the reports of two signal guns in quick succession. A bombardment from one hundred and fifty cannon commenced and was replied to by eighty guns[540] of the Union Army whose convex line, advantageous in other respects, did not admit of their bringing into action a large part of their artillery. The Confederate fire was chiefly concentrated upon the Second Corps where Hancock had resumed command. It was, he wrote in his report, the heaviest artillery fire I have ever known. But it did little damage. The Union soldiers lay under the protection of stone walls, swells of the ground and earthworks and the projectiles of the enemy passed over their heads, sweeping the open ground in their rear. Hancock with his staff, his corps flag flying, rode deliberately along the front of his line and, by his coolness and his magnificent presence, inspired his men with courage and determination. One of his brigadiers, an old neighbor, said to him, General the corps commander ought not to risk his life in that way. Hancock replied, There are times when a corps commander's life does not count.[541] For an hour and a half this raging cannonade was kept up, when Meade, knowing that it was preliminary to an assault and desiring to lure the Confederates on, gave the order to cease firing, in which action he had been anticipated by Hunt, chief of the Union artillery, because his ammunition was running low.[542]

Meade's ruse was successful. Longstreet was inclined to think that the Confederate fire had been effective,[543] and Alexander, who commanded the Confederate artillery, felt sure that the enemy was feeling the punishment.[544] Pickett, who was to lead the attack, rode up to Longstreet for orders. I found him, Pickett wrote, like a great lion at bay. I have never seen him so grave and troubled. For several minutes after I had saluted him he looked at me without speaking. Then in an agonized voice he said: 'Pickett, I am being crucified at the thought of the sacrifice of life which this attack will make. I have instructed Alexander to watch the effect of our fire upon the enemy, and when it begins to tell he must take the responsibility and give you orders, for I can't.'[545]

---

[538] Letter of July 3, Pickett's Letters, 94.

[539] Hancock, O. R., XXVII, Pt. I, 372.

[540] T. L. Livermore, Milt. Hist. Soc., XIII, 536.

[541] Letter of T. L. Livermore, March 30, 1914. I acknowledge great indebtedness to Col. Livermore for his many papers and for intelligence conveyed in his letters and conversation.

[542] General Meade, II, 108; B. & L., III, 374.

[543] O. R., XXVII, Pt. II, 359.

[544] Alexander, 423.

[545] Pickett's Letters, 98.

Alexander had confidence in the attack because Lee had ordered it, although he shrank from the responsibility now thrust upon him; yet, having seen Pickett and found him cheerful and sanguine, he played his part. And when he dared wait no longer he sent a note to Pickett, who was still with Longstreet: For God's sake come quick. Come quick or my ammunition will not let me support you properly. Pickett read it, handed it to Longstreet and asked, Shall I obey and go forward? Longstreet, so Pickett wrote, looked at me for a moment, then held out his hand. Presently clasping his other hand over mine, without speaking, he bowed his head upon his breast. I shall never forget the look in his face nor the clasp of his hand when I said, 'Then, General, I shall lead my division on.'[546]

My brave boys, wrote Pickett, were full of hope and confident of victory as I led them forth, forming them in column of attack [at about 3:15] though officers and men alike knew what was before them. Over on Cemetery Ridge the Federals beheld an army forming in line of battle in full view, under their very eyes.[547] Hancock, who expected the attack and was prepared to meet it, wrote in his report, The enemy's lines were formed with a precision and steadiness that extorted the admiration of the witnesses of that memorable scene.[548]

Pickett's 15,000 had nearly a mile to go across the valley;[549] with banners flying they marched forward with the steadiness of a dress parade. Haskell of the Second Corps, against which the charge was directed, wrote: Every eye could see the enemy's legions, an overwhelming resistless tide of an ocean of armed men sweeping upon us! Regiment after regiment and brigade after brigade move from the woods and rapidly take their places in the line forming the assault. Pickett's proud division [5000] with some additional troops hold their right. The first line at short intervals is followed by a second, and that a third succeeds; and columns between support the lines. More than half a mile their front extends; more than a thousand yards the dull gray masses deploy, man touching man, rank pressing rank and line supporting line. The red flags wave, their horsemen gallop up and down; the arms of eighteen thousand men [15,000], barrel and bayonet, gleam in the sun, a sloping forest of flashing steel. Right on they move, as with one soul, in perfect order, without impediment of ditch or wall or stream, over ridge and slope, through orchard and meadow and cornfield, magnificent, grim, irresistible.[550] The

---

[546] Pickett's Letters, 98. I have made up this account from Pickett's letter of July 4 and Alexander's recollections, which differ slightly from Longstreet's report of July 27. Alexander (423) sent two notes to Pickett. I have used the second as fitting better Pickett's account.

[547] Pickett's Letters, 99, 100.

[548] O. R., XXVII, Pt. I, 373.

[549] "Longstreet sent forward Pickett's division of his corps and eight brigades of Hill's corps, numbering about 14,300 effectives, against about a mile of the Union line, which was held by about 10,100 effectives." ;T. L. Livermore, Milt. Hist. Soc., XIII, 536.

[550] Frank Haskell, 113.

Union artillery, which had been put in entire readiness to check such an onset, opened fire upon the advancing column at 700 yards and continued until it came to close quarters.[551] Still the Confederates advanced steadily and coolly. Their artillery had reopened over their heads in an effort to draw the deadly fire directed at them from Cemetery Ridge; but the Union guns made no change in aim and went on mowing down Pickett's men. A storm of canister came. The slaughter was terrible; but, nothing daunted, the remnant of Pickett's division of 5000 pressed on in the lead. The other brigades followed. Now the Union infantry opened fire[552] and the Confederates replied. General Garnett, just out of the sick ambulance and commanding a brigade in Pickett's division, rode immediately in the rear of his advancing line with great coolness and deliberation, and endeavored, so wrote Major Peyton, to keep his line well closed and dressed. He was shot from his horse while near the center of the brigade within about 25 paces of the stone wall. But our line much shattered still kept up the advance until within about twenty paces of the wall when, for a moment, it recoiled under the terrific fire that poured into our ranks both from their batteries and from their sheltered infantry. At this moment General Kemper came up on the right and General Armistead in rear, when the three lines joining in concert, rushed forward with unyielding determination and an apparent spirit of laudable rivalry to plant the Southern banner on the walls of the enemy. Armistead, wrote Colonel Aylett, was conspicuous to all. Fifty yards in advance of his brigade, waving his hat upon his sword, he led his men upon his enemy with a steady bearing. Far in advance of all he led the attack till he scaled the works of the enemy and fell wounded in their hands, but not until he had driven them from their position and seen his colors planted over their fortifications. The enemy's strongest and last line was gained, wrote Major Peyton; the Confederate battle flag waved over his defences and the fighting over the wall became hand to hand and of the most desperate character; but more than half having already fallen, our line was found too weak to rout the enemy.[553] The advancing mass was so deep and wide as to raise doubt whether the Union line could stand against its weight and momentum, but a brief contact with bayonets crossed and muskets clubbed solved this doubt. The Confederates threw

---

[551] T. L. Livermore, Milt. Hist. Soc., XIII, 536. The whole distance that the Confederates had to go was about 1400 yards.

[552] "The fire of the Union infantry which with great coolness was withheld for close work was opened from different parts of the line at 200 to 70 yards. Unfaltering under the destructive fire, the Confederates marched in such order and with such courage as to win the admiration of their opponents." ;T. L. Livermore, Milt. Hist. Soc., XIII, 537.

[553] The citations are from the only printed reports (so far as I know) of officers in Pickett's divisions, O. R., XXVII, Pt. II, 385, 999. They are dated respectively July 9, 12. Major Peyton was in Garnett's, Col. Aylett in Armistead's, brigade. Pickett made a report but, at the suggestion of General Lee, destroyed it, O. R., XXVII, Pt. III, 1075; Pickett's Letters, 100, 213.

down their arms as if they simultaneously realized that the battle was lost. Many surrendered while others who escaped the pursuing shots fled across the field to Seminary Ridge.[554]

I have never seen a more formidable attack, wrote Hancock to Meade on the day of the battle, with worse troops I should certainly have lost the day.[555] Haskell's detailed account confirms this judgment, as does the study of Colonel Thomas L. Livermore, who was in the battle. Meade, his face very white, the lines marked and earnest and full of care, rode up to Haskell and asked in a sharp eager voice, How is it going here? I believe, General, the enemy's attack is repulsed, was the reply. What! Is the assault already repulsed? It is, sir. Thank God! exclaimed Meade.[556]

Lee, entirely alone, rode forward to encourage and rally his broken troops. His earlier excitement had passed and he betrayed no bitterness in his disappointment; his composure was really extraordinary and the spirit in which he spoke of the disaster was nothing short of sublime. All this has been my fault, he said. It is I that have lost this fight.[557]

Again he said, this has been a sad day for us, a sad day.[558] The fate of two of Pickett's brigadiers has been recorded; the third, Kemper, was desperately wounded.[559] Seven of my colonels were killed, wrote Pickett, and one was mortally wounded. Nine of my lieutenant colonels were wounded and three were killed. Only one field officer of my whole command was unhurt and the loss of my company officers was in proportion.[560] Two of the three brigades were under the command of majors when the battle was over. The casualties of the division of 5000 were nearly 2900.

Pickett was unhurt and no one of his staff appears in the list of killed and wounded. He set forth at the head of his troops but did not go forward to the Union line; he stopped part way. The words he wrote to his betrothed on the following day have the ring of sincerity, Your soldier lives and mourns and but for you, he would rather, a million times rather, be back there with his dead to sleep for all time in an unknown grave.[561] Nevertheless the question was naturally raised in the South whether he might share in the glory won by his division that day. History answering must follow the judgment of General Lee, who knew all the circumstances and was a pre-eminently truthful and impartial man. On July 9 Lee wrote to Pickett, No one grieves more than I do at the loss suffered by your noble

---

[554] T. L. Livermore, Milt. Hist. Soc., XIII, 537.

[555] O. R., XXVII, Pt. II, 366.

[556] Frank Haskell, 136.

[557] Fremantle, 269.

[558] *Ibid.,* 268.

[559] After a long while Kemper recovered. Pickett's Men, Harrison, 103.

[560] Pickett's Letters, 107.

[561] *Ibid.,* 100.

division in the recent conflict or honors it more for its bravery and gallantry. In a later, undated letter, he said, You and your men have crowned yourselves with glory.[562]

Pickett's charge, though a hazardous enterprise, was by no means a hopeless one and might well have succeeded had not Meade and Hancock been thoroughly prepared for it and had they not shown generalship of a high order. With Hooker in command the irresolute Hooker of Chancellorsville there would have been a different story to relate. A comparison of the management of the two battles will confirm Halleck's judgment that Hooker would have lost the army and the capital.[563]

Moreover, Lee had to decide between an attack and an inglorious retreat. Divided, his army could live upon the country, but during a prolonged concentration it could not be fed. His decision was in keeping with his aggressive disposition, and his mistake seems to have been in underrating Meade's ability and in overestimating both the physical and moral damage done by his artillery fire. If the Confederates, who made the breach in the Union line could have held on, adequate support would undoubtedly have been given and Lee's idea of one determined and united blow[564] delivered by his whole line might have been realized. And if he could have thoroughly beaten the Army of the Potomac, Baltimore and Washington would have been at his mercy. Perhaps the risk was worth taking.

Whether Meade should at once have made a counter-charge across the valley, or attacked the Confederate right before dark on July 3, or occupied Lee's line of retreat that afternoon and made a general advance early next morning are questions frequently discussed by military writers. Meade's own idea is disclosed in these words of July 5 to his wife. The Confederates awaited one day expecting that flushed with success, I would attack them when they would play their old game of shooting us from behind breastworks.[565]

Under the cover of the night and heavy rain of July 4, Lee began his retreat. Meade followed. The strain on a commanding general during such a campaign is shown by these words to his wife on July 8: From the time I took command till to-day, now over ten days, I have not changed my clothes, have not had a regular night's rest and many nights not a wink of sleep and for several days did not even wash my face and hands, no regular food and all the time in a great state of mental anxiety. Indeed I think I have lived as much in this time as in the last thirty years. In this letter, which was written from Frederick, he said, I think we shall have another battle before Lee can cross the river.[566]

---

[562] O. R., XXVII, Pt. III, 987, 1075.

[563] O. R., XXIV, Pt. III, 498.

[564] Rec. and Letters of R. E. Lee, 102.

[565] General Meade, II, 125.

[566] Ibid., II, 132.

The heavy rains and resultant high water prevented Lee from crossing the Potomac at once and, by July 11, Meade in his pursuit had come within striking distance of the Confederate Army. While proceeding with great caution, he had determined to make an attack on July 13; but as he was wavering in mind and feeling oppressed by his great responsibility he called a council of war. Five out of six of his corps commanders were opposed to the projected attack, which caused him to delay giving the orders for it. Meade devoted July 13 to an examination of the enemy's position, strength and defensive works; and the next day, advancing his army for a reconnaissance in force, or an assault if the conditions should be favorable, he discovered that the Confederate army had crossed the Potomac in the night. The escape of Lee's army without another battle has created great dissatisfaction in the mind of the President, telegraphed Halleck [July 14]. Meade asked to be relieved of the command of the army: his application was refused.

During July 12 and 13, Lincoln was anxious and impatient and when, about noon of the 14th, he got word that Lee and his army were safely across the Potomac he was deeply grieved. And that, my God, is the last of this Army of the Potomac! he said. Meade has been pressed and urged, but only one of his generals was for an immediate attack, was ready to pounce on Lee; the rest held back. What does it mean, Mr. Welles? Great God! what does it mean?[567] We had them within our grasp, he said. We had only to stretch forth our hands and they were ours. And nothing I could say or do could make the army move.[568] In a later private letter he developed this opinion. I was deeply mortified, he said, by the escape of Lee across the Potomac, because the substantial destruction of his army would have ended the war and because I believed such destruction was perfectly easy. Perhaps my mortification was heightened because I had always believed making my belief a hobby possibly that the main rebel army going north of the Potomac could never return, if well attended to; and because I was so greatly flattered in this belief by the operations at Gettysburg.[569]

No one should accept this judgment of Lincoln's without considering Meade's defence. Had I attacked Lee the day I proposed to do so, the General wrote, and in the ignorance that then existed of his position, I have every reason to believe the attack would have been unsuccessful and would have resulted disastrously. This opinion is founded on the judgment of numerous distinguished officers after inspecting Lee's vacated works and position. I had great responsibility thrown on me. On one side were the known and important fruits of victory, and, on the other, the equally important and terrible consequences of a defeat.[570]

---

[567] Welles's Diary, July 14, I, 370.
[568] July 14, J. Hay, I, 85; N. & H., VII, 278.
[569] July 21, General Meade, II, 138.
[570] July 31, O. R., XXVII, Pt. I, 109.

In the end it was Lincoln himself who suggested the sanest possible view of the episode. In a letter of July 21 he wrote, I am now profoundly grateful for what was done without criticism for what was not done [at Gettysburg]. General Meade has my confidence as a brave and skilful officer and a true man. The change in Northern sentiment between July 1 and 4 reveals unmistakably the sense of a great deliverance.[571] Although indeed a great deliverance, the victory at Gettysburg had been gained by an army acting on the defensive, whilst the nature of the conflict required that the North should wage an aggressive war. And fortunately the aggressive leader had at last been found. On January 20, 1863, Grant had assumed the immediate command of the expedition against Vicksburg.

Before and during the war the Mississippi river possessed, as a channel of communication and commerce, a great importance, which has steadily diminished with the development of the railroad system of the West. The importance of gaining control of it was appreciated at the North from the first; such control being regarded in the East as a military advantage, whilst by the people of the Western States it was deemed indispensable to their existence, as providing an outlet for their products and an artery for their supply. The free navigation of the Mississippi were words to conjure with, not only in the Southwest, but everywhere west of the Alleghanies, except in the region directly tributary to the Great Lakes.[572] Lincoln, owing to the geographical situation of his home, had been brought up with this sentiment; in manhood his mind was thoroughly impregnated with it; and throughout the great crisis he never lost sight of its military and commercial significance. The capture of Forts Henry and Donelson and the resulting operations had freed the Mississippi north of Vicksburg; the capture of New Orleans had given the Union its mouth. But the Confederates were still in virtual possession of the two hundred miles of river between their two strong fortresses of Vicksburg and Port Hudson, thereby maintaining communication between Louisiana and Texas on the one side and the rest of the Confederacy on the other. Louisiana supplied them with sugar, while the great State of Texas furnished quantities of grain and beef, besides affording, through its contiguity to Mexico, an avenue for munitions of war received from Europe at the Mexican port of Matamoras a consideration of much weight, since the ports of the Southern States were now pretty effectually sealed by the Federal blockade. Of the two fastnesses, Vicksburg was by far the more important and the desire in the Confederacy to keep it was keen.

---

[571] Authorities: O. R., XXVII, Pt. I, II, III; General Meade; Frank Haskell; C. W., 1865, I; Pickett's Letters; W. R. Livermore; T. L. Livermore, Milt. Hist. Soc., XIII; IV; B. & L., III; Longstreet; Alexander; Welles's Diary; Schurz, Reminiscences; Pickett and his Men, L. S. Pickett; Pickett's Men, Harrison; Francis A. Walker; Pennypacker; Fitzhugh Lee; Fremantle; Hosmer's Appeal; Swinton, Army of the Potomac.

[572] California and Oregon are manifestly excepted from this general statement.

From the Union point of view the three most important strategic points in the South were Richmond, Vicksburg and Chattanooga. Vicksburg ranked second, for its capture would give the United States the control of the Mississippi River and cut the Confederacy asunder. An attempt had been made to take it by the navy, another by the army; both had failed.

Vicksburg, built for the most part upon a bluff two hundred feet above high-water mark of the river, presented a natural stronghold, strengthened by art and unassailable from the front. The problem was to reach the high ground on the east bank of the river so that it might be attacked or besieged from the side or rear. Many devices of artificial channels connecting natural water-courses were tried; apparently, indeed, every experiment was made that engineering skill or military initiative could suggest. Nearly two months were spent in such operations, all of which failed.

It had been a winter of heavy and continuous rains. The river had risen to an unusual height and in places the levees had given way. The whole country was covered with water. Troops could scarcely find dry ground on which to pitch their tents. Malarial fevers, measles and small-pox broke out among the men.[573] From newspaper correspondents, from letters which the soldiers wrote to their kinsmen and friends at home, from reports of visitors to the camps, the people of the North came to know in detail of the many attempts and failures, of the exceeding discomfort of the army and of the sickness which prevailed. Having in mind the Grant of Shiloh rather than the Grant of Donelson, they were prone to consider his operations in a fault-finding spirit and to believe the stories of his intemperance which were now in large measure revived. Nevertheless, Lincoln stood by his general faithfully.

Grant's despatches and letters at this time are evidently the work of a cool brain; his actions betoken a sound judgment and unflagging energy. Since the Battle of Shiloh [April 6, 7, 1862] he had, most of the time, had a responsible command, but had done nothing to attract public attention. His usefulness had been mainly in his capacity of commander of a Department, for his service in the field had been small and inconspicuous; but in these ten months he had observed and thought much about the conflict that tore his country. He was not a reader of military books, nor a close student of the campaigns of the great masters of his art, nor was he given to conning the principles of strategy and the rules of tactics; yet in his own way and within certain lines he was a deep thinker. Rebellion, he wrote, has assumed that shape now that it can only terminate by the complete subjugation of the South or the overthrow of the government. He must have believed that, if the chance should come, he could show the good stuff that was in him; and in organizing and taking command of the expedition against Vicksburg, he created such an opportunity. But fortune and the elements were at first against him and he must waste two months

---

[573] Grant, I, 458.

in fruitless efforts. Sensitive as he was to detraction, he felt keenly the calumnies that were propagated at the North. Said Lincoln, I think Grant has hardly a friend left except myself.[574]

The failure of the engineering expedients to turn or to supplement the courses of the waters and the realization that he must therefore accommodate himself to the natural features of the country and to the channel of the great river, left Grant in a state of grave perplexity. What should be tried next? The strategical way according to the rule, he wrote, would have been to go back to Memphis; establish that as a base of supplies and move from there along the line of the railroad. This was the advice of Sherman, his ablest and most trusted lieutenant. But, reasoned Grant, that is a backward movement and gravely objectionable, because it will intensify the discouragement with the war prevailing at the North. There was nothing left to be done, he said, but to go forward to a decisive victory.[575] Without a council of war, without even consulting any of his able officers, he formed his plan, and hoped for approval from Washington after he had begun to carry it out. He revealed it to his government in his despatches to Halleck, all of which are marked by courtesy and respect. From the confident and masterly tone of his communications, we may imagine with what satisfaction they were read by the President who, before the news of any signal success was received, authorized a despatch which gave Grant full and absolute authority to enforce his own commands and bore this further assurance, He has the full confidence of the government.[576]

On March 23, Grant ordered the concentration of his army at Milliken's Bend. On the 29th, the roads having dried up somewhat although still intolerably bad, he directed McClernand's corps to march to New Carthage, while Sherman and McPherson with their corps were in due time to follow. The movement was slow, for the transportation of supplies and ammunition and the progress of the artillery were exceedingly difficult. For the success of the enterprise, the co-operation of the navy was necessary and from acting-Admiral Porter Grant received efficient and generous support. Gunboats and other craft were needed for service below Vicksburg, more rations were required than could be hauled over a single, narrow and almost impassable road; hence gunboats and transports must run the batteries from a point above the town. On the night of April 16, such a movement was successfully made, and again, on the night of the 22d, six steamers towing twelve barges loaded with hay, corn and provisions steamed and drifted past Vicksburg, bringing an abundance of supplies to the army south of it.

Still remained the problem how to get on the high ground on the east bank of the river. McClernand's and McPherson's corps were set in motion for Hard Times,

---

[574] Nicolay, 253.
[575] Grant, I, 443.
[576] May 5, O. R., XXIV, Pt. I, 84.

part of them in the steamers and barges, the others afoot. It was necessary to proceed farther south, but the fortifications of Grand Gulf blocked the way of the transports and an assault of the gunboats failed to silence their batteries. Grant disembarked the troops that were on the transports at Hard Times and all marched to a point below, whence they were ferried across to Bruinsburg, high ground on the east bank of the Mississippi [April 30]. This point was selected in accordance with information supplied by a negro who had told Grant that there was a good road thence to Port Gibson. When the landing was seen to be feasible, Grant telegraphed to Halleck, I feel that the battle is now more than half won.[577] Yet all nature's obstacles had not been overcome. The country with its bayous, swamps and ravines, its timber, undergrowth, and almost impenetrable canebrakes and trailing shrubs rendered offensive operations difficult and hazardous. But the general exhorted and the soldiers pressed on. By two o'clock in the morning of May 1, while on the road to Port Gibson, they were in touch with the Confederates, whom they outnumbered. Skirmishing began, developing as it grew light into a general battle. The fighting continued all day, said Grant, and until after dark, over the most broken country I ever saw. The enemy were driven from point to point. They were sent in full retreat. Next day he had Port Gibson and the Confederates evacuated Grand Gulf. From that fort, Grant wrote a long despatch to Halleck, giving an account of his success. This army is in the highest health and spirits, he said. Since leaving Milliken's Bend they have marched as much by night as by day, through mud and rain, without tents or much other baggage and on irregular rations without a complaint and with less straggling than I have ever before witnessed.[578] Could the army have transmitted a collective despatch, they might have said, Our general has been subject to the same discomforts as we; he has shared all our hardships.

Grant, with his force of 43,000, had a secure base of supplies at Grand Gulf but he did not continue to supply his army from that point. Stopping only long enough to arrange for the transport of his ammunition and to get up what rations he could of hard bread, coffee and salt, he cut loose from his base and lived upon the country, where he found a sufficiency of beef, mutton, poultry, bacon, molasses and forage. Opposed to him were Pemberton, with probably 40,000 in Vicksburg and along the line of the railroad, and Joseph E. Johnston with nearly 15,000 in Jackson. Moving with extraordinary rapidity and throwing upon each detachment of the Confederates a superior force, Grant defeated them in detail and cleared the way to his final objective point. In nineteen days,[579] he had crossed the great river into the enemy's territory, had marched one hundred and eighty miles through a very difficult country, skirmishing constantly, had fought and won five distinct

---

[577] O. R., XXIV, Pt. I, 32.
[578] O.R., XXIV, Pt. I, 32; Grant, 484.
[579] April 30-May 18.

battles, inflicting a greater loss upon the enemy than he himself sustained and capturing many cannon and field-pieces, had taken the capital of the State and destroyed its arsenals and military manufactories, had been for ten days without communication with any base or his government,[580] and was now in the rear of Vicksburg. As Sherman, in company with Grant, rode up to the long-coveted, dry, high ground behind Vicksburg, looked down upon the Confederate fort and then upon the Federal fleet within easy supporting distance, and realized that they had secured a base of supplies which had safe and unobstructed communication with the North, as he perceived the full force of what they had gained and recalled the time when he had panted for this position, he gave vent to his enthusiasm in boundless terms, while Grant, imperturbable, thought and smoked on. To find a parallel in military history to the deeds of those eighteen days (or nineteen), wrote John Fiske, a good authority on both events, we must go back to the first Italian campaign of Napoleon in 1796.[581]

Grant made two unsuccessful attempts to carry the Confederate works by storm, after which he settled down to a regular siege. Mining, countermining and sapping went on as usual.[582] We are now approaching with pick and shovel, wrote General Sherman to his brother. We shell the town a little every day and keep the enemy constantly on the alert, said Grant in his despatch of June 3.[583] After the exciting active campaign, the siege operations were slow, heavy and exacting work which during the extreme hot weather of June induced a feeling of lassitude and depression among both officers and men.[584] Even Grant felt it and, on one occasion, yielded to his appetite for drink. On this occasion he invited Charles A. Dana to go with him to Satartia and the two went up the Yazoo river on a small steamboat. Grant fell ill and went to bed. When within two miles of Satartia, two gun-boats were met, whose officers came aboard and said that the General would run the risk of capture if he should proceed farther. Dana awakened Grant who, being too ill to decide, left the decision to Dana who ordered the steamer round-about. The next morning, as Dana related the story, Grant came out to breakfast fresh as a rose, clean shirt and all, quite himself. Well, Mr. Dana, he said, I suppose we are at Satartia now. No, general, was the reply, we are at Haynes's Bluff,[585] the point from which they had started on the steamer, the day before.

---

[580] Charles A. Dana wrote in his Reminiscences that the isolation of the army was complete for ten days. The gap in his despatches is between May 10 and 20. James H. Wilson in his Life of C. A. Dana (225) wrote, Communication "had been broken just ten days, during which time the army was operating without any base whatever." May 14, 15 Grant sent two despatches via Memphis to Halleck which reached him. O. R., XXIV, Pt. 1, 36.

[581] John Fiske, 242.

[582] *Ibid.*, 245

[583] IV, 312.

[584] Wilson's Under the Old Flag, 210.

This river excursion took place on June 6; at one A.M. of that day, John A. Rawlins, Grant's chief of staff, wrote a remarkable letter to his general. The great solicitude I feel for the safety of this army leads me to mention what I had hoped never again to do Rawlins wrote, the subject of your drinking. To-night I find you where the wine bottle has just been emptied, in company with those who drink and urge you to do likewise, and the lack of your usual promptness of decision and clearness in expressing yourself in writing tended to confirm my suspicions. You have the full control of your appetite and can let drinking alone. Had you not pledged me the sincerity of your honor early last March that you would drink no more during the war and kept that pledge during your recent campaign, you would not to-day have stood first in the world's history as a successful military leader. Your only salvation depends upon your strict adherence to that pledge. You cannot succeed in any other way.[586]

That same day Rawlins removed a box of wine from the front of Grant's tent that had been sent to him to celebrate his prospective entrance into Vicksburg, and next morning he searched every suspected tent for liquor and broke every bottle he found over a near-by stump.[587]

How much depends in military matters on one master mind! said Lincoln when Lee was invading Pennsylvania and Hooker was still in command of the Army of the Potomac.[588] A thorough study of the operations against Vicksburg brings the conviction that Grant alone of the Union generals could have conducted that brilliant campaign, discomfiting two Confederate Armies and establishing his own on the high ground behind Vicksburg, and that he alone could have prosecuted the siege to its successful conclusion. He was a greater general than Stonewall Jackson but he might have been still greater could he have said with Jackson, changing only the name of Federal to Confederate, I love whiskey but I never use it; I am more afraid of it than of Confederate bullets.

The anxiety of the President and his advisers over the Vicksburg campaign was intense and their dominant idea as expressed by a confidential friend of Stanton's was, If we keep Grant sober we shall take Vicksburg. Rawlins was a potent factor in the final success and he had the intelligent and sympathetic support of two men who fully comprehended the situation Lieutenant-Colonel James H. Wilson, of Grant's staff, and Charles A. Dana. Dana had been sent to the army by Stanton, with of course the President's consent, to watch Grant; known as the eyes of the government, he proved a faithful and considerate watchman. He estimated correctly not only Grant but acting-Admiral Porter, Sherman and McPherson; he seems to have won their confidence and did not abuse it. His despatches, written in

[585] Dana's Recollections, 83.
[586] W. F. Smith, 179.
[587] Rawlins's letter l. c.; Wilson's Under the Old Flag, I, 210.
[588] Welles's Diary, I, 344; *ante.*

the terse English of which he was a master, furnish an excellent history of the progress of the campaign.[589]

The rest of the story may be told briefly. Grant invested Vicksburg closely, maintaining at the same time a sufficient force to repel any attack that might be made on his rear. But Johnson was unable to relieve in any way the beleaguered garrison which was rapidly declining in efficiency through fatigue, illness and lack of food. Grant's army increased by re-enforcements to 72,000,[590] he steadily and grimly closed about the city and made ready for an attempt to take it by storm. Pemberton, thinking that he could not repel such an assault, gave up Vicksburg. At 10:30 on the morning of July 4, in the self-same hour when Lincoln announced to the country the result at Gettysburg, Grant sent this word to his government, The enemy surrendered this morning. The number of prisoners taken was 29,491, while the Confederate loss up to that time had probably reached 10,000. Moreover, 170 cannon and 50,000 small arms were captured. The muskets, being of an improved make recently obtained from Europe, were used to replace the inferior arms of many regiments in the Union Army. The result had been gained at small cost; Grant's loss during his whole campaign was 9362.

Of what occurred when the Federal troops took possession of the city and the Confederates marched out, accounts differ in detail but agree in essence. Grant wrote, Not a cheer went up, not a remark was made that would give pain. A Confederate officer of high rank recollects a hearty cheer from a division of the Union Army, but it was given for the gallant defenders of Vicksburg.[591]

General Sherman wrote nearly ten years after the close of the Civil War, The campaign of Vicksburg in its conception and execution, belonged exclusively to General Grant, not only in the great whole, but in the thousands of its details.[592]

When the news of the victory reached Port Hudson, the Confederate commander surrendered it to General Banks who had invested it with his army. On July 16 the steamboat Imperial, which had come directly from St. Louis, landed its commercial cargo on the levee at New Orleans. As Lincoln said, The Father of Waters again goes unvexed to the sea.[593]

Since the first of January the eyes of the North had been on Vicksburg. Hopes had been crushed, then had risen anew, only to meet with fresh disappointment; elation over Grant's May campaign and a false report that the fortress had fallen was followed by a period of weary suspense brightened withal by the glow of confident anticipation. When the final triumph was announced, the wave of gladness that swept the country ran all the higher for having been so long

---

[589] O.R., XXIV, Pt. I, 63 *et seq.*

[590] W. R. Livermore, 377.

[591] Grant, I, 570; Lockett, B. & L., III, 492.

[592] W. Sherman, I, 334.

[593] Lincoln, C. W., II, 398.

repressed; moreover, it was swelled by the coincidence of Gettysburg, especially as the popular mind might associate both victories with the Fourth of July, the day of the nation's birth. With Gettysburg and Vicksburg the war should have come to an end.[594] While the North took courage in that a great military leader had arisen to give aim to its resources, the South was profoundly depressed over her defeat in the two campaigns. Because of the failure of the invasion into Pennsylvania and the expressions of discontent in the public journals at the result of the expedition and the fear that such a feeling might extend to the soldiers, Lee earnestly requested Davis to supply his place as commander of the Army of Northern Virginia with a younger and abler man; but this request was promptly refused.[595]

---

[594] See authorities cited, IV, 320, note; Richard Taylor, Destruction and Reconstruction, 230; O. R., IV, II, 664. Gen. Wayne, C. S. A., son of Justice Wayne, said to Maj. H. L. Higginson in 1866, "After Vicksburg and Gettysburg most men, well-informed, knew that the contest was useless and wicked. Jo. Johnston held that opinion. But Davis and Lee disagreed with it and were much blamed on that account." Letter of H. L. Higginson, Feb. 16, 1905.

[595] Mrs. J. Davis, II, 393; O. R., XXIX, Pt. II, 639. Authorities for the Vicksburg campaign O. R., XXIV, Pts. I, III; IV; Grant; W. Sherman; W. R. Livermore; same Milt. Hist. Soc., IX; Welles's Diary, I; N. & H., VII; Wilson's Dana; Wilson's Under the Old Flag; Wilson's Life of Rawlins, M. S.; Dana's Recollections; W. F. Smith; John Fiske; Grant's private letters; Wister's Grant; Garland's Grant; Vilas, The Vicksburg Campaign.

Chapter VII

UNTIL the spring of 1862 the government of Great Britain preserved the neutrality which had been declared by the Queen's proclamation at the commencement of the war; and this neutrality would not have been violated had the feeling of the dominant classes been friendly to the North. The main body of the aristocracy and the highest of the middle class desired that the great democracy should fail, partly because it was a democracy, partly because it enacted high protective tariffs, partly because of sympathy with a people who desired release from what they deemed a position of irksome political subordination and partly because the division of a great power like the United States, which had frequently threatened Great Britain with war, would redound to their political advantage; but with the portion of the middle class engaged in commerce and manufactures, the desire that overshadowed all others was that the war should come to an end so that England could again secure cotton and resume the export of her manufactured goods to America. The North could terminate the war by the recognition of the Southern Confederacy; and the irritation was great over her persistence in the seemingly impossible task of conquering five and one-half millions of people. Conquer a free population of 3,000,000 souls? the thing is impossible, Chatham had said, and this was applied with force to the case in hand.

The friends of the North remained as sincere and active as in the previous autumn, but like the patriots at home they had days of discouragement at the small progress made towards a restoration of the Union. The most significant and touching feature of the situation was that the operatives of the North of England who suffered most from the lack of cotton, were frankly on the side of the United States. They knew that their misery came from the war, and were repeatedly told that it would cease in a day if the North would accept an accomplished fact; but discerning, in spite of their meagre intelligence, that the struggle was one of democracy against privilege, of freedom against slavery, they resisted all attempts to excite them to a demonstration against its continuance. They saw their work fall off, their savings dwindle, their families in want and threatened even with the lack of bread, yet they desired the North to fight out the contest.

If the indictment which Americans bring against the governing classes of England for their sympathy with the South is maintained at the bar of history, it will be because they sympathized with a slave power, and thereby seemed to admit their own government and people to have been wrong on the slavery question for a generation past. The attempt of Englishmen to persuade themselves that slavery was not the issue of the war was a case of wilful blindness. For the truth was patent to all observers: The South held slaves, the North was free. Lincoln had been elected President for the reason that he represented the opposition to the extension of slavery, and his election was the cause of the secession and the war. If the North won, slavery would certainly be restricted, would perhaps be abolished; if the South gained her independence, slavery would be ratified and extended and the African slave trade would probably be revived. The nature of the conflict and its possible consequences were stated to the English by Professor Cairnes and John Stuart Mill in logic impossible of refutation, yet a majority of the million voters remained unconvinced.[596] Nothing could be less candid than many of the current expressions. In 1861 when the avowed object of the war was the restoration of the Union, it was said, Make your war one against slavery and you will have the warm sympathy of the British public; yet Lincoln's plan of compensated emancipation was pronounced chimerical and its proposal insincere, as being for the purpose of affecting European opinion. Gladstone, a friend of the North in January, was later swayed by the sentiment of the powerful classes. On April 24, 1862, he told the men of Manchester that the deplorable struggle was the cause of their misery, but that if the heart of the South were set upon separation, she could not be conquered and Englishmen should therefore be careful not to alienate her 6,000,000 or 10,000,000. He argued against the call of sympathy for the North on the ground that the contest was between slavery and freedom, declaring, We have no faith in the propagation of free institutions at the point of the sword. When William E. Forster said in the House of Commons that he believed it was generally acknowledged that slavery was the cause of the war, he was answered with jeers and shouts of No, no! and The Tariff. When he insisted, Why Vice-President Stephens said that the South went to war to establish slavery as the corner stone of the new republic, his retort was apparently looked upon as only the usual House of Commons repartee.

The government of Great Britain was guilty of culpable negligence in permitting in March the sailing of the Florida, a vessel equipped for war, which had been built in Liverpool for the service of the Confederates. Sincere and diligent inquiry on the part of the authorities in Liverpool would have disclosed her true character and destination, and a friendly disposition towards the United States would have caused her detention until sufficient legal investigation could be made in proceedings for her condemnation.

A still more culpable act of negligence was that which permitted the escape of the Alabama. Adams asked Russell that she be prevented from sailing unless the fact should be established that her purpose was not inimical to the United States. The communication was referred to the proper department and in due course reached Liverpool, where the sympathy of the community with the Confederate States was notorious. The surveyor of the port, who undoubtedly suspected for

---

[596] The number registered at the last election, that of 1859, was 370,000, but probably a million had the right of suffrage.

whom the ship-of-war was intended, took care to shut his eyes to any condemnatory evidence, and made a colorless statement which was submitted by the Commissioners of Customs in London to their solicitor and was adjudged by him to be sufficient ground for advising against her seizure. The Commissioners in their communication to the Lords of the Treasury concurred in the opinion of their legal adviser, but said that the officers at Liverpool will keep a strict watch on the vessel. All these papers came to Earl Russell who, on the advice of the Attorney-General and Solicitor-General, suggested to Adams that the United States consul in Liverpool (Dudley) be instructed to submit to the collector of the port any evidence that confirmed his suspicion. Adams and Dudley were indefatigable and on July 9 Dudley addressed to the collector a letter which no impartial man could have read without being convinced that the vessel in question was designed for the Southern Confederacy. The greater part of his statements, wrote Chief Justice Cockburn afterwards in his opinion dissenting from the award of the Geneva Tribunal, could not have been made available in an English Court. But the moral evidence was complete and needed only time and opportunity to be converted into legal proof. It is hardly surprising, then, that historical analysis of the situation should lead to the conclusion that the collector, the solicitor and the Commissioners of Customs knew in their minds that the Alabama was intended for the Confederate government, wished in their hearts that she might get away, and, since they had not strictly a legal case against her, persuaded themselves that they were performing their official duty. Chief Justice Cockburn, who puts the best face possible upon the action of the English authorities, intimates that, at this juncture, these officials should have addressed an inquiry to the Messrs. Laird, demanding for whom this war-ship was designed. If this had been done, he added, the high character of these gentlemen would doubtless have insured either a refusal to answer or a truthful answer. The former would have helped materially to establish a case against the vessel, the latter would have justified her immediate seizure. This criticism is unanswerable. To require from Dudley direct proof which he must procure in a hostile community, with the quiet opposition probably of an unsympathetic and technical bureaucracy, was unfriendly and unreasonable.

Three weeks had passed since the customs officials in Liverpool and London had been enjoined to find out the truth, but, had they actually conspired to suppress it, they would hardly have acted differently. They showed no disposition to search for proof and carped at the evidence offered them. On July 17 Adams wrote to Dudley to employ a solicitor and secure affidavits to submit to the collector. Four days later Dudley and his solicitor brought to the collector documents amounting to a direct proof. Six persons deposed to the character and destination of the vessel; five of them showed it to be reasonably probable that the Alabama was destined for the Southern Confederacy, while the sixth, a mariner of Birkenhead, swore that it is well known by the hands on board that the vessel is going out as a privateer for the Confederate government to act against the United

States under a commission from Mr. Jefferson Davis. We cannot detain the vessel, says the collector. Insufficient evidence, says the solicitor of customs. You are both right, say the commissioners. The work of getting the Alabama ready went on with swiftness and zeal while the Circumlocution Office moved with the pace of a snail. The papers went to the Lords of the Treasury.

Meanwhile Adams had retained a Queen's counsel of eminence, Sir Robert P. Collier, to whom the six depositions and two additional ones were submitted. Collier's opinion is in no uncertain tone. I am of opinion, he wrote, that the collector of customs would be justified in detaining the vessel. Indeed I should think it his duty to detain her. It appears difficult to make out a stronger case of infringement of the Foreign Enlistment Act, which, if not enforced on this occasion, is little better than a dead letter. It well deserves consideration, whether, if the vessel be allowed to escape, the Federal government would not have serious grounds of remonstrance. This opinion went to the customs authorities in Liverpool. It was the duty of the collector of customs at Liverpool, declared Cockburn, as early as the 22nd of July to detain this vessel. The collector would not act and referred the matter to his superiors, the Commissioners of Customs. Insufficient evidence is still the word of the assistant solicitor of customs, who added, I cannot concur in Collier's views. At this stage in the proceedings, wrote Cockburn, it became in my opinion the duty of the Commissioners of Customs at once to direct the seizure to be made. Misled by advice which they ought to have rejected as palpably erroneous, they unfortunately refused to cause the vessel to be seized.

In the meantime Adams had sent the affidavits, Collier's opinion and many other papers relating to the case to Earl Russell. I ought to have been satisfied with the opinion of Sir Robert Collier, wrote Russell in after years, with a candor which does him honor, and to have given orders to detain the Alabama at Birkenhead.

Now ensues an episode which, useful as it would have been to the writer of an opera-bouffe libretto, or to Dickens for his account of the Circumlocution Office, completely baffles the descriptive pen of the historian. The papers received from the Commissioners of Customs and those which Adams had sent to Russell were submitted to the law officers of the Crown, one set reaching them July 23, the other July 26; that is to say, they reached the senior officer, the Queen's Advocate, on those days. Sir John Harding, who was then the Queen's Advocate, had been ill and incapacitated for business since the latter part of June; in fact, his excitable nerves and weak constitution had succumbed to the strain of work, and he was now verging on insanity. At his private house these papers lay for five days. Work on the Alabama went on briskly, and everybody in the kingdom was satisfied with having done his duty. The collector had referred the matter to the Commissioners; the Commissioners had referred it to the Lords of the Treasury; the Lords and Earl Russell had referred it to the law officers of the Crown. The papers on which perhaps depended war or peace between two great nations either received no notice whatever or were examined only by a lawyer who was going mad. Finally on July 28, the Attorney-General and Solicitor-General got hold of the papers. Their report was conclusive. We recommend, they said on July 29, that without loss of time the vessel be seized by the proper authorities. It was too late. The Alabama had left port that morning, and under pretence of a trial trip had gone out to sea. Yet she was still off the Welsh coast, only fifty miles from Liverpool, where the most ordinary energy on the part of the London and Liverpool authorities would have been sufficient to effect her apprehension before she started on the career which was to do so much in driving the American merchant marine from the high seas.

The Alabama left Liverpool without guns or munitions of war of any kind; these as well as coal were brought to her at the Azores by two British vessels which sailed from England about the middle of August.

However unfriendly the action of England was in the case of the Alabama, it must be borne in mind that the fault was one of omission. The British government, unlike the Emperor of the French, was during the whole war innocent of any overt unfriendly acts. The Queen's speech at the prorogation of Parliament on August 7, 1862 declared that her Majesty had still determined to take no part in the contest on the American continent.

Again, though the dominant sentiment of England toward the North is to be deplored and the want of due diligence in the performance of her duties as a neutral is unquestioned, her atonement has been ample. English books, magazines and newspapers are full of sincere admissions that the public opinion of the country took a wrong direction. In the treaty of Washington, the regret which Great Britain expressed at the escape of the Confederate cruisers is all that can be asked in the way of moral reparation from a high-spirited people conscious of their strength. As far as pecuniary damages were concerned, our case, already very strong, was made absolutely secure by the terms submitting the dispute to arbitration. That the score has been wiped out should be recognized at the bar of history. McClellan's failure on the Peninsula, Pope's inglorious campaign resulting in his crushing defeat at the second battle of Bull Run, during the summer of 1862, had a profound influence on the governors of England. The correspondence between Palmerston and Russell indicates that they were about ready to propose to the Cabinet that England should take the initiative and ask France, Russia and the other powers to join her in some intervention in the struggle in America. The Federals got a very complete smashing, wrote the Prime Minister on September 14; and if Washington or Baltimore fall into the hands of the Confederates, as seems not altogether unlikely, should not England and France address the contending parties and recommend an arrangement upon the basis of separation? Russell replied: I agree with you that the time has come for offering mediation to the United States Government with a view to the recognition of the Confederates. I agree further, that in case of failure, we ought ourselves to recognize the Southern States as an independent State. He suggested, moreover, a meeting of the Cabinet, and if a decision were arrived at, to propose, first, the intervention to France and then on the part of England and France to Russia and the other powers. When Palmerston replied to this letter, he was watching the Antietam campaign, and thought that if the Federals should sustain a great defeat it would be well to proceed with the project of mediation; but if they should have the best of it we may wait awhile and see what may follow.

Gladstone, the Chancellor of the Exchequer and the third member of the Cabinet in importance, was well aware of Palmerston's and Russell's attitude and, feeling certain that such would develop into the policy of the government, anticipated this probable event in a speech at Newcastle on October 7, wherein he expressed positively the view of the Prime Minister and Foreign Secretary as well as that of most of the aristocracy and higher middle class. There is no doubt, he declared, that Jefferson Davis and other leaders of the South have made an army; they are making, it appears, a navy; and they have made what is more than either they have made a nation. We may anticipate with certainty the success of the Southern States so far as their separation from the North is concerned.

An exchange of confidential letters between members of a ministry is a different affair from an announcement to the public of a policy which has not been fully determined upon, and, soon after the delivery of this speech, it was felt that Gladstone had committed an indiscretion; yet for the moment Palmerston and Russell were bent on the policy of mediation and probable subsequent recognition of the independence of the Confederate States. On October 13, Russell sent to his colleagues a confidential memorandum putting the question whether it is not a duty for Europe to ask both parties in the most friendly and conciliatory terms to agree to a suspension of arms.

Fortunately for the North there were differences in the Cabinet, and Gladstone's speech provoked a quasi-reply from Sir George Cornwall Lewis, the member of the Cabinet ranking next in importance to the Chancellor of the Exchequer. Addressing his constituents on October 14, he in effect asserted that the time had not yet arrived for the recognition of the Southern States and he followed this up by circulating among his Cabinet colleagues a confidential counter memorandum in reply to the circular letter of Earl Russell.

A Cabinet meeting was called for October 23. Previous to that time, the Prime Minister had changed his mind and did not travel to London from the country to keep the engagement. Hence no Cabinet meeting was held, but in the informal discussion among the ministers who had gathered, Russell and Gladstone were in favor of some sort of interference while the others held to the position formulated by Lewis. Adams saw the Foreign Secretary by appointment on the same afternoon and said to him: If I had entirely trusted to the construction given by the public to a late speech, I should have begun to think of packing my carpet-bag and trunks. His Lordship, as Adams proceeds to relate the conversation, at once embraced the allusion, and whilst endeavoring to excuse Mr. Gladstone, in fact admitted that his act had been regretted by Lord Palmerston and the other Cabinet officers. Still he could not disavow the sentiments of Mr. Gladstone so far as he understood them, which was not that ascribed to him by the public. Mr. Gladstone was himself willing to disclaim that. He had written to that effect to Lord Palmerston. His Lordship said that the policy of the Government was to adhere to a strict neutrality and to leave the struggle to settle itself. But he could not tell what a month would bring forth. I asked him if I was to understand that policy as not now to be changed. He said, Yes.

In the meantime, the Emperor of the French had made an attempt to conquer Mexico and place a European monarch upon her throne. For the success of his Mexican policy and because France wanted cotton for her manufacturing industries, he favored the Southern Confederacy. On October 30, 1862 he asked his Ambassadors at St. Petersburg and London to propose that the three governments exert their influence at Washington as well as with the Confederates to obtain an armistice for six months.

Earl Russell had shown discretion in warning Adams that he could not tell what a month would bring forth. At a Cabinet meeting in November,[597] he submitted the Emperor's proposition and although it was known that Russia had declined, in terms friendly to the North, to be a party to such a mediation, Russell advised that the proposal of France be accepted. Lewis gave this account of the meeting: Palmerston followed Lord John and supported him but did not say a great deal. The proposal was now thrown before the Cabinet, who proceeded to pick it to pieces. Everybody present threw a stone at it of greater or less size except Gladstone who supported it and two others who expressed no opinion. The principal objection was that the proposed armistice of six months by sea and land, involving a suspension of the commercial blockade, was so grossly unequal so decidedly in favor of the South, that there was no chance of the North agreeing to it. After a time Palmerston saw that the general feeling of the Cabinet was against being a party to the representation, and he capitulated. I do not think his support was very sincere: it certainly was not hearty. Gladstone also made a report. The United States affair has ended and not well, he wrote. Lord Russell rather turned tail. He gave way without resolutely fighting out his battle. Palmerston gave to Russell's proposal a feeble and half-hearted support.[598]

Two months later a combination of circumstances caused the Emperor to propose for his government alone a mediation between the two belligerents. The apparently crushing disaster of Fredericksburg satisfied him, as indeed it confirmed the public opinion of Europe, that the cause of the North was hopeless.

---

[597] Either Nov. 11 or 12.
[598] C. F. Adams, A crisis in Downing St., M. H. S., XLVII, 419, 420; Maxwell, Clarendon, II, 268; Morley, Gladstone, II, 85.

At the same time the distress in the cotton-manufacturing districts of France which had become acute was brought home as the winter wore on. More than a hundred thousand operatives in one department alone were out of work and in a condition of utter misery, subsisting, according to report, by roaming at night from house to house and demanding rather than asking alms. On January 9, the Emperor dictated a despatch, in which he offered courteously and diplomatically, the friendly mediation of his government between the two sections without the suggestion of an armistice which had been contained in his former proposition. This message went through the usual diplomatic channels and was presented, on February 3, 1863, by the French Minister at Washington to Seward, who, three days later, acting upon the President's instructions, declined the offer in a polite, gently argumentative and considerate letter. The Emperor lacked the courage to proceed further in his policy of intervention without the co-operation of Great Britain which was persistently withheld.

Lincoln's Emancipation Proclamation was received abroad with coldness and suspicion. The governing classes of England, whose organs in 1861 had asserted that, if the North should make her fight for the emancipation of the negro, she would commend her cause strongly to their sympathies, could now see in it nothing but an attempt to excite a servile insurrection. But the friends of the North comprehended it. John Stuart Mill wrote that no American could have exulted more than himself; John Bright said, I applaud the proclamation.[599] These utterances proved a prelude to the rise of anti-slavery sentiment toward the end of the year 1862. When the intelligence came that the President's emancipation policy was confirmed by the supplementary proclamation of January 1, the demonstrations of support were greater than had been known for any movement since the uprising for the abolition of the duties on corn. A deputation from the Emancipation Society waited on the American minister to offer to President Lincoln their warmest congratulations; Reverend Newman Hall, one of the speakers, asserted that the leading newspapers really did not represent the feelings of the masses. On a Sunday Spurgeon thus prayed before his congregation of many thousands, Now, O God! we turn our thoughts across the sea to the terrible conflict of which we knew not what to say; but now the voice of freedom shows where is right. We pray Thee give success to this glorious proclamation of liberty which comes to us from across the waters. We much feared our brethren were not in earnest and would not come to this. Bondage and the lash can claim no sympathy from us. God bless and strengthen the North, give victory to their arms. The immense congregation responded to this invocation in the midst of the prayer with a fervent Amen. Public meetings were constantly occurring. The Duke of Argyll and Milner Gibson, both Cabinet ministers, made speeches, indicating

---

[599] C. F. Adams, Trans-Atlantic Historical Solidarity, 112; C. F. Adams, 297; Index, Nov. 6, 1862.

greater confidence in the treatment of the American question and its relation to slavery. There was even a reaction at Liverpool, which town had witnessed with joy the departure of the Alabama. Bristol, the last port in Great Britain to relinquish the slave trade, addressed the President with respectful sympathy. On January 29, Exeter Hall was the scene of a more earnest demonstration of public opinion than had been known in London since the days of the Anti-Corn Law League. So vast was the crowd that an overflow meeting was held in a lower room and another in the open air. In the great hall, the mention of Jefferson Davis brought out manifestations of dislike, while the name of Abraham Lincoln was greeted with a burst of enthusiasm, the audience rising, cheering and waving hats and handkerchiefs. The resolutions adopted showed intelligence as well as fellow-feeling. On the same night a public meeting at Bradford, Yorkshire, declared that any intervention, physical or moral, on behalf of the slave power would be disgraceful, and closed its proceedings with three hearty cheers for President Lincoln. A large anti-slavery meeting in Gloucestershire, in a sympathetic address to the President, deplored any apparent complicity [of Englishmen] with the Southern States in the clandestine equipment of war ships. Everybody that I now meet, declared John Bright, says to me, 'public opinion seems to have undergone a considerable change.'

The month of February witnessed similar large meetings, which adopted like resolutions. There were gatherings at Leeds, Bath, Edinburgh, Paisley, Carlisle, Birmingham, Manchester, Liverpool, Merthyr Tydvil and many other places. A concourse of citizens in Glasgow said to the President in their address, We honor you and we congratulate you. On March 26, at a meeting of skilled laborers held in London at the call of the Trades-Unions, John Bright took the chair, and made an eloquent speech, in which he expressed the meaning of the assemblage and the spirit of their address to Abraham Lincoln. Privilege has shuddered, he said, at what might happen to old Europe if this grand experiment should succeed. But you, the workers you, striving after a better time you, struggling upwards toward the light with slow and painful steps you have no cause to look with jealousy upon a country which, menaced by the great nations of the globe, is that one where labor has met with the highest honor, and where it has reaped its greatest reward. This fearful struggle, he went on, is between one section where labor is honored more than elsewhere in the world and another section where labor is degraded and the laborer is made a chattel. He closed his speech with prophetic words: Impartial history will tell that, when your statesmen were hostile or coldly neutral, when many of your rich men were corrupt, when your press which ought to have instructed and defended was mainly written to betray, the fate of a continent and its vast population being in peril, you clung to freedom with an unfaltering trust that God in his infinite mercy will yet make it the heritage of all His children.

It is interesting to look, with the eyes of Adams, upon these expressions of a noble public opinion. Thus wrote he in his diary: January 17, 1863. It is quite clear that the current is now setting very strongly with us among the body of the people. January 30. Things are improving here. The manifestation made at Exeter Hall last night is reported as one of the most extraordinary ever made in London, and proves, pretty conclusively the spirit of the middle classes here as elsewhere. It will not change the temper of the higher classes but it will do something to moderate the manifestation of it. Speaking of a large and respectable delegation of the British and Foreign Anti-Slavery Society, he wrote: They left me with hearty shakes of the hand that marked the existence of active feeling at bottom. It was not the lukewarmness and indifference of the aristocracy but the genuine English heartiness of good-will. On February 26, The current is still setting strongly with us among the people.

These demonstrations show what potent arguments for the Northern side were the Emancipation Proclamation and the organized anti-slavery agitation. Those Englishmen who had espoused the cause of the South now became, by the logic of the situation, apologists for slavery. The Times presented the Biblical argument for the justification of it and told the story of Paul and Onesimus in the language and temper of the Southern planter. Slavery, it argued further, is no more at variance with the spirit of the gospel than sumptuous fare, purple and fine linen; and it said of the Proclamation that was arousing the enthusiasm of the masses, President Lincoln calls to his aid the execrable expedient of a servile insurrection. Egypt is destroyed but his heart is hardened and he will not let the people go. The Saturday Review urged that the laws dictated from on high, as recorded in the Old Testament, sanctioned and protected property in slaves. But the American law-giver not only confiscates his neighbor's slaves but orders the slaves to cut their master's throats. Nor is the matter left to the remote guidance of Old Testament precedent. St. Paul sent Onesimus, the fugitive slave of that time, back to his master Philemon; so that without the master's consent it was not competent, even in an Apostle, to release a slave. But what St. Paul might not do Abraham Lincoln may. Later it spoke of the movement which was ennobling the common people of England as a carnival of cant arousing agitation on behalf of the divine right of insurrection and massacre. The Times and Saturday Review, according to the Spectator, represented the higher intelligence of England, and their ground of reasoning revealed clearly the bond of sympathy between the two landed aristocracies separated by the sea. The Southern lords, by their system of labor, were relieved from the minute cares of money-making, were enabled to maintain an open and generous hospitality, and were afforded leisure for devotion to society and politics, thus obtaining a kind of community of life, tastes and aims with the English noblemen, who, in turn, had begun by looking kindly upon the Southern Confederacy, wishing for its success, and ended with taking up cudgels for negro slavery.

The sympathies of many of the eminent literary men were withheld from the North. Grote, who loved democracy in Greece and could palliate its excesses in

Athens, criticised with acrimony the Northern people, because they insisted that England had violated her declared neutrality and because their protests were not couched in courteous and polished language. Carlyle, who had received the first money for his French Revolution from Boston, when not a penny had been realized in England, and who was profoundly thankful for all that this implied, as well as for the needed money, had now no fellow-feeling with the North. No war ever raging in my time, he said, was to me more profoundly foolish looking. Neutral I am to a degree: I for one. Again he spoke of it as a smoky chimney which had taken fire, and when asked to publish something in regard to the conflict, he wrote his Ilias Americana in nuce. Peter of the North (to Paul of the South): Paul, you unaccountable scoundrel, I find you hire your servants for life, not by the month or year as I do. You are going straight to hell, you

Paul: Good Words, Peter. The risk is my own. I am willing to take the risk, Hire you your servants by the month or the day and get straight to heaven; leave me to my own method.

Peter: No, I won't. I will beat your brains out first!

(And is trying dreadfully ever since, but cannot yet manage it).

Dickens, who had brought tears and laughter into every household from the Atlantic to the Missouri river, who was loved in the free States as few writers have been loved, might have been expected from his vehement denunciation of slavery in the American Notes to see, now that the battle was joined, that the right would prevail. Yet when a friend of his returning from America in the spring of 1863 said that the North would ultimately triumph, he treated this opinion as a harmless hallucination. Indirectly and undesignedly he was a contributing cause to the view which the English higher classes took of the North, for his caricatures in Martin Chuzzlewit came to be regarded as a true portrayal of the character of the men and women who were now risking all for unity and freedom. But Anthony Trollope had an assured confidence that the North would win.[600] And Tennyson, the poet of the people, though filled with conventional horror at the war, was inspired by the hope of the abolition of slavery and used to sing with enthusiasm, Glory, glory hallelujah, His soul goes marching on. The most significant feature in the aspect of English sentiment during the spring of 1863 is the feeling of our friends that our cause was utterly hopeless. Queen Victoria and Disraeli were certain that the Union could not be restored.[601] The news of Hooker's disaster at Chancellorsville strengthened this belief. Then came the intelligence of Lee's invasion of Pennsylvania, fostering the rumors which were abroad that England and France would decide on intervention. Attempts were now made by assemblies of the people to stimulate and extend that phase of sentiment which favored recognition of the Southern Confederacy. Meetings were held in Manchester, Preston,

---

[600] Autobiography, 149; see North America, II, Chap. XVI.
[601] Review of Buckle's Disraeli, IV, Nation, July 27, 1916.

Sheffield and some other places which recommended this policy and were answered by other gatherings that protested against any interference.

On April 5, 1863, Earl Russell stopped the Alexandra, a gun-boat which was building at Birkenhead for the Southern Confederacy. His action was contested and although the decision in the Court of Exchequer was against the English government, the case remained for a long while in the Courts on one legal point and another, with the result that the vessel never got into Confederate hands to be used against American commerce.

The fluctuations of ministerial and House of Commons discussions during the spring and summer of 1863 need not here be reviewed; it should, however, be stated that a distinct line of demarcation is to be discerned between English sentiment and action before and after the victories of Gettysburg and Vicksburg, the news of which reached Europe soon after the middle of July.

In the meantime, work was proceeding on two steam iron-clad rams which the Lairds were building at Birkenhead for the Confederates. Adams was diligent in calling Earl Russell's attention to the transaction, and in furnishing him the evidence supplied by Dudley, our consul at Liverpool, which showed the character and destination of these vessels; and in pursuance of these communications, Earl Russell conscientiously set affairs in train to ascertain for whom the rams were building, his design being to stop them should there be warrant for such action under the law. While their construction was a matter of common knowledge, and while, as the Times remarked, ninety-nine people out of a hundred believe that these steam rams are 'intended to carry on hostilities sooner or later against the Federals,' Captain Bulloch, the able naval representative of the Southern Confederacy, who had contracted for these war-ships, as well as for the Alabama, and had been enlightened by the seizure of the Alexandra, was managing the business astutely, with the sympathetic co-operation of the Lairds. To a report that they were for the Emperor of the French, Palmerston, in an allusion in the House of Commons, gave some credence: when this was shown to be without foundation, it was stated to the English government that they were for the viceroy of Egypt. This was in turn denied. Representations were then made to the officials who were investigating the matter that they were owned by a firm of French merchants, and for this there was a legal basis, inasmuch as Bulloch, fearing the seizure of the vessels, had sold them in June to a French firm who had engaged to resell them to him when they should get beyond British jurisdiction.

Earl Russell caused all the facts which were submitted to him to be sifted with care by the Law officers of the Crown who gave him two positive opinions nearly a month apart, that there was no evidence capable of being presented to a Court of Justice, that the ships were intended for the Confederates, but that, on the other hand, the claim of French ownership seemed to be legally sustained: they could not, therefore, advise the government to detain the vessels. Still Russell was not satisfied, and he continued his inquiries, leaving no stone unturned to arrive at the truth; but, in spite of his suspicions, he could not get over the palpable tokens that they belonged to a firm of Paris merchants. He therefore wrote to Adams, on September 1, that the government was advised that they could not in any way interfere with these ships, but he promised that they would maintain a careful watch, and be ready to stop them should trustworthy evidence show any proceeding contrary to the statute. At this time, he was at his country-seat in Scotland, and his letter did not reach Adams until four o'clock in the afternoon of September 4.

Meanwhile our Minister had returned from an outing in Scotland, cheered by friendly intercourse with members of the government; but, on his arrival in London, he was immediately confronted with the critical question of the iron-clad rams, one of which, as Dudley had good reason to believe, might at any time go to sea. On September 3 Adams wrote to Russell, transmitting copies of further depositions and averring that there were no reasonable grounds for doubt that the vessels were intended for the Confederate service; and next day, hearing from Dudley that one of them was about to depart, he sent to the Foreign Office a last, solemn protest against the commission of such an act of hostility against a friendly nation. Soon afterwards he received Russell's note of September 1 which, as he wrote in his diary, affected me deeply. I clearly foresee that a collision must now come out of it. I must not, however, do anything to accelerate it, and yet must maintain the honor of my country with proper spirit. The issue must be properly made up before the world on its merits. The prospect is dark for poor America. After a night given to such reflections, My thoughts turned strongly upon the present crisis. My conclusion was that another note must be addressed to Lord Russell. So I drew one which I intended only to gain time previous to the inevitable result. This was his famous despatch of September 5: My Lord, he wrote, at this moment, when one of the iron-clad vessels is on the point of departure from this kingdom, on its hostile errand against the United States, I am honored with yours of the 1st instant. I trust I need not express how profound is my regret at the conclusion to which Her Majesty's Government have arrived. I can regard it no otherwise than as practically opening to the insurgents free liberty in this kingdom to execute a policy of attacking New York, Boston and Portland and of breaking our blockade. It would be superfluous in me to point out to your lordship that this is war.

As early as September 1, however, Russell was better than his word to Adams. Layard, the Under Secretary for Foreign Affairs, who was in London, wrote on that day to the Treasury: I am directed by Earl Russell to request that you will state to the Lord's Commissioners of her Majesty's Treasury that so much suspicion attaches to the iron-clad vessels at Birkenhead, that if sufficient evidence can be obtained to lead to the belief that they are intended for the Confederate States Lord Russell thinks the vessels ought to be detained until further examination can be made. Reflection, in which the belief that he had been tricked in the escape of the

Alabama undoubtedly played a part, led him, two days later [September 3], to direct that the iron-clad rams be prevented from sailing. On this day he wrote from Meikleour, Scotland: My dear Palmerston, the conduct of the gentlemen who have contracted for the two iron-clads at Birkenhead is so very suspicious that I have thought it necessary to direct that they should be detained. The Solicitor-General has been consulted, and concurs in the measure as one of policy, though not of strict law. We shall thus test the law and, if we have to pay damages, we have satisfied the opinion which prevails here as well as in America, that that kind of neutral hostility should not be allowed to go on without some attempt to stop it. If you do not approve, pray appoint a Cabinet for Tuesday or Wednesday next [the 8th or 9th]. Palmerston did not dissent and therefore called no meeting of the Cabinet. But Russell was not content to bide the slow course of the post or the approval of the Prime Minister, and on the same day [September 3] telegraphed to Layard to give direction to stop the iron-clads as soon as there is reason to believe that they are actually about to put to sea and to detain them until further orders. On September 4, he sent word to Adams that the matter is under the serious and anxious consideration of Her Majesty's Government; but this Adams did not receive until after he had despatched his note, saying, It would be superfluous in me to point out to your Lordship that this is war. On September 5 Russell ordered that the vessels be prevented from leaving Liverpool on a trial trip or on any other pretext until satisfactory evidence can be given as to their destination, and on the same day he sent a confidential note to the chargé d'affaires in Washington requesting that Secretary Seward be apprised that they had been stopped from leaving port; but for some unexplained reason he did not advise Adams of this action until three days later.

At the same time the Foreign Office made a systematic and careful investigation, demonstrating, to a moral certainty, that the French ownership was a blind, and that the iron-clad rams were intended for the Confederates. On October 8, by order of Earl Russell, the vessel the more advanced in construction was seized, and the next day the Broad Arrow was likewise put upon the other. The Lairds were annoyed at this action, and their operatives showed much ill feeling. In order to defeat any attempt at rescue the ships were watched by a powerful naval force. The question whether the iron-clads should be condemned was never passed upon by the courts. Neither the government nor the owners were eager to run the chances of a trial. In the end, as the best way out of the complication, the vessels were purchased by the British Admiralty.

Stopping these iron-clads is a question of life or death, wrote Fox, assistant Secretary of the Navy.[602] They were indeed formidable vessels of war and had they got away would undoubtedly have broken the blockade at Charleston and Wilmington; and as the blockade, constantly growing in efficiency, was a potent

---

[602] Life of J. M. Forbes, II, 22.

weapon on the Northern side, the harm would have been incalculable: the victories even of Gettysburg and Vicksburg might have been neutralized. Bulloch deemed that our iron-clads might sweep the blockading fleet from the sea front of every harbor, ascend the Potomac and render Washington itself untenable, and lay Portsmouth (N. H.) and Philadelphia under contribution. From some such damage, Earl Russell, by his careful and decisive action, had saved the North and thereby prevented a war between the United States and Great Britain, which the energy of Bulloch and the sympathy and cupidity of a firm of Birkenhead ship-builders had come near bringing about. The seizure of the rams was a serious blow to the Confederate cause.[603]

As early as January, Benjamin, the Confederate Secretary of State, complained, when writing to Slidell, that Mason had been discourteously treated by Earl Russell; in March, that the irritation against Great Britain is fast increasing; and in June he indulged in words almost abusive of the English government. On August 4, he wrote to Mason that the President was convinced, from the recent debates in Parliament, that England would not recognize the Confederacy, and he therefore instructed him to consider his mission as at an end and withdraw from London. Mason received this despatch on September 14, and after waiting a week to consult with Slidell, notified Earl Russell that in accordance with his instructions he should terminate his mission. Jefferson Davis in his message to his Congress in December, gave vent to his dissatisfaction with the conduct of the British government, two of his many grievances being that they respected the Federal blockade and had seized the iron-clad rams.

Although England's attitude toward us was not as just as ours toward her during the Crimean War, it should be borne in mind that our only well-wisher in Europe was Russia, and that the course of the British government if contrasted with that of the French will appear to border on friendliness. England, indeed, was the insurmountable obstacle to a recognition of the Southern Confederacy by France and other European nations. While the English Cabinet looked with regret on the operations of English merchants and ship-builders who, by selling arms, munitions and vessels to the South greatly embarrassed the government in its relations with the United States, Louis Napoleon was instigating the Confederates to construct two iron-clads and four clipper corvettes in France and giving an indirect assurance that they might be armed and equipped as well; but these vessels never got to sea under the Confederate flag, and in November, 1863, the Emperor altered his attitude toward the American war. While Russell declined to see Mason, subsequent to their first meeting shortly after his arrival in February, 1862, and Palmerston saw him only once at a time when all danger of foreign interference had passed, the Emperor accorded three interviews to Slidell and the Minister for

---

[603] In this account of the affair of the iron-clad rams I have been much assisted by an article by Brooks Adams printed in the M. H. S. Proceedings XLV, 243.

Foreign Affairs and other members of the imperial ministry and household maintained with him an unrestricted intercourse. Moreover Louis Napoleon conquered Mexico and placed a European monarch on her throne.[604]

[604] My authorities are IV, Chap. XXII with the various references; Charles F. Adams, Life of Adams; Trans-Atlantic Solidarity; A Crisis in Downing St., M. H. S., XLVII, 372; Brooks Adams. The Seizure of the Laird Rams, M. H. S., XLV, 243; Letters of Goldwin Smith to C. E. Norton, M. H. S., XLIX, 106; Diary of Benjamin Moran, M. H. S., XLVIII, 431; Morley's Gladstone, II; Maxwell's Clarendon, II; Fitzmaurice's Granville, I; The Public Life and Dip. Corr. of James M. Mason; Retrospection of an Active Life, John Bigelow, II; Life of John Bright, G. M. Trevelyan; Atkins, W. H. Russell; Dasent, Delane. I have not attempted to reconcile my account with Seward's declarations to Welles noted in the Diary under dates Aug. 12, 29, Sept. 17, 18, I, 399, 429, 435,437.

Chapter VIII

WITH superior resources, larger armies as well disciplined as those of the South and better equipped and supplied, with generals equal on the whole in ability, as may be asserted after Gettysburg and Vicksburg, the North was certain to win in the end provided it would with persistency and patience make the sacrifice of men and money necessary to subjugate the brave and high-spirited people of the Southern Confederacy, who were still determined on resistance. But volunteering had practically ceased, and only a pretty rigorous conscription could furnish the soldiers needed. Such a measure was contrary to the genius and habits of the people and could not be enforced unless the government were backed by public sentiment. Whether the President would receive this necessary support might have been momentarily doubted from what took place in New York City shortly after the victories of Gettysburg and Vicksburg.

During the enrolment under the Conscription Act of March 3, 1863, disturbances had occurred, but these had been speedily quelled, and though giving rise to local excitement, were not of a nature to indicate any extended and violent opposition to the policy of filling the armies of the North by compulsion. On July 7 the draft under the Conscription Act began in Rhode Island, next day in Massachusetts and proceeded quietly in various districts until Saturday, July 11, which had been the day appointed for the drawings to commence in New York City. Although the popular dissatisfaction with the draft was known and there were rumors of trouble and a large crowd had assembled at the provost-marshal's office, the drawing took place on this Saturday without any disturbance whatever; a spirit of positive good humor prevailed. But on the Sunday, publication in the newspapers of the names of the conscripts, who were seen to be nearly all mechanics and laborers, revealed the practical effect of the draft at the same time that it emphasized the provisions of the Act for compulsory military service during three years. Those who had already been drawn or were liable to be drawn on the following days became excited, then angry. Crowds gathered to discuss the provisions of the law and the opinion of prominent Democrats that it was unconstitutional. The provision which allowed a man to buy himself off for three hundred dollars was the main grievance. This had been introduced into the act at a time when the sum specified seemed sufficient as a bounty wherewith to procure a substitute. But now owing to the continued decline in the purchasing power of the paper currency, the demand for labor, the rise in wages, and the increased cost of living, a soldier could not be had for that amount. Hence the provision was denounced as an unworthy device to enable the rich to escape cheaply whilst the poor must take up their burden. At the end of this day of busy rumor and seething agitation the populace was convinced that the draft was unjust and ought to be resisted.

Monday dawned.[605] Aware of the commotion in the city, the authorities had taken some measures for protection. Shortly after seven the provost-marshal opened the head-quarters of the Ninth District, on the corner of Third avenue and Forty-sixth street, and made ready to continue the draft. The wheel was placed on the table. Slips of paper bearing the names of the men liable, rolled tightly and bound with a ring of india-rubber, were put into the wheel. One-fifth of the names were to be drawn, and each person so designated, unless physically or mentally unfit for service or exempt for other reasons under the law, if failing to furnish a substitute or pay three hundred dollars, must serve in the army for three years or until the end of the war. At ten o'clock the wheel began to turn, and at each revolution a man blindfolded drew out a name which the provost-marshal read to the comparatively orderly crowd of mechanics and laborers who filled the room. For half an hour the business proceeded. A hundred names had been drawn when a pistol was fired in the street, and a mass of brickbats and paving-stones came crashing through the windows and doors of the house, hurled by a mob of some thousands, which had been gathering since early in the day. The workmen of the Second and Sixth avenue street railroads and of many of the manufactories in the upper part of the city had stopped work and, parading the streets, had persuaded and compelled others to join their ranks. When their force had become a little army, they moved with one accord to the place where the drafting was going on and attacked and took possession of the house, driving the provost-marshal and his deputies away. The furniture was broken up, turpentine poured on the floor and the building set fire to; soon this and the adjoining houses in the block were ablaze. The superintendent of police came near on a tour of inspection, and, though not in uniform, was recognized, set upon and badly mauled; it was only by an exhibition of remarkable pluck that he escaped with his life. The provost-marshal's guard from the Invalid corps, hurrying to the scene, were stopped and pelted with stones by the dense crowd of rioters which now filled the streets for two squares from the burning buildings. The soldiers fired into the mob but with little effect; they were overpowered and deprived of their muskets and many of them were cruelly beaten. A strong squad of police appeared and received a volley of stones; they drew their clubs and revolvers and charged the mob, but after a fight lasting a few minutes were forced by vastly overpowering numbers to retreat.

Emboldened by these victories, the mob roamed about the city at will, showing especial wrath toward abolitionists and negroes on the ground that men were being drafted for an abolition war. On the Tuesday the riot was worse, as thieves and ruffians swelling the crowd went about bent on plunder under cover of the rioters' grievance; but effective defensive measures had now been undertaken by the

---

[605] July 13.

authorities. On Wednesday a notice that the draft had been suspended influenced many to retire to their homes; and, at the same time militia regiments that had been sent to Pennsylvania to resist Lee began to arrive and use harsh measures to suppress the mob. By Wednesday evening order was in the main restored and on Thursday what remained of the mob was suppressed by the Seventh and other militia regiments coming from Pennsylvania and by a force of United States infantry and cavalry.[606]

The draft was only temporarily interrupted. Strenuous precautions were taken to insure order during its continuance. Ten thousand infantry and three batteries of artillery picked troops including the regulars were sent to New York city from the Army of the Potomac; the First Division of the New York State National Guard was ordered upon duty; and the governor by proclamation counselled and admonished the citizens to submit to the execution of the law of Congress. On August 19 the draft was resumed and continued with entire peacefulness. It was operated generally throughout the country, and, although it did not actually furnish many soldiers to the army, owing to the numerous exemptions under the statute and the large number of those drafted who paid the commutation money, it stimulated enlistments by inducing States, counties, cities and towns to add to the government bounty other bounties sufficient to prevail upon men to volunteer and fill the respective quotas.[607] Ten days after the battle of Gettysburg, as we have already seen, Lee with his army crossed the Potomac into Virginia. Meade followed leisurely. A campaign of manoeuvres ensued with skirmishes and combats but no general battle. Lincoln had lost confidence in Meade's power of aggression. I have no faith that Meade will attack Lee, he said; nothing looks like it to me. I believe he can never have another as good opportunity as that which he trifled away. Everything since has dragged with him.[608] On September 21, Lincoln unbosomed himself to Welles. It is the same old story of the Army of the Potomac, he said. Imbecility, inefficiency don't want to do is defending the Capital. Oh it is terrible, terrible, this weakness, this indifference of our Potomac generals, with such armies of good and brave men.[609] On October 16, Lincoln gave Meade a warrant for action. If General Meade, he wrote in a letter to Halleck, can now attack Lee on a field no more than equal for us and will do so with all the skill and courage which he, his officers and men possess, the honor will be his if he succeeds and the blame may be mine if he fails.[610]

---

[606] IV: Welles's Diary, I; J. M. Forbes, II.

[607] IV, 330.

[608] July 26. Welles's Diary, I, 383. Taking everything into account this is hardly inconsistent with Lincoln's letter to Halleck, O. R., XXVII, Pt. I, 105; see Pennypacker, 223.

[609] Welles's Diary, I, 439; see O. R., XXIX, Pt. II, 207.

[610] G. Bradford, Am. Hist. Rev., 318; O. R., XXIX, Pt. II, 332.

Meade's private correspondence shows a timidity and hesitancy hardly to be looked for in one who had been known as a fighting general. He manoeuvred constantly with the aim not to fight Lee unless he obtained the better position. The source of this excessive caution as contrasted with his former attitude when as division and corps commander he criticised the general of the army for the same defect may have lain in the difference between the responsibility of the chief and the freedom of the subordinate, or it may be that Meade was no longer the man he had been before and during the Gettysburg campaign; that the stress of those days had impaired his nerve and diminished his aggressiveness. If we dwell on his remark that in ten days he had lived thirty years,[611] we may incline to this belief. At all events, during this campaign, nothing was done after Gettysburg toward bringing the war to an end. After the battle of Stone's river, Rosecrans remained inactive for nearly six months, recuperating and resupplying his army and fortifying Murfreesborough. The Government urged him forward and insisted that he should drive the Confederates out of Tennessee and take Chattanooga. The McClellan drama was played over again. The General complained of the lack of supplies, of forage, of revolving rifles for his mounted troops, of his great deficiency in cavalry as compared with his adversary; in the course of his correspondence with Stanton and Halleck, he displayed the art of a dexterous controversialist. At last, on June 24, he began to move and inaugurated a campaign of brilliant strategy which accomplished a momentous gain for Northern arms. Helped by the moral effect of Gettysburg and Vicksburg, he manoeuvred the Confederates under Bragg out of middle Tennessee, continued his advance through a very difficult country, and, without having been obliged to fight a battle, marched on the 9th of September into Chattanooga, which, with Richmond and Vicksburg, constituted the three most important strategic points of the Southern Confederacy.

Rosecrans was elated at the success of his strategy and thought that Bragg was retreating southward. Eager to strike at the Confederate army he ordered his troops in pursuit, and being under the necessity of crossing the mountains at gaps far apart he separated widely his different corps and divisions. But Bragg had not the slightest intention to retreat; on the contrary, he turned on his enemy. This movement placed Rosecrans in peril, and it became, as he himself related, a matter of life and death to effect the concentration of the army. For nearly a week he wrought with desperate energy, and by September 18 had accomplished the concentration, although not without some mischance; but the loss of sleep, the fear that Bragg might crush, one after another, his different detachments, as some now think he had it in his power to do, the intense anxiety on two successive nights for the safety of one of his corps, all these combined to unnerve the Union commander, who in the opinion of his army was whipped before he went into the

---

[611] *Ante.*

battle which the Confederate general was determined to bring on. Re-enforced by troops from Johnston's army, which became available after the fall of Vicksburg, by Buckner's corps from Knoxville and by Longstreet's corps from the Army of Northern Virginia, Bragg outnumbered his opponent and made on September 19 an indecisive attack.

Next day took place the fierce and bloody battle of Chickamauga, the great battle of the West. It would have been an undecided contest or a Union victory, since the defensive position and the intrenchments fully compensated for the disparity in numbers, had not Rosecrans lacked nerve for the contest. His force was the Army of the Cumberland, seasoned and intrepid soldiers, who, as their history shows, were able, under proper command, to accomplish wonders, but in this case were affected by the spirit, as indeed they were sacrificed by the orders, which emanated from headquarters. The battle was proceeding with variant fortune, when the execution of an ill-considered and unlucky order from the commanding general opened a gap in the line of battle, through which the Confederates poured and, throwing two divisions into confusion and routing two others, drove a mass of soldiers panic-stricken from the field. Rosecrans was carried away in the crowd of fugitives and, fearing that the whole army was vanquished, rode on into Chattanooga, twelve to fifteen miles away, for the purpose of taking measures for the defence of the city. He sent thence at five o'clock in the afternoon a despatch to Halleck saying: We have met with a serious disaster. Enemy overwhelmed us, drove our right, pierced our centre and scattered troops there. General George H. Thomas commanded the left wing of the army and with 25,000 men repulsed during the whole afternoon the assaults of a force double his number, holding his position with such steadiness that he earned the title of the Rock of Chickamauga. Later, under orders from Rosecrans, Thomas withdrew to Chattanooga, where was assembled the remainder of the army; the city was then fortified so that it could be taken only by a regular siege; this was forthwith commenced by Bragg.

Before the battle of Chickamauga, Grant had been ordered to send re-enforcements to Rosecrans from Vicksburg, but it had taken a week for the despatch to reach him and although two divisions were now on the way and two others were getting ready to move, all of them, under Sherman's command, word to this effect had not reached Washington. Telegrams from Rosecrans to the President and from Dana to Stanton, urging the necessity of immediate re-enforcements to hold Chattanooga and the Tennessee line, were received late in the evening of September 23; and Stanton, impressed with the need of prompt action, summoned a midnight conference. Lincoln, to whom John Hay brought the request at his summer abode, the Soldiers' Home, bestrode his horse and took his way this moonlight night to the War Department, where in addition to the Secretary and three of his subordinates, he met Halleck, Seward and Chase. Stanton proposed sending troops to Chattanooga from the Army of the Potomac;

and while the President and Halleck were at first averse to this project, he was so earnest in advocating it that, with the support of Seward and Chase, he overbore their opposition; in the end, the council agreed that if Meade did not purpose an advance at once, the Eleventh and Twelfth Corps under Hooker should be sent to Rosecrans. After conferring with Meade, these 16,000 men were brought from Culpeper Court House, Virginia, to Washington by rail, there transferred to the Baltimore and Ohio railroad and carried via Bellaire, Columbus, Indianapolis, Louisville and Nashville, to the Tennessee river. The time of transport, six days for the largest part of the force, showed for that period excellent work.

Yet something was necessary besides additional soldiers: another general must command. Rosecrans, who through his defeat at Chickamauga had lost all his buoyancy and prestige, became more irresolute than ever and showed himself unable to cope with the difficulties of the situation. The danger lay in lack of supplies; this might compel the evacuation of Chattanooga. The Confederates commanded the Tennessee river and the direct and good wagon roads on the south side of it; and though the Union Army held the country north of it, their supplies had to be wagoned over long, circuitous and rough mountain roads from Stevenson and Bridgeport, which had rail connections with Nashville. At best the line of communication was difficult, but with the autumn rains, it became exceedingly precarious. The army was verging on starvation. The roads, wrote Dana, are in such a state that wagons are eight days making the journey from Stevenson to Chattanooga. Though subsistence stores are so nearly exhausted here, the wagons are compelled to throw overboard portions of their precious cargo to get through at all. It does not seem possible to hold out here another week without a new avenue of supplies. Amid all this the practical incapacity of the general commanding is astonishing. His imbecility appears to be contagious and it is difficult for anyone to get anything done.

Two days before this telegram was received, the impression made by the despatches of Rosecrans himself and the information contained in Dana's frequent and circumstantial accounts had decided the Government to place Grant in supreme command of all the military operations in the West except those under Banks. Grant at once relieved Rosecrans and placed Thomas in command of the Army of the Cumberland telegraphing to Thomas from Louisville to hold Chattanooga at all hazards. Thomas replied promptly, We will hold the town till we starve. The force of this despatch, implying the straits in which the garrison lay, is illustrated by Wilson's and Dana's experience who, after a ride of fifty-five miles, reached Chattanooga shortly before midnight. They obtained at the headquarters of Captain Horace Porter a supper of his best one square of fried hard-tack with a small piece of salt pork and a cup of army coffee without milk or sugar. As it was, they fared better than their horses, who were each given two ears of corn but no hay.[612]

Rosecrans undoubtedly had in mind some plan for securing a better line of supply, but he lacked the energy and resolution to carry it into effect. Grant's wisdom in placing Thomas in command was immediately manifest. The change at headquarters here is already strikingly perceptible, wrote Dana from Chattanooga, October 23. Order prevails instead of universal chaos. William F. Smith, the Chief Engineer of the Army, had matured a plan for opening a short route of supplies from Bridgeport, which he now submitted to Thomas, who approved it and gave the necessary instructions for its execution.

Grant now repaired in person to the scene of action. Having proceeded as rapidly as possible by rail from Louisville to Bridgeport, he must thence ride fifty-five miles over the road which served as the main line of supply for the army. A number of weeks before, on a visit to New Orleans, he had had a fall from a runaway horse, receiving severe injuries which still kept him on crutches. Through a chilling rain-storm, he now rode with difficulty over the rough way where, owing to the heavy rains and the washouts from the mountains, the mud was often knee-deep; he was carried over places unsafe for him to cross on horseback. He related that the roads were strewn with the débris of broken wagons and the carcasses of thousands of starved mules and horses. On the night of October 23, he arrived at Chattanooga, wet, dirty, and well. His clear eye and clear face showed to his comrades-in-arms that he was mentally at his best; his energy and enterprise extending to the officers and diffused through the rank and file, the impetus communicated to the operations, the marvellous change from the régime of Rosecrans at once gave evidence that a compeller of men, like Cæsar and Napoleon, like Robert E. Lee, was at the head of affairs.

On the morning after his arrival Grant made a reconnaissance in company with Thomas and Smith, approved their project and urged its prompt execution. It proved eminently successful in securing supplies for the army. The seizure by the Union troops of this advantageous line of supply was a bitter disappointment to Bragg and he endeavored, without success, to recover it by a night attack.

On November 15, Sherman rode into Chattanooga; his soldiers, the Army of the Tennessee, were close behind him. Grant had already matured his plan of attack and, at the earliest possible moment put it in execution. Thomas, Sherman, William F. Smith and Hooker were efficient aids. The action of the three days, November 23, 24, 25, is called the battle of Chattanooga; its culminating and most dramatic episode was the battle of Missionary Ridge. About the middle of the afternoon (November 25) the word was given to Thomas's soldiers, who held the centre, to advance. They carried the first line of rifle-pits, and should have halted for further commands; but here they were exposed to a murderous fire, and would not fall back. Without orders, indeed in spite of orders, those twenty thousand

---

[612] Wilson's Dana, 279; Under the Old Flag, I, 270.

Western soldiers, conspicuous among whom was Sheridan, rushed up Missionary Ridge and carried it, driving the Confederates in panic before them.

At 4:30 P.M. Dana telegraphed to Stanton: Glory to God. The day is decisively ours; and a few hours later, Our men are frantic with joy and enthusiasm, and received Grant as he rode along the lines after the victory with tumultuous shouts. Bragg was in full retreat, burning his depots and bridges, telegraphed Dana next day.

The outcome of this campaign pointed significantly to the waning fortune of the Southern cause. The news of Missionary Ridge reached the people of the North on the last Thursday of November, and made possible the first genuine Thanksgiving since the outbreak of the Civil War.[613] The autumn elections of 1863 were favorable to the administration. Four days after the October States had voted (October 17), the President issued a proclamation calling for 300,000 volunteers for three years or the war, not however exceeding three years; if the number was not filled by volunteers, recourse should be had to the draft. Congress met at the usual time and took effective action toward filling the armies for the campaigns of 1864. By the Act of February 24,[614] the President was authorized to call for such number of men for the military service as the public exigencies may require; if a sufficient number of volunteers were not obtained he might order a draft.[615]

Congress furnished the President money by increasing the imposts, by a comprehensive act of internal taxation and by the authorization of loans.[616]

The growing dislike of military service and the greater rewards at home for labor and business ability were constantly making it more difficult to get a sufficient number of the proper kind of men. Congress, the President and the War Department did fairly well, on the whole as well perhaps as could be expected in a democracy where every man had an opinion and a vote and at a time when the coming presidential election in the autumn might not be lost sight of; but the results fell far short of what would have been obtained had the Prussian system been possible. Nevertheless the conscription went on with few, if any, disturbances of the peace, the people having learned to look upon the draft as a military necessity. The government, the States, the counties and other political divisions were munificent in their offers of bounties, of which a salient example is seen in the advertisement of the New York County Volunteer committee: 30,000 volunteers wanted. The following are the pecuniary inducements offered: County bounty, cash down $300; State bounty, $75; United States bounty to new recruits $302; additional to veteran soldiers $100, making totals respectively of $677 and

---

[613] Authorities: O. R., XXX, XXXI; C. W. supplement, Pt. I; IV; B. & L., III; Welles's Diary; Wilson's Dana; do., Under the Old Flag; do., W. F. Smith; Board of Army Officers' report; Dana's Recollections; Grant; W. Sherman; N. & H., VIII.

[614] 1864.

[615] The following were the calls, one of which was made before the Act of February 24:

[616] IV, 428.

$777 for service which would not exceed three years, was likely to be less, and turned out to be an active duty of little more than one year; in addition there was the private soldier's pay of $16 per month with clothing and rations. The bounty in New York County was more than that generally paid throughout the country, although in some districts it was even higher. The system was bad, for it fostered a class of substitute brokers whose business was to get recruits, and whose aim was to earn their brokerage without any regard to the physical or moral quality of the men they supplied. It brought into existence the crime of bounty jumping. Thieves, pickpockets and vagabonds would enlist, take whatever bounty was paid in cash, desert when opportunity offered, change their names, go to another district or State, re-enlist, collect another bounty, desert again and go on playing the same trick until they were caught, or until such chances of gain were no longer available. The Provost-Marshal-General stated in his final report that, A man now in the Albany penitentiary, undergoing an imprisonment of four years, confessed to having 'jumped the bounty' thirty-two times. It was stated that out of a detachment of 625 recruits sent to re-enforce a New Hampshire regiment in the Army of the Potomac, 137 deserted on the passage, 82 to the enemy's picket line and 36 to the rear, leaving but 370 men.

The vast area of the country, the feverish anxiety in each town and municipal ward to fill its quota, together with a certain lack of administrative system, made it difficult to detect the bounty-jumpers. The mischief promoted by substitute brokers and bounty jumping was seen at its worst in the large cities of the East where it brought into the ranks a number of criminals, bullies and vagrants; and as these came to be guarded as prisoners, many of them reached the front. Yet not a large proportion of the 1864 recruits were social outcasts. In the country districts, villages and smaller cities, the efforts of able business men, who engaged voluntarily in the work of filling the respective quotas, were brought to bear, with the result that attention was paid to the character of the men offering to serve; yet the recruits were on the whole inferior physically, morally and intellectually to those who had enlisted in 1861 and 1862 and were very largely mercenaries, although a considerable part of them were sturdy Canadians and brawny immigrants from Europe, tempted by the high wage offered for military service. Moreover though the rank and file were deteriorating, the process of weeding out political generals and those appointed to the lower commands by influence rather than by merit, left their places open to the better officers who had further improved by the lessons of experience. I will see, wrote General Sherman to his brother on April 5, that by May 1st I have on the Tennessee one of the best armies in the world. The result of his campaign fully justified his promise. Best of all, the North had developed four great generals, Grant, Sherman, Thomas, Sheridan, and in this respect was now superior to the South. In the death-grapple, as we shall see, Grant was to be matched against Lee, Sherman against Joseph E. Johnston, who had succeeded Bragg; and, with the exception of Lee and Johnston, no one in the

Confederacy showed the same ability in the command of an independent army as Thomas, nor did any prove the equal of Sheridan, whose singular prowess must have made Lee regret bitterly the loss of his Stonewall Jackson.[617]

---

[617] IV, 430 *et seq.* O. R., III, V, 673-675.

Chapter IX

IN a military point of view, thank Heaven! the 'coming man,' for whom we have so long been waiting, seems really to have come. So Motley wrote; so thought the President, Congress and the people. By an act of February 29, Congress revived the grade of Lieutenant-General and authorized the President to place the General whom he should appoint to fill it in command of the armies of the United States under his direction and during his pleasure. It was understood on all sides that the man whom the nation's representatives desired to honor and upon whom they wished to devolve the burden of military affairs was Grant. This action agreed entirely with Lincoln's wish. From the first he would have been glad to have some general whom he could trust with the responsibility of military operations. Scott was too old; McClellan lacked the requisite ability; and Halleck, deficient in the same respect, lost all nerve and pluck after Pope's disaster and became little more, so Lincoln said, than a first-rate clerk.[618] It was a welcome function for the President to send to the Senate the nomination of Grant as Lieutenant-General. This he did at once and the nomination was immediately confirmed.

Grant came to Washington and met Lincoln for the first time at a crowded reception in the White House. An appointment between the two was made for the next day (March 9), when in the presence of the Cabinet, General Halleck and three others, the President presented Grant with the commission of Lieutenant-General, saying, With this high honor devolves upon you also a corresponding responsibility. As the country herein trusts you, so under God, it will sustain you. Grant replied, I feel the full weight of the responsibilities now devolving upon me; and I know that if they are met, it will be due to those noble armies that have fought on so many fields for our common country, and, above all, to the favor of that Providence which leads both nations and men.[619]

Next day Grant was formally assigned to the command of the armies of the United States. Until his visit to Washington, he had intended to remain in the West, but he now saw that his place was with the Army of the Potomac. He went to the front and had a conference with Meade, in the course of which, after an interchange of views creditable to both, he decided that Meade should retain his present command. He then went to Nashville and discussed with Sherman, who succeeded him as chief of the Western army, the plan of operations in Tennessee

---

[618] J. Hay, I, 187.

[619] N. & H., VIII, 341, 342. The remarks are abridged and in Grant's reply a clause is transposed.

and Georgia, returning on March 23 to Washington. He was now without question the most popular man in the United States. Both parties and all factions vied with one another in his praise. He had met with obstacles in working up to his present position and had suffered many hours of pain at the obloquy with which he had been pursued. But Vicksburg and Chattanooga were victories which not only bore down all detraction but invested with glory the general who had won them. It happens to but few men of action to receive during their lifetime such plaudits as Grant received in the winter and early spring of 1864; there was hardly a murmuring voice; few grudged him his success. His modest and unaffected bearing commanded respect for his character as his great deeds had won admiration for his military genius. It is striking to contrast this almost universal applause of Grant with the abuse of Lincoln by the Democrats, the sharp criticism of him by some of the radical Republicans and by others the damning him with faint praise.

Grant had the charm of simplicity of character and in common with Lincoln felt that he was one of the plain people and wished to keep in touch with them. But this merit in him was carried to excess. Too often was he unwilling to keep himself to himself too often ready to lend his time in undesirable quarters too often lacking the dignity and reserve reasonably to be expected of the commander of those half million soldiers to whom the nation looked for its salvation. Shortly before he began his May campaign, Richard H. Dana saw him in Willard's Hotel, Washington, and described him as a short, round-shouldered man in a very tarnished major-general's uniform; nothing marked in his appearance an ordinary scrubby-looking man with a slightly seedy look. Dana expressed his astonishment to see him talking and smoking in the lower entry of Willard's, in that crowd, in such times the generalissimo of our armies, on whom the destiny of the empire seemed to hang. But he went on, his face looks firm and hard, and his eye is clear and resolute, and he is certainly natural, and clear of all appearance of self-consciousness. Impressed with Grant's supremacy and his hold on the country, he broke out, How war, how all great crises, bring us to the one-man power.[620]

It was not until after both Gettysburg and Vicksburg, wrote General Sherman, that the war professionally began. In 1864 and 1865, the campaigns and the battles were, as in the previous years, the events on which all else depended; but by this time the President and his generals had learned the lessons of war and begun to conduct it with professional skill.

The two salient features of Grant's plan were the destruction or capture of Lee's army by himself and his force of 122,000 and the crushing of Joseph E. Johnston by Sherman with his 99,000. From the nature of the situation, a collateral objective in the one case was Richmond, in the other, Atlanta. The winter and early spring had been spent largely in systematic and effective preparation. The people's

---

[620] Adams's Dana, II, 271.

confidence in Grant was so great that many were sanguine that the war would be over by midsummer.

On the night of May 3 the Army of the Potomac began its advance by crossing the Rapidan without molestation and encamping next day in the Wilderness,[621] where Hooker had last year come to grief. Grant had no desire to fight a battle in this jungle; but Lee, who had watched him intently, permitted him to traverse the river unopposed, thinking that, when he halted in the dense thicket, every inch of which was known to the Confederate general and soldiers, the Lord had delivered him into their hands. Lee ordered at once the concentration of his army and with Napoleonic swiftness marched forward to dispute the advance of his enemy. On May 5, the forces came together in the Wilderness and a hot battle raged. The Confederates numerically were one-half the Union strength but their better knowledge of the battle ground and the little use that could be made of the Federal artillery, rendered it an equal contest; neither side gained an advantage.

Grant perceived that he must fight his way through the Wilderness and next day prepared to take the offensive; but Lee had likewise determined on attack. Both desiring the initiative, the battle was on at an early hour. It progressed with varying fortune; each force gained successes at different moments and at different parts of the line. At one time the Confederate right wing was driven back and disaster seemed imminent, when Longstreet came up and saved the day. A Texas brigade of Longstreet's corps went forward to the charge, and Lee, who like his exemplar Washington was an eager warrior and loved the noise and excitement of battle, spurred onward his horse and, in his anxiety for the result, started to follow the Texans as they advanced in regular order. He was recognized, and from the entire line came the cry, Go back, General Lee! go back! This Confederate movement was stopped by the wounding of Longstreet by a shot from his own men, an accident similar to that by which Stonewall Jackson one year before had received his mortal hurt.

The fighting of these two days is called the battle of the Wilderness. Both generals claimed the advantage; both were disappointed in the result. Grant, who had expected that the passage of the Rapidan and the turning of the right of the Confederates would compel them to fall back, had hoped to march through the Wilderness unopposed, fight them in more open country and inflict upon them a heavy blow. Lee, in no way daunted because Grant had taken command in person

---

[621] The Wilderness is a gently undulating tract of low ridges and swampy swales alternating, covered with a dense second growth of small pines intermixed with oaks, ash and walnut, and thick matted underbrush in patches almost impenetrable. It is from ten to twelve miles across in any direction. The main roads which traverse it and a few clearings, widely separated, let but little daylight into the dense, gloomy and monotonous woods. Once off the roads it is exceedingly difficult to manoeuvre troops through this region and almost impossible to preserve their orderly formation or to keep them in any given direction when in motion." ;Hazard Stevens, Milt. Hist. Soc., IV, 187.

of the Army of the Potomac, thought, undoubtedly, that his Western victories had been due more to his opponent's lack of skill than to his own generalship, and had hoped to beat Grant as he had beaten McClellan, Pope, Burnside and Hooker, drive him back across the Rapidan and constrain him, like his predecessors, to abandon the campaign. Measured by casualties, the Confederates came the nearer to victory. The Union loss was 17,666; the Confederate certainly less, although an accurate report of it is lacking.

Next day Grant said to Meade, Joe Johnston would have retreated after two such days' punishment![622] In this remark was implied a wholesome respect for the redoubtable commander whom he had encountered for the first time. Neither general showed a disposition to attack, but Grant made arrangements to continue the movement by the left in a night march to Spottsylvania Court House. To James H. Wilson who, perturbed at the disaster to the Union right on the second day of the battle, had sought the General to bear information and seek comfort, he said, It's all right, Wilson; the army is moving toward Richmond![623] The troops set forth knowing of the slaughter of the past two days but unaware if they had been beaten or not, and when they came to the parting of the ways, the question uppermost in all minds was, would the orders be to turn northward and recross the river? But the command, File right, set the men's faces towards Richmond, and Grant in their estimation was exalted. The soldiers sang and stepped forward with a brisker tread. The spirits of men and officers are of the highest pitch of animation was the word which Dana sent to Stanton. Grant rode by and in spite of the darkness was recognized. The men burst into cheers, swung their hats, clapped their hands, threw up their arms and greeted their general as a comrade, so pleased were they that he was leading them on to Richmond instead of ordering them to fall back to the camp which they had just abandoned.

The Confederate soldiers, believing in their invincibility on their own soil, thought that Grant, like the other Federal generals, would give it up and fall back; and Lee at one time held the opinion that he was retiring on Fredericksburg. But the Confederate general was too sagacious to base his plans entirely on one supposition; surmising that Grant might move to Spottsylvania, he sent thither a portion of his force, which, having the shorter and easier line of march, arrived earlier than the Union Army, and took up a position across the path of their approach. The armies soon came in contact and fighting began. On May 11 Grant sent his celebrated despatch to Halleck: We have now ended the sixth day of very heavy fighting. I propose to fight it out on this line if it takes all summer.[624] After a furious battle next day at the Salient the so-called bloody angle there was a lull, owing principally to the heavy and constant rains, which made the roads deep with

---

[622] Theodore Lyman, Milt. Hist. Soc., IV, 171.
[623] Under the Old Flag, I, 389.
[624] O. R., XXXVI, Pt. 1, 13.

mud and impassable. It is true, however, that the Union Army needed rest and that Grant was desirous of re-enforcements to fill the gaps in his ranks caused by his heavy losses. In these battles at Spottsylvania he was almost invariably the attacking party; again and again he assailed the Confederates in front, where their intrenchments, defended by rifled muskets and artillery throughout, quadrupled their strength. It has been said that the hurling of his men against Lee in chosen and fortified positions was unnecessary as the roads in number and direction lent themselves to the operation of turning either flank of the Confederate Army. To assault 'all along the line,' wrote General Walker, as was so often done in the summer of 1864, is the very abdication of leadership.[625] But Grant was essentially an aggressive soldier, and an important feature of his plan of operations was, as he himself has stated it, to hammer continuously against the armed force of the enemy and his resources until by mere attrition, if in no other way, the South should be subdued.[626]

Before Spottsylvania an incident of the Wilderness fighting was repeated. Twice, when the Confederates were on the verge of disaster, Lee rode to the head of a column, intending to lead a charge which he thought might be necessary to save the day. On both occasions the soldiers refused to advance unless their general should go to the rear. Lee did not court danger and was bent on exposing himself in the one case only after his lines had been broken, and in the other when the struggle for the Salient demanded the utmost from general and men. Such incidents in Lee's career did not happen until Grant came to direct the movements of the Army of the Potomac.[627]

On May 19, Meade wrote to his wife, We did not have the big battle which I expected yesterday, as, on advancing, we found the enemy so strongly intrenched that even Grant thought it useless to knock our heads against a brick wall, and directed a suspension of the attack.[628]

As a result of one month's fighting, Grant had by June 2 advanced a considerable distance into Virginia, reaching the ground which one wing of McClellan's army had occupied in May and June, 1862. He took up a position near the scene of Fitz-John Porter's gallant fight of Gaines's Mill and almost in sight of the spires of the Confederate capital. Lee, about six miles from the exterior fortifications of Richmond, held a position naturally strong, which by intrenchments he had made practically impregnable. On the supposition that flanking movements were impracticable, Grant, with unjustifiable precipitation,

---

[625] Walker's Hancock, 193.

[626] O. R., XXXVI., Pt. 1, 13.

[627] On May 15, Meade wrote to his wife, "I think we have gained decided advantages over the enemy; nevertheless, he confronts us still and, owing to the strong position he occupies, and the works he is all the time throwing up, the task of overcoming him is a very difficult one, taxing all our energies." General Meade, II, 195.

[628] General Meade, II, 197.

ordered an assault in front. This was made at 4:30 in the morning of June 3, and is known as the battle of Cold Harbor the greatest blemish on his reputation as a general. The attack, which had at first been ordered for the afternoon of the 2d, was postponed till the morrow; this gave officers and men a chance to chew upon it, and both knew that the undertaking was hopeless. Horace Porter, one of Grant's aides, related that when walking among the troops on staff duty the evening before the battle he noticed many soldiers of one of the regiments, designated for the assault, pinning on the backs of their coats slips of paper on which were written their names and home addresses so that their dead bodies might be recognized on the field and their fate be known to their families at the North.

The soldiers sprang promptly to the assault. The experience of Hancock's corps, the Second, will suffice as an epitome of the action. In about twenty-two minutes its repulse was complete. It had lost over 3000 of its bravest and best, both of officers and men.[629] The total casualties in the Union Army were probably 7000. Grant regretted the attack. No advantage whatever, he wrote, was gained to compensate for the heavy loss we sustained.[630] After the battle of Cold Harbor he determined to move to a point south of the James with his headquarters at City Point, and between June 12 and 16, had his army successfully transferred to the new position. Up to this time, wrote Meade on June 6, our success has consisted only in compelling the enemy to draw in towards Richmond; our failure has been that we have not been able to overcome, destroy or bag his army.[631]

Grant's loss from May 4 to June 12 in the campaign from the Rapidan to the James was 54,926, a number nearly equal to Lee's whole army at the commencement of the Union advance; the Confederate loss is not known, but it was certainly very much less. Nor do the bare figures tell the whole story. To the total loss the flower of the Army of the Potomac contributed a disproportionate share. Fighting against odds of position and strategy, the high-spirited and capable officers were constantly in the thick of danger and the veterans of the rank and file were always at the front: they were the forlorn hope. The bounty-jumpers and mercenaries skulked to the rear. The morale of the soldiers was much lower than on the day when, in high spirits, they had crossed the Rapidan. Many officers lost confidence in Grant; the men said, It is no use. No matter who is given us, we can't whip Bobby Lee. I think, wrote Meade, Grant has had his eyes opened and is willing to admit now that Virginia and Lee's army is not Tennessee and Bragg's.[632]

In the judgment of many military critics Grant had not been equal to his opportunities, had not made the best use of his advantages, and had secured no gain commensurate with his loss. Yet the friends of McClellan who maintain that,

---

[629] XXXVI, Pt. i, 367.

[630] Grant, II, 276.

[631] Gen. Meade, II, 201.

[632] *Ibid.*, II, 201.

as this commander reached the same ground near Richmond with comparatively little sacrifice of life, his campaign had the greater merit, miss the main point of the situation, to wit, that the incessant hammering of Lee's army was a necessary concomitant of success. They regard the capture of the Confederate capital as tantamount to the subjugation of the South; this error blinds them to the fact that Grant was supremely right in making Lee's army his first objective and Richmond only his second. His strategy was superior to McClellan's in that he grasped the aim of the war, and resolutely and grimly stuck to his purpose in spite of defeat and losses which would have dismayed any but the stoutest soul; and criticism of him is not sound unless it proves, as perhaps it does, that there might have been the same persistent fighting of the Army of Northern Virginia without so great a slaughter of Northern soldiers. The case is certainly stronger for Grant if we compare his work even thus far with the operations of Pope, Burnside and Hooker. As for Meade, his name is so gratefully associated with the magnificent victory of Gettysburg that our judgment leans in his favor and would fain rate his achievements at the highest; but it is difficult to discover anything that he did afterwards in independent command towards bringing the war to a close. If the final outcome be anticipated in order to compare Grant's total losses to the day on which he received the surrender of Lee's army, with the combined losses of the rest of the commanders of the Army of the Potomac, the result arrived at is that his aggregate was less than theirs whilst his was the great achievement. The military literature of the South directly and by implication breathes a constant tribute to the effectiveness of his plan. It must not, however, be forgotten that McClellan and Meade had weakened in some measure the power of resistance of the Army of Northern Virginia.[633] Sherman, whose headquarters had been at Chattanooga, began his advance on May 6. He was at the head of three armies: those of the Cumberland, the Tennessee and the Ohio, commanded respectively by Thomas, McPherson and Schofield and aggregating 99,000 men. Joseph E. Johnston was at Dalton, Georgia, strongly intrenched with a force of 53,000. The campaign from Chattanooga to Atlanta, which now commenced, is remarkable for the vigor and pertinacity of the attack, the skill and obstinacy of the defence. Two giants met. Sherman's greater number corresponded to the greater difficulty of his task. For the invasion of the enemy's territory, with a constantly lengthening line of supply and a consequent dwindling of the main force through detachments necessary to protect this line, an army twice as great as the enemy's was required for accomplishing the object of the campaign, which was the destruction or the surrender of the opposing host. Johnston had not as able lieutenants as Sherman,

---

[633] Authorities, O. R., XXXVI; IV; Humphreys; Gen. Meade, II; Charles H. Porter, Theodore Lyman, Hazard Stevens, Ropes, T. L. Livermore in Milt. Hist. Soc., IV; Wilson's Dana; do. Under the Old Flag; do. W. F. Smith; do. Rawlins, M. S.; Alexander; T. L. Livermore; Longstreet; G. M. Dodge.

and did not win from them as great a measure of devotion, nor had he in other respects a personnel equal to that of the Union commander, whose army, moreover, had derived confidence for the future from its victory at Chattanooga. Taking everything into consideration, the conditions of the contest were about even. Sherman's work became easier, as will be seen, when he had as antagonist a commander of inferior parts. But it cannot be maintained with any show of reason that Johnston could have been driven constantly and steadily southward from position to position, by a general who did not possess a high order of ability. The more one studies this inch-by-inch struggle, the better will one realize that in the direction and supply of each of the opposing forces, there was a master mind, with the best of professional training, with the added advantage of three years of practical experience in warfare. The strife between the two was of the most honorable character even as it has been between all noble spirits who have fought to the end since Homer's time. Either would have regarded the killing of the other as a happy fortune of war, though indeed he might have apostrophized his dead body as Mark Antony did Brutus's; yet twenty-seven years later, when the victor in this campaign had succumbed to death, the magnanimous Johnston, though aged and feeble, travelled from Washington to New York to act as a pall-bearer and to grieve as a sincere mourner at his funeral.[634]

By systematic flanking and fighting, Sherman drove Johnston to Cassville, where the Confederate at first decided to accept battle; but learning that two of his corps commanders did not approve his plan, he did not deem it wise to risk a battle with a force so much his superior while lacking the unanimous and sympathetic support of his lieutenants; he therefore retreated south of the Etowah river. Yet he was right in wishing to try the fortune of war at this time and in this comparatively open country, for in his retreat he had been picking up detachments and receiving reenforcements, while Sherman, although also re-enforced, had less than his original army with him owing to the necessity of protecting the railroad in his rear, which was his only line of supply; in fact the two armies were now more nearly equal than at any other time during the campaign. Sherman had been eager for battle ever since the beginning of his advance, an eagerness shared by his men. Johnston's continual avoidance of it, the proffered gage, increased their confidence, which had been high from the outset, and they went forward sure of victory, enduring with patience the privations and hardships of the march. All this while news of the operations in Virginia was furnished to both armies, the one hearing of Union victories in the Wilderness and at Spottsylvania, the other that Lee has whipped Grant and General Lee beat Grant again.

On May 23 Sherman wrote from Kingston, I am already within fifty miles of Atlanta and have added one hundred miles to my railroad communications, every

---

[634] Sherman died Feb. 14, 1891; Johnston five weeks later of heart failure aggravated by a cold taken at Sherman's funeral.

mile of which is liable to attack by cavalry. This despatch gives some idea of the labor attending the invasion of the enemy's territory. The men needed not only marching and fighting qualities but the temper to endure with good grace the loss of many of the creature comforts of ordinary army life. Most of the baggage and tents had been left behind; a tent-fly was the shelter for brigade and division headquarters; but the food, consisting of meat, bread, coffee and sugar, was abundant and of good quality. All the supplies came over the single line of railroad running from Chattanooga to Atlanta, of which the track was torn up and the bridges burned by the Confederates, as they retreated. But the engineer corps in charge of the railway repairs were skilful and energetic, renewing bridges as if by magic, much to the amazement of Johnston's men, who under the illusion that their destruction would cause great delays were always startled to hear the whistle of the locomotive bringing up the supply trains in the rear of the Union Army.

At Kingston Sherman was in a country which, as lieutenant of artillery, he had ridden over on horseback twenty years before. Apprised by his early recollections that Johnston's position at Allatoona Pass was very strong and would be hard to force, he formed the design of turning it, and to that end left the railroad on May 25, made a circuit to the right and brought on the severe battle of New Hope Church, which accomplished his object, so that when he returned to the railroad he occupied it from Allatoona to Big Shanty in sight of Kenesaw Mountain. For some reason which is not altogether clear, Sherman now departed from his usual strategy and assaulted in front Johnston's almost impregnable position at Kenesaw Mountain, an operation which is admittedly a flaw in this otherwise well-conceived and admirably executed campaign. There is a tradition in the Army of the Cumberland that the decision was spasmodic, adopted in a state of excited restlessness; but if this was indeed Sherman's mood it did not preclude a careful preparation for the attack. Although he issued the orders on June 24, the onslaught was not actually made until three days later. The veteran soldiers entered upon the assault with great courage, but, soon discovering that one rifle in the trench was worth five in front of it, they were satisfied that the works could not be carried except by an immense sacrifice of life; with the consent of the division and corps commanders, they abandoned the attempt. Sherman's loss was nearly 3000, Johnston's 800.

The battle of Kenesaw Mountain brought to the surface the rooted difference between Sherman's and Thomas's characters and modes of operation. Sherman thought Thomas slow, with a disposition to act continually on the defensive when the nature of the campaign required that the Union Army should assail not defend. On the other hand the officers of the Army of the Cumberland for the most part believed that Sherman's restlessness and impetuosity, which had got them into trouble at Kenesaw, would have led them to other disasters had he not been restrained by Thomas's discretion and prudence. In this controversy the layman may hardly venture an opinion, but since the campaign was successful to the point which this account of it has now reached, and was eminently successful in its conclusion, he would like to believe that the differing gifts of Sherman and Thomas wrought together to advantage, and that the two men accomplished in their union, jarring though it was at times, what neither one alone would have done so completely and so well.[635] At the same time as these military operations, be it remembered, a political campaign was in progress; a President must be nominated and elected. The important question whether Lincoln should succeed himself could not be kept in abeyance even during the preceding year. He was in a measure held responsible for the military failures of 1862, for the disasters of Fredericksburg and Chancellorsville, so that many came to doubt whether he had the requisite ability and decision to carry on the great undertaking. But he came in for a share of the glory of Gettysburg and Vicksburg and thereafter was greatly strengthened in his political position. Yet the disaffection had been strong enough to seek a head and had found it in Chase, whose craving for the Presidency was exceedingly strong. Theoretically he might seem a formidable candidate. He was the representative of the radical Republicans and was regarded by them as the counterpoise to Lincoln, who, in his blows at slavery, had proceeded too slowly to suit them and was now arousing their antagonism in his policy for the reconstruction of the Union. Already successful in his management of the Treasury, Chase was in character and ability fit for the office of the President.

Lincoln had long known of Chase's striving for the Presidency and, though at times this may have caused him some concern, his attitude towards it after the victories of Gettysburg and Vicksburg is revealed in his remark of October, 1863, to his private secretary: I have determined to shut my eyes, so far as possible, to everything of the sort. Mr. Chase makes a good Secretary and I shall keep him where he is. If he becomes President, all right. I hope we may never have a worse man.[636]

In various ways before the assembling of the national convention, the Union and Republican party pronounced in favor of Lincoln's renomination. In spite of all that was urged against him by his opponents touching the manipulation by office-holders and politicians, there remains no doubt that the mass of citizens were lending aid to these movements. The President had gained the support of the plain people, of business men and of a goodly portion of the best intelligence of the country. Nothing in the study of popular sentiment can be more gratifying than this oneness of thought between farmers, small shop-keepers, salesmen, clerks, mechanics and the men who stood intellectually for the highest aspirations of the nation. Lowell wrote in the North American Review: History will rank Mr. Lincoln among the most prudent of statesmen and the most successful of rulers. If we wish to appreciate him, we have only to conceive the inevitable chaos in which

[635] O. R., XXXVII, Pts. 1, 4; IV
[636] N. & H., VIII, 316; J. Hay, I, 108.

we should now be weltering had a weak man or an unwise one been chosen in his stead. Homely, honest, ungainly Lincoln, wrote Asa Gray to Darwin, is the representative man of the country.[637]

General Grant, after the battle of Chattanooga, might indeed have been a formidable candidate if he had not positively refused to give his would-be backers any encouragement for the use of his name. In connection with the attempt to bring Grant forward, Lincoln exhibited his usual shrewdness. If he takes Richmond, he said, let him have it [the nomination].[638]

Those were exciting days between May 3, when Grant crossed the Rapidan, and June 7, when the National Union or Republican convention met. My hopes under God, wrote Chase, are almost wholly in Grant and his soldiers.[639] So thought the North. The bloody work of the Virginia campaign went on. Welles's record in his faithful Diary is a true index of public opinion. On May 17: A painful suspense in military operations. The intense anxiety is oppressive and almost unfits the mind for mental activity. On June 2: Great confidence is felt in Grant but the immense slaughter of our brave men chills and sickens us all. On June 7: We have had severe slaughter. Brave men have been killed and maimed most fearfully but Grant persists.[640] Lincoln was very anxious and sad during the battles of the Wilderness.[641] On May 7, Welles wrote, The President came into my room about 1 P.M., and told me he had slept none last night.[642] As the campaign went on he grew sanguine. On June 15, after he must have realized the extent of the Cold Harbor disaster and after Grant had announced his purpose of crossing to the south side of the James, he telegraphed to Grant, I begin to see it: you will succeed. God bless you all.[643]

The excellent and real progress of Sherman was not of a sufficiently striking character to distract the attention of the public mind, even in the Western States, whose sons made up his army, from the duel between Grant and Lee.

On June 7, Welles confided to his Diary, The Convention to-day is the absorbing theme. Lincoln was renominated, receiving all the votes except those of Missouri, which were given to Grant. As Lincoln explained the result, the Convention concluded that it is not best to swop horses while crossing the stream.[644]

---

[637] IV, 461.

[638] N. & H., IX, 59.

[639] Warden, 584.

[640] Welles's Diary, II, 33, 44, 46.

[641] Carpenter, 30.

[642] Welles's Diary, II, 25.

[643] Lincoln, C. W., II, 533.

[644] Lect. 190, n. 1.

Chapter X

WE left the Army of the Potomac on the James river. Grant had hoped to destroy or inflict a decisive defeat on Lee's army north of Richmond and, having failed to do either, he now decided to transfer his troops to the south side of the James with a view to besieging the Confederates in their capital. This movement, which began on June 12 and ended on the 16th, was very successfully accomplished. The precision of the march, the skilful work of the engineers in bridging the river, the orderly crossing showed how like a fine machine the Army of the Potomac, even in its crippled state, responded to efficient direction. Lee divined Grant's movement but did nothing to impede it.[645] Yet the capture of Petersburg, the possession of which would undoubtedly within a brief period compel the fall of the Confederate capital, was included in the Union general's plan and was within his grasp; and if everything had been properly ordered and carried out, the city might have been taken and the Appomattox river reached.

But this golden opportunity was allowed to slip. When Grant and Meade arrived upon the ground the Confederate works were pretty well manned. They ordered successive assaults[646] which failed to take Petersburg and resulted in a loss of about 10,000 men. The sequel of this rebuff is told in Grant's and Dana's despatches. Dana: General Grant has directed that no more assaults shall be made. He will now manoeuvre. Grant: I shall try to give the army a few days' rest, which they now stand much in need of.[647]

The Army of the Potomac was worn out. The continual fighting for forty-five days at a disadvantage and without success, and the frequent marches by night had exhausted and disheartened the men. Gallant and skilful officers by the score, brave veterans by the thousands, had fallen. The morale of the troops was distinctly lower even than the day after Cold Harbor. Re-enforcements were constantly sent to Grant but they were for the most part mercenaries, many of whom were diseased, immoral or cowardly. Such men were now in too large a proportion to insure efficient work. They needed months of drill and discipline to make good soldiers. Indeed a reconstitution and reorganization of the army had become necessary; this was effected during the many weeks of inaction from June 18 to the spring of 1865, a period covered by the siege of Petersburg, which now commenced.

---

[645] See Lee's Confidential Dispatches to Davis, 1862-65 (1915), 227.

[646] June 16, 17, 18.

[647] O. R., XL, Pt. 1, 14, 25.

At this time the President paid a visit to the army. The impression that I have tried to convey of the failure of Grant's costly operations and of the army's demoralization might lead the reader's imagination to construct a private interview between Lincoln and Grant, in which the President entreated the general to be more careful of his soldiers' lives and warned him that the country could not or would not repair the waste of another such campaign of attrition. So far, however, as I know, there is no evidence of such an entreaty or warning. It is unlikely that the thought of either entered Lincoln's head, inconsistent as it would have been with his despatch of six days earlier;[648] and nothing had since occurred to change his view except the unsuccessful assaults on the intrenchments of Petersburg; moreover, the failure to capture this stronghold was not at this time regarded as so serious a mishap as later it came to be. Kindness of heart and humanity rather than disappointment in his general were shown in his words when contemplated battles were spoken of. I cannot pretend to advise, he said, but I do sincerely hope that all may be accomplished with as little bloodshed as possible.[649]

Horace Porter has given an interesting account of this visit, which one loves to dwell upon for a moment in the midst of the gloom which had settled down on the Army of the Potomac and was soon to spread over the country. The President on horseback, wearing a high silk hat, a frock coat and black trousers, rode with Grant along the line. A civilian mounted was always an odd sight amid the crowd of uniformed and epauletted officers; and Lincoln, although a good horseman, was always awkward and, being now covered with dust, presented the appearance of a country farmer riding into town, wearing his Sunday clothes. But the character of the man disarmed the American soldiers' keen sense of the ridiculous and as the word was passed along the line that Uncle Abe is with us he was greeted with cheers and shouts that came from the heart. He visited a division of colored soldiers who had won distinction by their bravery in an assault on the works of Petersburg. They flocked around the liberator of their race, kissing his hands, touching his clothes for the virtue they conceived to be in them, cheering, laughing, singing hymns of praise, shouting, God bress Massa Lincoln. De Lord sabe Fader Abraham. De day of jubilee am come, shuah. His head was bare, his eyes were full of tears, his voice broke with emotion. As no picture of Lincoln would be complete without humor atop of pathos, we may see him the same evening, with a group of staff officers before the general's tent, a willing raconteur, plying his wit to teach them truth, pleased by their appreciation, egged on by their hearty laughs.

There is little or no evidence, so far as I know, of Grant being dejected over the failure of those high hopes which he had entertained on crossing the Rapidan. His sturdy disposition, his strong will and determination to succeed probably

---

[648] *Ante.*

[649] Horace Porter.

prevented any admission of failure even to himself; or if they did not, his stolid countenance concealed the fact. It is nevertheless true that the bitterness of disappointment drove him for a while to drink. Rawlins told Wilson soon after their first meeting that they must do all in their power to stay Grant from falling[650] and, in the period of tedious waiting before Petersburg, this faithful mentor and sturdy patriot served his country as no one else could have done. Rawlins's familiar letters to his wife exhibit his anxiety and his good influence on the general whom the North needed to bring the war to an end. Twice (on June 29 and on one of the last days of July) Grant, to use Rawlins's words, digressed from his true path;[651] but, after the last deviation, he pulled himself together and did not again falter. It was an unclouded brain that carried on the siege of Petersburg to its capture, forced the evacuation of Richmond and effected the final discomfiture of Lee and the ruin of the Southern Confederacy. For the moment, however, Lee was making a resolute fight. Encouraged by his victories over Grant and confident that with a diminished force, he could hold his ground against the crippled Army of the Potomac, he detached Early and his corps to drive the Union troops out of the Shenandoah Valley: this Early succeeded in doing and gained thereby an easy route to Maryland and the rear of the Federal capital. On July 9 he reached Frederick City, defeated the Union force opposed to him, and next day, at the head of 20,000 veterans, flushed with victory and spoils, advanced rapidly toward the capital itself. Washington and its fortifications had been denuded of troops for the purpose of re-enforcing Grant and was now defended only by invalids, state militia and District of Columbia volunteers, a total of 20,400, of whom nearly all were raw troops and a considerable portion unavailable. On the morning of July 11, Early, with his infantry and artillery, appeared on the Seventh street road north of Washington before the fortifications of the city and in sight of the dome of the Capitol. Communication between Washington and the Northern cities was cut; the general excitement and alarm were intense. On the night before the President, unmindful of personal danger, had ridden out as usual to his summer residence, the Soldiers' Home, which was directly in the line of the enemy's advance, but he was now brought back to the city upon the earnest insistence of the Secretary of War; also, unknown to Lincoln, Gustavus V. Fox, Assistant-Secretary of the Navy, had a vessel ready to transport him from the capital, should its fall become absolutely certain. If Early had profited by the moment of consternation, he could have gone into Washington on July 11, seized the money in the Treasury, the large stores of clothing, arms and ammunition, destroyed a large amount of Government property and, though he might not have been able to hold the place, he could have escaped without harm from the veteran troops now hastening to the rescue; he would thus have struck the prestige of the Union a staggering blow.

---

[650] Wilson's Under the Old Flag, I, 137.
[651] Wilson's Rawlins, M. S.; W. F. Smith.

The veterans of the Sixth Corps of the Army of the Potomac and of the Nineteenth Corps from New Orleans saved the country from the capture of its capital. It was, however, little to Grant's credit that Washington should be in so imminent danger, while Richmond was in none, and that the measures for its safety should have been so tardily taken. During these days, the commander seemed to be stunned. Although his frequent despatches bear witness to his diligence, they show, at the same time, that he did not realize the danger. He was not the man of prompt decision and ready purpose who commanded at Donelson, Vicksburg and Chattanooga; rather was he the remiss and lethargic general of Shiloh. At the very time when Early's troops were marching down the Shenandoah Valley he refused to believe that the self-same Confederate corps had left Petersburg. It was not until July 5 that he became convinced of the truth, and even then he failed to show a complete mastery of the situation. He displays little strategy or invention,[652] wrote Welles.

Yet in the result Grant had acted with sufficient promptness to save the capital, inasmuch as Early, by delay, let slip a great opportunity. The Confederate commander probably suspected that the veterans had already arrived, for he did not seize Fort Stevens, which guarded the entrance to Washington by the Seventh street road and which he might have had by simply saying the word. At noon of this day (July 11) two divisions of the Sixth Corps from City Point, with General Wright in command, arrived at the wharf in Washington and soon after four o'clock in the afternoon were in the neighborhood of Fort Stevens. The capital was saved. Next day a sharp skirmish took place, which was watched from the fort by the President, who was apparently oblivious of the sharpshooters' flying bullets, until the fall of a wounded officer near him caused General Wright to ask him peremptorily to retire to a safer spot. In the night of July 12 the Confederates withdrew. The rebs, so wrote Gustavus V. Fox, have just made off with more plunder than has entered all the blockaded ports since the war commenced. It was an attempt with 20,000 men to break up Grant; but he was too calm and persistent to be caught. It is rather humiliating but does not affect the campaign at all, the result of which is sure.[653] Not everyone had the same confidence in Grant. It is a tradition that, because of the failure and great loss of life in his campaign, over which the feeling of the country was intensified by the Confederate invasion of Maryland and the imminent danger of Washington, the question of his removal from command was mooted; but of this I have found no evidence, nor do I believe that such a thought ever occurred to the President. Indeed there was no one to take his place. Extenuation of his faults is unnecessary for arriving at the conviction that, so far as any military ability had been developed, Grant was the fittest of all the generals to command the armies of the United States. That the President had

---

[652] Welles's Diary, II, 68.
[653] Forbes, II, 99.

confidence in him is plainly manifest. During July and August, the usual pressure in time of disaster was exercised for the restoration of McClellan to command, but it is idle to suppose that Lincoln entertained the idea of displacing Grant in favor of McClellan or that such a change would have redounded to the benefit of the Union cause.[654]

On July 18, Lincoln issued a proclamation calling for 500,000 volunteers, by virtue of the Act of Congress of July 4, 1864,[655] the passage of which had been largely influenced by the great losses in the Wilderness, at Spottsylvania and at Cold Harbor; he further ordered a draft to take place immediately after September 5 for any unfilled quotas.

During July the North was plunged in gloom. Everybody was asking, Who shall revive the withered hopes that bloomed on the opening of Grant's campaign? And the most despondent were those who possessed the fullest information.

A resolution of Congress adopted July 2 was worthy of the Hebrews of the Old Testament or of the Puritans of the English Civil War. It requested the President to appoint a day for humiliation and prayer and to ask the people to convene at their usual places of worship in order that they may confess and repent of their manifold sins, implore the compassion and forgiveness of the Almighty, that, if consistent with his will the existing rebellion may be speedily suppressed and implore him as the supreme ruler of the world not to destroy us as a people. The President, cordially concurring in the penitential and pious sentiments expressed in that resolution, appointed the first Thursday of August to be observed by the people of the United States as a day of national humiliation and prayer.

Thomas A. Scott, who was always ready with efficient help for the Government in its times of trouble and who now offered the services of himself and the Pennsylvania railroad, telegraphed to Stanton from Philadelphia, The apathy in the public mind is fearful.[656] It might well be doubted if men in sufficient number and money in sufficient amount would be forthcoming to complete the work of conquering the South. The deplorable financial condition of the country may be measured by the fluctuations of the price of gold. On January 2 gold sold in New York at 152 and, when in April it reached 175, the Secretary of the Treasury endeavored to depress the price by the sale of about eleven millions; but the effect was only temporary. It soon resumed its advance and by June 17 had passed 197. On this day the President approved an act of Congress which aimed to prevent speculative sales of gold and proved about as effectual as human efforts to stay the flood. After this enactment the speculation became wilder than before and, owing

---

[654] O. R., XXXVII; IV; Welles's Diary, II; General Meade, II; Early.

[655] This act repealed the $300 exemption clause which had been a large factor in the incitement of the New York draft riots; if a man were drafted now, he must go into the service or furnish a substitute.

[656] O. R., XXXVII, Pt. 2, 255.

to the military failures and Chase's resignation as Secretary of the Treasury, gold touched on the last day of June 250. On July 2 the act intended to prevent speculation in gold was repealed. On July 11, when Early was before Washington and communication with that city had been cut, gold fetched 285, its highest price during the war; next day, the day of the skirmish near Fort Stevens and of the rumor in Philadelphia that the capital had fallen, it sold at 282. Such prices meant that the paper money in circulation was worth less than forty cents on the dollar. As the Government bonds were sold for this money, the United States were paying, with gold at 250 (at which price or higher it sold during the greater part of July and August), fifteen per cent on their loans. Nevertheless money could be had. The continued issue of legal tender notes had inflated the currency. Business, though feverish, was good; and many fortunes of our day had their origin in these excited business years of 1863 and 1864; when sales were easily made, most transactions were for cash, and nearly everyone engaged in trade or manufactures seemed to be getting rich. There must have been still considerable financial strength in reserve and, as the value of property depended largely on a stable government, ample funds for its maintenance would have been forthcoming in a supreme crisis. Even now, an element of confidence was to be seen in the large and constant purchases of our bonds by the Germans.

But the question of men was of far greater seriousness. In spite of the large immigration, labor was scarce and, in spite of the high cost of living, seemed to be well paid. The class of men who enlisted in 1861 and 1862 no longer came forward; the ranks were filled by mercenaries, part of whom were obtained from the steady influx of European immigrants and from robust sons of Canada, who contracted their service for a stipulated sum.[657] Notwithstanding these sources of supply, able-bodied men in sufficient number were difficult to obtain. Many of the veterans, men of all ranks in Sherman's army, the officers generally in all the armies; the militia from the Western States, originally organized as home guards, and now taking part in the defence of Washington, were from the best classes of their several communities; and sorrow now hanging over nearly every household from the casualties among these contingents, augmented the discouragement and gloom.[658]

Nor did Sherman's operations lift the country out of its despondency. Successful though they were, they lacked a striking character, and while steadily making for the destruction of Johnston's army and the capture of Atlanta, had as yet accomplished neither of these objects. On July 17, Sherman crossed the Chattahoochee river and began his movement directly against Atlanta. On the same day, Jefferson Davis materially assisted him by relieving Johnston from the command for the reason, in the words of the order, that you have failed to arrest

---

[657] The conditions of the narrative obliged me to state this previously.
[658] The conditions of the narrative obliged me to state this previously.

the advance of the enemy to the vicinity of Atlanta and express no confidence that you can defeat or repel him.[659] So masterly had been Johnston's strategy in retreat that his displacement was thoroughly relished by Sherman and by his officers and men. J. B. Hood, the new commander, had been personally known at West Point by McPherson, Schofield and Howard, and these three, together with Sherman, accurately took his measure, deciding that the change meant fight.[660] The logic of Johnston's removal was indeed that the Confederates must take the offensive, and Hood lost no time in carrying Davis's purpose into effect. Thrice he attacked and brought on a battle; thrice he was repulsed with severe loss. The chief feature of the second battle, that of Atlanta, which was fought within two and one-half miles of the city, was a vigorous and skilful Confederate attack which struck a portion of the Union line in the rear and would have caused a panic among any but sturdy veterans; but the soldiers of the Army of the Tennessee leaped over their breastworks and fought from the reverse side. McPherson, however, their commander, was killed. He had just left Sherman to investigate the unexplained firing in the rear and to make the necessary dispositions to meet it; he had already given a number of orders, when he rode into a wood and encountered there a line of Confederate skirmishers. By these he was summoned to surrender, but he wheeled his horse and tried to ride off: there was a volley of musketry and one of the noblest soldiers of the war fell dead. His sudden loss, telegraphed Sherman, was a heavy blow to me.[661] This misfortune, together with the Confederate claims of victory, undoubtedly accounted in some measure for the lack of comprehension of what had really been gained during the month of July; at all events a general impression seemed to prevail that Sherman had been checked before Atlanta. In point of fact Hood's army had been crippled and, after the third battle, he did not again attack Sherman for more than a month.

The general apathy and discouragement took form in certain quarters of a yearning for peace. The mercantile classes are longing for it, wrote Lowell. During July Horace Greeley thought that negotiations for peace should be opened and, commissioned by the President, made an effort in that direction. Lincoln was willing to make peace on the basis of the restoration of the Union and abandonment of slavery. Two self-constituted envoys, hoping to stop the war, went on an irregular mission to Richmond and had an interview with Jefferson Davis. Both of these attempts were barren of result.[662]

Though the military situation was already sufficiently depressing, the North had not yet come to the end of its misfortunes. A promising attempt to capture Petersburg through blowing up a portion of the Confederate works, by a huge

---

[659] Johnston, 349.
[660] W. Sherman, II, 72.
[661] O. R., XXXVIII, Pt. 5, 240.
[662] IV, 513-516.

mine charged with powder, failed through the inefficiency of a corps commander and the incompetence and cowardice of a division general, who were unequal to their opportunity after the mine had properly done its work. The casualties were great, the blundering was indisputable. This affair intensified the dejection in the Army of the Potomac and in the country at large. I feel rather down in the mouth, wrote Lowell to Norton on August 1. The war and its constant expectation and anxiety oppress me. I cannot think.[663]

Another manifestation of the general despondency was seen in the growing dissatisfaction with Lincoln. I beg you, implore you, wrote Greeley to Lincoln on August 9, to inaugurate or invite proposals for peace forthwith. And in case peace cannot now be made consent to an armistice for one year. In this private letter Greeley expressed the thoughts of very many men. Nine days later he wrote: Lincoln is already beaten. He cannot be elected. And we must have another ticket to save us from utter overthrow. Influential men of affairs in New York, Boston and the West were earnest in their belief that Lincoln should withdraw and make way for another candidate. This belief infected the Republican National Executive Committee, whose chairman, Henry J. Raymond, wrote to the President on August 22: The tide is setting strongly against us Nothing but the most resolute and decided action on the part of the Government and its friends can save the country from falling into hostile hands. This great reaction in public sentiment was due to the want of military successes and to the impression that Lincoln would not make peace save on the condition of the abandonment of slavery. So perturbed were the Committee that they went to Washington to plead with him. In a private letter of August 25 to Hay, Nicolay gave an account of their visit: The New York politicians have got a stampede on that is about to swamp everything. Raymond and the National Committee are here to-day. R. thinks a commission to Richmond is about the only salt to save us; while the Tycoon [Lincoln] sees and says it would be utter ruination. The matter is now undergoing consultation. Weak-kneed fools are in the movement for a new candidate to supplant the Tycoon. Everything is darkness and doubt and discouragement.[664] Lincoln himself thought it exceedingly probable that he would not be re-elected,[665] but he signified no intention of withdrawing and intimated that he would modify his policy in but one direction. He would undoubtedly have made peace on the basis of reunion, saying nothing about slavery, for he was convinced that slavery could never exist in the same form as before the War and that gradual emancipation was certain.[666]

Hay, on a visit to the West, had found some cheer, and in a private letter to Nicolay from Illinois set down the following accurate estimate of public sentiment

---

[663] Lowell, I, 339.
[664] Nicolay, 306.
[665] Aug. 23.
[666] IV, 513-522.

in that region: There is throughout the country, I mean the rural districts, a good healthy Union feeling and an intention to succeed in the military and the political contests; but everywhere in the towns the copperheads[667] are exultant and our own people either growling and despondent or sneakingly apologetic.[668]

Nicolay showed penetration when he wrote, Our men see giants in the airy and unsubstantial shadows of the opposition and are about to surrender without a fight.[669] As the Democrats had nominated no candidate there was in fact nothing to contend against. We are waiting with the greatest interest, Hay wrote, for the hatching of the big peace snake at Chicago.[670] Hay referred to the approaching Democratic convention which, when it met,[671] nominated McClellan for President and adopted a resolution that an earnest effort be made for peace. The nomination evoked a momentary burst of enthusiasm from the Democrats which corresponded to momentary disquietude among Republicans. Lincoln's yearning for military success betrayed itself in his vernacular of the prairie. Hold on with a bull dog grip, he telegraphed to Grant, and chew and choke.[672] His ardent desire was fulfilled. Better than any stump-speakers were two of his commanders on sea and on land.

On August 5, Farragut fought the battle of Mobile Bay. In making his entrance into the bay he must pass through a channel said to be mined with torpedoes, must run by the powerful Fort Morgan and then fight the iron-clad Tennessee. As his fleet advanced, a torpedo exploded under one of his monitors. She disappeared almost instantaneously beneath the waves carrying with her her gallant commander and nearly all her crew. A terrible disaster, Farragut called it.[673] Ahead were torpedoes, behind was retreat. O God, he prayed, who created man and gave him reason, direct me what to do. Shall I go on? And it seemed, he said, as if in answer a voice commanded, 'Go on!'[674] On he went, steering clear of the torpedoes, past Fort Morgan. The Tennessee attacked his fleet and, after a desperate battle, was beaten. She struck her flag and surrendered. One of the hardest earned victories of his life, as Farragut termed it, the crowning achievement of his naval career, as Mahan wrote, made him master of Mobile Bay. The surrender of Forts Gaines and Morgan (August 8th) followed.[675]

Mobile, now the most important port in the Gulf of Mexico remaining to the Confederates, was no longer available for blockade-running. Another door to the

---

[667] A popular name for the Democrats, see IV, 224.

[668] Aug. 25, J. Hay, I, 219.

[669] icolay, 306.

[670] J. Hay, I, 219.

[671] Aug. 29.

[672] Lincoln, C. W., II, 563.

[673] O. R. N., XXI, 415, 417.

[674] Mahan's Farragut, 277.

[675] O. R. N., XXI, 397 et seq.; Mahan's Farragut, Chap. X.

outside world was shut. The persistent work of the navy by the blockade and the capture of ports was reducing the South to a state of isolation.

The North in its general despondency failed at first to appreciate the magnitude of this victory; but the news received on September 3 that Sherman had captured Atlanta seemed to give Farragut's achievement a cumulative force. The taking of Atlanta was the culmination of the campaign from Chattanooga and was all the more glorious in that a victory is twice itself when the achiever brings home full numbers. The army which entered Atlanta was substantially the same as the army which Sherman had led out of Chattanooga.

The President, on September 3, issued a proclamation asking the people, when they assembled in their churches on next Sunday, to make a devout acknowledgment to the Supreme Being for the success of the fleet in Mobile harbor and the glorious achievements of the army in the State of Georgia; he issued orders of thanks to Farragut and Sherman, and ordered salutes of rejoicing to be fired from the navy-yards and arsenals of the country. On the Sunday appointed by the President, the people, with one accord, thanked God and took courage.

With epigrammatic brevity they had reduced the peace plank of the Democratic platform to the words, Resolved that the war is a failure,[676] and they now rejoiced that Farragut and Sherman had knocked out the underpinning of this platform.[677] On September 9, a letter of Grant's was made public in which he said: The rebels have now in their ranks their last man. They have robbed the cradle and the grave equally to get their present force. Besides what they lose in frequent skirmishes and battles, they are now losing from desertions and other causes, at least one regiment per day. With this drain upon them, the end is not far distant, if we will only be true to ourselves.

The State elections in Vermont and Maine during the first half of September showed that the disaffection to the administration was slight; they indicated a favorable result for Lincoln in November.

On September 15 Grant paid a visit to Sheridan, who had the command in the Shenandoah Valley, and gave him the order, Go in. Within a week Sheridan gained two brilliant victories over Early. These achievements appealed to the popular imagination as Stonewall Jackson's had done in 1862; but now it was the Northerner's turn to rejoice in a commander who, uniting dash and prudence, was giving them the long-wished-for but unexpected victories in the Shenandoah Valley that famous graveyard of Northern hopes with its open gateway for invasion from the South. Better than any campaign speeches were Sheridan's despatches telling the story of Confederate defeats. While such victories are

---

[676] The real expression was, "After four years of failure to restore the Union by the experiment of war."

[677] An alteration of Seward's remark, IV, 527.

gained, said one citizen to another as they shook hands and rejoiced, the war is not a failure; and victors in such battles do not ask for an armistice.

On October 11 State and congressional elections took place in Pennsylvania, Ohio and Indiana. Ohio went Union by a majority of 54,751; Indiana gave Morton for governor 20,883 more votes than were received by his Democratic opponent and all three States made material gains in Union members of Congress. These elections manifested a tendency of public opinion which pointed almost conclusively to Lincoln's election in November. The tide had turned and now it was again accelerated by Sheridan, who infused a considerable enthusiasm into the last weeks of the canvass by gaining a further and spectacular victory on the nineteenth of October. Sheridan's Ride, a poem written by Thomas Buchanan Read and read by Murdoch at many gatherings, not only won votes but made a lasting impression on the minds of men. With great pleasure, telegraphed Lincoln to Sheridan, I tender to you and your brave army the thanks of the nation and my own personal admiration and gratitude for the month's operations in the Shenandoah Valley; and especially for the splendid work of October 19, 1864.[678]

On November 8 the Presidential election took place. Lincoln carried States sufficient to give him 212 electoral votes, while McClellan would receive only 21, those of New Jersey, Delaware and Kentucky. In but one large State, New York, was there a close contest. Lincoln had a majority of the popular vote of 494,567. Moreover, the Lincoln party chose two-thirds of the House of Representatives.

I give you joy of the election, wrote Emerson to a friend. Seldom in history was so much staked on a popular vote. I suppose never in history.[679] Grant was deeply impressed with the vast importance and significance of the Presidential election the quiet and orderly character of the whole affair. There was, added Hay, no bloodshed or riot. It proves our worthiness of free institutions and our capability of preserving them without running into anarchy or despotism.[680]

In Lincoln's first election the people of the North had spoken, declaring their antagonism to slavery; if they were to remain true to their highest aspirations, they could not now turn back but must go resolutely forward. In spite of burdensome taxation, weariness of the war and mourning in every household, they decided on this election day of 1864 to finish the work they had begun.

---

[678] Lincoln, C. W., II, 589.
[679] Cabot, 609.
[680] J. Hay, I, 249.

Chapter XI

LIFE at the North during the war resembled that of most civilized communities which had full communication with the outside world. Business went on as usual, schools and colleges were full, churches were attended and men and women had their recreations. Progress was made in the mechanical sciences and arts. Men strove for wealth or learning; and the pursuit of fame was by no means confined to military and political circles. Nevertheless, that supreme business, the war, left its stamp on all private concerns and on every mode of thought. This was especially remarkable during the first eighteen months when the patriotic volunteers were individually encouraged by the sympathy and enthusiasm of those at home. What of the war! Isn't it grand! exclaimed Phillips Brooks in May, 1861. As late as the summer of 1862 the excellent character of the soldiers was noted. Our army, wrote Asa Gray on July 2, is largely composed of materials such as nothing but a high sense of duty could keep for a year in military life. Our best young men, said Agassiz in a private letter of August 15, are the first to enlist; if anything can be objected to these large numbers of soldiers, it is that it takes away the best material that the land possesses. In all the country districts the strong young men were gone.[681]

Times were hard at the commencement of the war and continued so until the autumn of 1862. People are getting dreadfully poor here, wrote Phillips Brooks from Philadelphia.[682] The New York Tribune referred to our paralyzed industry, obstructed commerce, our overloaded finances and our mangled railroads.[683] All sorts of economies were practised. Coffee and sugar rose enormously in price. Many families mixed roasted dandelion root with pure coffee while others made their morning beverage from parched corn or rye; some substituted brown for white sugar. One by one luxuries disappeared from the table and few were ashamed of their frugal repasts. The wearing of plain clothes became a fashion as well as a virtue. The North was for the most part a community of simple living. Opera was only occasional, theatres were few and the amusements took on a character adapted to the life. A popular lecture, a concert, a church sociable with a charade turning on some striking event of the war, a gathering of young men and women to scrape lint for the wounded, a visit perhaps to a neighboring camp to witness a dress parade of volunteers these were the diversions from the overpowering anxiety weighing upon the people. Personal grief was added to the

---

[681] V, 189. Fite, Social and Industrial Conditions during the Civil War, 5.
[682] June 29, 1861.
[683] Aug. 5, 1862.

national anxiety. In many of our dwellings, wrote Harriet Beecher Stowe, the very light of our lives has gone out.

With great trials were mingled petty inconveniences arising from derangement of the country's finances. Gold began to sell at a premium in January, 1862, and disappeared from circulation; but this was no hardship to the mass of the people for gold had not been used largely as currency and there was a ready substitute for it in State bank-notes and the United States legal tenders. But the advance in gold was followed by a similar advance in silver. Silver change became an article of speculation and was bought at a premium by brokers; much of it was sent to Canada and by July 1, 1862, it seems to have practically disappeared from circulation. Its sudden disappearance brought forth diverse remedies. Individuals, prompter in action than municipalities or the general government, flooded the country with shinplasters small notes in denominations of from 5 to 50 cents, promises to pay of hotels, restaurants, business houses and country dealers. For a short while copper and nickel cents commanded a premium and various metal tokens were issued by tradesmen to take their place as well as that of the small silver coins. Secretary Chase, in a letter of July 14, 1862, to the Chairman of the Committee of Ways and Means of the House of Representatives, said that the most serious inconveniences and evils are apprehended unless the issues of shinplasters and metal tokens can be checked and the small coins of the government kept in circulation or a substitute provided. He proposed either to debase the silver coinage of the fractional parts of a dollar or to legalize in effect the use of postage and other stamps as currency. Congress, by Act of July 17, 1862, prohibited the issue of shinplasters by private corporations or individuals, provided for the issuance to the public of postage and other stamps and declared that, under certain limitations, these were receivable in payment of dues to the United States and were redeemable in greenbacks. People naturally preferred the stamps to the promises to pay of private individuals and hastened to the post offices to be supplied therewith, but what they here gained in soundness they lost in convenience. The gummy back, flimsy texture, small surface and light weight of the stamps rendered them the most imperfect circulating medium ever known in the United States. For one thing, the making of change in the course of small transactions proved a laborious business because of the intrusion of a common denomination of 3 cents (the stamp most frequently employed and the one of which there was the greatest supply) into the convenient decimal system. The counting out of 2, 3, 5 and 10 cent stamps became intolerable when large quantities of change were required, so that in places where various sorts of tickets were sold, the stamps were put up in small envelopes marked in large figures, 10, 25 and 50 cents, as the case might be. This mitigated the nuisance only in part as cautious persons would insist on opening the envelopes and counting the stamps in order to see whether the contents tallied with the figure outside. The stamps became dirty and mutilated; losing their adhesive power they were unfit for postage. They had proved a poor substitute for shinplasters. But relief from both evils was afforded almost simultaneously by the Treasury Department and by various municipalities.

From the language of Chase's recommendation for the use of postage and other stamps as currency and from the provisions of the statute, it would be impossible to divine the relief which was eventually forthcoming. The Secretary, in accordance with the Act of July 17, 1862, had made an arrangement with the Postmaster-General for a supply of postage stamps, but it being soon discovered that stamps prepared for postage uses were not adapted to the purposes of currency, he proceeded to construe the law liberally and issue a postage currency. This was in the form of small notes of which the 25 and 50 cent denominations were about a quarter the size of a dollar bill, the 5 and 10 cent somewhat smaller. On the 5 cent note was a facsimile of the 5 cent postage stamp, the vignette being Jefferson's head; for the 25 cent note this vignette appeared five times. Of similar design were the 10 and 50 cent notes, the vignette on the 10 cent stamp being Washington's head. The color of the 5 and 25 cent notes was brown; that of the 10 and 50 cent, green; when new they were not ill-looking. To men and women who had been using shinplasters and soiled and worn postage and revenue stamps, they seemed a positive deliverance. The issue of this postage currency began August 21, 1862, and crowds of people waited patiently in long lines at the office of the Assistant-Treasurer in New York and other cities for their turn to secure some of these new and attractive notes.

By the act of March 3, 1863 Congress provided for the issue of fractional currency, in lieu of the postage currency, and limited the amount of both kinds to a circulation of fifty millions. The Secretary of the Treasury in issuing the new notes gave up the facsimile of the postage stamps, although the size of the notes remained substantially the same and their backs, at first brown, green, purple and red, were afterwards green for all the 3, 5, 10, 15, 25 and 50 cent notes. They were receivable for all dues to the United States less than $5, except customs, and were exchangeable for United States notes; they gradually supplanted the postage currency; in popular usage both were termed scrip. Although desirable at first as a relief for greater evils, the notes became so worn and filthy with constant passing from hand to hand as to be objectionable on the score of cleanliness and health. Most of the people were rejoiced when finally in 1876 they began to be replaced by subsidiary silver coin and gradually to disappear from circulation, although a few regretted the paper fractional currency because of its easy transmission by mail and its service in making up the fractional amounts of pay-rolls of mining and manufacturing concerns when the money for the men was put into envelopes as the best manner of its distribution. For a year, from July, 1862 to July, 1863, the people of the North suffered the bitterness of defeat. McClellan's failure on the Peninsula, Pope's defeat at the second battle of Bull Run, Burnside's disaster of Fredericksburg, Hooker's overthrow at Chancellorsville, only slightly relieved by the partial victories of Antietam and Stone's river, were a succession of calamities, the cumulative force of which would have broken the spirit of any except a resolute people who believed that their cause was just. Sumner comes to dinner, wrote Longfellow in his journal.[684] He is very gloomy and desponding; and sighs out every now and then, 'Poor country! poor, poor country!' During the dark days, when after some bloody reverse of our armies, Phillips Brooks met a friend on a street corner, he could only wring his hand and say, Isn't it horrible? and gloomily pass on. People who took counsel of their meaner fears cried for peace at any price. During that year social clubs ceased to meet. Men when they heard of a disaster would give up some festive entertainment, would forego even a quiet evening at cards. They had no disposition for mirth. Their hearts were with their dead and wounded fellow citizens on the Southern battle-field; they sat in quiet and brooded over their country's reverses. No thoughtful American opened his morning paper without dreading to find that he had no longer a country to love and honor.[685]

It is a striking fact that during this period of gloom, in the autumn of 1862, a revival of business began. From that time until the end of the war trade was active, factories busy, labor constantly employed and failures remarkably few. Railroad stocks had a sharp advance and the prices of the leading articles in the New York market rose steadily as measured in paper currency. Pig iron is often called the barometer of industrial activity: the production of it increased with regularity during the years 1862, 1863 and 1864 and its price rose in a still greater ratio. The average yearly price per ton of No. 1 anthracite foundry pig iron in Philadelphia was respectively $23.87, $35.25, $59.25. It was a period of money-making and accumulation of wealth. August Belmont wrote [May 7, 1863] of the eagerness with which, for the last two months, the people of all classes have invested their money in the securities of the government; for The North is united and prosperous. Harriet Beecher Stowe said, Old Hartford seems fat, rich and cosey stocks higher than ever, business plenty everything as tranquil as possible. John Sherman spoke of the wonderful prosperity of all classes, especially of laborers.[686]

The basis of prosperity in the United States was agriculture, and its steady growth at the North is one of the characteristics of the war. Despite the number of men who went into the army, good crops were made; the wheat crop was excellent during the years of the war and so was Indian corn, except for the partial failure in 1863. Three things saved the harvests, wrote Fite, the increased use of labor-saving machinery, the work of women in the fields and the continued influx of new population.[687] The wide use of mowing, reaping and threshing machines and the horse rake increased six-fold the efficiency of the farm laborer.

---

[684] Sept. 14, 1862.

[685] Lowell.

[686] November, 1863.

The women turned out to help. A missionary wrote from Iowa: I met more women driving teams on the road and saw more at work in the fields than men. They seem to have said to their husbands in the language of a favorite song, 'Just take your gun and go; For Ruth can drive the oxen, John, And I can use the hoe.'[688] Many of the immigrants went west. They were tempted by the ease and cheapness with which land could be acquired: the wise Homestead Act fostered the development of the West and the growing of food so important for the army and the people who were sustaining it. There was always a surplus of grain which was shipped largely to Great Britain where it was badly needed because of deficient harvests from 1860-62. This movement was beneficial to the exchanges between America and Europe.[689]

The story of the North during the war would not be complete without reference to certain infractions of the Constitution. Arbitrary arrests were made in the Northern States where the courts were open and where the regular administration of justice had not been interrupted by any overt acts of rebellion. Most of these arrests were made by order of the Secretary of State, the others by order of the Secretary of War. Sometimes the authority of the officer was a simple telegram; in no case was the warrant such as the Constitution required. The men arrested were charged with no offence, were examined by no magistrate and were confined in Fort Lafayette or Fort Warren as prisoners of state. The justification pleaded in the Senate for these stretches of authority was that the persons apprehended were, by treasonable speaking and writing, giving aid and comfort to the enemy and that their imprisonment was necessary for the safety of the republic. Yet the matter did not go unquestioned. Senator Trumbull introduced a resolution asking information from the Secretary of State in regard to these arrests and in his remarks supporting it pointed out the injustice and needlessness of such procedure. What are we coming to, he asked, if arrests may be made at the whim or caprice of a cabinet minister? and when Senator Hale demanded, Have not arrests been made in violation of the great principles of our Constitution? no one could deny that this was the fact.

Public sentiment, however, sustained the administration and it was only from a minority in the Senate and in the country that murmurs were heard. Nevertheless, the protests were emphatic and couched in irrefutable logic. They were directed against Seward, who was deemed responsible for the apprehension of men in Maine, Vermont, Connecticut and northern New York on suspicion that they were traitors, instead of leaving them to be dealt with by the public sentiment of their thoroughly loyal communities; and it was felt that his action savored rather of the capriciousness of an absolute monarch than of a desire to govern in a

---

[687] Fite, 6.

[688] Fite, 8.

[689] *Ibid., 17 et seq.*

constitutional manner. The mischief of this policy was immediately evident in that it gave a handle to the Democratic opposition, probably increasing its strength, and in that it furnished our critics over the sea an additional opportunity for detraction. The remote consequences which were feared that our people would lose some of their liberties, that we were beginning in very sooth to tread the well-worn path from democracy to despotism have not been realized.

It is true that the acts of a cabinet minister, unless disavowed by the President, become the President's own acts; in so far must Lincoln be held responsible for these arbitrary arrests. Nevertheless, it is improbable that Lincoln, of his own motion, would have ordered them; for, although at times he acted without warrant of the Constitution, he had at the same time a profound reverence for it, showing in all his procedure that he much preferred to keep within the strict limits of the letter and spirit of the organic law of the land and that whenever he exercised or permitted others to exercise arbitrary power he did so with keen regret. It was undoubtedly disagreeable to him to be called the Cæsar of the American Republic and a more unlimited despot than the world knows this side of China, and to be aware that Senator Grimes described a call at the White House for the purpose of seeing the President, as an attempt to approach the footstool of the power enthroned at the other end of the avenue. An order of the Secretary of War on February 14, 1862, directed the release of the political prisoners on parole that they would give no aid or comfort to the enemies of the United States and laid down the rule that henceforward arrests would be made under the direction of the military authorities alone.

The term Copperhead, which originated in the autumn of 1862, was used freely during the next year. It was an opprobrious epithet applied by Union men to those who adhered rigidly to the Democratic organization, strenuously opposed all the distinctive and vigorous war measures of the President and of Congress and, deeming it impossible to conquer the South, were therefore earnest advocates of peace. It might not be hardly exact to say that all who voted the Democratic ticket in 1863 were, in the parlance of the day, Copperheads, but this sweeping statement would be nearer the truth than one limiting the term to those who really wished for the military success of the South and organized or joined the secret order of Knights of the Golden Circle. In the Western States, at all events, the words Democrat and Copperhead became, after the middle of January [1863], practically synonymous, and the cognomen, applied as a reproach, was assumed with pride. The War Democrats, in contradistinction from those who favored peace, acted at elections in the main with the Republicans, voting the Union ticket, as it was called in most of the States. It may be safely said that practically all the men who adhered with fidelity and enthusiasm to the Democratic organization and name found a spokesman in either Horatio Seymour of New York or Clement L. Vallandigham of Ohio, both of whom had the peculiar ability required for political leadership. The tendency of the Eastern Democrats was to range themselves with

Seymour whilst the Western Democrats were attracted by the more extreme views of Vallandigham.

Under any constitutional government, where speech and the press are free, the necessity should be readily admitted of an opposition in time of war, even when the Ship of State is in distress. It is not difficult to define a correct policy for the Democrats during the civil conflict, when, as was conceded by everyone, the republic was in great danger. In Congress they should have co-operated to the full extent of their power with the dominant party in its effort to raise men and money to carry on the war; and in any opposition they ought to have taken the tone, not of party objection, but of friendly criticism, with the end in view of perfecting rather than defeating the necessary bills. While in the session of Congress that ended March 4, 1863, they failed to rise to this height, they did not, on the other hand, pursue a policy of obstruction that would be troublesome if not pernicious. For that matter it is doubtful if obstructive tactics could have prevailed against the able and despotic parliamentary leadership of the majority in the House by Thaddeus Stevens and prevented the passage at this session of the two bills which gave the President control of the sword and purse of the nation; but a serious attempt in that direction, with all that it involved, would have reduced the country to a state of panic. There must therefore be set down to the credit of the Democrats in Congress a measure of patriotism that almost always exists in an Anglo-Saxon minority, proving sufficient to preserve the commonwealth from destruction.

More severe criticism than is due for any positive action in the House or the Senate must be meted out to the leaders of the Democratic party for their speeches in and out of the legislative halls and to the influential Democratic newspapers in their effort to form and guide a public sentiment which should dictate the policy of the Government. One fact they ignored, that peace was impossible unless the Southern Confederacy were acknowledged and a boundary line agreed upon between what would then be two distinct nations. They pretended to a belief, for which there was absolutely no foundation, that if fighting ceased and a convention of the States were called, the Union might be restored. Hence proceeded their opposition to the President's emancipation policy as being an obstacle to the two sections becoming re-united. But men who loved their country better than their party ought to have perceived, for it was palpable at the time, that the Southern States had not the slightest intention of consenting on even the most favorable conditions to the Union as it was, and that the President had been brought to his decree against slavery by the logic of events. Apologists for slavery as the Democrats had been for so many years on the ground that it was a necessary evil, they could not give hearty support to emancipation; but, if they had allowed themselves to be influenced in a reasonable degree by their own conviction that slavery was morally wrong, they could, with patriotism and consistency, have adopted the position that the proclamation was a military order, and having been made, should be executed. If they had abandoned the pursuit of an impossible attainment and the policy of hindering the President and Congress in the exercise of their prerogatives, there would still have remained scope for a healthy opposition which would not have left the name Copperhead-Democrat a reproach for so many years; in truth, the Democrats might have deserved well of the muse of history. In point of fact they performed a real service to the country in advocating economy and integrity in the disposition of the public money, and they might have gone further and applauded Chase in his efforts to secure the one and Stanton in his determination to have the other. Their criticisms of the Executive for suspending the privilege of the writ of habeas corpus, for the arbitrary arrests and for the abridgment of the freedom of speech and of writing were justly taken, and undoubtedly had an influence for the good on legislation. Had they concentrated their opposition on these points their arguments would have carried greater force and would have attracted men who were disturbed by these infractions of personal liberty but who were repelled by the remainder of the Democratic program.

In consideration of our own practice, the decision of our courts, the opinions of our statesmen and jurists, and English precedents for two centuries, it may be affirmed that the right of suspending the privilege of the writ of habeas corpus was vested by the Constitution in Congress and not in the Executive. The President, in assuming that authority and applying the suspension to States beyond the sphere of hostile operations, arrogated power which became necessary to support the policy of arbitrary arrests, so diligently pursued by Seward at first and afterwards by Stanton. The defence made was necessity, and our own precedents were set aside because the State now stood in its greatest peril since the adoption of the Constitution.

By the Act of March 3, 1863, the Secretary of State and the Secretary of War were required to furnish lists of State or political prisoners to the judges of the United States Courts, but no lists, so far as I have been able to ascertain, were ever furnished; and in truth the aptitude for autocratic government had grown at such a pace that in September [1863] Chase discovered, to his surprise, that the provisions of this act were unfamiliar to the President and to all the members of the Cabinet except himself.

For my own part, after careful consideration, I do not hesitate to condemn the arbitrary arrests and the arbitrary interference with the freedom of the press[690] in States which were not included in the theatre of the war and in which the courts remained open. In arriving at this judgment I have not left out of account an unpatriotic speech of Vallandigham's in the House nor the still more dastardly writing in the Democratic newspapers, nor the Copperhead talk in the street, in public conveyances and in hotels, where prudence and restraint were cast to the winds; nor am I unmindful of the fact that the criticisms generally were increasing

---

[690] See IV, 253.

in virulence and that complaints of the utterance of treasonable sentiments were constantly being made to the authorities by patriotic men. Nevertheless, I am convinced that all this extrajudicial procedure was inexpedient, unnecessary and wrong and that the offenders thus summarily dealt with should have been prosecuted according to law or, if their offences were not indictable, permitted to go free. Abraham Lincoln, wrote James Bryce, wielded more authority than any single Englishman has done since Oliver Cromwell. My reading of English history and comparative study of our own have led me to the same conclusion, although it should be added that Cromwell's exercise of arbitrary power greatly exceeded Lincoln's and involved more important infractions of the Constitution of his country. Moreover, there was in Lincoln's nature so much of kindness and mercy as to mitigate the harshness of Seward's and Stanton's procedure. The pervasive and lingering influence of his personality, the respect for the Constitution and the law which history and tradition have ascribed to him, the greatness of his character and work, have prevented the generation that has grown up since the civil conflict from realizing the enormity of the acts done under his authority by direction of his Secretaries of State and War. I have not lighted on a single instance in which the President himself directed an arrest, yet he permitted them all; he stands responsible for the casting into prison of citizens of the United States on orders as arbitrary as the lettres-de-cachet of Louis XIV.[691] The technical experts of the War Department and of the Army may be justly criticised for not arming our infantry with breech-loading rifles. They were behindhand and not up to their opportunities. The Secretary of War in his report of December 1, 1859, had stated the result of the experiments in breech-loading arms: these arms were nearly if not entirely perfected, and he added: With the best breech-loading arm, one skilful man would be equal to two, probably three, armed with the ordinary muzzle-loading gun. True policy requires that steps should be taken to introduce these arms gradually into our service. But on October 22, 1864, the chief of ordnance reported to Stanton, The use of breech-loading arms in our service has, with few exceptions, been confined to mounted troops, and on December 5, 1864, he returned to the subject thus: The experience of the war has shown that breech-loading arms are greatly superior to muzzle-loaders for infantry as well as for cavalry, and that measures should immediately be taken to substitute a suitable breech-loading musket in place of the rifle musket which is now manufactured at the National Armory and by private concerns for this department. Some one ought to have known this at least three years earlier and to have made it his business to press the importance of it upon the President, the Secretary of War and Congress. The Prussians had used a breech-loading rifle in the Revolution of 1848 and again in the Schleswig-Holstein war of 1864 and the infantry of the Northern army ought

---

[691] For the most celebrated case of arbitrary arrests during the war, that of Vallandigham, see IV, 245.

to have been armed with a similar gun for their campaigns twelve months before Lee's surrender. Our few regiments which had repeating and breech-loading rifles did such effective execution that the dramatic scene of Königgratz a great battle between an army with breech-loaders and one with muzzle-loaders ought to have been anticipated by two years and played upon the field of Virginia or in the mountains of Georgia. In the art of war we showed ourselves inferior to the Prussians but the fault was not with American inventive talent. Excellent arms were offered to the Government and it is safe to say that, had its administration of technical affairs equalled that of the Pennsylvania Railroad or some of our large manufacturing establishments, the army would have had the improved weapons. The war gave a powerful impetus to the humanitarian spirit. Americans were essentially religious and Christ's teaching had sunk deep in their hearts. Non-combatants individually and through well-devised organizations were diligent in ministering to the wants and sufferings of the soldiers who were upholding the Northern cause in the field. This work of aid was well adapted to women whose energy, self-sacrifice and well-directed efforts proved them worthy of Lincoln's words spoken at one of the Sanitary fairs.[692] This extraordinary war, he said, in which we are engaged, falls heavily upon all classes of people, but the most heavily upon the soldier. For it has been said, all that a man hath will he give for his life; and while all contribute of their substance, the soldier puts his life at stake and often yields it up in his country's cause. The highest merit then is due to the soldier. In this extraordinary war, extraordinary developments have manifested themselves such as have not been seen in former wars; and amongst these manifestations nothing has been more remarkable than these fairs for the relief of suffering soldiers and their families. And the chief agents in these fairs are the women of America. I am not accustomed to the use of the language of eulogy; I have never studied the art of paying compliments to women; but I must say, that if all that has been said by orators and poets since the creation of the world in praise of women were applied to the women of America, it would not do them justice for their conduct during this war. I will close by saying, God bless the women of America. Despite the opinion of our Supreme Court that It follows from the very nature of war that trading between the belligerents should cease, there was a large overland trade between the South and the North; the South exchanged her cotton for money or needed supplies and this trade was encouraged by the Washington Government. The intention was good, and if the history of these transactions were to be written from the acts of Congress, the proclamations of the President, the instructions of the Secretary of the Treasury and the orders of the Secretaries of War and Navy, it might be affirmed that a difficult problem had been frankly met and solved. Special agents were appointed by the Secretary of the Treasury to collect captured and abandoned property in parts of the Confederacy occupied by

---

[692] For the Sanitary fairs see V, 257

our forces which should be sold for the benefit of the United States subject to the rights of ownership of loyal persons. Permits to trade in districts which had been recovered from the Confederacy were issued to proper and loyal persons by these agents and other officers of the Treasury Department, but all commercial intercourse beyond the lines of the National Army was strictly forbidden. The special agents were further ordered to confer with the generals commanding the respective departments and they and the authorized traders were in a measure responsible to the military authority but were under the immediate control and management of the Secretary of the Treasury, who supervised this limited commercial intercourse licensed by the President. No other trade was legal and all property coming into the United States through other means was ordered to be confiscated.

But the feverish business conditions of 1864 and a certain relaxation in morality were felt in the commercial intercourse between the South and the North. The price of cotton in Boston at the beginning of the year was eighty-one cents per pound; it advanced steadily until the close of August when it fetched $1.90 in United States currency. It could be bought in the Confederacy for from twelve to twenty cents per pound in gold. The enormous difference between the two values represented a profit so enticing that many men in responsible positions were led into trading beyond the restrictions imposed by the Government. If accurate statistics could be obtained, it would surprise no student of the subject to find that the North received more cotton from the internal commerce than did Great Britain from the blockade-runners;[693] the greater portion of this staple came from a region under the control of the Southern Confederacy, and in exchange for it the Southern Army and people obtained needed supplies. This trade was a greater advantage to the South than to the North. New England and the Middle States obtained cotton and probably ran their mills nearer to full time than if they had been entirely dependent on the foreign article, but any further curtailment of this manufacture would have caused no distress to the operatives. So extended was the demand for labor that work was readily to be found in other industries. In Lowell where, in 1862, the stoppage of spindles was proportionately the greatest, deposits in the savings-banks largely increased during that year. For the indispensable articles Indian cotton could have been used, as in Great Britain, and for other cotton fabrics woollen might have been substituted. On the other hand the South obtained salt, quinine, powder and arms, absolute necessaries for carrying on the war. The summer of 1864 brought almost crushing burdens. The failure of Grant's Virginia campaign and the doubts in regard to Lincoln's re-election intensified every other trouble and led many thoughtful persons to fear that the game was up. Governor Brough of Ohio wrote to Stanton on March 14, 1864 that he regarded our financial position as critical; every man whom we put into the army was costing us over

---

[693] *post.*

$300 and we were incurring a debt which we could not pay without scaling it down; such a measure would be our ruin. About the same time Chase was asked, What is the debt now in round numbers? About $2,500,000,000 was the reply. How much more can the country stand? If we do not suppress the rebellion, answered Chase, when it reaches $3,000,000,000 we shall have to give it up. Soon after Fessenden entered upon the duties of the Treasury Department,[694] he wrote to his friend Senator Grimes, Things must be taken as I find them and they are quite bad enough to appall any but a man as desperate as I am. Weed placed the situation plainly before an English friend. We are beset by dangers, he wrote, foremost of which is the presidential canvass. Regiments are returning home, worn, weary, maimed and depleted. Our cities and villages swarm with skulking, demoralized soldiers. You, my dear old friend, the Englishman replied, ought to settle your affairs before the crash comes. It may be that your government will be reunited for a time; but it cannot last after this era of tremendous passion. I should really like to go to the United States if only to see your Lincoln. But will he soon be in Fort Lafayette or here in exile? If this country gets ultimately through, wrote Francis Lieber in a private letter, safe and hale, no matter with how many scars, a great civil war with a presidential election in the very midst of it (while the enemy has to stand no such calamity) I shall set it down as the most wonderful miracle in the whole history of events. The memory of the New York draft riot of 1863 which had lasted four days was in every mind and there were now apprehensions of forcible resistance to the draft in New York, Pennsylvania, Ohio, Indiana, Illinois and Wisconsin; the different authorities in these States called upon the general government for troops to enforce the laws. But Grant sorely needed re-enforcements to fill his shattered ranks: to comply with the military exigencies and at the same time content the governors of the States was indeed a difficult problem.

The President and Secretary of War were obliged to work through the Federal system, the disadvantages of which for carrying on a war were largely overcome by the sympathetic co-operation of most of the governors, who, with few exceptions, belonged to the same party as the President. Many of them were men of ability and knew the local wants and capabilities. Conspicuous as one gathers from the Official Records were Morton of Indiana, Andrew of Massachusetts, Curtin of Pennsylvania, Tod and Brough successively of Ohio. At the same time patience and discretion were needed in handling affairs so that the dignity of these and of the other Northern governors should not be offended. They were all patriotic, desiring to assist the general government to the extent of their power, but each had his local pride and was zealous in looking after the interests of his own State. They were diligent in their communications to the War Department,

---

[694] Fessenden succeeded Chase on July 5, 1864. This is date of taking office. He was nominated, confirmed and commissioned on July 1.

reckoning closely the number of men they ought to furnish, and frequently claiming that their quotas were filled or that troops in excess had been contributed on one call which should be allowed on another. The State arithmeticians in their eagerness to have credit for every possible man were so adroit at computation that at one time, as Lincoln stated it, the aggregate of the credits due to all the States exceeded very considerably the number of men called for. This vexation was of a most trying nature since a vital condition of the President's success in the war was that he should have the active and zealous support of these governors. When he told the committee of the Rhode Island legislature that men and not an adjustment of balances was the object of the call for troops, he answered with his clear logic the reclamations that poured in upon Stanton and the provost-marshal general; nevertheless, he did not urge it to triumph in the argument but to persuade the committee and the country that he must have men. However, be the necessity never so dire, he purposed proceeding with the utmost fairness. The governors were forward in making suggestions and most of them felt that some things should be done differently. Maryland, Pennsylvania, Ohio, Indiana and Illinois were in constant danger of invasion; threatened raids from Canada and other British provinces kept the authorities of New York, Vermont and Maine in a state of alarm; all these and similar troubles were brought to the War Department with requests for succor and protection. The patience of Stanton when he replied to the claims and grievances of the governors exhibits another side of this man who was often irascible to an extraordinary degree. But it was the patience of a determined man who gave the cue to his department with the result that during the last two years of the war the commissary and quarter-master's departments were admirably managed and the transportation of troops and supplies well carried out. After Lincoln it was Stanton more than any other who smoothed the way for the governors to carry out their predilection for energetically upholding the national administration by helping the Secretary of War in various matters of detail which came within their sphere.

The Stanton of tradition is a stern man, standing at a high desk, busy and careworn, grumbling, fuming and swearing, approached by every subordinate with fear, by every officer except the highest with anxiety, by the delinquent with trepidation. The Stanton of the Official Records is a patient, tactful, unobtrusive man, who, bearing a heavy responsibility, disposes of business promptly, who takes a firm grasp of many and various facts and conditions and adapts himself to circumstances, keeping always in view the great result to be achieved. No one accustomed to affairs can go through the correspondence of the summer of 1864 without arriving at a high opinion of Stanton's executive ability. He was patient and consideration with those to whom Patience and consideration were due but, when he believed himself in the right, he was unyielding and resolute. He was wise in his conduct of affairs, but it is a wonder that on top of the trials of three years he and Lincoln were not crushed by the disappointments and cares which fell to their lot from May to September, 1864.

The burden of the war told perceptibly on Lincoln. His boisterous laughter, wrote John Hay, became less frequent year by year; the eye grew veiled by constant meditation on momentous subjects; the air of reserve and detachment from his surroundings increased. He aged with great rapidity. The change in Lincoln is shown in two life masks, one made in 1860, the other in the spring of 1865. The face of 1860 belongs to a strong healthy man, is full of life, of energy, of vivid aspiration. The other, continued Hay, is so sad and peaceful in its infinite repose that St. Gaudens insisted when he first saw it that it was a death mask. The lines are set as if the living face like the copy had been in bronze; the nose is thin and lengthened by the emaciation of the cheeks; the mouth is fixed like that of an archaic statue; a look as of one on whom sorrow and care had done their worst without victory, is on all the features; the whole expression is of unspeakable sadness and all-sufficing strength.

We of the North maintain that, after Sumter was fired upon, the war was unavoidable and just, but the summer of 1864 carries this lesson: given our system of government with its division of powers between the nation and the States and its partition of authority at Washington; given our frequent elections; given the independence and individuality of our people, it is clear that we are but poorly equipped for making war. The genius of the American Commonwealth lies in peace.[695]

---

[695] This chapter is based on III, p. 555 *et seq.*;Chapters XIX, IV, XXVII, V; and on Fite, Social and Industrial Conditions during the Civil War.

Chapter XII

CONDITIONS in the Southern Confederacy were novel in that the community was cut off by the blockade from any extensive intercourse with the outer world. As the North was the stronger naval power the blockade was clearly obvious and was proclaimed by the President one week after the firing on Sumter. Although at first not thorough it gradually increased in efficiency and proved one of the important agencies in deciding the war. But Lincoln and Grant saw plainly that peace could not be had until the Southern armies had been fought to a finish of destruction or surrender. To this end the patient work of the navy in blockading the Southern ports was a grateful and necessary aid to Grant and Sherman in their decisive operations. But the blockade of itself might have been maintained even unto the crack of doom if Lee's and Johnston's armies remained intact, living in a fertile country cultivated by a mass of negro non-combatants, clothed from an excess supply of cotton and a limited supply of wool. The relation between our army and navy during the Civil War was the same as between the British army and navy in 1914 when the English fleet had effectually blockaded the German ports and kept the German fleet in a safe harbor. Said the London Times, The Navy [is] our shield, the Army our sword.[696]

The blockade was a source of acute discomfort to the Southern people, cutting them off from most luxuries and many necessaries. Salt, coffee, tea, soap, candles, matches, glue advanced enormously in price and were extremely scarce. The blockade taught lessons of economy, causing highly bred young women of Charleston to dress in homespun and Richmond gentlemen to wear last year's clothes. Brooms, chairs, baskets, brushes, pails, tubs, kegs, slate pencils and knitting needles were scarce. Ink began to be made in the home by a crude process. In the news columns of the Charleston Courier, it was announced that a man in Caswell County (N. C.) was manufacturing writing ink which he would furnish in any quantity to those who would provide their own bottles. A Richmond apothecary advertised that he could not fill prescriptions unless persons requiring medicines should bring their own phials. But many common medicines were hard to get. The medical purveyor at Richmond appealed to the ladies of Virginia to cultivate the poppy so that opium might be had for the sick and wounded of the army. Various things were popularly suggested to take the place of quinine and other medicines. The surgeon-general sent out officially a formula for a compound tincture of dried dogwood, poplar and willow bark and whiskey to be issued as a

---

[696] Sept. 9. "Though the Navy can protect our shores, only an army and a well-trained army can bring a war to an end." Spectator, Sept. 12, 1914.

tonic and febrifuge and substitute as far as practicable for quinine. Quinine and morphia were articles greatly desired in the trade with the North. All possible means were used to obtain these and other drugs and a large amount of smuggling was at one time carried on from Cincinnati by men and women devoted to the Confederate cause. In October, 1862, when General Sherman was in command at Memphis, an imposing funeral headed by a handsome city hearse, with pall and plumes, was allowed by the guards to pass through the Union lines: the coffin which was borne by the hearse contained a lot of well-selected medicines for the Confederate army. A large doll filled with quinine was brought through the lines in a trunk from New Orleans; when it was scrutinized, the owner declared with tears in her eyes that the doll was for a poor crippled girl; this ruse was likewise successful in passing it through without the discovery of its precious burden.

No deprivation was felt so keenly as the lack of tea and coffee. Tea is beyond the reach of all save the most opulent, said the Charleston Courier in April, 1862. I have not tasted coffee or tea for more than a year, is an entry of Jones on February 4, 1864. Rich people even abstained from the use of tea in order that the small supply should be saved for those who were ill. The hospitals procured coffee for a while, but on December 2, 1863, the surgeon-general ordered its discontinuance as an article of diet for the sick. In consequence of the very limited supply, he added, it is essential that it be used solely for its medicinal effects as a stimulant. People resorted to all kinds of substitutes. Parched rye, wheat, corn, sweet potatoes, chestnuts, peanuts, chicory and cotton seed took the place of the Arabian berry, but all agreed that there was nothing coffee but coffee. For tea a decoction of dried currant, blackberry and sage leaves, of sassafras root or blossoms was drunk and some tried to make themselves believe that the substitute was as good as China tea. Fremantle, during his travels through the South, tasted no tea from April 6 to June 17, 1863, when some uncommonly good was offered him at President Davis's house.

In 1862, may be noted a scarcity of salt and anxiety as to a future supply, especially for the army, as salt meat was a large part of the army ration. The governor of Mississippi wrote to Davis that the destitution of salt is alarming, and the governor of Alabama, in a letter to the Secretary of War, said, The salt famine in our land is most lamentable. The earthen floors of smokehouses, saturated by the dripping of bacon, were dug up and boiled that no salty material be left unused. Sea-water was to a large extent utilized to provide for the deficiency, but a more valuable source of supply was the saline springs of southwestern Virginia. The commonwealth of Virginia embarked on the manufacture of salt and made regulations for its distribution to the public. Other States followed her example so that the salt famine was to some extent mitigated.

Another serious hardship arose from the scarcity of paper. Many of the newspapers were gradually reduced in size and were finally printed on half sheets. Sometimes one sheet would be brown, another wall paper. Even the white paper was frequently coarse; and this, together with inferior type, made the news sheet itself a daily record of the waning material fortunes of the Confederacy. The Richmond Examiner said that the editorials of the journals were written on brown paper, waste paper, backs of old letters and rejected essays, unpaid bills, bits of foolscap torn from the copy books of youth and the ledgers of the business men. An Alabama editor used a shingle; when one editorial was set up he would wipe it out and write another. Another editor employed in a similar way his schoolboy slate. An advertisement in the Charleston Courier ran that no more orders for Miller's Almanac for 1863 could be filled unless forty or fifty reams of printing paper could be purchased. Mrs. MacGuire could not get a blank-book in which to continue her diary and was obliged to use wrapping paper for the vivid account of her daily experiences. Mrs. Putnam states that their family and friendly letters were written on paper which they would hardly have used for wrapping paper before the war. Envelopes which had been received were frequently turned inside out and used for the reply. Curry relates that the tax receipts given for the produce of his farm in Alabama were written on brown paper and had a dingy archaic appearance. Citizens as a boon to the press and the public, nay the government itself were urged to send their accumulated rags to the paper manufacturers. There was danger of an iron famine and certain other metals were in short supply. Information came to the Charleston arsenal that many patriotic citizens were willing to contribute their lead window weights to the Government for war purposes and the captain of the corps of artillery in charge offered to replace them with iron. The editor of the Charleston Courier offered the lead water pipe in his residence as a free gift to my beloved and imperilled country. Other similar offers were made and church bells were proffered that their metal might be melted and cast into cannon.

Contemporary writings are full of complaints of lack of bread and meat. Hunger, wrote Professor Gildersleeve, was the dominant note of life in the Confederacy. While this was true of Virginia, which largely had Lee's army to feed and suffered from the devastation of the Northern armies, the rest of the Confederacy was, on the whole, pretty well supplied with food, although there was suffering from the short crop of cereals of 1862 in many States owing to a severe drought. But if the railroads had been in shape to do their proper work of distribution, all parts of the Confederacy would have been well supplied. During this year of 1862, Texas had a large crop of grain and was able to supply contiguous parts of the Confederacy with grain, beef and mutton, but next year such commerce would have been stopped by Grant's capture of Vicksburg and possession of the Mississippi river. While Virginia complained of scarcity, Sherman, in January, 1863, reported abundant supplies in Mississippi. We found cattle and fat ones feeding quietly, he wrote. The country everywhere abounds with corn. Grant's cutting loose from his base in May, 1863, and living upon the country is a well-known episode; and during the autumn of 1864, Sherman's army in Georgia revelled in plenty while

Lee's soldiers almost starved in Virginia. The whole difficulty was one of transportation.

In 1861 the railroads began to deteriorate, and as the years went on their condition got worse and worse. The wear and tear of a railroad is enormous and can be counteracted only by constant repair and renewal which in this case was impossible. In time of peace every article of railroad equipment had been purchased at the North. While freight cars were constructed at the South every bolt and rod, every wheel and axle, every nail, spike and screw, every sheet of tin, every ounce of solder, every gallon of oil and every pound of paint came from Northern workshops, and factories, as did likewise, for the most part, passenger cars and locomotives: if these last were sometimes made at the South, this concession to local patriotism or convenience cost much in money. At the same time with decay came increased business, one element in which was the transportation of food to great distances for the army and cities. In 1862 a good crop of Indian corn in southern Georgia and Florida and the poor one elsewhere east of Louisiana required equalization which the railroads were called upon to effect. They hauled a considerable amount of provisions and other freight but, in 1862 and the succeeding years, were utterly unable to satisfy the demands of the Government and the public. In April, 1863, there were 6300 miles of railroad in the Confederacy, exclusive of those in the hands of the enemy, which was enough considering that they were conveniently located to handle the Government traffic and serve the public to some extent, if they could be used to the full. But owing to the deterioration of the permanent way and lack of equipment, few trains were run and as compared with Northern practice at the same period, the train-load was light. From everywhere came complaints. Cities wanted food which the railroads could not bring. In January, 1864, it was said that Indian corn was selling at $1 and $2 a bushel in southwestern Georgia and at $12 or $15 in Virginia. Another Richmond authority, at the close of that year, was sure that everyone would have enough to eat if food could be properly distributed.

The possession of the railroads by the Northern armies as they advanced interfered with proper transportation. This is exemplified by a comparison of the railroad guides for 1863 and 1864. Under the head of certain railroads instead of the time table one may read The Yankees have possession of a portion of this road at present or The entire road is in the hands of the Yankees. These indications were more numerous in 1864 than in 1863.

Government work continually encroached on the ordinary business of the railroads, yet this was by no means well done. The public suffered as well as the army. Mails were irregular and long delayed; newspapers failed to be received or, when they came to hand, were many days old. The traveller on the railroad encountered difficulties and dangers, of which the two railroad guides published at the South gave no inkling. Consulting these, he might have expected in 1863 to make his journey at the rate of from fourteen to eighteen miles per hour, including stops, and, in 1864, at a rate not greatly less. But the indications of the guides were deceptive. The traveller was lucky if his train made a continued progress of from five to eight miles per hour. Trains were always late and connections were missed. Frequent accidents, many of which were fatal, happened because of the unstable condition of the permanent way and equipment. General Joseph E. Johnston, on his way from Richmond to Chattanooga in November, 1862, to take command of the new department assigned to him, was delayed by several railroad accidents. Fremantle gave a good-humored account of his experiences in June, 1863 between Charleston and Richmond. At Florence he was detained by the breakdown of another train, and when his own was at last ready he fought his way into some desperately crowded cars. After being transferred by boat at Wilmington, he had a hot and an oppressive all day's ride in a dreadfully crowded train. We changed cars again at Weldon, he wrote, where I had a terrific fight for a seat, but I succeeded, for experience had made me very quick at this sort of business. Travelling as continuously as possible, he was forty-one hours from Charleston to Richmond, a journey which is now made in ten. Another Englishman mentions the conventional joke that a journey from Wilmington to Richmond was almost as dangerous as an engagement with the enemy. According to the official estimate of the capacity and the schedules, one or two passenger trains ran daily each way on the railroads, but at times the Government compelled the suspension of all other service in favor of the transportation of provisions for the army and of officers and soldiers returning to their commands. In April, 1864, a certain minister was unable to keep his engagement to preach a sermon at the opening session of the Presbyterian Anniversary at Augusta as, by reason of the military necessity, ordinary travel on all the railroads between that city and Richmond had been prohibited. Vice President Stephens gave an interesting relation of his attempted journey in May, 1864 from his Georgia home to the capital of the Confederacy, when he travelled northward from Charlotte in a passenger car attached to a train loaded with bacon for the army. On one dark and rainy night, he ascertained that there was a train five minutes behind his and that the only precaution taken against a rear-end collision was the placing of a lamp on the rear platform of his car. The locomotive steamed slowly up the grades but dashed furiously down-hill. While going up a steep grade, the cars broke loose from the locomotive and ran down the grade at increasing speed for two miles until, having reached the foot of one hill, they began to ascend the other and finally came to a stop just in time to avoid colliding with the train behind. After a while the locomotive came back and Stephens proceeded on his journey. Stopped at Danville by a fatal accident ahead of him and learning that the railroad had been cut by the enemy between Danville and Richmond, he believed that it would be almost impossible to reach the capital and therefore decided to return home. Suffering unaccountable delays he travelled a part of the way on a train bearing a large number of Yankee prisoners and wounded Confederates from the battles of the Wilderness. He had one seat reserved for him in the single passenger car; the rest of the train was made up of box cars, which the Yankees filled inside and out, they being given the preference in despatch to the Confederates, who in their wrath swore that the Yankees ought to be killed; but instead of that they were cared more for than the men who had been wounded in defending their country. In September, 1864, Thomas Dabney wrote from Macon that in middle Georgia the railroads were in the hands of the Government and all private travel was excluded except on freight trains. As a special favor Governor Brown's wife was given passage in an express car, a close box. Dabney himself, desiring to take his family, servants and furniture from Macon to Jackson, Mississippi, chartered two box cars for several thousand dollars and they travelled thither on freight trains, stopping at night and not infrequently a whole day, consuming two weeks on a journey which with close connections could now be made in less than twenty hours.

For this defective transportation, from which the Government and public suffered, all sorts of remedies were suggested by Government officials and railroad presidents and superintendents, but most of them involved a development of manufacturing industries or an extension of commerce which was impossible. Lack of iron was the serious difficulty; if an adequate supply of this metal had been available, the railroads could have been kept in repair. How scarce it was is implied in the request that the Government impress the rails of an unprofitable railroad and give them to another company for the extension of its line. Indeed, such an expedient was afterwards resorted to. Army officers likewise frequently impressed cars and locomotives and ordered the rolling stock from one road to another without providing for its return. But on the other hand the Government made appropriations of money for the completion of certain lines of railroads.

A study of conditions in the South cannot fail to emphasize the dependence of modern civilization on iron; it will also cause surprise that practically nothing had been done to utilize the rich deposits of iron ore and the abundance of coking coal in many of the Southern States. Everywhere is one struck with a painful scarcity of iron. In a paper read before a railroad conference in Richmond, it was suggested that the Government make a public appeal for all the cast and wrought iron scrap on the farms, in the yards and houses of citizens of the Confederacy, and that it establish a system for the collection from the country, cities, towns and villages of broken or worn-out ploughs, plough-points, hoes, spades, axes, broken stoves, household and kitchen utensils with promise of adequate compensation. The rails of the street railroad in Richmond were taken up to be made into armor for a gunboat. The planters of Alabama in those very regions where iron ore in abundance existed underground could not get iron enough to make and repair their agricultural implements. The Charleston Courier complained that a sword could not be made in the Confederacy. A remark of a Union officer after the capture of Vicksburg offended the Confederate who reports it, yet it contains a pertinent criticism of a one-sided material development. The officer, noting on the iron stairway of the Vicksburg court-house the name of a Cincinnati manufacturer moulded on it, exclaimed, Confound the impudence of the people who thought they could whip the United States when they couldn't even make their own staircases. The war demand stimulated the manufacture of iron in the Confederacy; but a comparison of the iron industry at the South with that at the North under the same stimulus shows rude and early methods contrasted with a practice which, though wasteful and untechnical beside the European, did nevertheless meet the exigency of the moment and become the parent of the pre-eminently scientific and practical processes of the present day. The iron blast furnaces at the South were small and of antiquated construction. The fuel used was charcoal, no attempt having been made apparently to smelt the ores with coke or raw coal. In the oldest iron region, Virginia, the constant cutting of timber for a series of years had made it alarmingly scarce. Ore existed in pockets which were soon worked out, and many furnaces had but a precarious supply of it which was hauled to them for miles in wagons, in one case as far as ten miles. If ore was plenty, fuel was likely to be scarce or else the converse was the case. Even if both were at hand in sufficient quantity to make ten tons daily, which was considered a large product, it was impossible to feed the hands necessarily employed, who must depend on the immediate neighborhood for supplies of bread and meat, since transportation of these from a distance was out of the question. In Alabama the industry made a better showing. It was a new region; fuel and ore were abundant and food could be had. Of the large and improved furnaces, one owned by the Government made an average of thirteen tons daily for a month. Georgia and Tennessee were the other iron manufacturing States and, in all of them, the work was obstructed by the steady progress of the Union armies in the occupation of Southern territory. Within the year ending October 1, 1864, ten iron furnaces in Virginia, all but three in Tennessee, all in Georgia and four in Alabama had been burned by the enemy or abandoned because of his inroads. Yet in a report of November 20, 1864, it was stated that eighteen furnaces were in blast in Virginia although their work was very irregular. In return for certain privileges and assistance, the Government took one-half of the production of iron at a little above cost and had for the remaining half the preference over other purchasers. The amount of iron reported as received by the Nitre and Mining Bureau is surprisingly small and the figures cannot adequately measure the production, which, nevertheless, by a liberal estimate, must have been insignificant as compared with that of the North.

Despite the unfavorable conditions under which they labored, the Confederates did not lack munitions of war. Through home manufacture and imports by blockade-runners, they always had a sufficient supply of small arms and ordnance; the small arms came chiefly from abroad, the field, siege and sea-coast artillery were produced mainly in the arsenals and workshops of the Confederacy. Their rifles were equal in efficiency to those used by the Union soldiers and breech-loading carbines were made in Richmond for the cavalry. During the last two years of the war, the Northern artillery may have been superior to the Southern. In 1861 and 1862 the Confederates captured many arms from their enemy, but in 1863 the conditions were reversed and they lost at Gettysburg, Vicksburg and Port Hudson seventy-five thousand stand of small arms and in addition a considerable amount of ordnance.

England and France desired the cotton and tobacco which glutted the Southern markets whilst the South needed the arms, munitions of war and iron which England could furnish in abundance. This desirable exchange was prevented by the blockade; hence it became necessary to resort to blockade-running an enterprise which attracted capital by reason of its enormous profits when successful. This trade in 1861 was of an improvised character and was carried on by the Southern coasting steamers, whose regular business was gone, and by small craft which, though slow, had little difficulty at first in evading the blockade and reaching some near-by neutral port. Vessels laden with arms, munitions of war and merchandise cleared from Great Britain for some port in the West Indies, but their true destination was the Southern Confederacy and when their voyage was successful they brought back cargoes of the Southern staples. As adventurous business men in England and in the Confederacy became accustomed to the state of war and had constantly before their eyes the high price and scarcity of cotton in England and the low price and plenty in the Confederacy, with certain necessaries of war and articles of comfort in the reverse order, they discerned in these conditions a rare opportunity for profitable trade. Meanwhile the blockade was becoming steadily more stringent and the business of evading it grew from the haphazard methods of its earlier days into a regular system. Arms, munitions of war, blankets, army cloth, shoes, tea, soap, letter-paper and envelopes, fine fabrics of cotton, linen, wool and silk, cases and barrels of medicines, liquors, wines and other merchandise were shipped from England to Bermuda, Nassau or Havana, and there transferred to blockade-runners, which made their way to Wilmington, Charleston, Savannah, Mobile or Galveston. If these ports were soon reached, a quick and lucrative market was found for the cargo; and a return load of cotton or occasionally tobacco or turpentine, was brought to Nassau, Bermuda or Havana and there transshipped to the vessel which carried them to England. The blockade-runners were now specially constructed for their trade and a typical one of 1863. 1864 was a low, long, narrow, swift, side-wheel steamer with light draught and a capacity of four to six hundred tons. The hull was painted a dull gray or lead color, which rendered the vessel invisible, unless at short range, even in daylight. In order to avoid smoke, Pennsylvania anthracite was used when it could be had, otherwise Welsh semi-bituminous coal. Nassau was the most important neutral, and Charleston and Wilmington the most important Confederate, ports in this trade. The blockade-runner left Nassau at an hour that would bring her off Charleston or Wilmington at night and the running of the blockade was rarely attempted unless there was no moon. When near the blockading squadron all lights were put out, the engine-room hatchways and binnacle were covered with tarpaulin and the steamer made her way forward in utter darkness. No noise was permitted; necessary orders and reports of soundings were given in muffled voices; steam was blown off under water. Often the blockade-runners escaped without being seen; sometimes they were chased but escaped; sometimes the pursuit was so hard that they ran ashore or were captured. It was a keenly contested game between these and the blockaders, only to be played by those loving the sea.

The tales of the blockade-runners are highly interesting, full as they are of the spice of adventure. Battling with the sea in overloaded craft, specially constructed to avoid other danger; feeling their way through the blockading squadron; now painfully making their port without regularly set lights, now detected, pursued and resorting to all manner of tricks to elude the pursuers; loving fog, darkness and mystery they were cool, fearless, nervy men and their stories are highly romantic. Less thrilling the tale of the blockader. The blockade-runner chose his own time and had the excitement of the attempt, but the blockader must be ever vigilant throughout long periods of inaction. After days and nights of anxious watching, the emergency, lasting brief minutes, might come when least expected. The great extent of coast, much of it having a double line with numerous inlets, and the necessity for the blockading ships to ride out the gales at anchor, close to a hostile shore, made of this blockade an operation that for difficulty was probably without precedent: it was certainly the first time that the evaders of a blockade had the powerful help of steam. The eager desire to obtain cotton was another factor operating to the advantage of the blockade-runners as was likewise the proximity of friendly neutral ports. The effective work of the United States navy is measured by the number of captures and by the increasing difficulty of evading the blockade. Gradually port after port was practically closed until none were left but Charleston and Wilmington. Wilmington, owing to the peculiar configuration and character of the coast and the large island at the entrance of Cape Fear river, was the most difficult port of all to blockade and in 1863 and 1864 its trade with Nassau and Bermuda was large. On June 16, 1863, Fremantle, passing through Wilmington, counted eight large steamers, all handsome, leaden-colored vessels, which ply their trade with the greatest regularity. Blockade-running to and from port continued until the taking of Fort Fisher in January, 1865, but the risk of capture during the last six months of activity was great. Charleston remained open until Sherman's northward march compelled its evacuation, but for a long while before this only the best-constructed steamers could run the blockade and the success even of these was rare. The work of the United States navy in the blockade was an affair of long patience unrelieved by the prospect of brilliant exploits; lacking the stimulus of open battle it required discipline and character only the more. But the reward to the country was great for the blockade played an important part in the final outcome of the war.

The cotton crops were made by the negro slaves and one of the strange things in this eventful history is the peaceful labor of three and one-half million negro slaves whose presence in the South was the cause of the war and whose freedom was fought for after September, 1862, by the Northern soldiers. The evidence warrants the oft-repeated statement that the blacks made no move to rise. A thousand torches, Henry Grady declared, would have disbanded the Southern army but there was not one. Instead of rising they remained patiently submissive and faithful to their owners. It was their labor that produced food for the soldiers fighting to keep them in slavery, and without them the cotton could not have been grown, which brought supplies from Europe and the North. Our great strength, declared a Confederate Army staff officer, consists in our system of slave labor because it makes our 8,000,000 productive of fighting material equal to the 20,000,000 of the North. One owner or overseer to every twenty slaves was exempt from military service in order to secure the proper police of the country, but a study of the conditions indicates that these were needed not as a restraining influence but for the purposes of intelligent direction. As a matter of fact, the able-bodied negroes remained on the plantations of the sparsely settled country of the Confederacy while, with few exceptions, the white people in the neighborhood were old or diseased men, women and children. Here is a remarkable picture and one that discovers virtues in the Southern negroes and merit in the civilization under which they had been trained.

The slaves came to know of Lincoln's Proclamation of Emancipation and had a vague idea that the success of the Northern arms would set them free. As the Union armies penetrated into the country, negroes in great number, who had fanciful ideas of what freedom meant, followed them, often to the manifest inconvenience of the commanders. The slaves were friendly to the Union soldiers whom they encountered; they fed any who escaped from Southern prisons and, by handing them on from one to another, guided them to the Federal lines. At the same time they would conceal the valuables of their mistresses lest they should be stolen by the camp followers and stragglers of the Union Army, showing some craft in keeping the hiding-places secret. Thus they maintained a divided allegiance. Many Confederate officers were saved from death or capture by the care and devotion of their body-servants while other negroes served as guides to Union generals when important offensive movements were on foot.

The South came to conscription sooner than the North. An act of April 16, 1862, prompted by the Southern reverses, chief of which was the capture of Fort Donelson, placed in the military service all white men between the ages of eighteen and thirty-five. An act of September 27 of the same year extended the conscription to all white men between thirty-five and forty-five but at first only those of forty or under were enrolled, but directly after Gettysburg and Vicksburg, President Davis ordered that all between forty and forty-five should be included in the enrolment. On February 17, 1864, the Confederate Congress passed an act requiring that all white men between seventeen and fifty should be in the military service.[697] They have robbed the cradle and the grave, said Grant.

As men became weary of the war desertion was more common. Compulsory service was disliked and evaded by many whenever possible. Homesickness and the wretched fare in the army were prolific causes of this abandonment of duty. Gettysburg and Vicksburg were potent arguments with the Southern people. Dear Seddon,[698] wrote a friend from Mobile, we are without doubt gone up.[699] Soldiers deserted by the hundreds; even whole regiments left at a time. Deserters almost always carried their muskets and when halted and asked for their authority to be absent from the army would pat their guns and say defiantly, 'This is my furlough.' In the mountain fastnesses of South Carolina, bold and defiant deserters were banded together; with travelling threshing machines they worked their farms in common and congregated at still yards and houses where they distilled quantities of liquor and swore vengeance on any one who should attempt their arrest. Summing up the mass of evidence which came to the War Department, Judge Campbell[700] wrote, The condition of things in the mountain districts of North Carolina, South Carolina, Georgia and Alabama menaces the existence of the Confederacy as fatally as either of the armies of the United States.[701]

The much rarer references to desertion in the official papers of 1864, the somewhat satisfied tone of Seddon's report of April 28 of that year, the full ranks of Lee's and Johnston's armies and their heroic resistance are evidence that, through the influence of public sentiment and the persistently rigorous measures of the Government the evil of desertion had by that time been greatly mitigated. The military operations of the autumn of 1864, however, resulted in disaster to the Confederates whilst Lincoln's re-election amounted to a notification that there would be no cessation of the vigorous onward movement of the Northern armies. A weighty recommendation that conscription be given up and volunteering resorted to again to recruit the army, and the fact that there were 100,000 deserters, are not reasons for condemning the Confederate policy of conscription, but they are among the many indications that the Southern cause was lost. The Confederacy was practically supported, in so far as its strictly defined financial operations were concerned, by the issue of paper money and from the proceeds of bonds which were paid for in the paper currency; in this medium the holders of the bonds received their interest. Owing to the stringency of the blockade the revenue derived from the export duty on cotton and from duties on imports was inconsiderable. No large amount of money was raised by internal taxation. An

---

[697] Those between 17 and 18 and 45 and 50 should constitute a reserve for State defence and should not be called beyond the limits of their own State.

[698] The Secretary of War.

[699] July 24, 1863.

[700] Assistant Secretary of War.

[701] Sept. 7, 1863.

attempt to maintain specie payments would have been futile: $27,000,000 is an outside estimate of the receipts in specie of the Confederate government during its life of four years. Before the end of 1863, $700,000,000 of Treasury notes were in circulation and this amount was increased during the next year to $1,000,000,000, but the issues grew so enormously that apparently no exact amount of them was made public; it is even possible that the Treasury Department itself did not know the amount afloat. But this was not the extent of the inflation of the currency. The different States issued State Treasury notes; the banks expanded their circulation; Richmond, Charleston and other cities put out municipal treasury bills; railroad, turnpike and insurance companies, factories and savings-banks added to the mass of paper money. A large part of this municipal and corporation paper was issued in denominations below one dollar to supply the need for small change caused by the disappearance of fractional silver. In North Carolina ten-penny nails passed current at five cents apiece. At times postage stamps circulated. Tobacconists, grocers, barkeepers and milk dealers put out shinplasters. In 1862 the Confederate government began the issue of one-dollar and two-dollar bills and of fractional amounts under one dollar. It was a carnival of fiat money.

Early in 1864, it was conceded that something must be done to contract the currency. The financial history of the American Revolution and the French Revolution repeated itself on February 17 of that year in a measure of virtual repudiation. This was a provision for the compulsory funding of the notes into four per cent bonds; if the bonds were not taken, all notes of the denominations under one hundred dollars might be exchanged for new ones in the ratio of three dollars of old money for two dollars of the new. If neither exchange was made the old notes were to be taxed out of existence. This was really a confession of bankruptcy by the Confederate Congress and the President: the financial situation was hopeless unless independence could be won.

The people of the South recognized the superior resources of the North by accepting readily in trade United States greenbacks. They were quoted in Richmond and might be seen in the brokers' offices. Another symptom of the debasement of the Confederate currency was the resort to barter. Manufacturers and merchants advertised in the newspapers, offering their goods in exchange for farm and other products. To obtain supplies for the army, wrote Seddon to Lee on March 29, 1864, we must not recur to the most expensive and mischievous of all modes the issue of a redundant currency. I expect to introduce and to rely upon to a considerable extent a system of barter.

Accompanying the redundant currency were apparent high prices. Contemporary and later writings are full of the subject and indicate the impression made on people's minds by the advance of daily comforts and conveniences. Mrs. Jefferson Davis, drawing from her own domestic experiences and from private diaries, has presented many of the facts in an interesting manner. In July, 1862, when gold was worth $1.50, beef and mutton sold in Richmond for 37 1/2 cents a pound, potatoes

$6 a bushel, tea $5 a pound and boots $25 per pair. In the early part of 1864, when $1 in gold brought $22 in Confederate money, she reports the price of a turkey as $60, flour $300 per barrel and in July of that year shoes $150 per pair.

Gold increased steadily in value and most articles of consumption followed until the extravagant prices were reached which prevailed in the last days of the Confederacy. That money was cheap rather than articles of food dear is signified by the experiences of two Englishmen. Lieutenant-Colonel Fremantle was in Charleston during June, 1863, and wrote that the fare was good at the Charleston Hotel, the charge being $8 a day which was equivalent to but little over $1 in gold. A compatriot sojourning at the best hotel in Richmond in January, 1864, remarked that he had never lived so cheaply in any country. It is true that he paid $20 per day, but that was equal to only three shillings of his own money.

The great concern of the Confederate government was to feed the army and, when its financial system broke down, it resorted to the tax of one-tenth in kind of agricultural products, and collected this tax by the impressment of food [1863]. The impossibility of supplying the army by purchase alone being now clearly recognized, the act of impressment inaugurated a far-reaching system of taking private property for public use and authorized substantially, within certain limits, any officer of the army to seize any property anywhere in the Confederacy in order to accumulate supplies or for the good of the service.

The outcry against the operation of this law was bitter, widely extended and prolonged; and the evils of impressment were thoroughly appreciated by the War Department. Some attempt, which was probably futile, was made to correct the abuses; its operation was conceded to be harsh, unequal and odious but inexorable necessity had led to the adoption of the policy and would require its continuance.

High taxation, loans and the purchase of food at the market price was suggested as a policy in lieu of impressment: all had become impracticable. In 1863 the currency in which the taxes were received was redundant and steadily depreciating; in 1864 it was scarce but worth still less than in 1863. All sorts of bond issues were tried and as large an amount of loans was floated as the market would take. That the amount of bonds was smaller in proportion to the amount of Treasury notes than one would expect was not due to financial mismanagement but to the paucity of savings available at the South for such a permanent investment. The surplus capital, as is well known, had been constantly laid out in land and negroes. By January 1, 1863, it became apparent that primitive methods must supplant the modern mechanism of business operations. The South had practically no specie, or, in other words, no basis for a modern fiscal system, consisting of a redeemable currency and bonds. She had no credit. At the outbreak of the war she was in debt to the North and to Europe. With the closing of her ports by the blockade, her chance of getting any credits in the marts of the world was gone. One has only to look over many schedules of goods that went out and came in by the blockade-runners to understand how insignificant was the exchange of commodities through this precarious commerce. The blockade-running and the trade with the North brought in articles of prime necessity for carrying on the war and all the cotton which went out was absorbed in these indispensable transactions: there was not enough of it to establish credits or bring in specie. The resort then to the tithe and to impressment was unavoidable. The tithe was, under the circumstances, an admirable method of taxation and, though it bore hard on the farmers and was the cause of complaint, the bulk of the testimony is to the effect that it worked well. Like much of the other statecraft, both North and South, it was a policy too tardily adopted because of men's imperfect comprehension of the magnitude and duration of the struggle. It is now easy to see that it should have been imposed on the crop of 1862, which would have tended to make the later impressment operations less onerous. In 1863, affairs were at a pitch where impressment became imperative. The law was not at fault, but its administration was defective. A consideration of the grievances it gave rise to will show how a stringent law was rendered odious through negligence, lack of uniformity and undue harshness in execution. The sparsely settled region of the South presented grave obstacles to the efficient operation of the plan. The methods which had served this simple agricultural community in time of peace no longer availed: a system of administration by trained officials was needed to handle the enormous amount of business brought on by the war; and, in the ingenuity requisite to devise such a system, the South was far inferior to the North.

Yet though the South had no specie, no credits and no commerce that was not seriously hampered, she had land and laborers; and in utilizing these in a somewhat imperfect fashion she kept her armies and citizens from starvation and maintained the struggle for four years.

Richmond was near the seat of war and, after the battles, the wounded were brought to the city in such numbers as to demand unremitting labor to relieve their sufferings. In 1862, there were thirty-five public and private hospitals in Richmond; and churches were likewise converted into temporary abiding-places for those who had been shot in the field. Devotion to the Southern cause beat high in the hearts of their womankind, compelling well-born and fastidious ladies to the care of men wounded in every distressful and revolting manner and tormented by physical suffering, which, from lack of anæsthetics and morphine, the surgeons were often powerless to relieve. It was the case we all know When pain and anguish wring the brow A ministering angel thou! But old as it is there is always fresh inspiration in it to those who tell the tale of a cause they have embraced. Confederate writings are full of gratitude to the women; their works in Richmond were matched everywhere throughout the Confederacy.

Heavily as the war bore on Northern women the distress of Southern women had a wider range. In the Union there were many families who had no near relative in the war; in the Confederacy it was a rare exception when neither husband, father, son nor brother was in the army: hardly a household was not in mourning.

Moreover, the constant suspense affected a larger number than at the North. In Richmond, where intelligence of battles was received with comparative promptness, the frequent sounding of the tocsin, indicating the proximity of danger, increased the general disquietude, while those who lived in the country where newspapers were infrequent and mails irregular, felt they would have preferred living in the midst of alarms to having their anxious uncertainty thus prolonged. Physical privations are far from alleviating moral distress and the lack of luxuries and then of necessaries increased the harshness of woman's lot in the Confederacy. The tale of poverty in its every-day aspect is familiar to us all, but at the South the contrast between life before the war and afterwards is most unusual and striking. In the domestic establishments plenty had been the rule, even lavishness. Tables groaned under the weight of food. The Southerners had been extravagant in their living and generous in their entertainment. Servants were numerous. Southern ladies who had never taken thought where food came from, who had themselves never stooped to the least physical exertion, were now forced by the advance of the enemy to leave their luxurious homes and take refuge in Richmond; there they might be seen in line before the cheapest shop awaiting their chance to spend the scant wages of plain sewing or copying or clerical work in a Government office, for a pittance of flour or bacon. No clerkship was given to a woman unless she would aver that she was in want, and in the Treasury Department one vacancy would elicit a hundred applications, a number of which came from ladies of gentle birth and former affluence. Other ladies accustomed to luxury did the menial work of the household. Such labor was peculiarly distasteful to the Southern-bred woman, yet this and the insufficiency of wholesome food were borne with cheerfulness in the hope of independence and the preservation of their social institutions. It seemed to them that the North had undertaken a crusade against the social fabric under which they and their mothers had been reared and that the war which caused their sufferings had been forced upon the South which was now defending her vested rights. The devastation of country, the wanton destruction in cities, the pillage conducted by the more disreputable Northern soldiers exasperated them to a point where they could no longer control their feelings but gave vent to violent expressions of indignation, some of which are recorded in the diaries of the period. If all the words of hatred in every language, wrote a young Georgia woman, were lumped together into one huge epithet of detestation they could not tell how I hate Yankees.

Fully as noticeable as at the North was the profound religious sentiment pervading soldiers and people. A preacher spoke of the active piety which prevailed in the army and Seddon attested a large religious element and much devotional feeling.[702] George Cary Eggleston related that in the last year of the war a revival took place among Lee's soldiers. Prayer meetings were held in every

---

[702] Report of Apr. 28, 1864.

tent. Testaments were in every hand and a sort of religious ecstasy took possession of the army. In the annals of the Episcopal Church, an incident is recorded which serves pleasantly to relieve the general bitterness of the war. The bishops and clergy of the South appealed to their brethren at the North to send down two or three thousand prayer books and a quantity of church tracts for use in the Confederate Army: the United States Government gave permission for passing these through the lines of the Union Army. In concluding this survey, a comparison between South and North with respect to certain prepossessions of the two peoples naturally suggests itself. The Confederate Congress refused a number of times to make their Treasury notes a legal tender, construing the clause of the Constitution (alike in the Confederate and Federal) which related to the subject, more strictly than did the United States Congress: in the thorough discussions that took place, it was mainly the constitutional arguments which prevented such legislation, although this was advocated by many men of influence, among them General Lee.

In the practical application of the clause of the Constitution, The privilege of the writ of habeas corpus shall not be suspended unless when in cases of rebellion or invasion the public safety may require it, the Confederate government exhibited the greater regard for the liberty of the individual, and the Southern citizen the greater jealousy of the use of arbitrary power. Lincoln from the first assumed the right to suspend the writ by Executive decree, a right never claimed by Davis. It was generally conceded at the South that Congress alone possessed this power and the privilege was available to the citizens of the Confederacy except when curtailed by express statute. And the Confederate Congress asserted its rights boldly enough, declaring in the Act of February 15, 1864, that the power of suspending the privilege of said writ is vested solely in the Congress which is the exclusive judge of the necessity of such suspension. The war may be said to have lasted four years: the periods of suspension of the writ in the Confederacy amounted in the aggregate to one year, five months and two days, less than one-half of the war's duration. In the Union the writ was suspended or disregarded at any time and in any place where the Executive, or those to whom he delegated this power, deemed such action necessary. For anyone who in any manner or degree took an unfriendly attitude toward the recruitment of the army, for political prisoners, for persons suspected of any disloyal practice, the privilege did not exist. It was suspended for one year, ten months and twenty-one days by Executive assumption and for the rest of the period by the authorization of Congress.

The provocation for the use of arbitrary power was, all things considered, about equal in the Confederacy and the Union. In the Union the disloyal secret societies were larger and more dangerous, and the public criticism of the administration more copious and bitter. There was, too, the organized political party which made a focus for the opposition and developed Vallandigham, who had no counterpart at the South. But these considerations are balanced by the circumstance that in the

South was the seat of war which was never but for brief periods moved north of Mason and Dixon's line and the Ohio river. Civil administration is everywhere relaxed, wrote Judge Campbell as early as October, 1862, and has lost much of its energy, and our entire Confederacy is like a city in a state of siege, cut off from all intercourse with foreign nations and invaded by a superior force at every assailable point. Where armies stand in opposition disloyalty may give the enemy aid and comfort so substantial as to decide an impending battle; far from the front it is apt to spend itself in bluster, threats and secret midnight oaths. In the Confederacy there was practically no important place east of the Mississippi river which was not at one time or another invaded or threatened by the invader. The courts, it is true, were open in the South, but, owing to the disorganized state of society, the interruption of trade and the passage of stay laws by the States, they tried few commercial cases but confined themselves to criminal jurisdiction and to decisions sustaining the acts of Congress; or on the other hand to issuing writs of habeas corpus in favor of those who desired to escape military service.

The press was essentially free at the North, entirely so at the South, where no journals were suppressed as some had been in the Union. As the Southern papers had little news-gathering enterprise and borrowed a large part of their news from the Northern press, they did not offend the Confederate generals as the Union generals were offended by the publication of estimates of the strength of armies or shrewd guesses of projected movements. Sometimes the Richmond journals, upon request of General Lee or of the Secretary of War, refrained from publishing intelligence that might benefit the enemy, but no compulsion was employed. The right of public meeting was fully exercised in both sections, but the gatherings for free discussion were much more common at the North.

Southerners believed that the Federal government had degenerated into a military despotism. At the same time the general belief at the North was that the Confederate government was a tyranny which crushed all opposition. The bases for both these beliefs are apparent. Theoretically liberty seemed surer at the South than at the North, but practically the reverse was true. Few men either in the Union or in the Confederacy had actual need of the privilege of the writ of habeas corpus; but all able-bodied men at the South, who were not too old, were touched by the universal exaction of military service and all who had property were affected by the impressment of it at an arbitrary price fixed by the government. The Federal government may be called a dictatorship. Congress and the people surrendered certain of their powers and rights to a trusted man. The Confederacy was a grand socialized state in which the government did everything. It levied directly on the produce of the land and fixed prices; it managed the railroads; operated manufacturing establishments, owned merchant vessels and carried on a foreign commerce. It did all this by common consent and the public desired it to absorb even more activities. Frequent requests to extend the province of the general government, of the States and of the municipalities may be read in the newspapers and in the public and private letters of the time. The operations seemed too large for individual initiative and the sovereign power of the State came to be invoked.

It will always be an interesting question whether the affairs of the Confederacy, outside of the military department, were ably conducted. In the lower branches of administration, they certainly were not. Nor did the Secretary of the Treasury display sufficient capacity to cope with the difficulties which environed him. The post-office was badly managed and it boots little to inquire whether this was due to untoward circumstances or to the Postmaster-General's inefficiency. The State and Navy Departments seem to have availed themselves of their opportunities. Benjamin's[703] work was not confined to foreign affairs, for he was Davis's intimate friend and confidential adviser; but he was suspected of corruption and, through his cotton speculations, was believed to have carried to his credit in England a handsome sum of money. One part of this rumor was unfounded for, after Benjamin landed in England, he was for some time nearly penniless; and if he made illicit gains, he spent them in the Confederacy; indeed he was one of the men who had lived well throughout the war.

Davis naturally gave his attention to the War Department, of which the Secretary was said to be merely his chief clerk. If the frequently superfluous controversial letters of the Confederate President and Secretary of War be excepted, a study of the papers of Davis, Seddon and Judge Campbell will give one a high idea of their executive talents; indeed any government might be proud of the ability shown in these documents. A certain class of facts if considered alone can make us wonder how it was possible to subjugate the Confederates. And this would certainly have been impossible of accomplishment without great political capacity at the head of the Northern government and a sturdy support of Lincoln by the Northern people.

Lincoln was a man of much greater ability than Davis, yet Davis was a worthy foeman. Davis suffered constantly from ill health which was so persistent and so noised abroad that men were always conjecturing how the government would be carried on in the event of his death. In December, 1864, it was thought that he was suffering from brain disease and would surely die. His form was spare, his face emaciated and he looked older than his years. The cares of the Confederacy weighed heavily upon him. But he had a sweet domestic life and the devotion of a woman of brains and character. Those who like similitudes will recall that Lincoln and Davis each lost a beloved son during the war Willie, at the age of twelve, from an illness; Joseph, a little romping boy, died as the result of a fall from a portico to the brick pavement below.

But if Davis had won he would have been a hard master to the vanquished. Does anyone imagine, he asked in October, 1864, that we can conquer the Yankees by retreating before them or do you not all know that the only way to make spaniels civil is to whip them? The moral height of Lincoln's second inaugural address was

---

[703] J. P. Benjamin, Secretary of State.

beyond his reach. Perhaps one of the reasons for the success of the North is given in the words of Shakespeare's Henry V: When levity and cruelty play for a kingdom, the gentler gamester is the soonest winner.[704]

---

[704] This chapter is founded on Chap. XXVIII, Vol. V of my History and on a thesis written for me by D. M. Matteson "based upon a study of printed material to be found in the Harvard College Library and the Boston Public Library published since 1904." "In all," he writes, "I have examined about 70 books and perhaps 40 articles in magazines; and reports and proceedings." In the course of his thesis he refers to: The Journals of the Confederate Congress; Vol. II, Georgia Confederate Records; Correspondence of Toombs, Stephens and Cobb; Civil War and Reconstruction in Florida, W. W. Davis; Correspondence of Jon. Worth; Alderman and Gordon, J. L. Curry; South in the Building of the Nation; Civil War and Reconstruction in Alabama, W. L. Fleming; Autobiography of Joseph Le Conte; Mrs. Burton Harrison's Recollections, in Scribner's Magazine; Cal. of Confed. Papers, D. S. Freeman; Blockaded Family, P. A. Hague; Southern Historical Society Papers; Diary from Dixie, M. B. Chesnut; Miss. Hist. Soc. Pubs.; A Confed. Girl's Diary, S. M. Dawson; N. C. Hist. Commission Bulletin; Soldier's Letters, J. B. Polley; Soldier's Recollections, R. H. McKim; King and Queen Co., Alfred Bagby; British Consuls in Confederacy, Bonham; Va. Girl in Civil War, Avary; Doctor Quintard, A. H. Noll; War Time Journal, E. F. Andrews; Reminiscences, Mrs. R. A. Pryor; A. H. Stephens, Pendleton; S. Atlantic Quarterly; R. H. Wilmer, W. C. Whitaker; William and Mary Quarterly; Orange Co., Va., W. W. Scott; Thomas Smyth, Autobiography; Atlantic Monthly; Southern Girl in 1861, D. G. Wright; Julie le Grand, Journal; J. P. Benjamin, P. Butler; Autobiography of Brantley York; J. H. Reagan, Memoirs; Gulf State Hist. Magazine.

Chapter XIII

OUR story left William T. Sherman in camp at Atlanta during September, 1864. Mentally and bodily in his prime of forty-four, he had added to an ample book-knowledge of his profession three years of fruitful experience in the field, whilst his warm friendship with Grant had proved of great advantage to each and to their country. Now his busy brain planned an extraordinary movement, a march to the sea. He proposed to leave Thomas to cope with Hood while, to use his own words, he should make Georgia howl. But the President felt much solicitude at his leaving Hood in his rear, believing that a misstep might be fatal to his army. Meanwhile Hood crossed the Tennessee river and invaded Tennessee: this movement made Grant doubt the wisdom of the plan and he asked Sherman whether he had not better destroy Hood's army before starting southward. But Sherman, anticipating this objection, had already sent a despatch to Grant allaying his misgivings and drawing from him the word, Go as you propose.

The march to the sea, the march northward from Savannah and Thomas's operations in Tennessee are a combination of bold and effective strategy, possible only after the Chattanooga-Atlanta campaign and a fit sequel to it. A hundred persons may have conceived the design of advancing to the ocean but the genius of the general lay in foreseeing the possible moves of his adversary, in guarding against them and in his estimate of the physical and moral results of cutting the Confederacy in twain. Wise in precaution and fully conscious of the difficulties of the venture, Sherman showed the same boldness and tenacity in sticking to his purpose when others shook their heads as Grant had shown in his Vicksburg campaign. No general who lacked daring and resolution would have persisted in his determination to advance through Georgia after Hood had crossed the Tennessee river, especially when Grant himself for a while doubted the wisdom of the movement. Sherman was the commander and, even as he knew his men and comprehended the conditions, he knew he could expect no success unless Thomas should defeat Hood. Therein, as the affair turned out, lay the risk. But Sherman knew Thomas through and through. Classmates at West Point, they had ever since been friends and had been drawn closer together by the vicissitudes of the Civil War despite differences of opinion arising from their diverse temperaments. Sherman had implicit confidence in Thomas, thought that he had furnished him a force sufficient for all emergencies and that the defence of Tennessee was not left to chance. If I had Schofield, Thomas telegraphed, I should feel perfectly safe.[705] Sherman had already detached Schofield's corps from his army and sent it

---

[705] Nov. 1, O. R., XXXIX, Pt. 3, 582.

northward with instructions to report to Thomas for orders. On the day that Sherman started for the sea, Thomas sent this word: I have no fear that Beauregard[706] [Hood] can do us any harm now, and if he attempts to follow you, I will follow him as far as possible. If he does not follow you I will then thoroughly organize my troops and I believe I shall have men enough to ruin him unless he gets out of the way very rapidly.[707]

At this time the Union commanders were uncertain whether Hood would follow Sherman or move north toward Nashville. The army that marched to the sea proved unnecessarily large and 10,000 men more with Schofield would have saved some trial of soul, yet, as the problem appeared at the time, Sherman must be sufficiently strong to defeat Hood and the scattered forces of uncertain number which would gather to protect Georgia. Moreover, as his ultimate aim was to re-enforce our armies in Virginia he must have troops enough to oppose Lee until Grant should be at his heels. He reckoned that the force left in Tennessee was numerically greater than Hood's.[708] Considering everything that could have been known between November 1 and 12, it seems clear beyond dispute that he made a fair division of his army between himself and Thomas.

Sherman reviewed his decision with deliberation, care and foresight; until within six days of his start southward, he held himself ready, if need were, to co-operate with Thomas in the pursuit of Hood, the one moving directly against the Confederates and the other endeavoring to cut off their retreat, for he admitted that the first object should be the destruction of that army;[709] but, as the days wore on, he came to believe that the advantages of the march to the sea outweighed those of any other plan and he took the irrevocable step. Stopping at Cartersville on November 12 on his progress southward he received Thomas's last despatch[710] and replied all right:[711] a bridge was burned, severing the telegraph wire and all communication with Thomas and his government. As was the case with Julian, who plunged into the recesses of the Marcian or Black forest, so was Sherman's fate for many days unknown to the world.[712] No direct intelligence from him reached the North from November 12 to December 14. I will not attempt to send carriers back, he had written to Grant, but trust to the Richmond papers to keep you well advised.[713] For these thirty-two days, Lincoln and Grant had no other information of this important movement than what they could glean from the Southern journals.

---

[706] Beauregard had been placed in command of the Department and was Hood's superior.

[707] Nov. 12, O. R., XXXIX, Pt. 3, 756.

[708] O. R., XXXIX, Pt. 3, 659, 660.

[709] *Ibid.,* 659.

[710] That of Nov. 12, *ante.*

[711] O. R., XXXIX, Pt. 3, 757.

[712] Gibbon, Chap. XXII.

[713] O. R., XXXIX, Pt. 3, 661.

Sherman's imagination was vividly impressed with the strangeness of the situation: two hostile armies were marching in opposite directions, each in the full belief that it was achieving a final and conclusive result in the great war.[714] It would be impossible to show an entire consistency in the utterances of this great general; a single aspect of the campaign often claimed his attention to the exclusion of all others and he was so fertile in thought and fluent in expression that the idea uppermost in his brain was apt to burst forth without regard for what else remained behind. As with almost all men of action, the speculation of to-day might supersede that of yesterday only to disappear under that of to-morrow, yet this did not impair his capacity for making a correct decision nor his steadfastness in the execution of a plan. Grant, more reticent and not at all expansive, is not chargeable in the same degree with inconsistency in his written words. He lacked imagination and did not worry. A remark of Sherman's provides an acute estimate of their different temperaments: Grant does not care for what the enemy does out of his sight but it scares me.[715]

While the army was concentrating at Atlanta, the railway station, machine shops and other buildings of that city which might be useful to the enemy in his military operations were destroyed. The right wing and one corps of the left wing having started the day before, Sherman rode out of Atlanta on November 16 with the Fourteenth Corps: he had in all 62,000 able-bodied, experienced soldiers, well armed, well equipped and provided, as far as human foresight could, with all the essentials of life, strength and vigorous action.[716] One of the bands happening to play John Brown's body lies a-mouldering in the grave, the men sang the well-known song, giving to the chorus, Glory, glory hallelujah, his soul is marching on, a force full of meaning, as their minds reverted to the events which had taken place since that December day in 1859 when he who was now a saint in their calendar had suffered death on the scaffold. When the march to the sea began, the weather was fine, the air bracing and the movement to the south and east exhilarated the men. Many of the common soldiers called out to their general, Uncle Billy, I guess Grant is waiting for us at Richmond. There was a 'devil-may-care' feeling pervading officers and men, related Sherman, that made me feel the full load of responsibility.[717] The tale of the march is not one of battle and inch-by-inch progress as was the campaign from Chattanooga to Atlanta. As to the 'lion' in our path, wrote Sherman after he had reached Savannah, we never met him.[718] Officers and men looked upon the march as a picnic, a vast holiday frolic.[719] The burden was on the general in command. He was in the enemy's country; he must show his

---

[714] W. Sherman, II, 170.

[715] Wilson's Under the Old Flag, II, 17.

[716] W. Sherman, II, 172.

[717] Ibid., II, 179.

[718] O. R., XLIV, 793.

[719] J. D. Cox, 42.

skill by keeping this large army supplied. When the army set out it had approximately supplies of bread for twenty days, sugar, coffee and salt for forty and about three days' forage in grain; it had also a sufficient quantity of ammunition; all this was carried in 2500 wagons with a team of six mules to each. Droves of cattle, enough to insure fresh meat for more than a month, were part of the commissariat. The ambulances were 600 in number; the artillery had been reduced to 65 guns. Pontoon trains were carried along, as the invading host had many rivers to cross. The right wing was composed of the Fifteenth and Seventeenth Corps, the left, of the Fourteenth and Twentieth; each corps marched on a separate road. The division of the wagon trains gave each corps about 800 wagons, which occupied on the march five miles or more of road. The artillery and wagons with their advance and rear guards had the right of way, the men taking improvised paths at their side. The troops began their daily march at dawn and pitched their camp soon after noon, having covered ordinarily ten to fifteen miles. Milledgeville, the capital of the State, was reached by the left wing in seven days. This march through the heart of Georgia so alarmed the Confederates lest either Macon or Augusta or both might be attacked that they divided their forces; and, when it finally became clear that Savannah was the point aimed at, they found it impossible for various reasons to concentrate a large number of troops for defence. By December 10, the enemy was driven within his lines at Savannah, the march of 300 miles was over and the siege began.

The special field order of November 9 said, The army will forage liberally on the country during the march.[720] As the State was sparsely settled and the plan of making requisitions on the civil authorities therefore impracticable, this was the only possible mode of supplying the troops. The arrangements for the foraging were made and carried out with military precision. Each brigade sent out a party of about fifty men on foot who would return mounted, driving cattle and mules and hauling wagons or family carriages loaded with fresh mutton, smoked bacon, turkeys, chickens, ducks, corn meal, jugs of molasses and sweet potatoes. As the crop was large, and had just been gathered and laid by for the winter, and as the region had never before been visited by a hostile army, the land was rich in provisions and forage. While Sherman and his officers sincerely endeavored to have the foraging done in an orderly way, the men were often riotous in seizing food on their own account. A soldier passed me, so related the General, with a ham on his musket, a jug of sorghum molasses under his arm and a big piece of honey in his hand, from which he was eating and, catching my eye he remarked in a low voice to a comrade, 'Forage liberally on the country.' Sherman reproved the man as he did others when similar acts of lawlessness fell under his observation,

---

[720] O. R., XXXIX, Pt. 3, 713. "We give express charge, that in our marches through the country, there be nothing compelled from the villages, nothing taken but paid for, none of the French upbraided or abused in disdainful language." Henry V, Act III, sc. VI.

explaining that foraging must be limited to the regular parties properly detailed.[721] Full of pride in his soldiers and elated at their manifestations of confidence in him, he had for them after the completion of the march only this mild censure, A little loose in foraging they 'did some things they ought not to have done.'[722] A spirit of fun pervaded the army which exhibited itself in innocent frolics, typical of which was the meeting of some officers in the Hall of Representatives at Milledgeville where they constituted themselves the Legislature of the State of Georgia, elected a speaker and after a formal debate repealed by a fair vote the Ordinance of Secession.

Destruction was a part of the business of the march, especially as Lee's army drew its supplies of provisions largely from Georgia. The State of Georgia alone, said Jefferson Davis in a speech at Augusta, produces food enough not only for her own people and the army within it but feeds too the Army of Virginia. It became of the utmost importance to sever the railroad communication between the Gulf States and Richmond and to this Sherman gave his personal attention. The bridges and trestles were burned, the masonry of the culverts blown up. In the destruction of the iron rails mechanical skill vied with native ingenuity in doing the most effective work. The chief engineer designed a machine for twisting the rails after heating them in the fires made by burning the ties: this was used by Michigan and Missouri engineers. But the infantry with the mania for destruction which pervaded the army joined in the work, carrying the rails when they came to a red heat to the nearest trees and twisting them about the trunks or warping them in some fantastic way so that they were useless except as old iron and, even as such, in unmanageable shape for working in a mill. About 265 miles of railroad were thus destroyed. This in the heart of Jeff. Davis's empire, as Sherman called it, effected a damage almost irreparable owing to the scarcity of factories which could make rails for renewals and to the embargo on imports by the blockade of the Southern ports. Stations and machine shops along the lines were burned. Many thousand bales of cotton and a large number of cotton gins and presses were destroyed. At Milledgeville, Sherman reported, I burned the railroad buildings and the arsenals; the state-house and Governor's mansion I left unharmed.[723] The penitentiary had been burned by the convicts before the arrival of the army. A negro, from whom Sherman asked information regarding the operations of the right wing, thus described what he had seen, First there come along some cavalrymen and they burned the depot; then come along some infantry men and they tore up the track and burned it; and just before I left they set fire to the well.[724] In the main, the General forebore destroying private property but, in nearly all his

---

[721] W. Sherman, II, 181.

[722] Jan. 1, 1865, O. R., XLIV, 14.

[723] O. R., XLIV, 789.

[724] W. Sherman, II, 191.

despatches after he had reached the sea, he gloated over the destruction along the line of his march, writing from Savannah: We have consumed the corn and fodder in the region of country thirty miles on either side of a line from Atlanta to Savannah as also the sweet potatoes, cattle, hogs, sheep and poultry and have carried away more than 10,000 horses and mules as well as a countless number of their slaves. I estimate the damage done to the State of Georgia and its military resources at $100,000,000; at least $20,000,000 of which has inured to our advantage and the remainder is simple waste and destruction. This may seem a hard species of warfare but it brings the sad realities of war home to those who have been directly or indirectly instrumental in involving us in its attendant calamities.[725] Well might he say afterwards, War is hell.

Various orders given from time to time show that there was not only lawless foraging but that there was an unwarranted burning of buildings. A more serious charge against these men of the western army is pillage. Sherman admitted the truth of it as did likewise General Cox. After the campaign, Sherman heard of jewelry being taken from women and was of the opinion that these depredations were committed by parties of foragers usually called bummers. Cox dubbed with that name the habitual stragglers to whom he ascribed a large part of the irregular acts. Some of the pilfering was undoubtedly due to the uncontrollable American desire for mementos of places connected with great events. Moreover, while three and one-half years of civil war had built up an effective fighting machine, they had caused a relaxation in the rules of orderly conduct among its members so that it had come to be considered proper to despoil anyone living in the enemy's country; but the commander and his officers sincerely desired to restrain the soldiers within the limits of civilized usage. The lofty personal character of most of the men in high command and the severity of the punishment threatened for breaches of discipline are evidence of this; nor should it be overlooked that much of the plundering charged to Sherman's men was actually done by Confederate bands. From my general characterization of the Union officers one notable exception must be made. Kilpatrick, the commander of the cavalry, was notorious for his immorality and rapacity, and his escapades, winked at by Sherman on account of his military efficiency, were demoralizing to the army at the time, and have since tended to give it a bad name. With no purpose of extenuation it is pleasant to record some of Sherman's words which should be read in the light of his honesty of soul and truthfulness of statement. I never heard, he wrote, of any cases of murder or rape.[726]

Sherman's campaign struck slavery a staggering blow. Everywhere the negroes received the Northern soldiers with joy. Near Covington an old gray-haired negro

---

[725] O. R., XLIV, 13. These are undoubtedly exaggerated estimates. The assessed value of real estate and personal property in Georgia in 1860 was $618,232,387.

[726] W. Sherman, II, 183.

said to Sherman that he had been looking for the angel of the Lord ever since he was knee-high and he supposed that the success of the Northern army would bring him freedom. Another who was spokesman for a large number of fellow-slaves said to an aide-de-camp of the General's, Ise hope de Lord will prosper you Yankees and Mr. Sherman because I tinks and we'se all tinks dat you'se down here in our interests. At Milledgeville the negroes in their ecstasy shouted, Bress de Lord! tanks be to Almighty God, the Yanks is come! de day ob jubilee hab arribed.[727] Negro men, women and children joined the column at every mile of our march, reported the commander of the left wing. The desire to realize their freedom at once was keen and the number would have been far greater had not Sherman discouraged the negroes from following the army, as all but the young and able-bodied, who were put to use, were a serious drawback, increasing the number of mouths to be fed and causing constant apprehension lest they should hamper the movement of the troops in the event that the enemy were encountered in formidable array. But the tidings that President Lincoln had proclaimed them all free was spread far and wide.

The moral effect of the march to the sea was very great. Sherman's campaign has produced bad effect on our people, wrote Jefferson Davis.[728] At first it was popularly supposed at the South that the operation was hazardous and that the Union Army might be checked or even destroyed. The Union force was underrated; the Confederate means of defence were estimated too high, especially as they were so disposed as to be ineffective. The marching columns met with little resistance. The victorious progress of this modern Attila, as Sherman was called, brought out indications that many people in the South were tired of the war.

During the thirty-two days when the world lost sight of Sherman, the only news of him was from the Richmond newspapers which came through Grant's lines and from other Southern journals, copious extracts from which were printed in the Northern dailies. The President was apprehensive for his safety; and, if Grant's recollection be correct, there was for a time considerable anxiety among people at the North who had husbands, sons or brothers in the invading army. The first word of his security was received in Washington on the evening of December 14; four days later came a despatch from Sherman himself, saying that he had opened communication with the fleet. On the night of December 20 the Confederates evacuated Savannah. Sherman took possession of the city and sent his celebrated despatch to President Lincoln, who received it opportunely on the evening of Christmas Day. I beg to present you, the General said, as a Christmas gift the city of Savannah with 150 heavy guns and plenty of ammunition and also about 25,000 bales of cotton.[729]

---

[727] Nichols, 56, 60
[728] O. R., XLV, Pt. 2, 778.
[729] Authorities: O. R., XXXIX, Pts. 1, 2, 3; XLIV; XLV, Pt. 2; V; W. Sherman; J. D.

When the balance of probabilities seemed to indicate that Hood would invade Tennessee, Sherman, on parting with General J. D. Cox, whom he was sending northward, said, If there's to be any hard fighting you will have it to do.[730] This turned out to be the case. Tempted by the division of the Union Army and aiming to distract Sherman's advance into Georgia,[731] Hood on November 21 took the offensive and began his movement upon Nashville. His energy and alertness secured for him the advantage of superior numbers over General John M. Schofield, who endeavored to retard the Confederate advance so that Thomas might gain time for a concentration of the Union troops. Aware of his inferiority, Schofield executed a masterly retreat and, through strenuous exertions of officers and men, arrived safely at Franklin, where the impetuous Hood forced him to fight with a river at his back. Hood made a desperate frontal attack and was repulsed with terrible slaughter. General J. D. Cox shared with Schofield the credit for the brilliant victory.[732] The Union troops, under orders from Thomas, marched to Nashville.

Hood followed Schofield to Nashville and sat down before the city with an army now reduced to 26,000, inviting his doom.[733] The reason he gave for continuing his advance northward was stated in his report of December 11, to force the enemy to take the initiative.[734] Thomas had now at Nashville 49,000 men.

Thomas understood the position of affairs and knew that he should attack Hood. Feeling pretty sure that Hood would not attempt an advance to the Ohio river, or retreat southward, he was making his preparations complete with the aim of striking the Confederates a crushing blow. Meanwhile Grant was growing impatient the more so as personally he did not like Thomas. The two were unsympathetic and their view of military movements was diverse. Grant loved Sherman and Sheridan and was always ready to overlook their short-comings, but his attitude toward Thomas during these December days was that of an unrelenting fault-finder. Knowing that Hood's defeat was necessary for the success of Sherman's campaign he could not control his annoyance at the delay. Attack Hood at once was his order of December 6. As no attack was made, he purposed relieving Thomas and placing Schofield in command; but suspending, for a space, the issuance of an order to this effect he telegraphed to Thomas on December 11, Let there be no further delay. Meanwhile a storm of sleet had converted the hills about Nashville into slopes of slippery ice rendering any movement impossible until there should be a thaw: this was reported to Grant, who appeared to see in the intelligence only a further excuse for delay. In his unreasonable mood, he ordered

Cox; Force; Nichols; Whitelaw Reid, I.

[730] J. D. Cox, 21; do. Reminiscences, II, 326.
[731] O. R., XLV, Pt. 1, 1215.
[732] O. R., XLV, Pt. 1, 343.
[733] Van Horne's Thomas, 316.
[734] O. R., XLV, Pt. 1, 658.

General Logan to proceed to Nashville for the purpose of superseding Thomas in command of the Army of the Cumberland;[735] then, growing still more anxious, he decided to go thither himself and had reached Washington on the way when he received word that Thomas had made the attack.

Grant had been unjust to Thomas, looking at only one side of his character. While Thomas was deliberate unto slowness he had the situation well in hand after the battle of Franklin and was admirably fitted to cope with an impetuous general like Hood. This Sherman had divined when placing upon him such a weight of responsibility. Moreover, he had the confidence and devotion of his soldiers. In whatever way the circumstances may be regarded there was no justification for superseding him by Schofield or Logan; and the sequel showed that he was abundantly equal to the demands made upon him.

On December 15 Thomas attacked Hood and in the course of that day and the next struck him a crushing blow.

When in the spring of 1864, Grant took command of all the armies of the United States, the two salient features of his plan were the destruction or capture of Lee's army and the crushing of the Confederate force in the Southwest. Before the close of the year one-half of the work had been accomplished. Hood's army was disintegrated. Not all, to be sure, of that compact and well-disciplined force of 53,000 with which Johnston had begun to resist Sherman's advance in May had been killed, wounded or made prisoners, but through casualties, desertions and forced furloughs, practically none of it was left as a fighting body. As an army it is no longer known in the annals of the war, although two detachments of it appear to recall to us its wrecked fortunes. Nine thousand of these discouraged and partially equipped soldiers turned up under Johnston in North Carolina and 1692 went to Mobile

Jefferson Davis had unwittingly helped to bring about the destruction of the Confederate force in the Southwest by removing Joseph E. Johnston and placing Hood in command. Sherman began the ruin of Hood's army about Atlanta; Schofield gave it a severe blow at Franklin; Thomas completed the work at Nashville. There was good generalship; there were brave, devoted and energetic officers and men. Of course Sherman's successful march to the sea would have been a bitter disappointment to the North without Thomas's victory at Nashville; but the two together formed an important part of the grand scheme which broke down the military resistance of the South. The great achievement, the capture of Lee's army, still remained. While the people were rejoicing in the merriest season of the year over the success of Sherman and of Thomas, the President, Grant and Sherman were evolving the plan which should end the Civil War.[736] The President

---

[735] This and the Army of the Ohio (Schofield's) made up Thomas's command.

[736] Authorities: O. R., XXXIX, Pt. 3; XLIV; XLV, Pts. 1, 2; V; Wilson's Under the Old Flag.

earnestly desired the adoption of a constitutional amendment abolishing slavery in the United States forever. Such an amendment had passed the Senate at the previous session but it had failed to secure the requisite two-thirds vote in the House. It was still the same House of Representatives but the President pointed out that the voice of the people as manifested in the national election was for the amendment and that the House, which should come into being on March 4, 1865, would certainly pass it: therefore, as it is certain to go to the States for their action, may we not agree that the sooner the better. He recommended the reconsideration and passage of the amendment.[737] On January 31, 1865, his ardent wish was gratified. When the Speaker announced that the constitutional majority of two-thirds had voted in the affirmative, there was great enthusiasm. In honor of the immortal and sublime event, the House adjourned.[738] This amendment, which is now known as the Thirteenth, was in due time ratified by three-fourths of the States. To contrast the amendment, which Congress intended in March, 1861, to have numbered XIII, with the existing addition to our organic act is to comprehend the mighty revolution of four years. That of 1861 reads: No amendment shall be made to the Constitution which will authorize or give to Congress the power to abolish or interfere within any State with the domestic institutions thereof including that of persons held to labor or service by the laws of said State. That of 1865, which is a part of our Constitution: Neither slavery nor involuntary servitude shall exist within the United States or any place subject to their jurisdiction. The South was approaching exhaustion. Sherman's march through Georgia and Hood's defeat at Nashville had bred a feeling of despondency far and wide. Lee called attention to the alarming frequency of desertions from his army which were due mainly to the insufficiency of food and non-payment of the troops.[739] Even the Confederate paper money was not to be had, although this was fast losing value. Sixty dollars of it were needed to buy one dollar in gold. Beef sold for $6 a pound and flour for $1000 a barrel. The weather was cold and fuel scarce. Jones makes a record of the mercury at zero and wood selling at $5 a stick.[740] In the midst of this distress came the news that Fort Fisher had fallen.[741] This closed Wilmington, North Carolina, the last open port of the Confederacy. Blockade-running was now at an end. The trade with Europe of cotton and tobacco for needed supplies, on which the South had lived and carried on the war, must now cease. As the existence of the Confederacy depended on Lee's army, the most serious feature of a very grave situation was the lack of food for his soldiers. Sherman's march had cut off the supplies from Georgia, but meat and corn could be obtained from

---

[737] Lincoln, C. W., II, 613.
[738] Globe, 531.
[739] Jan. 27, O. R., XLVI, Pt. 2, 1143.
[740] Jan. 11, 13, 14, 27. Jones, II, 383, 384, 386, 400.
[741] Jan. 16.

southwest Virginia and the Carolinas. The permanent way, however, of the Richmond and Danville Railroad, on which the transportation of this food depended, had not been kept up; the locomotives, cars and machinery generally were out of repair so that the daily wants of the commissariat could hardly be met. Lee reported that the whole country within reach of his army had been swept clear. The Commissary-General wrote that for several months the Army of Northern Virginia had been living literally from hand to mouth.[742] The overpowering difficulty was the lack of money. In North Carolina producers refused to sell, as they feared the Government would not pay. In a number of Virginia counties along the Potomac the people, who had formerly held that patriotism required them to take Confederate money and refuse greenbacks, would now sell their cattle and hogs only for United States currency, cotton or gold. In Virginia generally gold or greenbacks were necessary to obtain horses. The value of the paper currency of a nation is a symptom of the nation's stability, and men had it thus brought home to them in the common operations of life, that the financial system of the Confederacy had broken down while the enemy's money was eagerly sought for within its borders. A natural step in reasoning led to a distrust of the whole Southern enterprise. Traffic across the lines with country under control of the Union forces was an important source of supply for Lee's army. This traffic, which consisted in the exchange of cotton for subsistence stores, was carried on largely by agents of the Confederate government.

Despondency and discontent filled the public mind. President Davis was discontented with his Congress and Congress was equally discontented with him; and many people were dissatisfied with both. The General Assembly of Virginia by a unanimous vote expressed the opinion that Lee's appointment to the command of all the armies would promote their efficiency and reanimate the spirit of both soldiers and people. This was communicated deferentially and in confidence to Davis who, with ready sympathy, replied that he fully agreed with the Assembly; shortly afterwards he appointed Lee General-in-chief.[743] It is significant that all men, no matter how they might differ in other respects, turned with one accord to Lee as their saviour if indeed salvation were to be had. His personal influence is illustrated by a circumstance occurring at this time. Heavy rains had destroyed a part of the Richmond and Danville railroad, which was the main source of supply for his army, so that food could not be transported over it for a number of days. On a suggestion from the War Department, Lee made a personal appeal to the farmers, millers and other citizens to give him food, and although it was probable that nothing could have been impressed in that section, these men willingly brought in supplies sufficient to tide the army over its difficulty.

[742] Jan. 11, Feb. 9, O. R., XLVI, Pt. 2, 1035, 1211.
[743] Jan. 17, 18, O. R., XLVI, Pt. 2, 1084, 1091.

Far below Lee in the public estimation came Jefferson Davis, yet next to Lee he was the strongest individual influence in this time of distress. The power which he exercised by virtue of his office, together with the fact that his opponents lacked a leader, make it difficult to discern what was public opinion. All yearned for peace and everybody would have been willing to give the North liberal conditions if she would grant independence to the Confederacy. This view was shared by Davis who, however, did not fully comprehend the widespread demoralization of the South.[744] His hopefulness gave him strength to rise above illness and a constant debility. He was inflexible and lacked tact in a eminent degree. Criticism was rife and various plans were proposed but, with rare exceptions, men failed to grasp the actual situation: that by superior resources and more efficient management the North had beaten the South. But it is impossible to tell how many saw the inevitable, that there could be no peace except by reunion and the abolition of slavery, and were willing to submit to these conditions. Thus matters were allowed to drift. The only feasible plan from a military point of view was to confer freedom on all slaves who would take up arms for the Confederacy.

During the year 1864 the enlistment of slaves began to be mooted; and, on January 11, 1865, this policy received the sanction of General Lee, who proposed immediate freedom to all who should enlist and at the same time recommended a well-digested plan of gradual and general emancipation.[745] Congress did not act promptly on Lee's recommendation and, if there was any virtue in such a policy, it was now too late to avail anything. The enlistment of the slaves was strongly opposed and Howell Cobb, who at the commencement of the war owned a thousand negroes, argued against it with force. The day you make soldiers of them [the negroes], he wrote, is the beginning of the end of the revolution. If slaves will make good soldiers our whole theory of slavery is wrong.[746] In truth it might have been asked, if we are voluntarily going to free our slaves, wherefore did we secede and go to war? But in January, 1865, nearly all Southerners, if asked, What are you fighting for? would have answered, For our independence and against subjugation.

Through the officious interference of Francis P. Blair, Sr., a conference was brought about between Lincoln and Seward on the one side and Vice-President Stephens, Judge Campbell and Senator Hunter on the other. Known as the Hampton Roads Conference, it took place on board a United States steamer anchored near Fort Monroe [February 3]. When personal courtesies had been passed and Whig memories revived between Lincoln and Stephens, Stephens asked, Mr. President, is there no way of putting an end to the present trouble? Lincoln replied in substance that there is but one way I know of an that is for those

[744] Alfriend, 597.

[745] Jan. 11, O. R., IV, III, 1013.

[746] Jan. 8, O. R., IV, III, 1009.

who are resisting the laws of the Union to cease that resistance. The restoration of the Union is a sine qua non with me. Judge Campbell inquired how restoration was to take place supposing that the Confederate States consented to it. Lincoln replied, by disbanding their armies and permitting the national authorities to resume their functions. Slavery was discussed; the President said that he never would change or modify the terms of the Proclamation in the slightest particular and Seward told the Southerners that the Thirteenth Amendment abolishing slavery had just been passed by Congress.

If the Confederate States were to abandon the war, asked Stephens, would they be admitted to representation in Congress? Lincoln replied that he thought that they ought to be but he could not enter into any stipulation upon the subject. When Stephens pressed the point that there should be some understanding, Lincoln said that he could not treat with parties in arms against the government. Hunter said that this had been often done, especially by Charles I when at civil war with the British Parliament. Lincoln replied: I do not profess to be posted in history. On all such matters I will turn you over to Seward. All I distinctly recollect about the case of Charles I is that he lost his head in the end. After further discussion Lincoln burst out: Stephens, if I resided in Georgia with my present sentiments, I'll tell you what I would do if I were in your place: I would go home and get the Governor of the State to call the Legislature together and get them to recall all the State troops from the war; elect Senators and members to Congress and ratify this Constitutional Amendment [the Thirteenth] prospectively, so as to take effect say in five years. Whatever may have been the views of your people before the war, they must be convinced now that slavery is doomed. It cannot last long in any event and the best course it seems to me, for your public men to pursue, would be to adopt such a policy as will avoid, as far as possible, the evils of immediate emancipation. This would be my course if I were in your place.

Hunter summed up the talk, saying that nothing had been offered them but unconditional submission to the mercy of the conquerors. This Seward disclaimed in courteous terms and Lincoln said that as far as the Confiscation Acts and other penal acts were concerned, their enforcement was left entirely with him and on that point he was perfectly willing to be full and explicit and on his assurance perfect reliance might be placed. He should exercise the power of the Executive with the utmost liberality. He went on to say that he would be willing to be taxed to remunerate the Southern people for their slaves. He believed the people of the North were as responsible for slavery as people of the South, and if the war should then cease, with the voluntary abolition of slavery by the States, he should be in favor, individually, of the Government paying a fair indemnity for the loss to their owners. He said he believed this feeling had an extensive existence at the North. He knew some who were in favor of an appropriation as high as four hundred million dollars for this purpose. But on this subject he said he could give no assurance enter into no stipulation. He barely expressed his own feelings and views and what he believed to be the views of others on the subject. In the President's report to the House of Representatives he said, The Conference ended without result.[747]

Two men, Lee and Davis, acting together, could have led the Confederate Congress and the South. Lee's caution, his deference to his superior and his aversion to assuming a responsibility that was not clearly his, probably prevented him from urging his President to negotiate a peace; but, if the memories of private conversation may be believed, he had lost all hope of success. It was Jefferson Davis who in this matter imposed his will on all his subordinates and it was he more than anybody else who stood in the way of an attempt to secure favorable terms for the South in a reconstruction of the Union.

If Davis, Lee and the Confederate Congress could have made up their minds to sue for peace, the contemporaneous occurrences in Washington reveal the magnanimous spirit in which they would have been met by Abraham Lincoln.

Two days after the Hampton Roads Conference, on Sunday evening, February 5, the President called his Cabinet together to consult them in regard to a message he proposed to send recommending that Congress empower him to pay to the eleven slave States of the Southern Confederacy then in arms against the Union and to the five Union slave States four hundred million dollars as compensation for their slaves provided that all resistance to the national authority should cease on April first next. The Cabinet unanimously disapproved this project and Lincoln with a deep sigh said, You are all opposed to me and I will not send the message. Such a proposal to the Southern Confederacy, tottering to her fall, only sixty-three days before Lee's surrender to Grant would have shown magnanimous foresight. Had the Confederate States accepted it, there would have been an immediate fraternal union after the Civil War. Had they rejected it, the President and Congress would have made a noble record. The offer, however, was too wise and too generous to be widely approved of men; Lincoln of all those in authority had reached a moral height where he must dwell alone and impotent. But when reflecting on the events from 1865 to 1877, men may well wish that the offer had been made. A month later, in the spirit of this Sunday, Lincoln uttered the sublime words of his second inaugural address, the greatest of presidential inaugurals, one of the noblest of State papers.[748]

---

[747] V, 68-71.
[748] V; N. & H., X; Lincoln, C. W., II; Welles's Dairy, II.

Chapter XIV

SHERMAN with an army of 60,000, which was substantially the same as that which he had led from Atlanta to Savannah, started northward from Savannah on February 1, in the execution of a plan devised by himself, and on March 23 reached Goldsborough, North Carolina, having covered the 425 miles in fifty days. His progress to the sea had been a frolic; the march northward a long wrestle with the elements. At the outset the first division encountered a deluging rain, causing a rise in the Savannah river which burst its dikes, washed over the road and nearly drowned many of the troops. Waiting until this flood abated and passing successfully the difficulties occasioned by the high water in the neighborhood of Savannah, the army plunged into the swamps of the Combahee and Edisto, and floundered through the flat quagmires of the river countries of the Pedee and Cape Fear. They crossed five large navigable rivers, which the almost continuous rains of the winter had converted into lakes, at times marching through icy water waist deep. One day, as Sherman related the incident, while my men were wading a river which was surrounded for miles by swamps on each side, after they had been in the water for about an hour without much prospect of reaching the other side, one of them cried out to his chum, 'Say, Tommy, I'm blowed if I don't believe we've struck this river lengthways!'[749] Where the country was not actually under water, there was deep mud; the incessant downpour made roads which were always difficult almost impassable, turned swampy ways into deep quagmires. It was chaos come again wrote Cox, but the chaos was bridged for hundreds of miles[750] by this indomitable army. The roads were corduroyed; the streams and rivers were crossed on pontoon and trestle bridges. It would have been a difficult region for an army to march through had the inhabitants been friendly and no enemy near; but, under the direction of Wheeler's cavalry, details of negro laborers had felled trees, burned bridges and made obstructions to impede Sherman's progress.[751] To gain possession of the long causeways through the swamps it was necessary to outflank the enemy and drive him off. For this and other reasons there were skirmishes nearly every day, yet the army marched at the average daily rate of ten miles. Sherman seems to have everything his own way, wrote Lee from Petersburg.[752] I made up my mind, said Joseph E. Johnston, that there had been no such army since the days of Julius Cæsar.[753]

---

[749] Horace Porter, Century, Sept. 1897, 739.

[750] J. D. Cox, 172.

[751] O. R., XLVII, Pt. 1, 19.

[752] Feb. 19, *ib.,* 1044.

The 2500 wagons of the army carried a full supply of ammunition and a large number of Government rations. The initial food supply was eked out and systematic foraging upon the country was carried on in the manner which had proved so successful in the campaign from Atlanta to the sea. The march began in South Carolina, continued directly through the centre of the State and was marked by a line of buildings and cotton bales afire. The soldiers tore up the railroads, applied the torch to their woodwork, twisted the rails and destroyed all water-tanks, engines and machinery. The Confederates set fire to cotton to prevent its falling into the hands of the Union Army and what they spared was burned by the Northern soldiers in the territory which they were merely traversing and could not hope to occupy permanently. In the high circles of the army a bitter feeling existed against South Carolina as the cause of all the trouble of the past four years. The whole army, Sherman wrote, is burning with an insatiable desire to wreak vengeance upon South Carolina. I almost tremble at her fate but feel that she deserves all that seems in store for her.[754] With such sentiments at headquarters it is little wonder that the rank and file thought it legitimate to despoil the enemy and set fire to his houses: still most of these irregular acts were committed by stragglers. Sherman's orders may probably be justified from the military point of view but they left loopholes for the mania for destruction; and the necessities of the case and the burden of responsibility resting upon him may have caused him to wink at the havoc wrought by his army. The evidence shows, however, that many of the general officers did their best to stop the depredations of their soldiers and some punishments were inflicted. From this statement must again be excepted Kilpatrick, whose command suffered no restraint and were forward in destruction and pillage.

The most notorious occurrence during this march was the partial destruction by fire of Columbia, the capital of South Carolina; but this was due neither to Sherman nor Wade Hampton nor any other Federal or Confederate officer.[755]

The occupation of Columbia by Sherman compelled the abandonment of Charleston on February 18 by the Confederates. Efforts were made to collect a force which should be able to resist the Union Army but, in view of the steadily advancing host, they seem to have been puny and at any rate were of no avail. When Davis heard that the evacuation of Charleston was necessary, he wrote, I had hoped for other and better results and the disappointment is to me extremely bitter.[756]

In Charleston much property was destroyed, but it was the Confederates who, through accident or design, were the agents of destruction. The Federal troops on

---

[753] J. D. Cox, 168, Reminiscences, II, 531.

[754] Dec. 24, 1864, O. R., XLIV, 741.

[755] V, 90 *et seq.* Rhodes, Historical Essays.

[756] O. R., XLVII, Pt. 2, 1201.

entering the city found public buildings, stores, warehouses, railroad bridges, private dwellings and cotton afire but they afterwards wreaked their vengeance on this cradle of secession by robbery and pillage. Probably the majority of Northern people at the time had no other idea of Charleston's distress than that it was abundantly deserved; but the suffering and want in this former abode of wealth and refinement must evoke in us now sympathy with the community on whom the horrors of war were visited.

To understand the march through South Carolina, the hatred of officers and soldiers for the State which had taken the lead in the secession movement must be borne constantly in mind. This undoubtedly led many of them into transgressions which they had not committed in Georgia and from which they afterwards refrained in North Carolina, while it furnished the stragglers a ready excuse for their robberies and outrages. General Blair reported on March 7 that every house on his line of march to-day was pillaged, trunks broken open, jewelry, silver, etc., taken.[757] Cox had evidence after the war of robberies and even partial hanging to extort the disclosure of a place where money and valuables were hidden. Stragglers, deserters from either army, marauders, bummers, and strolling vagabonds, negroes and whites committed outrages upon the inhabitants; three cases of rape and one of murder were reported.[758] In some cases punishment was inflicted. Howard directed that a soldier who had violently taken a watch from a citizen should have his head shaved and be drummed out of the service. Cox, who commanded the Twenty-third Corps in Schofield's army,[759] executed the death sentence pronounced by court-martial for a rape; the culprit, according to his recollection, was a bounty-jumper. A military commission, having found a private soldier guilty of the murder of a North Carolina citizen, sentenced him to be shot to death with musketry; two days later the sentence was executed.[760] Sherman asserted generally that whenever individuals were detected in theft they were punished; but, in going over the evidence, one cannot fail to note many offences and few penalties. Yet despite the general lawlessness, of which we obtain glimpses from time to time, outrages on the persons of women were rare. Sherman testified under oath that in the whole of the march he heard of but two cases of rape.

The tendency of Federal officers, apart from the contemporary documents, has been to minimize the depredations, and the tendency of many Northern writers has been to gloss them over, so that even if every instance brought to light by Northern testimony be mentioned, the Union armies will suffer no injustice by the seeming redundancy of facts. So much of the Southern evidence is not specific and all of it

---

[757] O. R., XLVII, Pt. 2, 714.

[758] O. R., XLVII, Pt. 3, 79.

[759] Schofield had come to North Carolina.

[760] O. R., XLVII, Pt. 3, 470.

is so pervaded with intense feeling that I have preferred to develop this subject from Northern sources, leaving the natural inference to be drawn that, if all had been told, the evidence against Sherman's army would have been somewhat greater.[761] The men who followed Sherman were probably more humane generally than those in almost any European army that had marched and fought before our Civil War, but any invading host in the country of the enemy is a terrible scourge.

Sherman reached Fayetteville (N. C.) on March 11 and, by means of a steam tug, which had come up the Cape Fear river from Wilmington, was placed in communication with Schofield[762] and therefore with Grant and Stanton. Up to February 22 Grant, through the Richmond newspapers, had kept pretty well informed of Sherman's progress, but on that day the newspapers were requested by the authorities not to publish any news connected with the pending military movements in the Carolinas, so that afterwards he could cull from them only meagre and unsatisfactory information. In his letter to Grant, Sherman said, The army is in splendid health, condition and spirit although we have had foul weather and roads that would have stopped travel to almost any other body of men I ever read of.[763]

On March 21 Schofield reached Goldsborough (N. C.) where, two days later, Sherman's army made with him the desired junction. Were I to express my measure of the relative importance of the march to the sea and of that from Savannah northward, wrote Sherman, I would place the former at one and the latter at ten or the maximum.[764] He might have continued in Napoleon's words written during his Austrian campaign, I have destroyed the enemy merely by marches.[765]

Sherman himself went to City Point to have a consultation with Grant and there met President Lincoln. The three had two interviews, one on the afternoon of March 27 and the other next day when they discussed the past operations, the harbinger of their success, and the approaching end of the war. Lincoln and Sherman did most of the talking while Grant listened and ruminated. According to Sherman's recollection of the interviews the two generals were agreed in their opinion that one or the other of them would have to fight one more bloody battle and that it would be the last. Lincoln said more than once that enough of blood had been shed and asked if another battle could not be avoided, to which Sherman made answer that they could not control that event; it rested with Jefferson Davis and General Lee whether or not the two armies should meet again in a desperate and bloody battle.[766]

---

[761] See Whitelaw Reid, Ohio in the War, I.

[762] Schofield had come from Thomas's army in Tennessee by river and rail to Washington, thence by sea to the vicinity of Wilmington, N. C.

[763] O. R., XLVII, Pt. 2, 794.

[764] W. Sherman, II, 221.

[765] Sloane, II, 235. Authorities: O. R., XLVII; V; W. Sherman; Cox's Reminiscences.

In truth these masters of State and war the three men to whom above all others we owe the successful termination of the conflict could not without gladness review the military operations of the last year and look forward to the promise of the future; but they appreciated too well the magnitude of the business in hand to give way to undue elation. As in May, 1864, Grant was confronted by Lee and Sherman by Johnston;[767] but Grant had fought his way from the Rapidan to the James and the Appomattox, while Sherman, after a contested progress from Dalton to Atlanta, had made a holiday march to the sea followed by a march northward with the elements for his bitterest foes. He had achieved his purpose and was now at Goldsborough (N. C.) with 80,000 men preparing to advance against Johnston, who lay between him and Raleigh with an army of about 33,000. In other parts of the theatre of war, there were large and well-appointed Union forces bent on aggressive operations, working under Grant's efficient direction with the common purpose of dealing the enemy a final blow. But it was confidently believed that if Lee and Johnston could be forced to surrender, the rest of the military resistance would collapse.

In this final encounter, the generals were well matched in intellectual ability but the material resources on the Union side were vastly greater. Yet the latent power of resistance in soldiers, skilfully and honestly led, who believe that they are fighting against the subjugation of their people, must be rated high, as so many instances in history attest. The more profound the study of the last days of the Confederacy, the firmer will be the conviction that the best of management was required of the North to assure the end of the war in the spring of 1865. In one respect fortune had signally favored the Union. Although distributing, in the last two years of the war, the favors of military skill with an equal hand, she had at the same time given to the United States a great ruler. Manifestly superior as had been Davis's advantages in family, breeding, training and experience, he fell far below Lincoln as a compeller of men. We have seen Lincoln in times of adversity and gloom and have marvelled at his self-effacement and we have seen him listening to words of advice, warning and even reproof such as are rarely spoken to men wielding immense power; and throughout he has preserved his native dignity and emerged from nearly every trial a stronger and more admirable man.

Grant appears at his best in the final operations of his army. He is the Grant of Donelson, Vicksburg and Chattanooga with a judgment developed through larger experience and the discipline of adversity. The full reports and detailed despatches admit us to the actual operations of his mind as he surveyed the vast field over which his armies, always in touch with him, moved to their several tasks in his grand scheme of strategy. He combined self-confidence with caution. He did not underestimate his enemy; he did not, as he perceived the successful operation of

[766] W. Sherman, II, 326; Horace Porter, Sept., 1897, 739.

[767] Johnston had been placed in command by Lee.

his plans, give way to elation, thinking the work already done which was only half done. But he was not too cautious to move forward boldly and without fear of the result. In Sherman and Sheridan he had helpers on whom he could rely as if each were another self. Seeing things alike they were in complete sympathy with him; they comprehended his orders and carried them out in letter and spirit as did no other of his subordinates. Sherman's marching and fighting were now over but Sheridan was to be to Grant a prop and a weapon such as Stonewall Jackson had been to Lee in his earlier campaigns. With the force immediately under him, Grant had, besides Sheridan, an efficient coadjutor in Meade, and good corps commanders in Warren, Humphreys, Ord, Wright and Parke. At the commencement of the Appomattox campaign, he had in this army 116,000 effectives while Lee mustered 52,000.[768]

Since the summer of 1864 Grant had besieged Richmond and Petersburg. The progress of the siege had been slow but persistent until, soon after the middle of February, Lee began to consider the eventuality of abandoning both cities. While in the freedom of private conversation he may have expressed himself in a despairing tone, his despatches indicated a belief that there was still a chance of success in fighting on; moreover, he made it clear that he would resist the foe as long as resistance was possible unless he were advised to yield by the superior civil authority. He infused an energy into his sortie of March 25, which, though the attempt was unsuccessful, demonstrated that there was still a great deal of fight in him and his army. The Union lines did not encircle Richmond and Petersburg, but left open an avenue of escape to the west and southwest. The Richmond and Danville railroad and its Petersburg connection, the Southside or Lynchburg railroad, which were the lines of supply for Richmond and Petersburg, were in operation. Grant spent days of anxiety lest Lee should abandon these places and, after getting away from him, either make a junction with Johnston, or, retreating by way of Lynchburg, secure himself in the mountain fastnesses and make a raid into East Tennessee. Should the two Confederates unite their forces he feared a long, tedious and expensive campaign consuming most of the summer.[769] Lee considered the two alternatives and preferred the union with Johnston; but, if Davis's memory may be trusted, Lee never contemplated surrender but, in emulation of a plan of Washington's, purposed as a last resort retreating to the Virginia mountains where he thought that he might carry on the war for twenty years.[770] Taking all conditions into account the game was equal and was played with skill on each side.

On March 29, Grant began his movement on his own left and at night had an unbroken line from the Appomattox river to Dinwiddie Court-House. From his

---

[768] T. L. Livermore, Milt. Hist. Soc., VI, 451.

[769] O. R., XLVI, Pt. 1, 47, 50, 52.

[770] J. Davis, II, 656.

headquarters in the field he wrote to Sheridan, I now feel like ending the matter if it is possible to do so without going back. Two nights and a day of heavy rain interrupted operations, but on the 31st the advance was resumed, when Lee attacked the Fifth Corps and the Union cavalry and gained a temporary success. Sheridan in falling back, wrote Grant, displayed great generalship. On April 1 Sheridan fought in a masterful way the battle of Five Forks, which resulted in disaster to the Confederates. He has carried everything before him is Grant's account of this action. The General-in-Chief received the intelligence of the victory of Five Forks at nine in the evening and immediately ordered an assault on the enemy's line, which was made at an early hour next day; his army won a decisive victory.[771] On the night of April 2, Lee evacuated Richmond and Petersburg, with the intention of concentrating his troops at Amelia Court-House, and making his way to Danville whence he would effect a junction with Johnston's army. After him, next morning, followed the Union forces in eager pursuit.

As late as April 1, Davis apparently thought that there was no immediate necessity for the abandonment of Richmond. On the morning of Sunday the 2d he was at St. Paul's listening to the noble liturgy of the Episcopal Church; the clergyman was reading for the last time in his ministry the prayer for the President of the Confederate States. Here Davis was apprised by a messenger from the War Department of the gravity of the military situation. He left his pew quietly and walked out of the church with dignity to receive Lee's telegram which gave an account of his disaster and advised that Richmond be abandoned. The news spread rapidly, and so unexpectedly had it come upon the city that the greatest confusion and excitement prevailed as functionaries and citizens made ready for flight. Davis with all the members of his cabinet (except the Secretary of War), a number of his staff and other officials, got away at eleven o'clock in the evening on a train of the Richmond and Danville railroad and reached Danville next afternoon in safety. Under Lee's previous order, Ewell, who was in command of the troops in Richmond, directed that the tobacco in the city should be burned and that all stores which could not be removed should be destroyed. It is probable that the fires lighted in pursuance of this order spread to shops and houses and it is certain that in the early morning of April 3 a mob of both colors and both sexes set fire to buildings and began to plunder the city. Ewell said in his report that by daylight the riot was subdued and Jones wrote that at seven o'clock in the morning men went to the liquor shops in execution of an order of the city government and commanded that the spirits be poured into the streets. The gutters ran with liquor from which pitchers and buckets were filled by black and white women and boys. By seven o'clock also the evacuation of Richmond by the Confederates was completed.

---

[771] O. R., XLVI, Pt. 1, 53, 54, Pt. 3, 394.

The Union troops passed cautiously the first line of the Confederate works but as they met with no opposition, they went by the next lines at a double quick, and when the spires of the city came into view, they unfurled a national banner, and their bands striking up Rally Round the Flag, they sent up cheer on cheer as they marched in triumph through the streets. But they found confusion, an extensive conflagration and a reign of pillage and disorder. Their commander, Weitzel, received the surrender of Richmond at the city hall at quarter past eight, and, by two o'clock in the afternoon, they had quelled the tumult and put out the fires but not before a considerable portion of the city had been destroyed.

The Union soldiers were received by the white people gratefully and by the negroes with joy. Full of meaning was the visit of President Lincoln to Richmond, which was made from City Point next day in an unostentatious and careless manner. Proper arrangements had been made for his conveyance and escort but, owing to two accidents, the President completed his river journey in a twelve-oared barge and walked about a mile and a half through the Richmond streets accompanied by Admiral Porter and three other officers with a guard of only ten sailors armed with carbines. He was received with demonstrations of joy by the negroes and, though the city was full of drunken civilians, he met with neither molestation nor indignity. He went to the house which Davis had occupied as a residence, now Weitzel's headquarters and, if we may believe some personal recollections, looked about the house and sat in Davis's chair with boyish delight. Lincoln passed the night in Richmond and on April 5 returned to City Point. Under that date Jones reported perfect order in the city and Dana telegraphed from Richmond, Whig appeared yesterday as Union paper. Theatre opens here to-night.[772]

The Army of Northern Virginia evacuated Richmond and Petersburg during the night of April 2 and the early morning of the 3d. Grant, without tarrying for a visit to Richmond, set after them in hot pursuit. After a chase of eighty miles he hemmed them in and compelled their surrender.[773] When Lee became convinced that further resistance was useless he said, Then there is nothing left me but to go and see General Grant and I would rather die a thousand deaths. He ordered the white flag to be displayed, requested by letter a suspension of hostilities and an interview with Grant. The two generals met at McLean's house in the little village of Appomattox Court-House. Lee wore a new full-dress uniform of Confederate

---

[772] O. R., XLVI, Pt. 3, 575.

[773] T. L. Livermore wrote on Jan. 8. 1906: "During the Appomattox campaign, March 29 to April 9, 1865, with a force of about 116,000 effectives, Grant manoeuvred and drove out of their intrenchments in front of Richmond and Petersburg about 52,000 Confederates and then with 72,000 men pursuing for eighty miles the remainder of the Confederate army estimated at 37,000, captured, dispersed, or put *hors de combat* on the way about 9000, and finally surrounded and received the surrender of 28,231. In no other modern campaign has an army ever pursued, surrounded and captured so many men in full flight." Milt. Hist. Soc., VI, 451.

gray buttoned to the throat and a handsome sword, the hilt of which was studded with jewels, while Grant had on a blouse of dark-blue flannel unbuttoned in front and carried no sword.[774] In my rough travelling suit, wrote Grant, the uniform of a private with the straps of lieutenant-general, I must have contrasted very strangely with a man so handsomely dressed, six feet high and of faultless form.[775] Although jubilant over his victory Grant, on coming into personal contact with Lee, felt like anything rather than rejoicing at the downfall of a foe who had fought so long and valiantly.[776] Grant was magnanimous; Lee heroic in his adversity. Generous terms were offered and the paper signed that ended the war.

The number of men surrendered was 28,231. The Confederates had been living for the last few days principally upon parched corn and were badly in need of food. Grant supplied them with rations. As soon as the Union soldiers heard of the surrender they commenced firing salutes at different points along the lines. He ordered these stopped saying, The war is over; the rebels are our countrymen again; and the best sign of rejoicing after the victory will be to abstain from all demonstrations in the field.[777]

Lee rode back sorrowfully to his soldiers. With eyes full of tears he said, We have fought through the war together. I have done the best I could for you. My heart is too full to say more.[778] On the morrow he issued a farewell address to the Army of Northern Virginia and rode away to Richmond. The army disbanded and dispersed to their homes.[779]

The news of Lee's surrender was received in Washington at nine o'clock on Sunday evening, April 9, and at a somewhat later hour in other cities. While the people had exulted at the occupation of Richmond, they perceived that the possession of the capital of the Confederacy did not imply the end of the war. But now it was in everybody's mouth, the great captain of the rebellion had surrendered: this imported that slavery was dead, the Union restored and that the nation lived. So pregnant an event ought to be made known speedily to Europe; accordingly the Inman line despatched a special steamer on the Monday to carry the intelligence across the ocean. The people of the North rejoiced on the night of the 9th and during the day and evening of the 10th as they had never rejoiced before, nor did they on any occasion during the remainder of the century show such an exuberance of gladness. Business was suspended and the courts adjourned. Cannons fired, bells rang, flags floated, houses and shops were gay with the red, white and blue. There were illuminations and bonfires. The streets of the cities and

---

[774] H. Porter, Oct. 1897, 883.

[775] Grant, II, 490. Grant was 5 feet 8 in. high, with shoulders slightly stooped. He was nearly 43, Lee 58.

[776] Grant, II, 489.

[777] Horace Porter, Oct. 1897, 886, 887.

[778] Life of Lee, Cooke, 463.

[779] See V, *passim*.

towns were filled with men who shook hands warmly, embraced each other, shouted, laughed and cheered and were indeed beside themselves in their great joy. There were pledges in generous wine and much common drinking in bar-rooms and liquor shops. There were fantastic processions, grotesque performances and some tomfoolery. Grave and old gentlemen forgot their age and dignity and played the pranks of school-boys. But always above these foolish and bibulous excesses sounded the patriotic and religious note of the jubilee. Praise God from Whom all blessings flow were the words most frequently sung in the street, the Board of Trade and the Stock Exchange. One writer recorded that in the bar-room of Willard's Hotel, Washington, when the news arrived, an elderly gentleman sprang upon the bar and led the crowd in singing with unwonted fervor the well-known doxology. Twenty thousand men in Wall Street sang it with uncovered heads. On the Tuesday, Trinity Church, New York, was crowded for a special service. The choir chanted the Te Deum and at the bidding of the clergyman the congregation rose and, inspired by the great organ and guided by the choir, sang the noble anthem Gloria in Excelsis. These opening words, Glory be to God on high and on earth peace, good will towards men had a peculiar significance to the Northern people who during these days of rejoicing were for the most part full of generous feeling for the South. Patriotism expressed itself in the songs John Brown's Body, My Country, 'tis of Thee, Rally Round the Flag, and the Star-spangled Banner. Lowell instinctively put into words what his countrymen had in their hearts: The news, my dear Charles, is from Heaven. I felt a strange and tender exaltation. I wanted to laugh and I wanted to cry and ended by holding my peace and feeling devoutly thankful. There is something magnificent in having a country to love.[780]

The surrender of Johnston to Sherman naturally followed Lee's surrender. The war was over.

Between these two events our country suffered the greatest disaster in its history. Lincoln was assassinated.

Walt Whitman sang: O Captain! my Captain! our fearful trip is done, The ship has weathered every rack, the prize we sought is won. O Captain! my Captain! rise up and hear the bells; Rise up for you the flag is flung for you the bugle trills. My Captain does not answer, his lips are pale and still. Although exasperated by Lincoln's assassination, the North was at the same time inspired by the grandeur of Grant's conduct at Appomattox. Nobody was hanged for a political crime,[781] no land of the vanquished Confederates confiscated. Since the Americans' most noble closing of the Civil War, wrote George Meredith, I have looked to them as the hope of our civilization.[782]

---

[780] To C. E. Norton, Lowell, I, 344.

[781] "It has been eloquently said that the grass soon grows over blood shed upon the battlefield but never over blood shed upon the scaffold." Froude's Elizabeth, IV, 368.

The great man of the Civil War was Lincoln. Lacking him the North would have abandoned the contest. His love of country and abnegation of self made him a worthy leader. Other rulers of great power have remorselessly crushed those who stood in their way. He said, I am not in favor of crushing anybody out. Give every man a chance.

Lincoln is not as Mommsen wrote of Cæsar the entire and perfect man who worked and created as never any mortal did before or after him. Verily Cæsar created Cæsarism for the modern world, the autocracy of the super-man. But which is the better policy to transmit to mankind, despotism or liberty? the better injunction, Submit yourselves unto Cæsar, or Give every man a chance? In intellect Cæsar and Lincoln are not to be compared. We speak of the mighty Cæsar, never of the mighty Lincoln. But nobody speaks of honest Julius, while Honest Old Abe will live through the ages.

---

[782] Lect., 193, n. 1; see V, *passim.*